T0271464

Application Architecture Patterns for Web 3.0

Over the past three years, the landscape of blockchain technology has undergone remarkable transformation, extending far beyond its association with cryptocurrencies especially with the emergence of Web3 applications.

Web 3.0 is built using artificial intelligence, machine learning, and the semantic web. It uses all this to process and interpret information with human-like intelligence. And for security, Web 3.0 uses the blockchain security system to keep information secure. This book aims to provide an overview of the evolution of blockchain technology, highlighting its expanding use cases and exploring the latest trends and news that have shaped the blockchain landscape in recent years. The timing of this book is ideal. NFTs, DeFi, and in general the emergence of the architectural concept of "Web3" are defining and will define the future of web applications.

The book takes the reader on a journey across the innovative use cases of blockchain technology, with a focus on building the technical foundation of such applications, in order to enable entrepreneurs and blockchain architects to create state-of-the-art Web3 solutions.

Stefano Tempesta is a technologist working at the crossroad of Web2 and Web3, to make the Internet a more accessible, meaningful, and inclusive space. Stefano is an ambassador of the use of AI and blockchain technologies for good humanitarian purposes. A former advisor to the Department of Industry and Science, Australia, on the National Blockchain Roadmap, he is co-founder of Aetlas Protocol, a climate fintech integrating blockchain contracts into fully digitized green bonds, simplifying and automating project financing for carbon removal infrastructure.

Application Architecture Patterns for Web 3.0

Design Patterns and Use Cases for Modern and Secure Web3 Applications

With foreword by Stephen Ashurst

Stefano Tempesta

Routledge
Taylor & Francis Group

A PRODUCTIVITY PRESS BOOK

First published 2025
by Routledge
605 Third Avenue, New York, NY 10158

and by Routledge
4 Park Square, Milton Park, Abingdon, Oxon, OX14 4RN

Routledge is an imprint of the Taylor & Francis Group, an informa business

Names: Tempesta, Stefano, author.
Title: Application architecture patterns for web 3.0: design patterns
and use cases for modern and secure web3 applications / Stefano Tempesta.
Description: New York, NY: Routledge, 2025. | Includes bibliographical
references and index. | Summary: "Over the past three years, the
landscape of blockchain technology has undergone remarkable
transformation, extending far beyond its association with
cryptocurrencies especially with the emergence of Web3 applications.
Web 3.0 is built using artificial intelligence, machine learning, and the
semantic web. It uses all this to process and interpret information with
human-like intelligence. And for security, Web 3.0 uses the blockchain
security system to keep information secure. This book aims to provide an
overview of the evolution of blockchain technology, highlighting its
expanding use cases and exploring the latest trends and news that have
shaped the blockchain landscape in recent years. The timing for this
book is ideal. NFTs, DeFi, and in general the emergence of the
architectural concept of "Web3" is defining and will define the future
of web applications. The book takes the reader on a journey across the
innovative use cases of blockchain technology, with a focus on building
the technical foundation of such applications, in order to enable
entrepreneurs and blockchain architects to create state-of-art Web3
solutions"– Provided by publisher.
Identifiers: LCCN 2024033859 (print) | LCCN 2024033860 (ebook) |
ISBN 9781032794327 (hardback) | ISBN 9781032794310 (paperback) |
ISBN 9781003491934 (ebook)
Subjects: LCSH: Computer architecture. | Electronic data processing. |
Software architecture. | Application software–Development.
Classification: LCC QA76.9.A73 T46 2025 (print) | LCC QA76.9.A73 (ebook) |
DDC 004.2/2–dc23/eng/20240828
LC record available at https://lccn.loc.gov/2024033859
LC ebook record available at https://lccn.loc.gov/2024033860

ISBN: 978-1-032-79432-7 (hbk)
ISBN: 978-1-032-79431-0 (pbk)
ISBN: 978-1-003-49193-4 (ebk)

DOI: 10.4324/9781003491934

Typeset in Garamond
by Deanta Global Publishing Services, Chennai, India

To the pioneers and dreamers of the decentralized future, this book is dedicated to those who envision a world where technology empowers individuals, where trust is inherent, and where the boundaries of innovation are continually pushed.

Contents

Acknowledgments

Writing *Application Architecture Patterns for Web 3.0* has been a journey of discovery, collaboration, and learning. This book would not have been possible without the support, encouragement, and contributions of many individuals and communities.

First and foremost, I would like to express my deepest gratitude to the Australian Computer Society (ACS) blockchain team. Your innovative spirit, community contributions, and relentless pursuit of decentralization have been a constant source of inspiration. The insights and feedback from numerous developers, researchers, and enthusiasts have enriched this book immensely.

I am also grateful to the pioneers in the blockchain and decentralized technologies space whose groundbreaking work laid the foundation for Web3. Your vision and dedication have paved the way for a new era of the internet.

To my family, thank you for your unwavering support and patience. Your encouragement kept me motivated during the countless hours spent researching and writing.

Finally, I would like to acknowledge the technical reviewers and editors whose meticulous attention to detail ensured the accuracy and clarity of the material presented in this book.

Thank you all for being a part of this journey. This book is a testament to our collective efforts and shared belief in the transformative potential of Web3.

Preface

Where were we? Since publishing *Blockchain Applied – Practical Technology and Use Cases of Enterprise Blockchain for the Real World* in 2021, the authors have continued their journey across multiple applications of blockchain technology to real-world scenarios.

Three years forward, I am thrilled to present a comprehensive guide to a new frontier in software development. This book is the culmination of years of research, experimentation, and collaboration within the vibrant and rapidly evolving Web3 community.

The journey that led to this book began with my fascination with blockchain technology and its potential to redefine how we interact with digital systems. Like many of you, I started exploring decentralized applications (dApps) with a mix of curiosity and skepticism. It became clear that while the promise of Web3 was immense, the path to realizing that promise was fraught with challenges. Traditional design patterns and methodologies often fell short when applied to decentralized environments, and the need for new paradigms was evident.

As I delved deeper into the world of Web3, I encountered numerous developers and architects grappling with similar issues. We were all trying to navigate this uncharted territory, learning through trial and error, and sharing insights within our communities. These interactions highlighted a significant gap in the available resources – a definitive guide that could provide structured solutions to the unique challenges posed by Web3.

Driven by this realization, I set out to compile and codify the knowledge and experiences amassed by myself and my peers. The goal was to create a resource that could serve as a beacon for developers entering the Web3 space, as well as a reference for seasoned professionals looking to refine their approaches. This book is the result of that effort, a synthesis of practical patterns, best practices, and theoretical foundations that underpin successful Web3 application development.

Writing this book was an enriching experience, as it allowed me to engage with some of the brightest minds in the industry. I had the privilege of collaborating with developers who were pioneering new solutions, participating in forums and hackathons, and learning from the collective wisdom of the Web3 community. Each pattern and principle discussed in this book has been tested and validated through real-world applications, ensuring that they are both practical and reliable.

The structure of this book reflects the diverse aspects of Web3 development. We begin with foundational concepts, exploring the principles of decentralization, blockchain mechanics, and smart contract design. From there, we delve into specific design patterns, each accompanied by detailed examples and case studies. The aim is to provide you with not just theoretical knowledge but also actionable insights that you can apply to your projects immediately.

One of the most exciting aspects of Web3 is its potential for innovation and positive impact. By decentralizing control and empowering users, Web3 applications can create more equitable and transparent systems. It is my hope that this book will inspire you to harness this potential, building applications that push the boundaries of what is possible and contribute to a more decentralized and democratized internet.

I would like to extend my deepest gratitude to everyone who contributed to this book – my colleagues, the developers who shared their experiences, and the vibrant Web3 community that continues to push the envelope. Your insights and feedback were invaluable in shaping this work.

As you embark on your journey through *Application Architecture Patterns for Web 3.0*, I encourage you to experiment, innovate, and share your discoveries. The Web3 landscape is still in its early days, and each one of us has a role to play in shaping its future. May this book serve as a guide and a source of inspiration as you explore the limitless possibilities of decentralized applications.

Welcome to the next generation of the Web!

Foreword

This book is all about *Web3*, a small word that represents a big change in the way we conceive and engineer digital ecosystems. Web3 is not an incremental update on what came before. It is a fundamental transformation.

Web3 has decentralization, transparency, and user empowerment at its core. Web3 is driven by equitable access, transparency, and trust. And ownership, smart contracts, and control. These attributes return the spirit and energy of the original internet to us, engineers, consumers, and communities.

As with any paradigm shift, the transition to Web3 presents unique challenges and opportunities for software engineers and architects. Traditional design patterns that served the engineering community well in previous eras (Web2) are often inadequate in addressing the nuances and complexities of Web3's decentralized systems.

This book, *Application Architecture Patterns for Web 3.0*, seeks to bridge that gap. The author sets out to provide a comprehensive guide to the principles and practices that underpin effective Web3 application development.

The importance of design patterns and principles in software engineering cannot be overstated. Patterns offer tried and tested solutions to common problems. Principles provide a shared basis for engineers to communicate ideas and collaborate more reliably and effectively. In the context of Web3, where decentralization introduces novel architectural considerations, the need for well-defined design patterns and principles is even more critical.

This book assesses Web3 patterns and principles that have emerged from the deployment and engineering of real-world Web3 applications (and the rigorous experimentation behind them) and presents these to the reader in an easily accessible and clear format.

Whether the reader is seasoned blockchain engineer or a newcomer, student, or manager eager to explore the possibilities of decentralized applications, this book offers valuable insights into the design and implementation of robust, scalable, and secure Web3 solutions. From consensus mechanisms and smart contract architectures to decentralized identity and tokenomics, the patterns and principles covered in the book will equip you with some of the knowledge and tools required to navigate the intricacies of Web3 engineering and architecture.

The author has taken great care to ensure that the patterns and principles presented are not only technically sound but also contextually relevant. Each is accompanied by practical examples, case studies, and best practice commentary making it easier for engineers to apply these concepts to their own projects.

The goal of the book is to educate and empower software architects and engineers to build applications that are not only functional but also align with the principles of decentralization and user sovereignty that define Web3. By mastering the design patterns and principles in this book, the reader will be well-positioned to participate in this exciting Web3 evolution and help shape the future of the internet.

Web3 promises to reshape industries, democratize access to information and services, and create new, trustable, and transparent economic models that benefit all participants.

We stand on the cusp of a new digital frontier – Web3.
The potential for innovation is boundless.

Welcome to the future of application design. Welcome to Web3

Stephen Ashurst
Co-founder and CEO, Tokenbridge
www.tokenbridge.co.uk

Chapter 1

The Blockchain Landscape in the Past Three Years

Over the past years, the landscape of blockchain technology has undergone a remarkable transformation, extending far beyond its association with cryptocurrencies. Originally introduced as the underlying technology powering Bitcoin, blockchain has since emerged as a powerful tool with a vast array of real-world applications. This first chapter aims to provide an overview of the evolution of blockchain technology, highlighting its expanding use cases and exploring the latest trends and news that have shaped the blockchain landscape in recent years.

Diversification of Use Cases

While cryptocurrencies remain an important aspect of the blockchain ecosystem, the technology has found utility in various sectors beyond finance. Blockchain's inherent characteristics, such as decentralization, immutability, and transparency, have sparked interest in industries seeking to enhance security, streamline processes, and foster trust among participants.

In the first edition of our book, we identified some prominent use cases of blockchain technology, including:

- **Supply Chain Management**: Blockchain enables end-to-end visibility and traceability in supply chains, combating issues like counterfeit products, ensuring product authenticity, and enhancing efficiency.
- **Healthcare**: Blockchain can securely store and share medical records, enable interoperability among healthcare providers, and facilitate secure and confidential data exchange.
- **Voting Systems**: Blockchain offers a tamper-resistant platform for secure and transparent voting, potentially eliminating fraud and ensuring the integrity of democratic processes.
- **Intellectual Property**: Blockchain can establish verifiable proof of ownership, timestamp creations, and automate royalty payments, revolutionizing intellectual property management.
- **Energy Sector**: Blockchain enables peer-to-peer energy trading, facilitates transparent tracking of renewable energy credits, and improves the overall efficiency of energy markets.

DOI: 10.4324/9781003491934-1

Whilst these scenarios remain absolutely valid for the application of blockchain technology, the last few years have seen an expansion of blockchain-based solutions to fields that could not even be foreseen before. As we will expand in the next chapters, based on our individual experiences, DeFi (Decentralized Finance), Central Bank Digital Currency (CBDC), Non-fungible Tokens (NFT), Carbon Tokenization, and the Metaverse have all brought the industry to a significant transformation.

Interoperability and Scalability Solutions

As blockchain adoption expands, the need for interoperability and scalability has become increasingly apparent. Interoperability allows different blockchain networks to communicate and exchange information seamlessly, while scalability addresses the challenge of handling a high volume of transactions. Several projects have emerged to tackle these issues, as illustrated in Figure 1.1, which we can summarize as:

- **Cross-Chain Bridges**: Projects like Polkadot, Cosmos, and ICON aim to enable interoperability by connecting multiple blockchain networks, allowing them to exchange assets and data.
- **Layer 2 Scaling Solutions**: Technologies like Lightning Network for Bitcoin and Ethereum's Layer 2 solutions like Optimistic Rollups and Plasma provide off-chain scaling to enhance transaction throughput and reduce costs.
- **Zero Knowledge (ZK) Proof**: Zero knowledge proofs (also called ZK proofs or ZKPs) use a cryptographic proof protocol for authentication. They can be executed on a decentralized blockchain network where data is non-custodial.
- **Wallets**: Wallets protect your digital assets, cryptocurrencies, and any other type of digital token. Wallets are the entry gate to Web3 solutions, and they also provide a mechanism for user authentication using decentralized identities.

In the next sections, we will look at each solution individually and identify the foundational technology at the core of each approach, and the inevitable challenges that it brings.

Cross-Chain Bridges

Blockchain technology has seen the emergence of various blockchain networks, each with its own set of features, functionalities, and native assets. However, these networks often operate in isolation, lacking the ability to communicate and transfer assets seamlessly. Cross-chain bridges

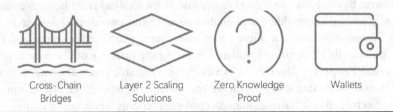

Cross-Chain   Layer 2 Scaling   Zero Knowledge   Wallets
Bridges   Solutions   Proof

Figure 1.1   Interoperability and scalability solutions for blockchain networks

are solutions designed to address the challenge of interoperability, enabling the exchange of assets and data between different blockchain networks. This section explores the challenges of interoperability, the need for cross-chain bridges, and the different approaches employed to resolve this problem.

Challenges in Interoperability

Each blockchain network operates independently, utilizing its consensus mechanism, smart contract functionality, and native assets. This leads to very isolated networks with little or no communication among each other. The challenges in interoperability are:

- **Siloed Blockchains**: This lack of interoperability restricts the movement of assets and data across different chains, hindering seamless interaction and collaboration between blockchain networks.
- **Fragmented Liquidity**: The fragmentation of liquidity across multiple blockchain networks limits the efficiency of decentralized exchanges and liquidity pools. Users are often required to navigate different platforms and networks to access various assets, leading to suboptimal trading experiences and increased complexity.
- **Asset Portability**: The inability to transfer assets between different blockchain networks hampers liquidity, as users may be confined to a particular blockchain ecosystem and unable to leverage assets on other networks. This restricts the potential utility and fungibility of assets across different blockchain platforms.

The Need for Cross-Chain Bridges

Cross-chain bridges play a vital role in addressing the challenges of interoperability and unlocking the full potential of blockchain technology. By enabling seamless communication and asset transfer between different blockchain networks, cross-chain bridges offer several benefits:

- **Asset Interoperability**: Cross-chain bridges allow the transfer of assets between different blockchain networks, promoting liquidity and enhancing the utility of assets. Users can seamlessly move tokens from one network to another, increasing flexibility and fostering cross-chain collaboration.
- **Enhanced Liquidity**: Cross-chain bridges facilitate the aggregation of liquidity from multiple blockchain networks, creating more efficient decentralized exchanges and liquidity pools. This leads to improved price discovery and better trading experiences for users.
- **Access to Diverse Ecosystems**: Cross-chain bridges enable users to access and interact with a broader range of decentralized applications (dApps) and services across multiple blockchain networks. This promotes innovation, interoperability, and cross-chain composability of dApps.

Approaches to Cross-Chain Bridges

How do cross-chain bridges help address the challenges identified before? A few approaches, depicted in Figure 1.2, have been explored over time and adopted by different blockchain networks. Examples include:

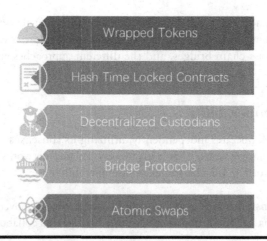

Figure 1.2 Approaches to cross-chain bridges

- **Wrapped Tokens**: Wrapped tokens are representations of assets from one blockchain network that are created on another blockchain. These tokens are backed by the original assets held in custody and allow for their transfer and utilization on different chains. Examples include Wrapped Bitcoin (WBTC) on Ethereum, which represents Bitcoin on the Ethereum network.
- **Hash Time Locked Contracts (HTLC)**: HTLCs enable the secure transfer of assets between blockchain networks by leveraging hash functions and time locks. HTLCs require participants to fulfill certain conditions, such as revealing a pre-image, within a specified time window to complete the transfer of assets across chains.
- **Decentralized Custodians**: Decentralized custodians act as trusted intermediaries between different blockchain networks, holding assets in custody and issuing corresponding tokens on the destination chain. These custodians facilitate the transfer of assets across chains, ensuring security and integrity.
- **Bridge Protocols**: Bridge protocols are dedicated protocols built specifically to facilitate cross-chain asset transfers. These protocols establish standardized methods for asset lockup, custody, verification, and release across different blockchain networks. Examples include Polkadot's XCMP (Cross-Chain Message Passing) and Cosmos' Inter-Blockchain Communication (IBC) protocol.
- **Atomic Swaps**: Atomic swaps enable the direct peer-to-peer exchange of assets between different blockchain networks without the need for intermediaries. This technology utilizes smart contracts and ensures the simultaneous and irreversible transfer of assets between participants.

Interoperability is a critical challenge in the blockchain space, hindering the seamless transfer of assets and data across different networks. Cross-chain bridges provide solutions to overcome these challenges, enabling asset interoperability, enhanced liquidity, and access to diverse blockchain ecosystems. Wrapped tokens, HTLCs, decentralized custodians, bridge protocols, and atomic swaps are different approaches used to facilitate cross-chain asset transfers. By bridging the gap between blockchain networks, cross-chain bridges unlock new opportunities for collaboration, innovation, and the seamless flow of assets and data in the blockchain landscape.

Layer 2 Scaling Solutions

Scalability has been a persistent challenge for blockchain technology, particularly in terms of handling a high volume of transactions. As the adoption of blockchain expands, the need for efficient scaling solutions becomes increasingly critical. Layer 2 scaling solutions aim to address these challenges by moving some of the transaction processing off the main blockchain, thereby improving throughput and reducing costs. This section explores the challenges faced by blockchain scalability, the need for layer 2 solutions, and the different approaches employed to resolve these problems.

Challenges in Blockchain Scalability

Layer 2 solutions aim to alleviate the challenges of blockchain scalability by enabling off-chain transaction processing while leveraging the security and trust of the underlying main blockchain. By moving some transactions off the main blockchain, layer 2 solutions can significantly increase the transaction throughput, reduce fees, and enhance the overall scalability of the blockchain ecosystem. These approaches will help with the following:

■ **Transaction Throughput**: Public blockchains like Bitcoin and Ethereum have limitations on their transaction processing capacity. Bitcoin, for instance, has a block time of approximately 10 minutes, allowing only a limited number of transactions to be included in each block. This results in slower confirmation times and low transaction throughput.
■ **Network Congestion and High Fees**: As blockchain networks experience increased usage, congestion can occur, leading to network slowdowns and rising transaction fees. This undermines the user experience and limits the scalability of blockchain platforms.
■ **Data Storage and Bandwidth Requirements**: The storage and bandwidth requirements for maintaining a full copy of the blockchain can be significant. As more transactions are added to the blockchain, the size of the data grows, making it challenging for nodes to keep up with storage and bandwidth demands.

Different Approaches to Layer 2 Scaling

Several approaches are commonly used within Layer 2 network, each of them bringing significant advantages. Figure 1.3 illustrates the common approaches described hereafter:

■ **State Channels**: State channels are off-chain channels where participants can conduct multiple transactions privately and securely. Only the final state of the channel is recorded on the main blockchain, reducing the need for on-chain transactions. State channels are well-suited for use cases involving frequent and rapid transactions, such as micropayments or gaming applications.
■ **Payment Channels**: Payment channels are a type of state channel specifically designed to enable fast and low-cost payments. They allow users to open payment channels with each other and conduct numerous transactions off-chain. Once the payment channel is closed, the final settlement is recorded on the main blockchain.
■ **Sidechains**: Sidechains are separate blockchain networks that are connected to the main blockchain, allowing for the transfer of assets between the main chain and the sidechain.

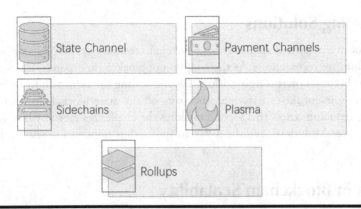

Figure 1.3   Different approaches to layer 2 scaling

Sidechains enable faster transaction processing and increased capacity, as they operate with their consensus mechanisms and block time.

■ **Plasma**: Plasma is a framework for creating scalable and secure decentralized applications (dApps) on top of existing blockchains. It works by creating hierarchical tree structures of sidechains, known as "plasma chains", which can handle a large number of transactions off the main blockchain. The plasma framework offers enhanced scalability while maintaining the security of the main chain.

■ **Rollups**: Rollups are Layer 2 solutions that aggregate multiple transactions into a single transaction, known as a "rollup", which is then submitted to the main blockchain. Rollups can either be optimistic rollups or zk-rollups. Optimistic rollups rely on fraud-proof mechanisms, where transactions are initially processed off-chain and later validated on the main chain if no fraud is detected. zk-rollups use zero-knowledge proofs to compress and validate multiple transactions on the main chain.

Blockchain scalability has been a significant challenge hindering the widespread adoption of blockchain technology. Layer 2 scaling solutions offer promising approaches to address these challenges by moving some transaction processing off the main blockchain. State channels, payment channels, sidechains, Plasma, and rollups are different techniques employed in layer 2 solutions, each with its unique advantages and trade-offs. By implementing layer 2 solutions, blockchain networks can significantly enhance transaction throughput, reduce fees, and unlock the potential for broader and more efficient blockchain-based applications.

Zero Knowledge (ZK) Proofs

Zero Knowledge Proofs (ZKPs) are cryptographic protocols that enable one party, the prover, to prove to another party, the verifier, that a statement is true without revealing any additional information beyond the validity of the statement. ZKPs have gained significant attention for their potential to address privacy and confidentiality challenges in various domains. This section explores the challenges ZKPs aim to address, the need for ZKPs, and the different approaches employed to resolve this problem.

Challenges in Privacy and Confidentiality

The challenges in privacy and confidentiality encompass data privacy, authentication and identity, and secure transactions. No industry is exempt from such challenges, and no technical solutions can ever be considered fully protected. Before proceeding any further, we want to understand better what these challenges are about, and how ZKPs may help mitigate the risks they bring:

- **Data Privacy**: In many scenarios, parties need to prove the validity of certain statements or transactions without revealing sensitive underlying data. Traditional proof mechanisms often require sharing extensive information, jeopardizing individual privacy and data confidentiality.
- **Authentication and Identity**: Verifying one's identity or membership in a specific group typically involves sharing personal information. This process raises concerns about privacy and the potential misuse or unauthorized access to sensitive personal data.
- **Secure Transactions**: In financial and transactional systems, ensuring the integrity and validity of transactions while maintaining privacy is a challenge. Parties often need to prove the correctness of a transaction without exposing the transaction details to unauthorized parties.

The Need for Zero Knowledge Proofs

ZKPs offer a compelling solution to the challenges mentioned above by allowing individuals to prove knowledge or the validity of statements without revealing any additional information beyond what is necessary. ZKPs provide several benefits:

- **Privacy and Confidentiality**: ZKPs enable individuals to prove statements without disclosing the underlying data, ensuring privacy and confidentiality. This is particularly valuable when dealing with sensitive information, such as personal data or confidential business transactions.
- **Trust and Security**: ZKPs allow parties to verify the integrity and correctness of transactions or claims without the need for trust in a centralized authority. By relying on cryptographic protocols, ZKPs ensure the validity of statements while preserving data privacy.
- **User Control**: ZKPs empower individuals to retain control over their data by providing a mechanism to validate claims or statements without sharing sensitive information. Users have greater agency and can selectively disclose only what is necessary, enhancing their control over personal data.

Approaches to Zero Knowledge Proofs

ZKPs are emerging as a technology for ensuring confidentiality in transactions. Several approaches are currently being experimented with the different blockchains in the market, and a lot of good learning is happening across businesses and the academy. Here are the most common techniques being used, depicted also in Figure 1.4:

- **Interactive Proofs**: In interactive ZKPs, the prover and verifier engage in a back-and-forth communication protocol. The prover aims to convince the verifier of the statement's validity without revealing additional information. Examples include Schnorr protocol and Fiat-Shamir heuristic.

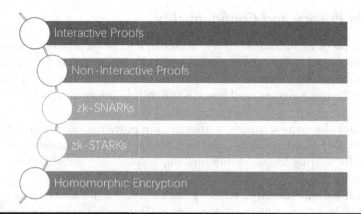

Figure 1.4 Approaches to zero knowledge proofs

- **Non-Interactive Proofs**: Non-Interactive Zero Knowledge Proofs (NIZKPs) are protocols where the prover can generate a proof that can be verified by the verifier without any further interaction. NIZKPs are efficient and useful in scenarios where interactive communication is not feasible. Examples include zk-SNARKs (Zero-Knowledge Succinct Non-Interactive Arguments of Knowledge) and Bulletproofs.
- **zk-SNARKs**: zk-SNARKs are a type of NIZKP that allows for the efficient verification of complex statements or computations. They enable the creation of succinct proofs and have been utilized in various blockchain applications, including privacy-focused cryptocurrencies like Zcash.
- **zk-STARKs**: zk-STARKs (Zero-Knowledge Scalable Transparent Arguments of Knowledge) are a more recent advancement in ZKPs. They offer scalability and transparency while providing strong security guarantees. zk-STARKs are being explored for applications in blockchain, finance, and other domains.
- **Homomorphic Encryption**: Homomorphic encryption allows computations to be performed on encrypted data, preserving the confidentiality of the input while obtaining an encrypted result. It can be leveraged to construct ZKPs, enabling privacy-preserving computations.

ZKPs offer a powerful solution to the challenges of privacy, confidentiality, and secure authentication. By allowing individuals to prove the validity of statements without revealing additional information, ZKPs ensure privacy, enhance trust, and provide greater user control over sensitive data. Interactive and non-interactive ZKPs, such as zk-SNARKs and zk-STARKs, provide efficient and scalable approaches to ZKPs, enabling applications in domains like cryptocurrencies, authentication, and secure transactions. Leveraging ZKPs and cryptographic protocols, individuals can prove knowledge or transactions while safeguarding their privacy and preserving data confidentiality.

Wallets

Cryptocurrency wallets are software applications or physical devices that enable users to securely store, manage, and interact with their digital assets. They play a crucial role in the adoption and usability of cryptocurrencies, providing a means for individuals to control their funds and engage in various transactions. This section explores the challenges wallets address, the need for wallets, and the different approaches employed to resolve these problems.

Challenges in Managing Cryptocurrency Assets

Managing cryptocurrency assets presents several challenges. The lack of regulation and oversight can lead to market volatility and potential monetary loss. Additionally, the anonymity of transactions can make it difficult to trace illicit activities or recover lost assets. Furthermore, tax implications and reporting requirements for cryptocurrency are still evolving and can be complex to navigate. In addition to this, the following challenges are specific to the way we interact with and store cryptocurrency:

■ **Security**: Cryptocurrency assets are digital and can be susceptible to theft or loss if not properly secured. As cryptocurrencies operate on decentralized networks, there is no central authority to recover lost or stolen funds. Thus, ensuring the security of private keys and protecting against unauthorized access is essential.

■ **User Experience**: Cryptocurrency wallets need to provide a user-friendly experience to encourage widespread adoption. Users should be able to easily navigate the wallet interface, manage their assets, and conduct transactions with minimal friction. Improving user experience is crucial for attracting new users and simplifying the complexities of interacting with blockchain-based assets.

■ **Interoperability**: With the existence of multiple blockchain networks and distinct types of cryptocurrencies, wallets must support interoperability. Users may hold different cryptocurrencies across different networks, and wallets should provide a unified interface to manage and transact with these assets seamlessly.

The Need for Wallets

Wallets address the challenges mentioned above and fulfill several crucial functions:

■ **Asset Storage**: Wallets provide a secure storage solution for cryptographic assets, such as cryptocurrencies. They generate and store the private keys required to access and control these assets. Wallets can be either software-based (e.g., desktop, mobile, or web wallets) or hardware devices (e.g., hardware wallets) designed specifically for enhanced security.

■ **Transaction Management**: Wallets enable users to send, receive, and manage their cryptocurrency transactions. They facilitate the creation of digital signatures and interact with the blockchain networks to initiate and verify transactions. Wallets also allow users to track their transaction history and manage transaction fees.

■ **Security and Key Management**: Wallets employ cryptographic techniques to secure private keys and ensure the integrity of transactions. They provide mechanisms for securely storing private keys, such as encryption and hardware-based solutions. Wallets also offer backup and recovery options to prevent the loss of funds in case of device failure or theft.

■ **Interoperability and Multi-Currency Support**: Wallets support various cryptocurrencies and blockchain networks, enabling users to manage and transact with diverse types of digital assets from a single interface. This interoperability simplifies the user experience and facilitates the adoption of multiple cryptocurrencies.

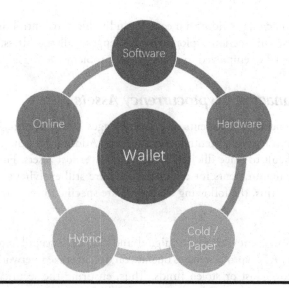

Figure 1.5   Types of wallets

Types of Wallets

Figure 1.5 lists the types of cryptographic wallets that are commonly used with blockchain networks, for securing cryptocurrency as well as different types of tokens. Here is a very high-level description of each type:

- **Software Wallets**: Software wallets encompass desktop, mobile, and web-based applications that store private keys on a user's device. They offer convenience and accessibility, allowing users to manage their assets from any compatible device with an internet connection. Examples include MetaMask (web wallet) and Exodus (desktop and mobile wallet).
- **Hardware Wallets**: Hardware wallets are physical devices specifically designed for storing private keys and conducting secure transactions offline. These wallets provide an extra layer of security by keeping private keys isolated from internet-connected devices, minimizing the risk of exposure to potential threats. Popular hardware wallets include Ledger and Trezor.
- **Cold or Paper Wallets**: Paper wallets involve printing the public and private keys on a physical medium, such as paper. While less convenient for regular transactions, paper wallets offer offline storage and are immune to hacking attacks. However, they require careful handling to protect against physical damage or loss.
- **Online Wallets**: Online wallets, also known as custodial wallets, store users' private keys on a third-party server. These wallets offer convenience and accessibility, but they entail the risk of trusting the custodian with the security of the assets. Popular online wallets include exchanges like Coinbase and Binance, which offer integrated wallet services.
- **Hybrid Wallets**: Hybrid wallets combine the benefits of software and hardware wallets. They use a mobile or desktop application to interact with the blockchain network while securely storing private keys on a hardware device. This approach balances security and convenience, offering a user-friendly experience with enhanced asset protection.

Cryptocurrency wallets address the challenges of securing, managing, and transacting with digital assets. They provide a secure storage solution for private keys, facilitate transaction management, and enhance user experience. Software wallets, hardware wallets, paper wallets, online wallets, and hybrid wallets offer different approaches to address the needs of users with varying security and convenience preferences. Wallets play a crucial role in the adoption and usability of cryptocurrencies, empowering individuals to control their digital assets and engage in decentralized financial activities securely.

Wallets are also differentiated as *custodial* and *self-custodial*. The difference between custodial and self-custodial wallets lies in the control and ownership of private keys, which are crucial for accessing and managing cryptocurrency assets.

Key Characteristics of Custodial Wallets

Custodial wallets, also known as hosted wallets or centralized wallets, are wallets where a third-party service provider holds and manages the users' private keys on their behalf. When using a custodial wallet, users trust the service provider to securely store their private keys and manage their funds. Examples of custodial wallets include wallets provided by centralized exchanges like Coinbase, Binance, or Kraken. They provide:

- **Private Key Control**: In custodial wallets, users do not have direct control over their private keys. Instead, the service provider manages and controls the keys on behalf of the users.
- **Convenience**: Custodial wallets often offer a user-friendly and intuitive interface, making it easier for beginners to use and navigate the wallet. They may also provide additional features like integrated exchange services.
- **Security Responsibility**: The security of funds in custodial wallets relies on the service provider's security practices. Users must trust that the custodian maintains adequate security measures to protect against theft or unauthorized access.
- **Third-Party Risk**: Since the custodial wallet provider holds the private keys, users are exposed to the risk of the service provider being hacked, becoming insolvent, or engaging in malicious activities.

Key Characteristics of Self-custodial Wallets

Self-custodial wallets, also known as non-custodial wallets or decentralized wallets, put the user in full control of their private keys. In this type of wallet, the user generates and manages their private keys, typically through software applications or hardware devices. Examples of self-custodial wallets include MetaMask, Ledger Live, MyEtherWallet, and Exodus. They provide:

- **Private Key Control**: Self-custodial wallets grant users complete control over their private keys. Users generate and store their keys securely, either using a software application on their device or on a dedicated hardware wallet.
- **Security and Responsibility**: Users are responsible for the security of their private keys and must take precautions to protect them from loss or unauthorized access. They have the freedom to back up and securely store their keys to maintain control over their funds.
- **Privacy and Anonymity**: Self-custodial wallets offer greater privacy since users do not need to provide personal information to a third-party service provider. Transactions are conducted directly on the blockchain, preserving anonymity.
- **Trustless Nature**: Self-custodial wallets operate in a trustless manner, as users do not need to rely on a third party to access or manage their funds. They can independently verify transactions and participate in the decentralized ecosystem.

It is important to note that while self-custodial wallets provide users with greater control and privacy, they also require users to take responsibility for the security of their private keys. Proper backup measures and secure storage practices are essential to prevent the loss of funds.

Latest Trends and News

To stay abreast of the rapidly evolving blockchain landscape, it is crucial to be aware of the latest trends and developments. Some notable trends and news in recent years include:

- **Decentralized Finance (DeFi)**: DeFi is an emerging financial technology that challenges the current centralized banking system. DeFi eliminates the fees that banks and other financial companies charge for using their services and promotes the use of peer-to-peer, or P2P, transactions.
- **Central Bank Digital Currencies (CBDC)**: Several countries, including China, the Bahamas, and Sweden, have made considerable progress in developing and piloting CBDCs, exploring blockchain's potential for issuing digital currencies backed by central banks.
- **Non-fungible Tokens (NFT)**: NFTs have gained considerable attention for their ability to tokenize unique digital assets, such as art, collectibles, and virtual real estate, enabling provenance, ownership verification, and new monetization models.
- **Sustainability and Green Blockchains**: As environmental concerns surrounding energy consumption of blockchain networks grow, efforts are being made to develop more energy-efficient consensus mechanisms and promote sustainable practices in the blockchain industry.
- **Regulatory Developments**: Governments and regulatory bodies worldwide are actively exploring frameworks and guidelines to regulate blockchain and cryptocurrencies, aiming to strike a balance between innovation and consumer protection.

Decentralized Finance

DeFi has emerged as a transformative application of blockchain technology, revolutionizing traditional financial systems. DeFi encompasses various financial services, including lending, borrowing, decentralized exchanges (DEXs), and stablecoins, all powered by smart contracts and blockchain networks. It offers individuals worldwide access to financial services without intermediaries, allowing for greater financial inclusion and opportunities for innovation.

Blockchain technology has unleashed a wave of innovation in the financial sector, leading to the rise of DeFi. DeFi encompasses a range of financial applications built on decentralized blockchain platforms, enabling peer-to-peer transactions, eliminating intermediaries, and providing individuals with greater control over their financial activities. This section delves into the opportunities, risks, and key players associated with DeFi.

Opportunities in DeFi

DeFi offers opportunities for financial inclusivity, transparency, and efficiency. It enables peer-to-peer transactions, bypassing traditional intermediaries, and provides access to financial services to unbanked populations. DeFi also fosters innovation in financial products and services, as in the following cases:

- **Financial Inclusion**: DeFi has the potential to provide financial services to the unbanked and underbanked populations worldwide. With just an internet connection, individuals can access a variety of financial instruments, including lending, borrowing, and earning interest on digital assets, without needing a traditional bank account.
- **Interoperability and Openness**: DeFi protocols are often built on open source blockchain platforms, allowing interoperability between different projects. This fosters innovation, as developers can build on existing infrastructure and integrate various applications, creating a vibrant ecosystem.
- **Programmable Money**: Smart contracts enable the automation of financial agreements and transactions, providing programmable money. This flexibility allows for the creation of complex financial products, such as DEXs, prediction markets, and yield farming strategies.
- **Transparency and Security**: Blockchain's transparent and immutable nature enhances the security and trustworthiness of financial transactions. Users can independently verify and audit transactions, reducing the need for blind trust in intermediaries.

Risks and Challenges in DeFi

As for any technology, DeFi faces risks such as smart contract vulnerabilities, hacking, and fraud due to its reliance on blockchain technology. Market volatility, lack of regulatory oversight, and the potential for financial loss are significant challenges. Additionally, the complexity of DeFi platforms can deter widespread adoption. As a quick recap:

- **Smart Contract Vulnerabilities**: Smart contracts are subject to bugs and vulnerabilities, which can be exploited by malicious actors. The absence of a central authority or regulatory oversight means users must be diligent in assessing the security and reliability of DeFi protocols before participating.
- **Price Volatility and Market Risks**: Many DeFi projects are built on cryptocurrencies, which are known for their price volatility. Users should be aware of the risks associated with fluctuating asset values and potential losses incurred due to market volatility.
- **Regulatory Uncertainty**: DeFi operates in a rapidly evolving regulatory landscape. Regulatory bodies are working to define guidelines and frameworks for DeFi, aiming to strike a balance between innovation and consumer protection. The uncertain regulatory environment may impact the future growth and development of DeFi.
- **Economic and Financial Risks**: DeFi protocols are not immune to economic risks, such as liquidity risks, smart contract failures, and vulnerabilities in underlying assets. Users should exercise caution and perform due diligence when engaging in DeFi activities.

Key Players in DeFi

Key players in DeFi, including developers, users, and regulators, shape its landscape. Developers create innovative platforms and applications. Users, ranging from individual investors to institutions, drive adoption and liquidity. Regulators play a crucial role in providing oversight, ensuring market integrity, and protecting consumer interests. There are many names to mention here, but going with the biggest ones, here is a list of key technology solutions in the DeFi space:

- **Ethereum (ETH)**: Ethereum is the most prominent blockchain platform for DeFi applications. It offers a robust infrastructure for building decentralized applications (dApps) and supports a wide range of DeFi projects, including DEXs like Uniswap and lending platforms like Aave.
- **Binance Smart Chain (BSC)**: BSC is a blockchain platform developed by Binance, which has gained significant traction in the DeFi space. BSC offers lower transaction fees and faster block times compared to Ethereum, attracting numerous DeFi projects and users.
- **Solana (SOL)**: Solana is a high-performance blockchain platform that has gained attention for its scalability and low transaction costs. It has seen the emergence of DeFi projects like Serum, a DEX, and lending platform.
- **Compound Finance**: Compound is a lending and borrowing protocol built on Ethereum. It allows users to earn interest by lending their digital assets or borrow assets by providing collateral. Compound paved the way for the lending market in DeFi.
- **MakerDAO**: MakerDAO is a decentralized autonomous organization (DAO) that operates the Maker protocol. It enables the creation of a stablecoin called DAI, pegged to the value of the U.S. dollar. Users can generate DAI by locking collateral and use it for various DeFi activities.
- **Uniswap**: Uniswap is a DEX protocol that allows users to trade Ethereum Request for Comment 20 (ERC-20) tokens directly from their wallets. It utilizes an automated market maker (AMM) model and has become one of the most popular DEXs in DeFi.
- **Chainlink**: Chainlink is an oracle network that connects smart contracts with real-world data. Oracles play a crucial role in DeFi by providing external data to decentralized applications, ensuring accurate and reliable information for financial transactions.

Decentralized Finance presents significant opportunities to reshape the financial landscape, offering financial inclusion, programmable money, transparency, and security. However, DeFi also faces risks, including smart contract vulnerabilities, market volatility, regulatory uncertainty, and economic risks. Ethereum, BSC, and Solana are key blockchain platforms facilitating DeFi innovation, while projects like Compound Finance, MakerDAO, Uniswap, and Chainlink are prominent players in the DeFi ecosystem. As DeFi continues to evolve, it will be essential to navigate the opportunities and risks to harness the full potential of decentralized finance.

Central Bank Digital Currencies

CBDCs are digital representations of a country's fiat currency issued and regulated by the central bank. CBDCs leverage blockchain or distributed ledger technology to enable secure and efficient digital transactions while maintaining central bank control over monetary policy. This section explores the opportunities, risks, and key players associated with CBDCs.

Opportunities of CBDCs

CBDCs present opportunities for improved financial efficiency, transparency, and inclusivity. They can streamline payments, reduce transaction costs, and provide access to financial services for the unbanked. CBDCs also offer the potential for better monetary policy implementation and financial stability:

- **Financial Inclusion**: CBDCs have the potential to increase financial inclusion by providing individuals without access to traditional banking services an opportunity to participate in the digital economy. CBDCs can be accessible to anyone with a smartphone or internet connection, enabling financial services for the unbanked and underbanked populations.
- **Efficiency and Cost Reduction**: CBDCs can streamline payment systems, reducing transaction costs and settlement times. Digital transactions using CBDCs can be processed more efficiently compared to traditional payment methods, potentially enhancing economic efficiency, and reducing the reliance on intermediaries.
- **Monetary Policy Tools**: CBDCs offer central banks new tools for implementing monetary policy. With CBDCs, central banks can have a more direct and immediate influence on the money supply, potentially enhancing their ability to manage inflation, interest rates, and economic stability.
- **Enhanced Security and Transparency**: CBDC transactions can be recorded on a blockchain or distributed ledger, providing a transparent and auditable record of transactions. This transparency can reduce the risk of fraud, money laundering, and corruption, enhancing the integrity of the financial system.

Risks and Challenges of CBDCs

CBDCs face challenges such as technological complexity, security risks, and potential disruption to traditional financial systems. They also pose risks related to privacy, digital exclusion, and the potential for misuse in illicit activities. Regulatory and legal frameworks for CBDCs are still evolving, adding to the uncertainty. In a nutshell:

- **Privacy and Surveillance**: Implementing CBDCs requires careful consideration of privacy concerns. While transaction transparency can be beneficial in combating illicit activities, it also raises concerns about surveillance and the potential for infringement on individuals' financial privacy.
- **Systemic Risk and Stability**: The introduction of CBDCs could impact the stability of the financial system. Designing robust and secure infrastructure, ensuring resilience against cyber threats, and managing potential systemic risks are crucial challenges for central banks.
- **Technological and Operational Challenges**: Developing and deploying CBDCs involves significant technological and operational challenges. Central banks need to ensure scalability, security, and interoperability across various platforms and networks, considering factors like transaction speed, user experience, and network resilience.
- **Impact on Financial Intermediaries**: The introduction of CBDCs could have implications for traditional financial intermediaries, such as commercial banks and payment processors. Disintermediation risks may arise, potentially altering the financial ecosystem and requiring careful transitional arrangements.

Key Players and Developments

Key players in CBDC include central banks, technology providers, and users. Central banks issue and regulate CBDCs, technology providers develop the infrastructure, and users drive adoption. Developments in CBDC involve technological advancements, regulatory frameworks, pilot projects, and research into potential impacts on financial stability and monetary policy. A few notable examples include:

- **People's Bank of China (PBOC)**: China's central bank has been at the forefront of CBDC development, piloting its digital currency, the Digital Currency Electronic Payment (DCEP). The PBOC has conducted trials and tests of the digital yuan, exploring use cases in various sectors.
- **Eastern Caribbean Central Bank (ECCB)**: The ECCB became the first central bank to launch a digital currency in collaboration with blockchain company Bitt. The digital currency, known as the Digital Eastern Caribbean Dollar (DXCD), aims to enhance financial inclusion and facilitate digital transactions within the Eastern Caribbean Currency Union.
- **European Central Bank (ECB)**: The ECB has been actively researching and exploring the potential introduction of a digital euro. The ECB has launched a public consultation and is examining the technical, legal, and policy aspects of a digital euro.
- **Federal Reserve (Fed)**: The U.S. Federal Reserve has been studying the implications and potential use cases of a digital dollar. The Fed has been engaging in research and public discussions to understand the benefits and risks associated with a digital currency.
- **Other Central Banks**: Several other central banks, including the Bank of Canada, Bank of England, Bank of Japan, and Reserve Bank of Australia, are actively researching and exploring the possibility of CBDCs. These central banks are examining the opportunities and challenges associated with digital currencies within their respective jurisdictions.

CBDCs present opportunities for financial inclusion, efficiency, and enhanced monetary policy tools. However, they also pose risks related to privacy, systemic stability, and technological challenges. Key players such as the People's Bank of China, Eastern Caribbean Central Bank, European Central Bank, Federal Reserve, and other central banks are actively researching and exploring CBDCs. As CBDCs continue to evolve, striking the right balance between innovation, privacy, security, and regulatory considerations will be crucial in realizing the potential benefits of digital currencies.

Non-fungible Tokens

NFTs are unique digital assets that represent ownership or proof of authenticity of a specific item or piece of content. Unlike cryptocurrencies such as Bitcoin or Ether, which are fungible and interchangeable, NFTs are indivisible and have distinct characteristics. This section explores the opportunities, risks, and key players associated with NFTs.

Opportunities of NFTs

NFTs offer opportunities for digital ownership, creativity, and monetization. They enable artists to sell their work directly to consumers, provide proof of authenticity, and earn royalties. NFTs also open avenues for virtual real estate, gaming assets, and collectibles, fostering innovation in the digital economy. By expanding on each of these points:

- **Digital Ownership and Authenticity**: NFTs provide a means to prove ownership and authenticity of digital assets, including artwork, collectibles, virtual real estate, music, and more. NFTs enable creators and artists to monetize their digital works and establish a direct relationship with their audience.

- **Increased Transparency and Traceability**: NFTs leverage blockchain technology, providing a transparent and immutable record of ownership and transaction history. This transparency enhances trust and enables users to verify the provenance and authenticity of digital assets.
- **New Revenue Streams for Creators**: NFTs introduce novel ways for creators to monetize their work. Artists can sell limited editions, fractional ownership, or receive royalties through smart contracts embedded within NFTs, potentially reshaping traditional revenue models.
- **Gamification and Virtual Worlds**: NFTs can be utilized in gaming and virtual worlds to represent unique in-game items, characters, or land ownership. Players can buy, sell, and trade NFTs within the game ecosystem, creating vibrant economies and fostering user engagement.

Risks and Challenges of NFTs

NFTs face challenges such as potential for fraud, copyright infringement, and market volatility. The environmental impact of blockchain technology used for NFTs is also a concern. Additionally, the legal and regulatory landscape for NFTs is still evolving, adding to the uncertainty and risk for investors. A quick list of these risks include:

- **Market Volatility and Speculation**: The NFT market has experienced significant volatility, with prices fluctuating dramatically. This volatility raises concerns about speculative bubbles and the potential for unsustainable valuations.
- **Copyright and Intellectual Property Issues**: NFTs can raise legal and copyright challenges, particularly when it comes to the ownership and rights associated with digital assets. The ease of tokenizing and trading digital content may lead to copyright infringement or disputes over ownership.
- **Environmental Impact**: NFTs have received criticism for their environmental impact, especially when minted on blockchains with high energy consumption, such as Ethereum. The energy-intensive mining processes involved in minting and trading NFTs contribute to carbon emissions and environmental concerns.
- **Lack of Regulation and Investor Protection**: The NFT market is relatively new and largely unregulated, which raises concerns about fraud and investor protection. Market participants must exercise caution and conduct due diligence when engaging in NFT transactions.

Key Players in the NFT Space

Key players in the NFT space include artists, collectors, marketplaces, and developers. Artists create and tokenize digital assets, collectors buy and trade these assets, marketplaces facilitate transactions, and developers build the underlying blockchain infrastructure. These players collectively drive the growth, innovation, and dynamics of the NFT market:

- **Ethereum**: Ethereum is the most widely used blockchain for NFTs, providing the infrastructure and standards (such as ERC-721 and ERC-1155) that enable the creation and trading of NFTs. Many NFT marketplaces and projects are built on the Ethereum blockchain.
- **Binance Smart Chain (BSC)**: BSC has gained popularity as an alternative blockchain platform for NFTs due to its lower transaction fees and faster transaction times compared to Ethereum. Several NFT projects and marketplaces have emerged on BSC.

- **OpenSea**: OpenSea is one of the largest NFT marketplaces, supporting a wide range of digital assets, including art, collectibles, virtual land, and more. It serves as a platform for buying, selling, and trading NFTs from various blockchain networks.
- **NBA Top Shot**: NBA Top Shot, developed by Dapper Labs, is an NFT platform that offers digital collectibles in the form of basketball highlights, known as "moments". It has gained significant attention and popularity, showcasing the potential of NFTs in the sports industry.
- **CryptoPunks**: CryptoPunks is an early and influential NFT project consisting of 10,000 unique algorithmically generated pixel art characters. Each CryptoPunk is a distinct NFT, with some rarities commanding high values in the market.
- **Beeple**: Beeple, an artist known for his digital artwork, gained significant attention for selling an NFT titled "Everydays: The First 5000 Days" at auction for a record-breaking price. The sale highlighted the potential value and demand for digital art NFTs.

NFTs present opportunities for digital ownership, authenticity verification, new revenue streams for creators, and innovation in various industries. However, risks such as market volatility, copyright issues, environmental impact, and the need for regulatory frameworks pose challenges to the NFT ecosystem. Ethereum and BSC serve as prominent blockchain platforms for NFTs, while platforms like OpenSea, NBA Top Shot, CryptoPunks, and artists like Beeple have played significant roles in shaping the NFT landscape. As the NFT market evolves, careful consideration of risks and responsible participation will be essential in realizing the full potential of NFTs in the digital economy.

Sustainability and Green Blockchains

As the popularity of blockchain technology grows, concerns about its environmental impact have emerged due to the energy consumption associated with certain consensus mechanisms, such as Proof of Work (PoW). Sustainability and green blockchains aim to mitigate the environmental footprint of blockchain networks while harnessing the benefits of decentralized systems. This section explores the opportunities, risks, and key players associated with sustainability and green blockchains.

Opportunities of Sustainability in Green Blockchains

Sustainability and green blockchains offer opportunities for energy-efficient transactions, reducing the environmental impact of blockchain technology. They foster sustainable practices in industries like supply chain and energy. Green blockchains also attract environmentally conscious investors, driving innovation toward more sustainable decentralized technologies and applications. We can summarize these opportunities as follows:

- **Energy Efficiency**: Green blockchains aim to improve energy efficiency by utilizing alternative consensus mechanisms that require less computational power than traditional PoW. This can reduce the environmental impact associated with blockchain networks.
- **Environmental Sustainability**: Sustainable blockchains strive to minimize carbon emissions and decrease reliance on non-renewable energy sources. By promoting energy-efficient practices, renewable energy adoption, and carbon offsetting initiatives, green blockchains contribute to environmental sustainability goals.

- **Enhanced Reputation and Adoption**: Embracing sustainability and green initiatives can enhance the reputation and credibility of blockchain projects and organizations. By demonstrating a commitment to environmental responsibility, they can attract environmentally conscious users and stakeholders.
- **Innovation in Energy Sector**: Green blockchains can drive innovation in the energy sector by facilitating peer-to-peer energy trading, renewable energy certificate tracking, and efficient supply chain management. They provide new opportunities for decentralized and sustainable energy solutions.

Risks and Challenges of Sustainability in Green Blockchains

Sustainability in green blockchains faces challenges such as technological complexity, scalability, and adoption barriers. The transition from energy-intensive to green blockchains can be difficult. Additionally, the effectiveness of green solutions in reducing environmental impact is still under scrutiny. Regulatory and standardization issues also pose significant challenges. In summary:

- **Scalability and Performance**: Implementing alternative consensus mechanisms that are more energy-efficient may present challenges in terms of scalability and network performance. Ensuring that sustainability measures do not compromise the speed and scalability of blockchain networks is a key challenge.
- **Network Security**: Transitioning to alternative consensus mechanisms may impact the security of blockchain networks. It is crucial to design mechanisms that maintain the integrity and security of transactions while reducing energy consumption.
- **Regulatory Uncertainty**: The evolving regulatory landscape surrounding sustainability and green initiatives can create uncertainty for blockchain projects. Compliance with emerging environmental regulations and the development of standardized frameworks can pose challenges.
- **Adoption and Awareness**: Encouraging adoption of sustainable and green blockchains requires raising awareness among developers, users, and businesses about the environmental impact of blockchain technology and the benefits of sustainable practices.

Key Players in Sustainability in Green Blockchains

Key players in sustainability in green blockchains include developers, users, and regulators. Developers create energy-efficient blockchain technologies, users adopt these sustainable practices, and regulators establish standards and policies for green blockchains. Together, they drive the transition toward more sustainable, decentralized technologies and applications. A few examples include:

- **Ethereum 2.0**: Ethereum has transitioned from a PoW consensus mechanism to a Proof of Stake (PoS) mechanism with the Ethereum 2.0 upgrade. This transition aimed to significantly reduce energy consumption and improve the sustainability of the network.
- **Cardano**: Cardano is a blockchain platform that utilizes a PoS consensus mechanism. It aims to be a sustainable and energy-efficient blockchain network while providing scalability and security.
- **Energy Web Foundation (EWF)**: The EWF focuses on building open source blockchain platforms and tools for the energy sector. Their focus is on enabling peer-to-peer energy

trading, renewable energy certificates, and energy asset management using sustainable blockchain solutions.

■ **Chia Network**: Chia Network is a blockchain platform developed by Bram Cohen, the creator of BitTorrent. It utilizes a consensus mechanism called Proof of Space and Time (PoST), which relies on available disk space rather than computational power, aiming for a greener alternative to PoW.

■ **Climate Ledger Initiative**: The Climate Ledger Initiative is an international coalition of organizations exploring the potential of blockchain technology for climate and sustainability challenges. It aims to foster collaboration, research, and implementation of blockchain solutions for climate action.

Sustainability and green blockchains present opportunities to reduce the environmental impact of blockchain technology while driving innovation in various sectors. Energy efficiency, environmental sustainability, enhanced reputation, and innovation in the energy sector are among the potential benefits. However, challenges related to scalability, network security, regulatory uncertainty, and adoption must be addressed. Key players like Ethereum 2.0, Cardano, Energy Web Foundation, Chia Network, and the Climate Ledger Initiative are actively working toward sustainable blockchain solutions. By prioritizing sustainability and embracing green initiatives, blockchain networks can contribute to a more sustainable and environmentally responsible future.

Regulatory Developments

Regulatory developments in blockchain are crucial for establishing a clear legal framework, ensuring consumer protection, fostering innovation, and addressing risks associated with blockchain technology. As the adoption of blockchain expands across various industries, regulators recognize the need to adapt existing regulations or introduce new ones to address the unique characteristics and challenges posed by decentralized systems. Some key reasons for regulatory developments in blockchain include:

■ **Investor Protection**: Regulations help protect investors from fraudulent activities and market manipulation. They establish standards for transparency, disclosure, and fair practices in blockchain-based investments, Initial Coin Offerings (ICOs), and security token offerings.

■ **Anti-Money Laundering (AML) and Know Your Customer (KYC)**: AML and KYC regulations are critical for preventing money laundering, terrorist financing, and other illicit activities facilitated through cryptocurrencies and blockchain networks. Regulators work to ensure compliance with these regulations to maintain the integrity of the financial system.

■ **Consumer Protection**: Regulations aim to protect consumers in blockchain transactions, including digital asset purchases, smart contract interactions, and decentralized applications (dApps). They provide guidelines for disclosures, dispute resolution mechanisms, and liability frameworks to safeguard consumer interests.

■ **Data Privacy and Security**: With the increasing use of blockchain for storing and processing personal data, regulations such as the General Data Protection Regulation (GDPR) in the European Union help ensure privacy and data protection. Regulators work to strike a balance between the transparency of blockchain and individuals' right to control their personal information.

■ **Market Integrity and Fair Competition**: Regulations help maintain fair competition, prevent market abuse, and ensure the integrity of blockchain-based markets. They address issues such as insider trading, market manipulation, and fraudulent practices to foster trust and confidence in the blockchain ecosystem.

Opportunities for Regulatory Developments

Regulatory developments in blockchain offer opportunities for legal clarity, consumer protection, and innovation. They can foster trust, promote responsible use of blockchain technology, and mitigate associated risks. Regulatory advancements also pave the way for institutional adoption and integration of blockchain into mainstream financial systems. Opportunities arising from regulatory developments in blockchain include:

■ **Clarity and Certainty**: Well-defined regulations provide clarity to businesses, investors, and users, enabling them to navigate the legal landscape with confidence. Clear guidelines can encourage innovation and attract more traditional financial institutions into the blockchain space.

■ **Institutional Adoption**: Regulatory developments can facilitate the entry of institutional investors and financial institutions into the blockchain market. Robust regulations that address risks and provide a stable legal environment can boost trust and encourage institutional participation.

■ **Global Interoperability**: Regulatory developments at an international level can lead to harmonization of standards and regulations, facilitating global interoperability and cross-border transactions. This can unlock new opportunities for trade, financial inclusion, and collaboration between different jurisdictions.

Risks and Challenges for Regulatory Developments

Regulatory developments in blockchain face challenges such as keeping pace with rapid technological advancements, ensuring global coordination, and addressing jurisdictional complexities. They also risk stifling innovation if regulations are overly restrictive. Balancing consumer protection with fostering innovation is a significant challenge in formulating effective blockchain regulations. Risks associated with regulatory developments include:

■ **Overregulation**: Excessive or burdensome regulations can stifle innovation and hinder the development of blockchain applications. Striking a balance between regulatory oversight and allowing room for technological advancement is crucial.

■ **Regulatory Arbitrage**: Different regulatory approaches across jurisdictions can lead to regulatory arbitrage, where businesses may choose to operate in areas with less stringent regulations. This can create challenges in maintaining a level playing field and consistent regulatory standards.

■ **Compliance Complexity**: The rapidly evolving nature of blockchain technology makes it challenging to create regulations that keep pace with technological advancements. Compliance requirements may become complex, especially for small businesses and start-ups, impeding their ability to enter the market.

Key Players for Regulatory Developments

Key players in regulatory developments for blockchain include regulators, policymakers, blockchain companies, and users. Regulators and policymakers formulate and enforce regulations. Blockchain companies comply with these regulations and influence policy through advocacy. Users' needs and behaviors also shape regulatory developments, ensuring practical and effective governance. Some notable regulatory associations are:

- **Financial Stability Board (FSB)**: The FSB is an international body that monitors and makes recommendations about the global financial system. It has been actively involved in assessing the risks and regulatory implications of cryptocurrencies and blockchain technology.
- **Financial Action Task Force (FATF)**: FATF is an intergovernmental organization that sets global standards for combating money laundering, terrorist financing, and other related threats. It has issued guidance on AML and KYC requirements for virtual assets and service providers.
- **Securities and Exchange Commission (SEC)**: The SEC, in the United States, plays a significant role in regulating securities and digital assets. It has provided guidance and enforcement actions to address issues related to ICOs, security tokens, and market manipulation.
- **European Securities and Markets Authority (ESMA)**: ESMA is responsible for developing and implementing regulations for securities and financial markets within the European Union. It has been actively monitoring and providing guidance on ICOs, crypto-assets, and distributed ledger technology.
- **National Blockchain Associations and Consortia**: Numerous blockchain associations and consortia, such as the Blockchain Association, Global Blockchain Business Council, and Global Digital Finance, advocate for blockchain-friendly regulations, industry standards, and best practices.

Regulatory developments in blockchain are essential for protecting investors, ensuring consumer safety, promoting fair competition, and facilitating innovation. Clear regulations can provide certainty, attract institutional investors, and foster global interoperability. However, striking the right balance between regulation and innovation, avoiding overregulation, and ensuring consistency across jurisdictions are ongoing challenges. Key players such as the FSB, FATF, SEC, ESMA, and industry associations play significant roles in shaping regulatory developments and fostering a conducive environment for blockchain technology to thrive. Continued collaboration between regulators, industry participants, and the blockchain community is crucial to strike the right regulatory balance and unlock the full potential of blockchain technology.

Conclusion

The past three years have witnessed a remarkable expansion of blockchain technology, transcending its origins in cryptocurrencies. With a diverse range of real-world applications and a rapidly evolving landscape, blockchain is poised to reshape industries, revolutionize financial systems, and foster trust in an increasingly digital world. Understanding the latest trends and staying informed about emerging news is essential for grasping the full potential of blockchain technology and its transformative impact.

Chapter 2

Web3 Oriented Architecture Patterns

As Web3 gains momentum and ushers in the era of decentralized applications and blockchain technology, developers are faced with new challenges in designing robust and scalable architectures. Service Oriented Architecture (SOA) is a proven architectural pattern that provides a solution for building modular, interoperable, and scalable systems. In this chapter, we explore SOA in general, its benefits and challenges, and discuss how this architecture pattern can be applied to Web3 applications.

Understanding Service Oriented Architecture (SOA)

SOA is an architectural style that promotes the creation of modular and loosely coupled services, which can be independently deployed and scaled. Services in an SOA are self-contained units of functionality that can be accessed and utilized by other services or client applications over a network. These services communicate through well-defined interfaces using standard protocols such as HTTP or message queues.

Benefits of SOA

SOA promotes reusability, flexibility, and interoperability. It allows for easy integration of diverse systems, reducing development time and costs. SOA improves scalability and simplifies maintenance by modularizing services. It enhances business agility, enabling quick adaptation to changing business needs. Lastly, it fosters innovation by allowing independent service evolution. Figure 2.1 illustrates the following four key benefits of SOA:

- **Modularity and Reusability**: SOA enables the development of services as independent modules, making them reusable across multiple applications. This modularity facilitates flexibility, as changes in one service do not affect others.

DOI: 10.4324/9781003491934-2

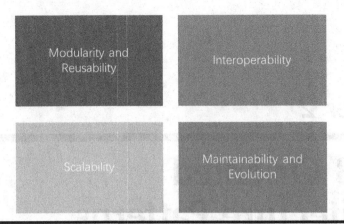

Figure 2.1 Benefits of Service Oriented Architecture

- **Interoperability**: Services in an SOA can be developed using different technologies and platforms, as long as they adhere to the defined interfaces and protocols. This allows for seamless integration of services across heterogeneous environments.
- **Scalability**: SOA enables scaling individual services independently based on their specific demands, improving performance and resource utilization. This flexibility is crucial in Web3 applications that may experience unpredictable traffic patterns or require scalability for handling blockchain interactions.
- **Maintainability and Evolution**: SOA promotes loose coupling between services, enabling easier maintenance and evolution of individual components without impacting the entire system. This makes it easier to introduce new features or modify existing functionality in Web3 applications.

Challenges of SOA

SOA can face challenges such as complexity in service management, increased initial investment, and potential performance overhead. It requires careful design to avoid tight coupling. Security can be complex due to distributed services. Lastly, achieving organizational alignment for SOA adoption can be difficult, requiring significant change management. To summarize, the top three challenges experienced by organizations adopting SOA are:

- **Service Discovery and Governance**: Managing and discovering services in an SOA can be complex, especially in large-scale systems. Proper governance practices, including service registries and policies, are necessary to ensure service availability and manage versioning.
- **Data Consistency and Integrity**: Maintaining data consistency across distributed services can be challenging. Careful consideration must be given to data synchronization, transaction management, and error handling mechanisms in Web3 applications utilizing SOA.
- **Performance Overhead**: The communication overhead between services can impact performance, especially when multiple services need to collaborate to fulfill a request. Efficient protocols, caching strategies, and optimization techniques are crucial for mitigating this challenge.

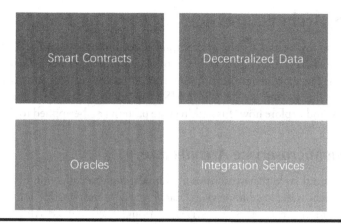

Figure 2.2   Applications of SOA principles to Web3

Applying SOA to Web3 Applications

Web3 applications, built on blockchain and decentralized technologies, can benefit from the principles of SOA. Applying SOA to Web3 applications can enhance decentralization and interoperability. It allows services to be shared across different blockchain networks. SOA can facilitate the integration of legacy systems with blockchain, promoting adoption. However, it requires careful design to ensure security and performance in the decentralized and trustless Web3 environment. The following four Web3 technologies, summarized in Figure 2.2, show how SOA principles can be applied to Web3:

- **Smart Contracts**: In a Web3 application, smart contracts can be encapsulated as services, providing specific functionality to other components. These services can expose APIs to interact with the smart contracts, enabling seamless integration with other services or client applications.
- **Decentralized Data**: Web3 applications often rely on distributed storage systems like InterPlanetary File System (IPFS) or Swarm. Services can be designed to interact with these decentralized storage systems, abstracting the complexity and providing a consistent and reliable data access layer.
- **Oracles**: Oracles are essential for accessing real-world data in Web3 applications. By implementing oracles as services, developers can decouple their applications from specific oracle providers, facilitating interoperability and allowing for easy switching between different oracle solutions.
- **Integration Services**: Web3 applications often need to interact with external systems or protocols. Integration services can be developed to bridge the gap between the Web3 ecosystem and traditional web services, enabling smooth interoperability and data exchange.

SOA offers a flexible and modular approach to building Web3 applications. Its benefits, such as modularity, interoperability, scalability, and maintainability, align well with the requirements of decentralized applications. By adopting SOA principles and leveraging services for various Web3 components, developers can design robust and future-proof architectures that can adapt to the evolving landscape of decentralized technologies.

Microservice Architecture

As Web3 applications evolve and embrace decentralized technologies, architects and developers are searching for effective ways to design scalable, modular, and maintainable systems. Microservice Architecture (MSA) has gained significant popularity in recent years due to its ability to address these challenges. In this section, we delve into MSA, discussing its fundamental principles, benefits, and challenges, and explore how this architecture pattern can be applied to Web3 applications.

Understanding Microservice Architecture

MSA is an architectural style that structures an application as a collection of small, loosely coupled, and independently deployable services. Each service is responsible for a specific business capability and communicates with other services through well-defined APIs or messaging protocols. Unlike monolithic architectures, where the entire application is tightly integrated, MSA promotes a decentralized and distributed approach.

MSAs, compared to SOA, offer higher flexibility and scalability. They allow independent deployment and scaling of services, reducing the impact of changes. Microservices can use different technologies per service, fostering innovation. They simplify continuous delivery and deployment. However, they may increase complexity due to the need for inter-service communication management.

Benefits of MSAs include:

- **Scalability and Performance**: Microservices enable horizontal scaling by allowing individual services to be scaled independently based on demand. This flexibility is especially valuable in Web3 applications where scalability is essential for handling decentralized networks, smart contract interactions, and potentially unpredictable traffic patterns.
- **Modularity and Maintainability**: Services in an MSA are independently deployable and maintainable. Developers can make changes to individual services without impacting the entire application. This modular approach makes it easier to add new features, fix bugs, or upgrade services without disrupting the entire system.
- **Technology Diversity**: Microservices can be built using different technologies, frameworks, and programming languages. This flexibility allows developers to choose the most suitable tools for each service, promoting innovation, and leveraging the strengths of different technologies in Web3 applications.
- **Team Autonomy and Scalability**: Microservices promote the division of labor among development teams, allowing them to work independently on different services. This autonomy facilitates faster development cycles, improved productivity, and better alignment with decentralized development methodologies such as agile and DevOps.

The following Figure 2.3 visualizes the four benefits in a single figure.

Challenges of Microservice Architecture

MSA can face challenges such as managing inter-service communication, data consistency, and distributed system complexity. It requires robust service discovery and fault tolerance mechanisms. Testing can be complex due to service dependencies. Lastly, it requires a cultural shift toward decentralized governance and responsibility, which can be challenging to implement. Organizations that adopt MSA will typically experience the following:

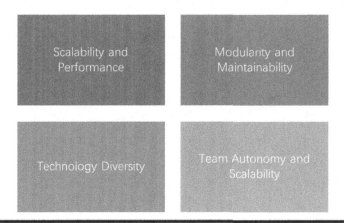

Figure 2.3   Benefits of Microservice Architecture

- **Distributed System Complexity**: Building and managing a distributed system introduces inherent complexity. Communication between services, data consistency, fault tolerance, and maintaining transactional integrity requires careful design, implementation, and operational considerations.
- **Service Discovery and Orchestration**: In an MSA, services need to discover and communicate with each other. Implementing service discovery mechanisms and effective orchestration techniques is essential to enable seamless communication and coordination in Web3 applications.
- **Data Management and Consistency**: Maintaining data consistency across multiple services can be challenging in a distributed environment. Strategies such as event-driven architectures, eventual consistency, and distributed transactions must be employed to ensure data integrity in Web3 applications utilizing MSA.
- **Operational Overhead**: With multiple services running independently, operational tasks such as monitoring, logging, deployment, and scaling become more complex. Robust DevOps practices and automation are crucial to manage the operational overhead of an MSA-based Web3 application.

Applying Microservice Architecture to Web3 Applications

MSA can be effectively applied to Web3 applications, capitalizing on its strengths, and addressing the specific requirements of decentralized systems. Here, and illustrated in Figure 2.4, are a few scenarios where MSA can be leveraged:

- **Blockchain Interactions**: Web3 applications interact with blockchains through various protocols and smart contracts. Designing services specifically responsible for blockchain interactions, transaction handling, and event management can provide a modular and scalable approach to integrate blockchain capabilities into the application.
- **Decentralized Storage and File Sharing**: Web3 applications often utilize decentralized storage systems like IPFS or Swarm. Services can be designed to interact with these storage networks, providing abstraction and standardization for file handling, retrieval, and data integrity.

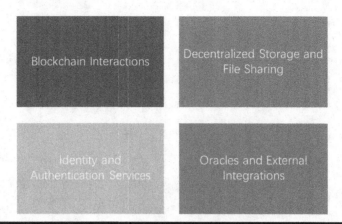

Figure 2.4 Application of Microservice Architecture to Web3

- **Identity and Authentication Services**: Web3 applications require robust identity management and authentication mechanisms. By developing separate services for user authentication, decentralized identity management, and access control, developers can ensure modular and interoperable solutions that align with Web3 standards.
- **Oracles and External Integrations**: Web3 applications frequently rely on oracles to access off-chain data or interact with external systems. Microservices can be dedicated to managing these integrations, abstracting the complexity, and providing a standardized interface for data retrieval and integration.

MSA offers a powerful approach to building scalable and modular Web3 applications. By embracing the benefits of scalability, modularity, technology diversity, and team autonomy, developers can create robust and adaptable systems capable of leveraging the full potential of decentralized technologies. However, it is important to address the challenges associated with distributed systems, service discovery, data management, and operational overhead to ensure the successful implementation of MSA in Web3 applications.

Cloud Architecture Patterns

Cloud computing has revolutionized the way applications are designed and deployed, providing scalability, flexibility, and cost-efficiency. Cloud architecture design patterns are established solutions to common problems faced in cloud-based systems. In this section, we explore some common cloud architecture design patterns, discuss the problems they address, and examine how these patterns can also be applied to Web3 applications.

Scalable Load Balancer

CONTEXT

As application traffic increases, distributing the load across multiple servers becomes essential to ensure optimal performance and availability.

PROBLEM

Handling increased traffic and preventing single points of failure.

SOLUTION

A load balancer distributes incoming requests across multiple servers, improving performance, and enabling horizontal scaling. It can be implemented using services like Elastic Load Balancer (ELB) in AWS or Application Gateway in Azure.

APPLICATION IN WEB3

Web3 applications often experience unpredictable traffic patterns due to blockchain interactions. Scalable load balancers can handle increased traffic and distribute requests to services responsible for blockchain interactions, ensuring responsiveness and availability.

Auto Scaling

CONTEXT

Applications may experience varying levels of traffic and resource demands, requiring dynamic scaling to meet demand.

PROBLEM

Ensuring application availability and optimal resource utilization during peak times while minimizing costs during low traffic periods.

SOLUTION

Auto Scaling automatically adjusts the number of computing resources (e.g., virtual machines or containers) based on defined thresholds. It can be achieved using services like Auto Scaling Groups in AWS or Virtual Machine Scale Sets in Azure.

APPLICATION IN WEB3

Web3 applications often face sporadic bursts of traffic during Initial Coin Offering (ICOs), token sales, or popular events. Auto Scaling enables Web3 applications to dynamically scale resources, ensuring adequate capacity during peak loads while optimizing costs during periods of low demand.

Database Replication

CONTEXT

Ensuring high availability, data durability, and read scalability for applications with heavy read loads or geographically dispersed users.

PROBLEM

Single points of failure, data loss, and latency issues.

SOLUTION

Database replication replicates data across multiple database instances, enabling high availability, data redundancy, and read scalability. Replication mechanisms like primary-secondary devices or primary-primary replication can be implemented using technologies like Amazon RDS or Azure SQL Database.

APPLICATION IN WEB3

Web3 applications may require high availability and data durability for blockchain-related data. Database replication can be employed to ensure redundant copies of blockchain data, enabling faster access, disaster recovery, and improved performance for Web3 applications.

Caching

CONTEXT

Accelerating access to frequently accessed data and reducing the load on backend systems.

PROBLEM

Slow response times and increased load on backend services.

SOLUTION

Caching stores frequently accessed data in a high-speed cache, reducing the need to fetch data from the backend on every request. Caching mechanisms like Redis or Memcached can be utilized.

APPLICATION IN WEB3

Web3 applications often interact with blockchain networks or external APIs. Caching can be employed to store frequently accessed blockchain data, smart contract responses, or API responses, improving response times and reducing load on the underlying systems.

Event-Driven Architecture

CONTEXT

Building loosely coupled and scalable systems that can handle asynchronous and real-time events.

PROBLEM

Ensuring system responsiveness and scalability while decoupling components.

SOLUTION

Event-driven architecture allows components to communicate through events, facilitating loose coupling, scalability, and real-time processing. Technologies like Apache Kafka or AWS EventBridge can be used for event-driven communication.

APPLICATION IN WEB3

Web3 applications often rely on events emitted by smart contracts or blockchain networks. Implementing an event-driven architecture enables seamless processing of blockchain events, allowing applications to react to changes in the blockchain state in real-time.

Cloud architecture design patterns provide proven solutions to common challenges in building scalable and resilient systems in the cloud. While originally designed for traditional cloud-based applications, many of these patterns can be effectively applied to Web3 applications. Scalable load balancers, auto scaling, database replication, caching, and event-driven architecture are just a few examples of patterns that can enhance the scalability, performance, and availability of Web3 applications. By leveraging these patterns, developers can build robust and efficient architectures that harness the benefits of cloud computing while meeting the unique requirements of decentralized technologies in Web3.

Web3 Native Design Patterns

Web3 applications, built on blockchain and decentralized technologies, present unique challenges that require specialized design patterns. In this section, we explore specific design patterns tailored for Web3 applications, highlighting the problems they address and their benefits in solving these challenges.

Blockchain Interoperability Pattern

PROBLEM

Web3 applications often need to interact with multiple blockchains or distributed ledgers to access different assets, protocols, or smart contracts.

SOLUTION

The Blockchain Interoperability pattern enables seamless integration and interoperability across multiple blockchains. It involves building abstraction layers or adapters that translate and standardize interactions with different blockchain networks, simplifying the development and maintenance of Web3 applications.

BENEFITS

- Facilitates cross-chain asset transfers and interoperability.
- Reduces development complexity by providing a consistent interface for interacting with multiple blockchains.
- Future proves applications by allowing easy integration with new blockchain networks as they emerge.

Decentralized Identity Pattern

PROBLEM

Web3 applications require robust identity management systems that preserve privacy, security, and user ownership of personal data.

SOLUTION

The Decentralized Identity pattern leverages decentralized identity frameworks, such as Self-Sovereign Identity (SSI), to enable users to control and manage their own identities. It involves the use of blockchain-based or decentralized protocols to store and verify user identity information, eliminating the need for central authorities or intermediaries.

BENEFITS

- Enhances privacy and security by giving users control over their personal data.
- Enables seamless and secure authentication across different Web3 applications.
- Promotes interoperability by allowing users to carry their identities across various platforms and services.

Tokenization Pattern

PROBLEM

Web3 applications often deal with digital assets, tokens, and cryptocurrencies, requiring efficient management, transfer, and tracking of these assets.

SOLUTION

The Tokenization pattern involves representing real-world or digital assets as tokens on a blockchain. It leverages smart contracts and token standards, such as ERC-20 or ERC-721, to create fungible or non-fungible tokens (NFTs). This pattern facilitates secure ownership, transferability, and traceability of assets within Web3 applications.

BENEFITS

- Enables fractional ownership and efficient transfer of assets.
- Simplifies the integration of assets into various Web3 applications and ecosystems.
- Enables the development of decentralized marketplaces and peer-to-peer asset exchange platforms.

Oracles Pattern

PROBLEM

Web3 applications often require access to external data sources, real-world events, or off-chain information to perform specific functions or make informed decisions.

SOLUTION

The Oracles pattern involves integrating oracles, which are services that provide external data to the blockchain. Oracles act as bridges between the blockchain and off-chain systems, enabling the secure and reliable flow of external information into Web3 applications.

BENEFITS

- Facilitates real-world data integration, enabling Web3 applications to interact with off-chain systems.
- Supports the automation of smart contract execution based on external events or conditions.
- Enhances trust and transparency by ensuring verifiability and tamper resistance of off-chain data.

Governance Pattern

PROBLEM

Web3 applications often require decentralized decision-making processes and mechanisms for protocol upgrades, consensus, and community governance.

SOLUTION

The Governance pattern involves designing and implementing decentralized governance systems within Web3 applications. These systems leverage decentralized voting mechanisms, token-based governance models, or consensus protocols to allow stakeholders to participate in decision-making processes.

BENEFITS

- Empowers community members to participate in the decision-making and evolution of Web3 applications.
- Enhances transparency and trust by enabling open and decentralized governance processes.
- Supports protocol upgrades, parameter changes, and consensus rule modifications in a decentralized manner.

Web3 applications demand specialized design patterns to address the unique challenges of decentralized technologies. The Blockchain Interoperability pattern, Decentralized Identity pattern, Tokenization pattern, Oracles pattern, and Governance pattern are just a few examples of design patterns tailored for Web3 applications. By leveraging these patterns, developers can overcome challenges related to interoperability, identity management, asset management, data integration, and decentralized decision-making, creating robust and innovative Web3 applications that harness the full potential of blockchain and decentralized technologies.

Wallet Connection and Interaction Patterns

We have seen wallets in Chapter 1 and described the types of wallets most commonly used in Web3 applications. Wallets are the mechanism for storing assets, cryptocurrency, and digital tokens. There are some key architecture patterns implemented by wallets, which are:

- Custodial wallets
- Self-custodial wallets
- App connection and integration
- Asymmetric cryptography

We will dive into cryptography in Chapter 4 in detail, so for now let's focus on the custody vs self-custody of assets comparison, and how Web3 apps can connect to and interact with wallets.

Custodial Wallets

Custodial wallets are digital wallets where a third-party entity, often an exchange platform, manages the private keys on behalf of the user. These wallets generally require KYC (know-your-customer) and use the same type of recoverability features similar to your email provider. However, this comes with the requirement of trusting the third party with their private keys and assets.

Despite this, custodial wallets offer the same features that non-custodial wallets provide, such as interacting with smart contracts. In contrast to non-custodial wallets, where users have full control over their keys, custodial wallets entrust the custody of private keys to a third party. This means that the user does not have direct control over their assets, and instead, relies on the third party to manage and secure their assets.

It's important to note that while custodial wallets can provide a level of convenience, they also come with risks, such as the potential for the third party to be hacked or go out of business. Therefore, users should carefully consider these factors when choosing between custodial and non-custodial wallets.

Figure 2.5 illustrates the user flow for custodial wallets, where the custody of the private keys used to sign transactions is with a third-party authority, on behalf of the user:

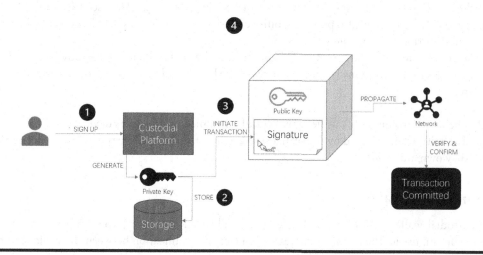

Figure 2.5   Custodial wallet user flow

1. Upon signing up into a custodial platform, the platform generates a **private key** for the user.
2. The private key is typically stored by the platform in a secure cloud storage system. To further protect the private key from access by the cloud service provider, technologies such as hardware secure modules (HSM) or multi-party computing (MPC) are implemented.
3. When the user initiates a transaction, the wallet uses the user's private key to generate a **digital signature**. This signature, along with the **public key**, is sent to the blockchain network. Public keys are not stored in the same way as private keys. Instead, they are derived from the private key and can be regenerated whenever needed. The public key can also be used to generate a **public address**, which is shared with others to receive assets. This public address is like a digital identity tag. It can be tied to a decentralized name service, making it easier for others to remember and interact with a wallet's public key.
4. The network uses the public key to **verify** the authenticity of the signature and **confirm** that the transaction was indeed initiated by the holder of the private key.

Self-Custodial Wallets

A self-custodial, also known as non-custodial, wallet is a type of wallet where the user holds the private keys and has full control over their assets (they have full custody of). This means that the user is solely responsible for the security of their cryptocurrency and tokens, and no third party, including the wallet provider, has access to them.

Non-custodial wallets rely on a public and private key pair to provide users with full control over their assets. The private key is used to sign transactions sent on the blockchain, ensuring that only the private key owner can access and control the associated assets.

It's crucial to keep the private key safe and secure because losing access to it will result in the loss of access to the assets. Non-custodial wallets can be stored in browser extensions or mobile apps and are classified as hot wallets since they are connected to the internet. Hardware versions also exist, often in the form of a USB memory flash drive.

In contrast to custodial wallets, non-custodial wallets do not entrust the custody of private keys to a third party. Instead, users maintain full control and responsibility over keys and assets within the wallet.

Non-custodial wallets are considered to be more secure than custodial wallets, as they eliminate the risk of the funds being compromised or lost due to the actions or security breaches of a third party. However, they also pose a usability challenge as the user is solely responsible for managing and securing their private keys.

Figure 2.6 illustrates the user flow for non-custodial wallets, where the custody of the private keys used to sign transactions is with the user only. The key differences with the custodial wallet flow are:

1. The user signs up with a wallet app, typically installed on the user's device.
2. The private key is issued by the wallet software itself, and stored by the user on a device that they own and control.

Connect to a Wallet

Self-custodial wallets run on your device, and you'll need to connect your wallet to your app before you can use it. The connection creates a line of communication between the wallet and the app or website.

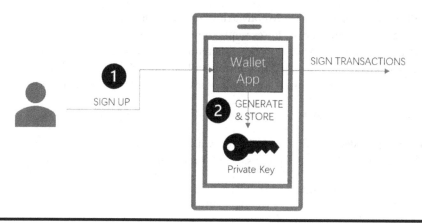

Figure 2.6   Non-custodial wallet user flow

Connecting a wallet like MetaMask (https://metamask.io/) to a website makes the wallet able to interact with the blockchain network, Ethereum for example. The connection process is a common Web3 design pattern that leverages libraries such as **web3.js** (https://web3js.org/). Below is an example of how to connect MetaMask to a web page using JavaScript.

Step 1: Include the web3.js library
Add the following script tag in the <head> section of your HTML file to include the web3.js library:

```
<script
src="https://cdn.jsdelivr.net/npm/web3/dist/web3.min.js"></script>
```

Step 2: Check if MetaMask is installed and enabled
Before using MetaMask, you need to check if the wallet is installed and enabled in the user's browser. Use the following JavaScript code to detect MetaMask:

```
if (typeof window.ethereum !== 'undefined') {
  // MetaMask is installed
}
```

Step 3: Request the user's permission to connect to MetaMask
To connect to the user's MetaMask wallet, you need to create an instance of the **Web3** object and request the user's permission to access their accounts. Use the following JavaScript code:

```
async function connectToMetaMask() {
  try {
    // Request access to the user's accounts
    await window.ethereum.enable();
    // Create a Web3 instance
    const web3 = new Web3(window.ethereum);
  } catch (error) {
  console.error('Failed to connect to MetaMask:', error);
  }
}
```

Step 4: Initiate the connection to MetaMask from the web page

To initiate the connection process, for example to request access to the user's Ethereum account, you can call the **request** function on the Ethereum object when an event (e.g., button click) occurs. In the HTML page you can add a button with an onclick handler (this is a simple HTML example, feel free to use any relevant web framework you're more comfortable with):

```
<button onclick="connectWallet()">Connect Wallet</button>
```

And the **connectWallet()** function will deal with the communication with the wallet directly, by requesting access to the user's accounts on the Ethereum network:

```
async function connectWallet() {
  const accounts = await window.ethereum.request({ method:
  'eth_requestAccounts' });
  console.log('Connected', accounts[0]);
}
```

That's it! When the user clicks the "Connect Wallet" button, MetaMask will prompt them to allow the website access to their accounts. Once connected, you can use the web3 object to interact with the Ethereum network, such as querying account balances, sending transactions, or interacting with smart contracts, as we'll see in the next section.

Note: Make sure to handle errors and provide appropriate feedback to the user throughout the connection process.

Interact with Smart Contracts

Once the wallet is connected to the user's app, you can make it interact with Ethereum smart contracts. You can keep on using the web3.js library, in your JavaScript code. After connecting to the Ethereum network, you need to define an instance of the smart contract. This is done with another common pattern for wallet interaction, which relies on the Application Binary Interface (**ABI**) and the network's address of a smart contract.

An ABI is an interface between two binary program modules. It defines how data structures or computational routines are accessed in machine code, which is a low-level, hardware-dependent format. In contrast, an Application Programming Interface (API) defines this access in source code, which is a relatively high-level, hardware-independent, often human-readable format.

In the context of blockchain and smart contracts, an ABI is essentially a JavaScript Object Notation (JSON) representation that defines available methods, specifies formatting requirements for data, and provides instructions on the proper procedures for executing function calls on the smart contract.

The other piece of information you need to connect to a smart contract on Ethereum is its **network address**. A smart contract's address is a unique identifier on the blockchain that allows users and other contracts to interact with it. It's similar to how an email address allows you to send and receive messages. Users can send transactions to this address to execute the contract's functions.

Step 1: Define a contract instance

Use the following JavaScript code to create an instance of the Web3 object and connect to a smart contract defined at a specified address:

```
// Create a Web3 instance
const web3 = new Web3(window.ethereum);

// Define the contract ABI
const contractABI = [ /* Contract ABI goes here */ ];

// Replace with the actual contract address
const contractAddress = '0x...';

// Create a contract instance
const contract = new web3.eth.Contract(contractABI, contractAddress);
```

Step 3: Interact with smart contract methods

You can now interact with the methods of the smart contract by calling them through the contract instance. Here's an example of how to call a read-only function called **readValue**, which is a function that reads a value in the contract but doesn't make any change to its state:

```
contract.methods.readValue().call()
  .then((result) => {
    console.log('Result:', result);
  })
  .catch((error) => {
    console.error('Error:', error);
  });
```

And this an example of calling a write function called **writeValue**, which alters the contract's state and returns a hash value of the transaction:

```
contract.methods.writeValue(parameter1).send({ from: '0x...' })
  .then((transactionHash) => {
    console.log('Transaction Hash:', transactionHash);
  })
  .catch((error) => {
    console.error('Error:', error);
  });
```

As noted before, remember to include the necessary error handling and additional logic as per your specific requirements.

Build a Web3 UX

There are specific patterns and paradigms for designing user experiences (UX) in Web3 applications. These patterns and paradigms take into account the unique characteristics of decentralized technologies, such as blockchain, smart contracts, and tokenized ecosystems. In this section, we'll explore some common patterns and paradigms for Web3 UX designs.

Wallet-Centric Design

Web3 applications heavily rely on user wallets to interact with blockchain networks and manage digital assets. Wallet-centric design focuses on creating seamless and intuitive user experiences around wallet interactions. This includes easy integration with popular wallets, clear instructions for connecting wallets, and streamlined processes for transactions, account management, and asset tracking.

Onboarding and Education

Given the novelty and complexity of Web3 technologies, onboarding and education play a crucial role in improving user adoption and engagement. UX designs should incorporate intuitive and informative onboarding processes that guide users through key concepts, such as wallet setup, token usage, and transaction flow. Interactive tutorials, tooltips, and contextual help can enhance user understanding and confidence.

Visualizing Blockchain Data

Web3 applications often involve interaction with blockchain data, including transaction histories, smart contract states, or token balances. Effective UX design should visualize this data in a clear and understandable manner, using charts, graphs, or interactive elements. Visualizations can help users comprehend complex blockchain data and facilitate decision-making processes.

Security and Trust

Security and trust are paramount in Web3 applications. UX designs should prioritize conveying the security measures in place, such as encryption, multi-factor authentication, and user control over private keys. Clear indications of transaction confirmations, gas fees, and smart contract permissions enhance user trust. Designing for secure interactions and seamless user experiences while maintaining user control over personal data and assets is essential.

Community Engagement

Web3 ecosystems thrive on community participation and engagement. UX designs should encourage and facilitate community interaction through features such as chat forums, voting mechanisms, decentralized governance interfaces, or NFT marketplaces. Integrating social elements, reputation systems, and incentivizing user contributions can foster an active and vibrant community experience.

Gamification and Incentives

Gamification techniques and token-based incentives can enhance user engagement and promote desired behaviors within Web3 applications. UX designs can incorporate elements such as rewards, badges, leaderboards, and achievements to incentivize user participation, exploration, and contribution to the ecosystem.

Interoperability and Integration

Web3 applications often need to interact with other decentralized protocols, platforms, or wallets. UX designs should consider seamless integration with popular protocols, standards, and third-party services. Offering integrations with widely used tools, such as decentralized exchanges (DEXs), identity providers, or oracle networks, enhances usability and convenience for users.

Mobile-First and Responsive Design

As the usage of mobile devices continues to rise, designing Web3 applications with a mobile-first approach is crucial. UX designs should prioritize responsive and adaptive interfaces that provide a consistent and user-friendly experience across different devices and screen sizes.

It's important to note that these patterns and paradigms are not exhaustive, and the specific design requirements may vary based on the nature and objectives of the Web3 application. UX designers should consider the target audience, usability testing, and feedback loops to continuously refine and improve the user experience in the evolving landscape of Web3 technologies.

DevOps

DevOps practices for Web3 applications, dApps (decentralized applications), and smart contracts encompass a set of techniques and approaches to ensure efficient development, deployment, and operation of these decentralized systems. Writing about DevOps for Web3 would likely require a book on its own (and this is probably a good idea for a new book!). Here, we'll describe at a high level a few common practices for DevOps. Most of them are not peculiar to Web3 apps only, and indeed they reflect best practices for DevOps in web applications in general. A few patterns are specific to Web3 apps because they deal with the immutability of data and code on a blockchain, as we shall see in this section.

Version Control

Use a version control system, such as Git, to track changes to your codebase, including smart contracts, dApp frontend/backend, and infrastructure configuration. Maintain separate repositories for different components to enable independent versioning and easy collaboration among team members.

Continuous Integration and Deployment (CI/CD)

Implement CI/CD pipelines to automate the building, testing, and deployment of your Web3 applications. CI/CD ensures that code changes are thoroughly tested, integrated, and deployed in a controlled and repeatable manner. Automated deployments enable faster and more reliable release cycles while minimizing the risk of human error.

Infrastructure as Code (IaC)

Adopt Infrastructure as Code practices using tools like Terraform or AWS CloudFormation to define and manage your Web3 application's infrastructure. IaC allows for versioning, reproducibility, and easy scaling of the underlying infrastructure components, including servers, networks, storage, and blockchain nodes.

Continuous Monitoring

Implement robust monitoring and logging solutions to gain insights into the performance, availability, and security of your Web3 application. Use tools like Prometheus, Grafana, or ELK stack to monitor key metrics, visualize data, and set up alerting mechanisms to detect and respond to issues promptly. Monitoring can include blockchain-specific metrics, such as pending transactions, gas usage, or contract interactions.

Security and Auditing

Pay close attention to security practices when dealing with Web3 applications. Ensure secure handling of private keys, implement authentication mechanisms, and follow best practices for secure smart contract development. Regularly perform security audits and penetration testing to identify and mitigate vulnerabilities in your application and infrastructure.

Automated Testing

Develop and maintain a comprehensive suite of automated tests for your Web3 application, including unit tests, integration tests, and end-to-end tests. Test both frontend and backend components as well as the interaction with smart contracts and blockchain networks. Automated testing ensures the reliability and correctness of your application, reduces manual effort, and prevents regressions during updates.

Containerization and Orchestration

Containerization with tools like Docker and orchestration with platforms like Kubernetes provide efficient deployment and scalability options for Web3 applications. Containerizing your application components allows for consistent environments across different stages and simplifies the management of dependencies. Orchestration frameworks enable scaling, resilience, and efficient resource utilization in distributed and decentralized architectures.

Disaster Recovery and Backups

Implement backup and disaster recovery strategies to protect critical data and ensure business continuity. Regularly back up data, including blockchain state, databases, and configuration files. Establish recovery plans and test them periodically to ensure reliable and swift recovery in case of unforeseen events or failures.

Secrets Management

For sensitive information like access keys, API tokens, or private keys, use a secrets management tool to securely store and access them within your workflows. Many cloud service providers offer secret management capability which is hardware protected with a Hardware Secure Module (HSM), making access to secrets opaque even to the cloud provider itself.

Figure 2.7 depicts the collections of typical DevOps practices for automation of tasks and infrastructure deployment.

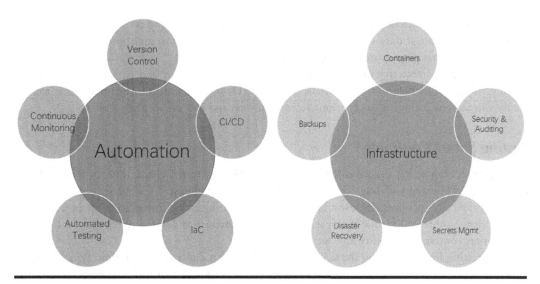

Figure 2.7   DevOps best practices

These practices provide a foundation for effective DevOps in any web development context. Adapt and refine them based on your specific requirements, team structure, and technology stack. In the next section we will focus on the evolving Web3 landscape and the importance of adopting the most effective DevOps practices for Web3 apps and smart contracts.

The Blockchain Challenge for DevOps

Blockchain technology brings unique challenges to DevOps practices, requiring a shift from traditional development, operations, and continuous integration/continuous deployment pipelines. These challenges arise from blockchain's inherent features, such as immutability, decentralization, consensus mechanisms, and the need for integration between on-chain and off-chain systems. In this section, we will delve into these challenges and their implications for DevOps.

Immutability and Consensus

The challenge of dealing with **immutable data structures** comes from the fact that blockchain data, once added to the chain, cannot be modified or removed. This immutability is crucial for the trust and security that blockchain provides but poses difficulties in version control, data correction, and updates.

Furthermore, the **consensus mechanism** in blockchain networks presents another challenge. These networks use consensus mechanisms, like Proof of Work (PoW) or Proof of Stake (PoS), to validate transactions. These mechanisms have implications for performance, scalability, and security. For instance, DevOps needs to consider the latency and throughput limitations of blockchain networks, which can significantly vary based on the consensus mechanism. This could influence application design, necessitating optimizations for transaction processing and state management.

When it comes to integrating **off-chain and on-chain data**, aspects like data synchronization, integrity, security, and privacy have significant implications for DevOps. It is crucial to maintain the integrity and consistency of data transitioning between on-chain and off-chain environments. This necessitates robust data validation, synchronization mechanisms, and potentially the use of oracles (services that provide external data to the blockchain).

On the topic of **security and privacy**: The points of integration between on-chain and off-chain systems can be potential weak spots. Therefore, DevOps practices must incorporate robust security measures, including encryption, access controls, and routine security audits.

Testing Smart Contracts

Testing smart contracts is crucial due to their immutable nature and the significant financial and operational implications of bugs or vulnerabilities. A comprehensive testing strategy for smart contracts typically encompasses several layers, including unit testing, integration testing, and, for highly critical contracts, formal verification. Each of these testing layers targets different aspects of the smart contract's reliability and security.

Unit testing involves testing the smallest parts of a smart contract in isolation, typically individual functions or methods, to ensure that they perform as expected under various conditions. Strategies include the following:

- **Mocking External Calls**: Use mocking frameworks to simulate external calls and dependencies, allowing developers to test the contract's logic in isolation.
- **Parameterized Testing**: Employ parameterized tests to cover a wide range of inputs, including edge cases, to ensure functions handle all expected and unexpected inputs correctly.
- **Automated Test Suites**: Utilize automated testing frameworks (e.g., Truffle, Hardhat for Ethereum, etc.) to write and run unit tests, ensuring they are executed regularly.

Integration testing assesses the interactions between different parts of the smart contract system, including interactions between multiple contracts and the interaction with the blockchain itself. Strategies include the following:

- **Testing Contract Interactions**: Ensure that contracts work together as expected, simulating real-world scenarios where contracts call each other or pass data.
- **Simulating Blockchain Conditions**: Use blockchain simulation tools to test contracts in an environment that closely mirrors live blockchain conditions, including gas usage and transaction ordering.
- **Cross-contract Dependencies**: Test how your contract responds to changes in contracts it depends on, if applicable, ensuring that your system is resilient to changes in external contracts.

In the blockchain space, there is a process known as **contract auditing** that utilizes mathematical methods to prove the correctness of smart contracts or protocols. It involves using formal methods, such as mathematical logic and automated reasoning techniques, to verify that a smart contract or protocol behaves as intended under all possible scenarios. Formal verification is particularly useful for mission-critical contracts where the cost of failure is high. Strategies include the following:

- **Modeling Contract Logic**: Translate smart contract logic into a formal model that can be analyzed mathematically. This often involves using specialized languages and tools.

- **Property Specification**: Clearly define the properties and invariants a contract must maintain (e.g., no unauthorized access, conservation of value, etc.) and use formal verification tools to prove these properties are always upheld.
- **Tooling**: Leverage formal verification tools and platforms (e.g., K Framework, CertiK, etc.) designed for smart contracts.

A comprehensive testing strategy for smart contracts is essential for ensuring their reliability and security. By combining unit tests, integration tests, and formal verification methods, developers can address different aspects of contract functionality and security. Integrating these testing practices into a continuous development and deployment pipeline, complemented by peer reviews and professional audits, maximizes the reliability and security of smart contracts in the blockchain ecosystem.

Testing Data

While the core principles of DevOps remain unchanged, the distributed nature and immutable ledger of blockchain bring about specific considerations on how data is handled "on chain" (i.e., stored inside the blockchain network). These considerations demand careful evaluation when adapting a DevOps approach for blockchain solutions. As previously mentioned, one common challenge with testing smart contracts is generating sample data. Populating a blockchain with test data is more complex than other databases. In a conventional database, scripts can be used to create tables and populate them with data. However, in a blockchain, the process is not as simple. The addition of new blocks is a complex process, as it involves validation by all network participants. While scripting can be effective, it requires meticulous coordination and sequencing, particularly when multiple parties are involved. A prevalent approach for testing is to **fork** an existing blockchain, essentially creating a copy, and using that for testing. This method can eliminate the need to create fake transactions from scratch.

Consider a blockchain as a highway, where every car represents a transaction. Forking is akin to constructing a detour, a new route for the cars to follow. Sometimes, the detour is temporary, like for road repairs, which is a **soft fork**. Other times, the detour becomes the new highway, and the old one is discarded, which is a **hard fork**. In both scenarios, the cars (transactions) must decide which route to take. Figure 2.8 illustrates how a hard fork diverges from the original blockchain, forming a new chain of its own.

When a soft fork happens, the blockchain protocol keeps the rules defined on the network backward compatible. Blocks in the forked chain will follow the old rules as well as the new rules.

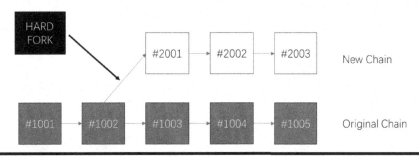

Figure 2.8   Hard fork of a blockchain

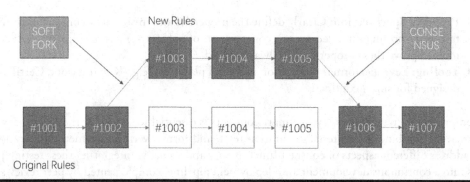

Figure 2.9   Soft work of a blockchain

Blocks in the original chain will continue to follow the old rules. Figure 2.9 depicts the alternate chain, which rejoins the original one when a consensus is reached.

More information about hard and soft forking as a strategy for test data generation can be found in the **DevOps for Blockchain Smart Contracts** article written by the author: https:// learn.microsoft.com/en-us/archive/msdn-magazine/2019/october/blockchain-devops-for-block-chain-smart-contracts.

As we looked at most common patterns for Web3 applications, our journey into the Web3 realm now progresses with the next two chapters that will introduce two critical aspects of this technology: all aspects of cyber security in Chapter 3, and the cryptographic foundation of block-chain in Chapter 4.

Chapter 3

Cybersecurity for Web3 Applications

Web3 applications, which are built on blockchain and decentralized technologies, introduce a unique set of security threats compared to traditional web applications. In this chapter we are going to look at some common security threats for Web3 applications and best practices to mitigate these risks.

Common Threats for Web3 Applications

Web3 applications, also known as decentralized applications (dApps), operate on blockchain technology and offer a new paradigm of user interaction and data management. However, this innovative approach does not render them immune to security threats. In fact, the decentralized nature of Web3 can introduce unique vulnerabilities that are non-existent in traditional web environments. This section delves into the common threats faced by Web3 applications, listed in Figure 3.1, ranging from smart contract exploits to front-end vulnerabilities. We then discuss common patterns for mitigation strategies and the importance of robust security measures to safeguard these platforms from malicious actors.

Let's dig into each threat more in detail now.

Smart Contract Vulnerabilities

Smart contracts are the backbone of many Web3 applications. They can be susceptible to various vulnerabilities, such as reentrancy attacks, integer overflow/underflow, and unhandled exceptions. To mitigate these risks, it is crucial to follow best practices like conducting extensive code audits, using well-tested libraries, implementing security mechanisms like access controls and input validation, and regularly updating contracts to patch known vulnerabilities.

DOI: 10.4324/9781003491934-3

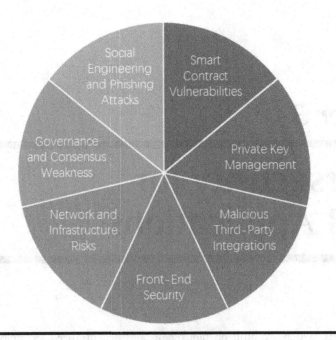

Figure 3.1   Common threats for Web3 applications

Private Key Management

Web3 applications rely on private keys to sign transactions and interact with blockchain networks. Inadequate private key management can lead to unauthorized access and asset theft. Best practices include using hardware wallets or secure key storage solutions, enforcing strong password policies, enabling two-factor authentication (2FA), and educating users about secure key management practices.

Malicious Third-Party Integrations

Web3 applications often integrate with external services, such as oracles or decentralized exchanges. However, these integrations can introduce security risks. It is essential to thoroughly vet and audit third-party services, review their security practices and track records, and minimize the permissions granted to external integrations. Additionally, implementing secure communication channels (e.g., HTTPS) and validating data received from external sources can help prevent data tampering and injection attacks.

Front-End Security

Web3 applications have a front-end component that interacts with the blockchain. Protecting the front-end against attacks like cross-site scripting (XSS) and cross-site request forgery (CSRF) is crucial. Employ best practices such as input validation, output encoding, and strict content security policies (CSP) to mitigate these risks. Regularly patching and updating dependencies is also important to address any known vulnerabilities.

Network and Infrastructure Risks

Web3 applications interact with various networks, including blockchain networks, decentralized storage systems, and peer-to-peer networks. To mitigate risks associated with network attacks, it is important to use secure communication protocols (e.g., Transport Layer Security (TLS)), implement strong network segmentation, regularly update and patch network infrastructure, and use firewalls and intrusion detection systems (IDS) to monitor and protect against network-based attacks.

Governance and Consensus Weakness

Web3 applications that utilize decentralized governance or consensus mechanisms may face security risks related to these mechanisms. Ensuring robust governance processes, conducting security audits of consensus algorithms, and following best practices for decentralized decision-making can help mitigate these risks.

Social Engineering and Phishing Attacks

Web3 applications may be targeted by social engineering attacks to trick users into revealing their private keys or other sensitive information. Implementing user education programs to raise awareness about common attack vectors, enabling multi-factor authentication, and using secure communication channels (e.g., HTTPS) can help protect against social engineering and phishing attacks.

These are just a few examples of the security threats and best practices for Web3 applications. It is essential to stay updated on the latest security trends, follow industry best practices, and conduct regular security audits to ensure the ongoing protection of Web3 applications.

Security Development Lifecycle

Developing a robust software development lifecycle (SDLC) for Web3 apps that prioritizes security is crucial for protecting dApps and smart contracts from attacks. There are many phases in a robust SDLC, and often requirements like security, identity protection, data privacy, are neglected or considered at a later stage. Security is *not* a feature to add to a software application. Security is a fundamental design principle to embed into the SDLC from the very beginning and to consider at each step. Figure 3.2 visually summarizes the initial stages of a solid SDLC, with the addition of Web3-specific activities.

Let's expand each phase with more context:

1. **Requirements Gathering**: Begin by gathering detailed requirements for your Web3 application. Consider security requirements, such as authentication, authorization, access controls, and data privacy.
2. **Threat Modeling**: Perform a comprehensive threat modeling exercise to identify potential security threats and vulnerabilities specific to your Web3 application. This involves analyzing the application's architecture, data flows, and potential attack vectors.
3. **Design Phase**: Based on the threat modeling results, design the architecture, smart contracts, and application components with security in mind. Implement secure coding practices, including input validation, output encoding, and appropriate access controls.

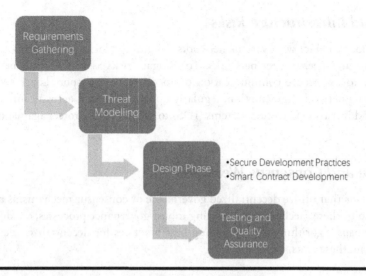

Figure 3.2 Requirements to QA in a Web3 software development lifecycle

4. **Secure Development Practices**: Emphasize secure development practices throughout the development process. This includes enforcing secure coding guidelines, conducting regular code reviews, using version control systems, and employing static code analysis tools to catch potential security issues.

5. **Smart Contract Development**: Follow secure coding practices when developing smart contracts. Use well-tested libraries, conduct thorough code reviews, and perform extensive testing to identify and fix potential vulnerabilities. Consider using formal verification tools to enhance contract security.

6. **Testing and Quality Assurance**: Conduct thorough security testing and quality assurance procedures. This includes unit testing, integration testing, and security-specific testing such as penetration testing, vulnerability scanning, and fuzz testing. Test the resilience of smart contracts against known attack vectors.

At this point, many software practices make the mistake of considering the SDLC complete. The software application is "done", that is developed and fully tested, and so it is their job "done". But it is not. A complete SDLC carries on as visualized in Figure 3.3.

Specifically, each additional stage can be described as follows:

7. **Deployment and Configuration Management**: Implement secure deployment and configuration management practices. Utilize secure infrastructure and cloud services, follow hardening guidelines for servers and network devices, and regularly update and patch all software components.

8. **Continuous Monitoring**: Implement monitoring mechanisms to detect and respond to security incidents promptly. Monitor the blockchain network for unusual activities, leverage security information and event management (SIEM) systems, and implement real-time alerting to mitigate potential threats.

9. **Ongoing Maintenance and Upgrades**: Maintain an active security posture even after deployment. Keep up with security best practices, monitor for emerging vulnerabilities and patches, and proactively address security issues by releasing timely upgrades and patches.

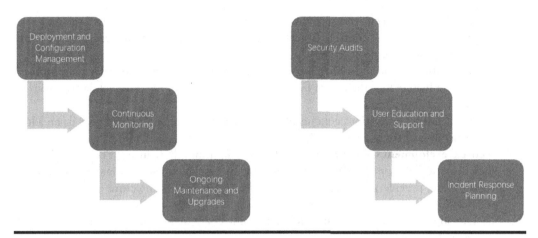

Figure 3.3   Additional stages of an end-to-end SDLC

10. **Security Audits**: Regularly engage third-party security auditors to perform comprehensive security audits of your smart contracts and the overall Web3 application. These auditors can identify vulnerabilities and provide recommendations for improving the application's security posture.
11. **User Education and Support**: Educate users about security best practices, including secure key management, identifying phishing attempts, and exercising caution when interacting with Web3 applications. Provide robust support channels to address security concerns and promptly respond to user inquiries.
12. **Incident Response Planning**: Develop a comprehensive incident response plan to handle security incidents effectively. Define roles and responsibilities, establish communication channels, and regularly test and update the incident response plan.

By incorporating these steps into your software development lifecycle, you can enhance the security of your Web3 application and protect it from potential attacks on both the dApp and smart contract levels. Remember that security is an ongoing process, and it is crucial to stay updated on the latest security trends and vulnerabilities to ensure continuous protection.

Security Audits

Organizations working on public facing Web3 solutions may need to engage third-party security auditors to perform comprehensive security audits of their smart contracts. These auditors can identify vulnerabilities, recommend best practices, and provide guidance for improving contract security.

ConsenSys Diligence (https://consensys.net/diligence) is a comprehensive smart contract audit service that helps businesses develop secure and reliable Ethereum blockchain applications. The service is aimed at enhancing the security, reliability, and trustworthiness of blockchain projects. In general, such auditing firms are worth considering for the following services:

■ **Security Audits**: Certified auditors conduct comprehensive security audits of smart contracts, protocols, and blockchain systems. Their experienced team of security experts thoroughly assesses the codebase, identifies vulnerabilities, and provides detailed recommendations to mitigate risks. Benefits include:

a. Identification of security vulnerabilities to uncover potential security flaws, such as reentrancy issues, access control vulnerabilities, or arithmetic errors, improving the overall resilience of the project.

b. Risk mitigation by addressing security vulnerabilities early in the development process; this can help reduce the risk of financial losses, exploits, or reputational damage caused by security breaches.

c. Independent verifications conducted by an external and reputable firm provide an additional layer of confidence to project stakeholders, investors, and users.

■ **Secure Development Consulting**: In addition to auditing, those firms offer consulting services to assist development teams in building secure blockchain applications and protocols. Their experts provide guidance on secure coding practices, architecture design, and best practices for secure development methodologies.

a. Development teams can learn and adopt industry best practices to build robust and secure blockchain solutions.

b. Web3 architects can design solution architectures that minimize attack vectors, implement appropriate access controls, and ensure secure data handling.

■ **Threat Modeling**: A thorough security audit helps projects identify potential threats and security risks through threat modeling. They assess the system from an attacker's perspective, identify attack vectors, and provide recommendations for risk mitigation.

a. Proactive risk management: By conducting threat modeling, projects can proactively identify and address potential security risks, reducing the likelihood of successful attacks.

b. Defense-in-depth: Projects can implement multiple layers of security controls and countermeasures to protect against different types of threats.

■ **Governance and Compliance**: Not less important, guidance on governance processes, compliance frameworks, and regulatory considerations can be introduced for blockchain projects. Auditors will assist in aligning projects with applicable regulations and ensuring compliance with industry standards.

a. Projects can navigate complex regulatory landscapes and adopt compliance frameworks specific to their industry or jurisdiction.

b. Web3 project/product managers can gain insights into governance best practices, ensuring projects adhere to transparent decision-making processes and accountability frameworks.

As a guidance, you may want to consider engaging a security auditing firm in any of the following situations:

■ **Pre-launch**: Prior to the launch of a blockchain project conduct a thorough security audit, address vulnerabilities, and ensure the project is well-prepared for deployment.

■ **Critical Systems**: For projects dealing with critical financial transactions, user funds, or sensitive data, security audits and secure development consulting can provide an extra layer of protection.

■ **Compliance and Governance**: Projects aiming to comply with regulatory requirements or seeking guidance on governance and compliance frameworks can benefit from expertise in these areas.

Continuous Monitoring and Incident Response

Implementing monitoring solutions to detect unusual activities and potential security incidents is a critical stage of the SDLC. Having a process in place will help establish an incident response plan to respond promptly and effectively to any security breaches or vulnerabilities discovered.

Real-time monitoring and detection of unusual activities and potential security incidents in Web3 apps involves a combination of tools, techniques, and best practices. Here are some tangible examples and products/tools you can use:

- **Event Log Analysis:**
  a. Monitor and analyze event logs emitted by your smart contracts to detect suspicious or unexpected behavior.
  b. Tools like Elasticsearch, Logstash, and Kibana (ELK Stack) can be utilized for log management and analysis.
- **Blockchain Explorers:**
  a. Use blockchain explorers to monitor on-chain transactions, addresses, and smart contract interactions.
  b. Popular blockchain explorers include Etherscan, Blockchair, and Etherchain.
- **Security Information and Event Management (SIEM) Systems:**
  a. SIEM systems aggregate and analyze logs from various sources, providing centralized monitoring and detection capabilities.
  b. Tools like Splunk, Elastic SIEM, or LogRhythm can be employed for real-time log analysis and incident detection.
- **Intrusion Detection Systems (IDS) and Intrusion Prevention Systems (IPS):**
  a. IDS/IPS solutions monitor network traffic and system logs, actively looking for suspicious or malicious activities.
  b. Examples of IDS/IPS tools include Snort, Suricata, and Bro/Zeek.
- **Anomaly Detection and Machine Learning:**
  a. Utilize machine learning techniques to detect anomalies and patterns in application behavior.
  b. Tools such as TensorFlow, scikit-learn, or Apache Spark can be employed for anomaly detection and predictive analysis.
- **Application Performance Monitoring (APM):**
  a. APM tools help monitor the performance, response times, and health of your application's components.
  b. Examples of APM tools include New Relic, Datadog, and Dynatrace.
- **Security Token Platform Monitoring:**
  a. If your Web3 app involves security tokens, consider using specialized security token platform monitoring tools like Solidified, TokenSoft, or Harbor.
- **Threat Intelligence Feeds:**
  a. Integrate threat intelligence feeds into your monitoring systems to receive real-time information about known malicious actors, indicators of compromise (IOCs), or emerging threats.
  b. Services like AlienVault OTX, IBM X-Force, or Recorded Future offer threat intelligence feeds.

Remember, the specific tools and solutions to use depend on your application's architecture, infrastructure, and monitoring requirements. It is crucial to tailor your monitoring approach based on the unique characteristics of your Web3 app and stay up to date with emerging security trends and practices in the blockchain space.

By incorporating these best practices, you can enhance the security of Ethereum smart contracts and mitigate the common threats associated with their development and deployment. Additionally, staying updated on the latest security practices, community feedback, and emerging vulnerabilities is crucial to maintaining a secure smart contract ecosystem, as we're going to explore in the next section.

Security Protection Patterns for Smart Contracts

Let's dive more specifically into typical development patterns for enhancing the security of smart contracts. Smart contracts are self-executing contracts with the terms of the agreement directly written into code. They are stored on the blockchain and are immutable once deployed. This means that any vulnerabilities or bugs in the code cannot be easily rectified, making them a prime target for hackers.

Securing smart contracts is therefore crucial, and the risks of not writing secure code may lead to reputation damage, failure to meet regulatory compliance, or even financial loss. For example, security breaches can lead to a loss of trust in the dApp or the underlying blockchain platform, damaging the reputation of the developers and the community. Depending on the jurisdiction and the specific use case, smart contracts might need to comply with certain regulatory requirements. A breach could lead to legal consequences. Smart contracts often handle and store cryptocurrency. If a smart contract is exploited, it can lead to funds being stolen.

When working with Ethereum smart contracts, it is essential to consider several common threats and security considerations, here described along with best practices for addressing them.

Reentrancy Attacks

Reentrancy attacks occur when a contract invokes an external contract that maliciously re-enters the calling contract before the initial invocation completes. To prevent such attacks, adopt the **checks-effects-interactions pattern**, where critical state changes and accounting are done before calling external contracts. Implement mutex locks to prevent multiple invocations of external contracts during a single function call.

Let's consider a simple example of a smart contract that represents a basic token transfer functionality, and how it can be vulnerable to a reentrancy attack. Here is an example in Solidity, the programming language of smart contracts in the Ethereum platform:

```
contract SimpleToken {
    mapping(address => uint256) balances;

    function transfer(address recipient, uint256 amount) public {
        uint256 balance = balances[msg.sender];
        require(balance >= amount, "Insufficient balance");

        // Vulnerable code: the recipient's contract can call back the
            transfer function
        recipient.call{value: amount}("");
```

```
        balances[msg.sender] -= amount;
        balances[recipient] += amount;
    }
}
```

In this example, the transfer function is vulnerable to a **reentrancy attack**. The attacker can create a malicious contract and invoke the transfer function repeatedly before the balances are updated. This can result in the attacker draining the contract's balance by repeatedly executing the callback function.

To mitigate this reentrancy attack, you can follow the checks-effects-interactions pattern and perform the interaction after updating the balance. In this way, any call will always occur after the balance has been updated with the latest amount. Here's an updated version of the contract with a solution:

```
contract SecureToken {
    mapping(address => uint256) balances;

    function transfer(address recipient, uint256 amount) public {
        uint256 balance = balances[msg.sender];
        require(balance >= amount, "Insufficient balance");

        balances[msg.sender] -= amount;
        balances[recipient] += amount;

        // Non-vulnerable code: perform the interaction after state
            changes
        (bool success, ) = recipient.call{value: amount}("");
        require(success, "Transfer failed");
    }
}
```

In this updated version, the state changes (updating balances) are performed before the interaction with the recipient's contract. By ensuring that the state changes are made before any external call, the contract prevents reentrancy attacks because the attacker's contract will no longer be able to re-enter the transfer function.

It is important to note that adopting the checks-effects-interactions pattern alone is not always sufficient to prevent all reentrancy attacks. Complex interactions and interdependencies between contracts can introduce other vulnerabilities. It is crucial to conduct thorough security audits, follow best practices, and consider advanced techniques such as reentrancy guards, mutex locks, or state machines to ensure robust protection against reentrancy attacks in smart contracts.

Integer Overflow/Underflow

Integer overflow and underflow can lead to unexpected behavior and vulnerabilities. Use safe mathematical libraries like **OpenZeppelin SafeMath** (https://docs.openzeppelin.com/contracts /2.x/api/math) to perform arithmetic operations and prevent such vulnerabilities.

The following example of a Solidity smart contract illustrates the issue and demonstrates the usage of SafeMath to prevent it.

```solidity
pragma solidity ^0.8.0;

import "@openzeppelin/contracts/utils/math/SafeMath.sol";

contract IntegerOverflowExample {
    using SafeMath for uint256;

    uint256 public maxValue = uint256(-1);

    function increase(uint256 amount) public {
        uint256 newValue = maxValue.add(amount);
        require(newValue >= maxValue, "Integer overflow");

        maxValue = newValue;
    }

    function decrease(uint256 amount) public {
        uint256 newValue = maxValue.sub(amount);
        require(newValue <= maxValue, "Integer underflow");

        maxValue = newValue;
    }
}
```

In this example, we have a contract called IntegerOverflowExample that utilizes the SafeMath library from OpenZeppelin. The contract keeps track of a maxValue variable and provides two functions: increase and decrease.

In the increase function, we use SafeMath's add function to increment maxValue by the specified amount. The SafeMath library checks for integer overflow, and if the addition operation causes an overflow, it throws an exception with the error message "Integer overflow".

Similarly, in the decrease function, we use SafeMath's sub-function to decrease maxValue by the specified amount. The SafeMath library checks for integer underflow, and if the subtraction operation causes an underflow (resulting in a negative value), it throws an exception with the error message "Integer underflow".

By utilizing SafeMath's secure arithmetic operations, we can prevent integer overflow and underflow vulnerabilities, ensuring that the arithmetic operations are performed safely and as intended.

It is important to note that the OpenZeppelin SafeMath library is just one example of a library that provides secure arithmetic operations. Similar libraries and implementations can be found in various Solidity development frameworks and toolkits. When using such libraries, it is crucial to review and verify their security and suitability for your specific use case and adhere to best practices for secure smart contract development.

Denial-of-Service (DoS) Attacks

Contracts with inefficient or unbounded loops can be exploited for DoS attacks. Implement gas limits on loops and recursive functions to prevent excessive gas consumption and ensure contract availability.

Protecting smart contracts from DoS attacks involves implementing strategies to mitigate excessive resource consumption and ensure contract availability. Here's an example of how you can protect a smart contract from DoS attacks:

```
contract DosProtectionExample {
    mapping(address => uint256) public balances;
    mapping(address => uint256) public withdrawalTimestamps;

    uint256 public withdrawalLimit = 1 ether;
    uint256 public withdrawalCooldown = 1 minutes;

    function withdraw(uint256 amount) public {
        require(amount <= withdrawalLimit, "Exceeded withdrawal limit");
        require(block.timestamp >= withdrawalTimestamps[msg.sender],
            "Withdrawal cooldown not expired");

        withdrawalTimestamps[msg.sender] = block.timestamp +
            withdrawalCooldown;

        // Perform the withdrawal
        balances[msg.sender] -= amount;
        // Send the funds to the user's address
        payable(msg.sender).transfer(amount);
    }
}
```

In this example, we have a DosProtectionExample contract that includes mitigation techniques against DoS attacks. Here is how it works:

1. **WithdrawalLimit**: The contract sets a withdrawal limit to restrict the maximum amount that can be withdrawn in a single transaction. In this case, the limit is set to 1 ether (withdrawalLimit = 1 ether).
2. **WithdrawalCooldown**: The contract implements a cooldown period between consecutive withdrawals for the same address. The withdrawalCooldown value represents the duration of the cooldown period, set to 1 minute (withdrawalCooldown = 1 minute).
3. **WithdrawalTimestamps Mapping**: The contract maintains a mapping called withdrawalTimestamps, which tracks the expiration timestamp of the withdrawal cooldown for each address.
4. **Withdrawal Function**: The withdraw function enforces the withdrawal limit and cooldown period. It first checks if the withdrawal amount is within the specified limit and whether the cooldown period for the sender's address has expired. If the conditions are met, it updates the withdrawal timestamp to the current time plus the cooldown period, effectively resetting the cooldown for the address. After the checks, the function performs the withdrawal by deducting the amount from the sender's balance and transferring the funds to the sender's address using the transfer function.

By implementing a withdrawal limit and cooldown period, this contract protects against DoS attacks by limiting the number and frequency of withdrawals that can be made. These mechanisms help prevent excessive resource consumption and ensure fair access to contract functionality.

It is worth noting that the specific mitigation strategies may vary depending on the contract's requirements and the nature of the DoS attack being targeted. Different techniques, such as gas limits, circuit breakers, or rate limiters, can also be employed to protect against various types of DoS attacks.

Access Control and Authorization

Incorrectly implemented access controls can lead to unauthorized access and misuse of contract functionality. One of the best practices is to implement proper access control mechanisms using role-based access control (RBAC) or attribute-based access control (ABAC). This principle is called "**defense in depth**" because it implements multiple layers of access controls.

The following example shows how you can implement RBAC and ABAC in a smart contract:

```
contract AccessControlExample {
    mapping(address => bool) private admins;
    mapping(address => bool) private editors;

    constructor() {
        // Contract deployer is the admin
        admins[msg.sender] = true;
    }

    // RBAC: Admin role can add editors
    function addEditor(address editor) public {
        require(admins[msg.sender], "Only admins can add editors");
        editors[editor] = true;
    }

    // ABAC: Only editors can perform specific action
    function performAction() public {
        require(editors[msg.sender], "Only editors can perform
            this action");

        // Action logic
    }

    // RBAC: Admin role can remove editors
    function removeEditor(address editor) public {
        require(admins[msg.sender], "Only admins can remove
            editors");
        editors[editor] = false;
    }

    // RBAC: Check if an address has admin role
    function isAdmin(address user) public view returns (bool) {
        return admins[user];
    }

    // ABAC: Check if an address has editor role
    function isEditor(address user) public view returns (bool) {
        return editors[user];
    }
}
```

In this example, the AccessControlExample contract demonstrates RBAC and ABAC mechanisms by implementing the following control logic:

■ **RBAC** (Role-Based Access Control):
   a. The contract maintains a mapping called admins to track admin addresses. Only admins have permission to add or remove editors.
   b. The contract deployer is initially set as an admin in the constructor.

c. The addEditor function allows admins to add editors to the editors mapping.

d. The removeEditor function allows admins to remove editors by updating the editors mapping.

e. The isAdmin function checks if an address has the admin role.

■ **ABAC** (Attribute-Based Access Control):

a. The performAction function is restricted to addresses listed as editors in the editors mapping.

b. Only addresses marked as editors in the editors mapping can execute the action logic within the function.

c. The isEditor function checks if an address has the editor role.

By combining RBAC and ABAC mechanisms, this contract allows for granular access control. Admins have the authority to manage editors, while editors have permissions to perform specific actions. These mechanisms ensure that only authorized entities can perform certain operations within the contract.

It's important to note that the RBAC and ABAC implementations shown here are simplified examples. In practical scenarios, access control mechanisms may involve more complex role hierarchies, permissions, and conditions. Smart contract developers should carefully design access control systems based on their specific requirements, considering potential attack vectors and regularly auditing and updating access control logic to maintain a secure environment.

Front-Running

Front-running occurs when an attacker exploits the order of transaction execution to gain an advantage. You can minimize the risk of front-running by using techniques such as transaction ordering mechanisms, commit-reveal schemes, or using pre-signed transactions.

Front-running is a vulnerability in smart contracts where an attacker exploits the order of transactions to gain an unfair advantage. Let's look at an example that demonstrates the front-running risk and explore some mitigation strategies:

```
contract FrontRunningExample {
    mapping(address => uint256) public balances;

    function buyTokens(uint256 amount) public payable {
        uint256 tokenPrice = 1 ether;
        uint256 requiredAmount = tokenPrice * amount;

        require(msg.value >= requiredAmount, "Insufficient funds");

        // Deduct tokens from contract balance
        balances[msg.sender] += amount;

        // Perform additional logic or external interactions
        // ...

        // Send the remaining Ether back to the buyer
        payable(msg.sender).transfer(msg.value - requiredAmount);
    }
}
```

In this example, we have a simple FrontRunningExample contract that allows users to buy tokens by sending ether to the contract. However, this contract is vulnerable to front-running attacks. An attacker can observe a pending transaction and quickly create a new transaction with a higher gas price to have their transaction executed before the original one, taking advantage of the knowledge gained from the pending transaction.

To mitigate front-running risks, here are a few strategies:

- **Use Commit-Reveal Schemes**: Implement a commit-reveal scheme where users commit to their actions first, and then reveal the committed values at a later time. This prevents attackers from front-running transactions since the committed values are not publicly known until the reveal phase.
- **Use Order Matching or Batch Auctions**: Employ order matching mechanisms or batch auctions where all transactions are executed simultaneously or in random order. This makes it difficult for attackers to determine the order of transactions and front-run specific transactions.
- **Implement Time-Locking**: Introduce time-locking mechanisms that delay the execution of transactions for a predefined period. This reduces the window of opportunity for attackers to front-run transactions.
- **Use Encryption or Secret Sharing**: Encrypt sensitive information or use secret sharing techniques to split critical data across multiple transactions. This makes it difficult for attackers to gain complete knowledge of the transaction content to exploit front-running opportunities.
- **Gas Price Limitations**: Consider implementing gas price limitations to prevent transactions with significantly higher gas prices from being prioritized. This helps minimize the potential for front-running attacks based solely on gas price manipulation.

It's worth noting that front-running attacks are complex and continually evolving. Employing a combination of these strategies, along with thorough security audits and continuous monitoring, can help mitigate the risk of front-running in smart contracts. However, no mitigation technique can completely eliminate the possibility of front-running, so it's essential to stay informed about the latest developments and emerging attack vectors in the blockchain space.

External Dependency Risks

Smart contracts often rely on external data sources or *oracles*, which can introduce security risks. Although the advice is to use reputable and audited oracle services, this is not always possible. As a best practice, you should always implement strict validation of external data, and consider using multiple oracles or decentralized oracle networks to mitigate risks.

Table 3.1 lists the risks of using external data sources in blockchain solutions, and guidance on mitigating the associated security risks.

By carefully selecting trusted oracles, implementing data verification mechanisms, diversifying data sources, and considering decentralized oracles, smart contract developers can mitigate the security risks associated with external data sources. Continuous monitoring, auditing, and staying informed about emerging oracle technologies and best practices are essential to maintaining the security and integrity of smart contract operations.

Solidity Compiler and Versioning

Upgrades to Solidity compilers or changes in language versions can introduce unintended vulnerabilities. As a rule of thumb, it's always advisable to regularly update your contracts to the latest

Table 3.1   Risks and mitigation strategies for the use of external data sources

Data Source	Risk	Mitigation
Unreliable Oracles	Using oracles that are not reputable or trustworthy may lead to incorrect or manipulated data, compromising the integrity and reliability of smart contract operations.	Engage with trusted and well-established oracle providers. Perform due diligence on the reputation, track record, and security practices of potential oracles. Consider decentralized oracle networks or multiple oracles to reduce single points of failure and enhance data reliability.
Manipulated Data Feeds	Attackers may attempt to manipulate the data being fed into the smart contract through compromised oracles. This can lead to malicious outcomes or financial losses.	Implement data verification mechanisms within the smart contract to ensure the accuracy and integrity of the received data. Employ cryptographic proofs, such as digital signatures or zero-knowledge proofs, to verify the authenticity of the data provided by the oracle. Use multiple independent oracles to cross-validate data and identify inconsistencies or anomalies.
Centralized Oracles	Relying on a single centralized oracle introduces a single point of failure. If the centralized oracle is compromised or experiences downtime, it can impact the functionality and security of the smart contract.	Consider using decentralized oracle networks or distributed consensus mechanisms to eliminate central points of failure. Employ oracle designs that utilize multiple independent nodes to fetch and validate data. Implement redundancy and failover mechanisms to handle oracle failures and ensure uninterrupted operation.
Data Source Vulnerabilities	The data sources that oracles rely on, may themselves be vulnerable to attacks, manipulation, or unauthorized access. Compromised data sources can lead to inaccurate or malicious data being fed into the smart contract.	Assess the security practices and data source reliability when selecting oracles. Utilize trusted and reputable data sources with strong security measures. Consider implementing multi-sourced data aggregation, where data from multiple trusted sources is combined to reduce the reliance on a single vulnerable data source.
Lack of Confidentiality	In certain cases, sensitive data from off-chain sources may need to be transmitted to the blockchain, potentially exposing it to unauthorized access or privacy breaches.	Employ privacy-enhancing techniques, such as encryption or secure multiparty computation, when transmitting sensitive data to the blockchain. Ensure that appropriate data access controls and encryption protocols are implemented to protect data confidentiality.

Table 3.1 (Continued) Risks and mitigation strategies for the use of external data sources

Data Source	Risk	Mitigation
Regular Oracle Auditing	Oracles may undergo changes over time, including updates to their infrastructure, codebase, or data sources. These changes can introduce vulnerabilities or compromise the security and reliability of the oracle.	Regularly audit and monitor the oracles used in the smart contract ecosystem. Stay updated with changes in the oracle infrastructure and ensure compatibility with the smart contract. Perform security assessments and code reviews of the oracle's implementation and monitor for any suspicious activities or changes.

version of the Solidity compiler and thoroughly test for any breaking changes or vulnerabilities introduced by the new version.

There have been a few breaking changes introduced in newer versions of the Solidity programming language, which are summarized in Table 3.2.

It's important to note that breaking changes in Solidity are introduced to improve the language's security, efficiency, and functionality. When migrating existing contracts to newer versions, it's crucial to carefully review the release notes, documentation, and follow the migration guides provided by the Solidity team to ensure compatibility and address any breaking changes effectively.

Table 3.2 Change log of the Solidity programming language

Version	Changes
Solidity 0.5.0	Introduction of the ABIEncoderV2 pragma: This version introduced the ABIEncoderV2 pragma, which changed the default encoding and decoding mechanism for function parameters and return values. It required explicit specification of the encoding type for structs and arrays.
Solidity 0.6.0	Changes in explicit data location syntax: Solidity 0.6.0 introduced a new syntax for specifying explicit data locations, such as storage, memory, or call data, for function parameters and state variables. This syntax change required modifications in existing contracts to adhere to the new syntax.
Solidity 0.8.0	Removal of the "fallback" function: Solidity 0.8.0 removed the automatic fallback function that was triggered when a contract received ether without a matching function call. Instead, contracts were required to explicitly define a receive() function for fallback functionality.
Solidity 0.8.6	Changes to visibility modifiers: Solidity 0.8.6 introduced stricter rules for visibility modifiers. External visibility was enforced on functions that interacted with other contracts, and internal visibility was enforced on functions that were only called within the contract.
Solidity 0.8.9	Removal of "override" keyword for interface functions: Solidity 0.8.9 removed the requirement to use the override keyword when implementing interface functions. This change simplified the syntax for implementing interfaces.

Although the introduction of new versions of the Solidity programming language aims to address vulnerabilities and enhance security, there can be instances where new versions inadvertently introduce vulnerabilities or risks. Here are a few examples:

Integer Overflow and Underflow

Solidity versions prior to 0.8.0 did not include built-in checks for integer overflow and underflow, which could lead to vulnerabilities. However, with the introduction of version 0.8.0, arithmetic operations on integer types now include automatic checks for overflow and underflow, reducing the risk of vulnerabilities related to these issues.

Reentrancy Attacks

Reentrancy attacks occur when a contract calls an external contract that, in turn, calls back into the original contract before completing its execution. Solidity versions prior to 0.8.0 did not explicitly address reentrancy vulnerabilities.

Solidity version 0.8.0 introduced the "nonReentrant" modifier, which allows developers to protect critical functions from reentrancy attacks by preventing reentrant calls within the same contract.

Time Manipulation

Time manipulation vulnerabilities occur when contracts rely on block timestamps for critical operations, and malicious actors manipulate the block timestamp to their advantage. Solidity versions, including the latest ones, do not inherently address time manipulation vulnerabilities.

Developers need to employ best practices, such as using block numbers instead of timestamps or utilizing external timestamp oracles, to mitigate time manipulation risks.

Unchecked External Calls

Solidity versions prior to 0.6.0 did not require explicit handling of the return value of external contract calls, which could lead to vulnerabilities if the return value is not properly checked or handled.

Solidity version 0.6.0 introduced the "unchecked" keyword, which allows developers to explicitly indicate that they have considered the potential issues of not checking the return value. This helps highlight the need for careful handling of external calls.

Gas Limit and Out-of-Gas Errors

Solidity versions are not directly responsible for gas limit vulnerabilities or out-of-gas errors, which are inherent to the Ethereum Virtual Machine (EVM). These issues can arise if developers do not properly estimate gas requirements for contract functions or fail to handle out-of-gas exceptions.

Developers should conduct thorough gas estimations, implement gas-efficient code, and include appropriate error-handling mechanisms to mitigate gas limit vulnerabilities.

It is crucial for developers to stay updated with the latest Solidity releases, follow security best practices, and conduct comprehensive testing and auditing of their smart contracts to identify and address any vulnerabilities introduced by new language versions. Regular security assessments and code reviews are essential for maintaining robust and secure smart contract deployments.

Contract Upgradability

Poorly implemented contract upgradability mechanisms can introduce security risks. The recommendation is to implement upgradability patterns carefully, considering the potential impact on contract integrity and security. Mechanisms like **proxy contracts** or **modular design patterns** allow for upgradability while maintaining security.

The most commonly used upgradability patterns are:

- ■ **Proxy Contracts:**
  a. Use a proxy contract as an intermediary between the client and the implementation contract.
  b. Store the contract logic separately from the proxy contract, enabling the logic to be upgraded while keeping the proxy contract intact.
  c. The proxy contract delegates function calls to the implementation contract, allowing for seamless upgradability.
- ■ **External Storage:**
  a. Separate the contract's state data from its logic.
  b. Use a storage contract to store the contract's state variables.
  c. When upgrading the contract logic, the storage contract remains intact, preserving the stored data.
- ■ **Upgradeable Libraries:**
  a. Extract reusable and upgradable logic into separate libraries.
  b. The main contract references the library and delegates functionality to it.
  c. By upgrading the library, the contract can benefit from enhanced or modified logic while maintaining the state and storage.
- ■ **Versioning and Interface Contracts:**
  a. Implement versioning to manage the compatibility of upgraded contracts.
  b. Use interface contracts to define a standard for interacting with the contract.
  c. When upgrading the contract, maintain backward compatibility by adhering to the defined interface.

Have a look at the Proxy contract available in the following GitHub repository. The file name is Chapter3_ProxyContract.sol.

https://github.com/stefanotempesta/Application_Architecture_Patterns_Web3

In this example, the Proxy contract acts as an intermediary between the client and the implementation contract. The fallback function delegates all calls to the implementation contract using delegatecall. The implementation contract address is stored in a storage slot. The setImplementation function allows setting the implementation contract address.

Note that this is a simplified example, and in a real-world scenario, additional functionality like access control and security measures should be implemented to ensure the integrity and security of the proxy contract and the upgrade process.

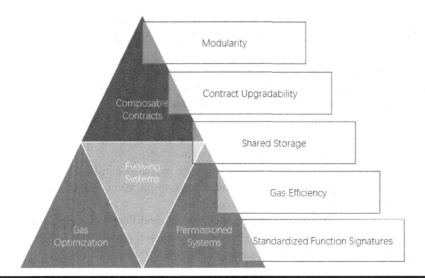

Figure 3.4   Features and benefits of the diamond pattern

Diamonds, or the Multi-Facet Proxy

The **diamond pattern** is an architectural design pattern for smart contracts that allows for code modularity, contract upgradability, and gas efficiency. It is especially useful in situations where a smart contract system requires the ability to add, modify, or upgrade features without having to deploy an entirely new set of contracts or sacrificing gas efficiency.

Figure 3.4 provides a high-level overview of the diamond pattern and its benefits, which can be summarized as follows:

- **Modularity**: The diamond pattern enables the separation of concerns by dividing the functionality of a smart contract system into multiple smaller contracts called facets. Each facet focuses on a specific aspect or feature, making the overall system more modular and maintainable.
- **Contract Upgradability**: With the diamond pattern, individual facets can be added, modified, or upgraded without affecting the other facets or the main contract itself. This allows for selective upgrades and avoids the need to redeploy the entire contract system.
- **Shared Storage**: The diamond pattern employs a central contract called the Diamond contract, which serves as the entry point to the system and holds shared storage. Facets delegate their storage operations to the Diamond contract, allowing them to share and access common data efficiently.
- **Gas Efficiency**: By using the diamond pattern, redundant code and storage duplication are minimized. The shared storage and function delegation result in more efficient gas usage compared to traditional monolithic contracts. The pattern reduces redundancy, saves gas costs, and optimizes contract interactions.
- **Standardized Function Signatures**: The diamond pattern ensures consistent function signatures across facets by using function selectors. This allows clients to interact with the Diamond contract without needing to know the specifics of each individual facet.

The diamond pattern is well-suited for complex smart contract systems that require upgradability and modular design. It is particularly beneficial in the following scenarios:

■ **Composable Contracts**: When developing composable contracts where different functionality can be combined or reused across multiple projects, the diamond pattern allows for the creation of independent facets that can be mixed and matched as needed.

■ **Evolving Systems**: When building systems that are expected to evolve over time with new features or enhancements, the Diamond Pattern provides a flexible approach to upgrade specific facets without affecting the entire system.

■ **Gas Optimization**: Projects aiming to optimize gas costs can benefit from the diamond pattern. By avoiding redundant code and storage duplication, gas efficiency is improved, resulting in cost savings for contract interactions.

■ **Permissioned Systems**: In permissioned systems where different participants or roles require distinct functionality or access permissions, the diamond pattern can facilitate the segregation and management of features based on roles or permissions.

It is important to note that implementing the diamond pattern requires careful consideration of security, access control, and testing to ensure that the facets interact correctly and securely with the diamond contract and shared storage. Additionally, the use of the diamond pattern adds complexity, so it should be applied judiciously based on the specific requirements and trade-offs of the project.

An example of implementation of the diamond pattern can be found in the Chapter3_ DiamondContract.sol file in the GitHub repository of the book.

In this example, we have a Diamond contract that serves as the entry point to the system. It contains a mapping object, facetAddresses, which stores the addresses of different facets based on their function selectors. The fallback function is used to delegate calls to the respective facet based on the function selector.

We have two example facets, FacetA and FacetB. Each facet contains its own specific functionality. These facets can be added or updated dynamically in the Diamond contract using the setFacet function, which associates the function selectors with the respective facet addresses.

With this setup, clients can interact with the Diamond contract, calling functions from FacetA or FacetB seamlessly. The Diamond contract delegates the calls to the appropriate facets based on the function selectors stored in facetAddresses.

Note that this is a simplified example to demonstrate the diamond pattern. In a real-world scenario, you may have multiple facets with more complex functionality and additional considerations such as access control, security measures, and event handling.

EIP-2535

The diamond pattern is described by the **EIP-2535** available at: https://eips.ethereum.org/EIPS/ eip-2535.

In Ethereum, EIP stands for Ethereum Improvement Proposal. EIPs are formal documents that propose changes, enhancements, or new features to the Ethereum network. They serve as a means for the Ethereum community, including developers, researchers, and users, to discuss and propose improvements to the protocol, standards, or processes.

The EIP process was inspired by the Bitcoin Improvement Proposal (BIP) process and was established to encourage collaboration, transparency, and open discussions regarding the development and evolution of the Ethereum ecosystem.

EIPs can cover a wide range of topics, including:

1. **Protocol Enhancements**: Proposals that suggest modifications or additions to the Ethereum protocol to improve functionality, scalability, security, or efficiency.
2. **Standards**: Proposals for the creation or modification of Ethereum standards, such as ERC (Ethereum Request for Comments) standards, which define interfaces, contracts, or APIs for specific use cases like tokens, decentralized exchanges, or identity.
3. **Process and Governance**: Proposals related to the governance, decision-making processes, or overall management of the Ethereum network and ecosystem.
4. **Meta**: Proposals related to the EIP process itself, such as updates to the EIP format, guidelines, or best practices.

The EIP process provides a structured approach for proposing, reviewing, and accepting or rejecting proposals. EIPs go through various stages, including drafting, discussion, review, and ultimately being accepted or rejected. Accepted EIPs become part of the Ethereum ecosystem and can influence the future direction and development of the network.

The EIP repository on GitHub (https://github.com/ethereum/EIPs) serves as a central hub for proposing, discussing, and documenting EIPs. It provides a transparent and accessible platform for the Ethereum community to participate in the evolution of the network.

EIPs have played a significant role in the development and growth of Ethereum, fostering innovation and enabling collaboration among stakeholders. They have facilitated the introduction of major upgrades like Ethereum 2.0, and they continue to be an important mechanism for driving the advancement of the Ethereum ecosystem.

Eternal Storage Pattern

Separation of storage from the logic of a contract is an approach used in designing upgradeable smart contracts. In the **eternal storage pattern**, the storage with setters and getters is moved to a separate smart contract, and only the logic contract is allowed to read/write from it. The term "eternal storage" refers to the persistence layer of the smart contract, where data is stored indefinitely and can be accessed by successive versions of the contract logic.

File Chapter3_EternalStorageContract.sol in the GitHub repository contains an example of how you can store the contract logic separately from the proxy contract using this design pattern. In this example, the EternalStorage contract is responsible for storing the contract state data, and the Proxy contract acts as a bridge between the client and the logic contract. The Proxy contract references the EternalStorage contract to read and write data.

The Proxy contract's fallback function delegates all calls to the logic contract address stored in the EternalStorage contract. The setUpgradedLogicContract function allows setting the address of the upgraded logic contract in the EternalStorage contract. The LogicContract contract contains the implementation logic, including functions and state variables. It interacts with the EternalStorage contract to read and modify data.

By separating the contract logic from the proxy contract and utilizing the EternalStorage contract for data storage, you can upgrade the logic contract while preserving the state data stored in the EternalStorage contract.

Conclusion

This chapter has investigated common threats for Web3 applications and proposed a set of strategies and best practices for risk mitigation and security protection. From reentrancy attacks to denial of service, from security audits to continuous monitoring, Web3 applications are not immune from cyberattacks, as any software application. The combination of considering security a key design principle of the software development lifecycle, as well as introducing regular security testing and auditing, will help reduce the attack surface of your applications, and help build a more secure and attack resilient solution.

Our exploration of security's best practices continues also in the next chapter, where we are going to understand the foundation of cryptography in Web3 and its utilization for making data and transactions more secure.

Chapter 4

Cryptography for Web3 Applications

Cryptography plays a vital role in ensuring the security and privacy of blockchain networks, as well as Web3 dApps and wallets. This chapter describes some common cryptographic concepts and algorithms relevant to Web3, which include:

- **Hash Functions**: Hash functions transform data into fixed-length strings (hashes). In Web3, hashes are used to verify data integrity and create unique identifiers for transactions and blocks.
- **Public and Private Key Pairs**: Web3 relies on asymmetric encryption, where each user has a public key (used for encryption) and a corresponding private key (used for decryption). Public keys are openly shared, while private keys must remain confidential. Transactions and data integrity are secured using these key pairs.
- **Symmetric Encryption**: Symmetric encryption uses a single shared secret key for both encryption and decryption. While less common in Web3, it's still relevant for certain use cases.
- **Digital Signatures**: Digital signatures provide proof of authenticity and integrity. When a user signs a transaction with their private key, others can verify it using the associated public key.
- **Zero-Knowledge Proofs**: Zero-Knowledge Proofs are cryptographic protocols that allow one party (the prover) to prove the truth of a statement to another party (the verifier) without revealing any additional information beyond the statement's validity. In other words, ZKPs enable verification without disclosure.

In addition, we'll look at a couple of privacy-enabling technologies that are becoming very popular in protecting sensitive information on a blockchain (and not only):

- **Homomorphic Encryption**: Homomorphic encryption is a cryptographic technique that allows computations to be performed on encrypted data without first decrypting it. The result of such computations remains encrypted, ensuring privacy while enabling useful tasks in untrusted environments.

DOI: 10.4324/9781003491934-4

■ **Confidential Computing**: Confidential computing is a cloud computing technology that protects data during processing. It achieves this by isolating sensitive data within a protected CPU/GPU enclave, ensuring that the data remains confidential even while being processed.

When relevant, code snippets in C++ or C# programming languages are added as examples of implementation and usage of such techniques.

Hash Functions

Hash functions are used extensively in blockchain networks for various purposes, including creating digital fingerprints of data, verifying data integrity, and generating addresses for wallets. Commonly used hash functions include **Secure Hash Algorithm (SHA-256)**, **Keccak-256** (used in Ethereum), and **Blake2**.

Secure Hash Algorithm (SHA-256)

SHA-256, part of the SHA-2 family, is a cryptographic hash function that converts text into an almost-unique 256-bit alphanumeric hash value. It's widely used for digital signatures, password authentication, and in blockchain technology. SHA-256 plays a critical role, particularly in the context of Bitcoin and other major blockchain protocols:

■ **Proof-of-Work (PoW) Consensus Algorithm**: In the Bitcoin network, SHA-256 is the backbone of the PoW consensus algorithm. Miners use SHA-256 to validate transactions and secure the distributed ledger. When a new block is added to the blockchain, its hash contains the previous block's hash, creating an immutable chain.

■ **Transaction Verification**: SHA-256 ensures the integrity of transactions on the blockchain. Each transaction is hashed using SHA-256, creating a unique identifier (transaction hash). These hashes are used for verification and linking transactions together.

■ **Mining**: Miners compete to find a nonce (a random number) that, when combined with the transaction data, produces a hash with a specific pattern (difficulty). The SHA-256 hash of the entire block header (including the nonce) must meet the difficulty criteria. Successful miners create new blocks and earn rewards in Bitcoin.

In summary, SHA-256's robustness ensures the security, consistency, and authenticity of the blockchain. It's the cryptographic workhorse that underpins the decentralized revolution!

Here's an example of a SHA-256 hash function implementation in C#:

```
public class Sha256Hash
{
    public static byte[] CalculateHash(string input)
    {
        byte[] data = Encoding.UTF8.GetBytes(input);
        using var sha256 = SHA256.Create();
        return sha256.ComputeHash(data);
    }
}
```

```
public static string CalculateHashAsString(string input)
{
    byte[] hash = CalculateHash(input);
    return BitConverter.ToString(hash).Replace("-", "");
}
}
```

In this implementation, we use the **SHA256** class from the System.Security.Cryptography namespace. The CalculateHash method takes the input string, converts it to bytes using UTF-8 encoding, and then computes the SHA-256 hash. The result is returned as a byte array. The CalculateHashAsString method takes the same input but returns the hash as a hexadecimal string without any dashes.

Keccak-256

Keccak-256, a cryptographic function, is part of the SHA-3 Family. It computes the hash of an input to a fixed-length output, yielding a singular 32-byte hash from any number of inputs. Unlike reversible operations, this cryptographic hash function can only be used in one direction, ensuring data integrity and security. Ethereum utilizes Keccak-256 in its consensus engine called Ethash123.

Below is an example of a Keccak-256 hash function implemented in C#:

```
public class Keccak256
{
    public static string CalculateHash(string input)
    {
        byte[] data = Encoding.UTF8.GetBytes(input);
        using var sha3 = new SHA3Managed(256);
        byte[] hash = sha3.ComputeHash(data);
        return BitConverter.ToString(hash).Replace("-", "");
    }
}
```

Please note that this implementation uses the **SHA3Managed** class, which is part of the System.Security.Cryptography namespace in .NET. The SHA3Managed class provides SHA-3 (Keccak) hashing functionality. The input string is converted to bytes using UTF-8 encoding, and then the hash is computed. The resulting hash is returned as a hexadecimal string without any dashes.

BLAKE2

BLAKE2, a cryptographic hash function based on BLAKE, is faster than MD5, SHA-1, SHA-2, and SHA-3, yet is at least as secure as the latest standard SHA-3. It has been adopted by many projects due to its high speed, security, and simplicity.

The following is an example of a Blake2 hash function implementation in C#:

```
public class Blake2
{
    public static byte[] CalculateHash(string input, int
        hashSizeInBytes = 32)
    {
        byte[] data = Encoding.UTF8.GetBytes(input);
        using var blake2b = new Blake2bManaged { HashSizeInBytes =
        hashSizeInBytes };
        return blake2b.ComputeHash(data);
    }

    public static string CalculateHashAsString(string input, int
        hashSizeInBytes = 32)
    {
        byte[] hash = CalculateHash(input, hashSizeInBytes);
        return BitConverter.ToString(hash).Replace("-", "");
    }
}
```

In this implementation, we use the **Blake2bManaged** class from the System.Security. Cryptography namespace. The CalculateHash method takes the input string, converts it to bytes using UTF-8 encoding, and then computes the BLAKE2 hash. The result is returned as a byte array. The CalculateHashAsString method takes the same input but returns the hash as a hexadecimal string without any dashes. The default hash size used in this implementation is 32 bytes, but you can adjust it as needed by providing a different hashSizeInBytes parameter.

Differences and Considerations

SHA-256, Keccak-256, and BLAKE2 are all cryptographic hash functions, but they have some key differences in their design and properties. Table 4.1 explores the main differences between these hash functions and when it might be preferable to use one over the others:

For general-purpose hashing needs, SHA-256 is a safe and widely adopted choice. Its prevalence and standardization make it a solid option in most scenarios.

Keccak-256, being the winner of the SHA-3 competition and designed to be more resistant to certain attacks, is suitable for situations where stronger security and resistance to known attacks are desired.

BLAKE2b (256-bit output) is an excellent choice when you need strong security and performance. It is suitable for various cryptographic applications and is often used as a replacement for SHA-256 and other hash functions due to its speed and security properties.

In conclusion, the choice of which hash function to use depends on the specific requirements of the application, security considerations, and performance constraints. For most general scenarios, SHA-256 is still a solid and widely used choice. However, Keccak-256 and BLAKE2b offer specific advantages in certain contexts, making them preferable in those cases. Always consider the latest recommendations and consult with cryptographic experts if you're unsure about the best choice for your specific use case.

Table 4.1 Key differences of hash functions

Function	Properties
SHA-256	• SHA-256 (Secure Hash Algorithm 256-bit) is part of the SHA-2 family and was designed by the National Security Agency (NSA). • It produces a fixed-size 256-bit (32-byte) hash output. • SHA-256 is widely used and well-studied, making it a standard choice for many security applications. • Its security is based on the cryptographic strength of the underlying Merkle-Damgard construction, though it is vulnerable to length extension attacks. • It is suitable for most general-purpose cryptographic hashing needs, such as password hashing and digital signatures.
Keccak-256	• Keccak-256, also known as SHA-3, is the winning algorithm from the NIST SHA-3 competition. • Like SHA-256, it produces a fixed-size 256-bit (32-byte) hash output. • Keccak has a different internal structure than SHA-256, using a sponge construction. This makes it more resistant to certain types of attacks, such as length extension attacks, due to its inherent design. • Keccak is considered more secure against cryptanalysis than SHA-256, and it is well-suited for situations where resistance to certain attacks is critical. • While it is not as widely adopted as SHA-256, Keccak is gaining popularity and may become more prevalent in the future.
BLAKE2	• BLAKE2 is a cryptographic hash function based on the SHA-3 finalist, BLAKE, with several optimizations. • It is available in various output sizes (e.g., 256-bit, 512-bit) and offers better performance than SHA-256 and Keccak-256 for many use cases. • BLAKE2b is the variant that produces a 256-bit (32-byte) hash output, similar to SHA-256 and Keccak-256. • BLAKE2 is resistant to length extension attacks and provides strong security properties, making it suitable for various applications. • It is commonly used in modern applications for hashing, message authentication codes (MACs), and key derivation.

Asymmetric Cryptography

Asymmetric cryptography, also known as public key cryptography, is a fundamental component of blockchain networks and Web3 applications. It involves the use of key pairs: a public key for encryption and a private key for decryption and digital signatures, as illustrated in Figure 4.1 and described below.

1. **Key Pair Generation**: In asymmetric encryption, two distinct keys are generated: a public key and a private key. The public key can be shared openly, while the private key remains secret and known only to the owner.
2. **Encryption Process**: When a sender wants to send an encrypted message to a recipient, they use the recipient's public key. The sender encrypts the data using the recipient's public key. This ensures that only the recipient, with their corresponding private key, can decrypt and read the message.
3. **Decryption Process**: The recipient receives the encrypted message. To decrypt it, they use their private key. The private key reverses the encryption process, revealing the original data.

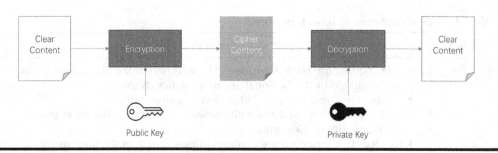

Figure 4.1   Asymmetric cryptography flow

Commonly used algorithms include:

- **Rivest-Shamir-Adleman (RSA)**: An algorithm for secure key exchange and digital signatures.
- **Elliptic Curve Cryptography (ECC)**: ECC algorithms, such as Elliptic Curve Digital Signature Algorithm (ECDSA), are widely used due to their efficiency and security. They are the basis for generating addresses and signing transactions in many blockchain networks, including Bitcoin and Ethereum.

Rivest-Shamir-Adleman (RSA)

RSA, named after its brilliant inventors Ron Rivest, Adi Shamir, and Leonard Adleman, is a public-key cryptosystem, one of the oldest widely used for secure data transmission. It relies on the practical difficulty of factoring large prime numbers and ensures secure communication via asymmetric encryption with a public key for encryption and a private key for decryption.

Below is an example of RSA encryption and decryption using the RSACryptoServiceProvider class in C#:

```
public class RSAEncryption
{
    public static byte[] EncryptData(byte[] data, RSAParameters
        publicKey)
    {
        using RSACryptoServiceProvider rsa = new RSACryptoService
            Provider();
        rsa.ImportParameters(publicKey);
        return rsa.Encrypt(data, true);
    }

    public static byte[] DecryptData(byte[] encryptedData, RSA
        Parameters privateKey)
    {
        using RSACryptoServiceProvider rsa = new RSACryptoService
            Provider();
        rsa.ImportParameters(privateKey);
        return rsa.Decrypt(encryptedData, true);
    }
}
```

In this example, we use the **RSACryptoServiceProvider** class from the System.Security. Cryptography namespace for RSA encryption and decryption. The EncryptData method takes the data to encrypt and the RSA public key parameters, while the DecryptData method takes the encrypted data and the RSA private key parameters. The true parameter in the methods specifies that we want to use OAEP padding (Optimal Asymmetric Encryption Padding) for better security. The example generates a new RSA key pair and uses the public key to encrypt the data and the private key to decrypt it. The original message is displayed along with the encrypted data and the decrypted message to show that the encryption and decryption process works correctly.

Elliptic Curve Cryptography (ECC)

Elliptic Curve Cryptography (ECC) is an approach to public-key cryptography based on the algebraic structure of elliptic curves over finite fields. ECC allows smaller keys compared to non-EC cryptography (based on plain Galois fields) to provide equivalent security.

The code snippet that follows is an example of ECC implementation using the ECDiffieHellmanCng class in C#:

```
public class ECCEncrytion
{
    public static byte[] GenerateECDHKey(out ECParameters publicKey)
    {
        using ECDiffieHellmanCng ecdh = new ECDiffieHellmanCng();
        publicKey = ecdh.ExportParameters(false);
        return ecdh.PublicKey.ToByteArray();
    }

    public static byte[] ComputeECDHSecret(byte[] publicKeyBytes)
    {
        using ECDiffieHellmanCng ecdh = new ECDiffieHellmanCng();
        ECParameters publicKey = new ECParameters
        {
          Curve = ecdh.Curve,
          Q = new ECPoint { X = publicKeyBytes }
        };
        ecdh.ImportParameters(publicKey);
        return ecdh.DeriveKeyMaterial(CngKeyBlobFormat.EccPublicBlob);
    }
}
```

In this example, we use the **ECDiffieHellmanCng** class from the System.Security. Cryptography namespace for ECC key generation and secret computation. The GenerateECDHKey method generates an ECC key pair, exports the public key parameters, and returns the public key as a byte array. The ComputeECDHSecret method takes a received public key as a byte array, creates an ECParameters structure with the public key, and then computes the shared secret using ECDH key agreement. The example demonstrates how two parties can generate their ECC key pairs, exchange their public keys, and then compute the shared secret using ECDH. Both parties should obtain the same shared secret if the key exchange process is successful.

Table 4.2   Key differences between RSA and ECC algorithms

Attribute	RSA	ECC
Key Size	RSA typically requires larger key sizes compared to ECC to achieve similar levels of security. For example, RSA-2048 provides roughly the same security level as ECC-256.	ECC offers the same level of security with much smaller key sizes compared to RSA. For example, ECC-256 provides roughly the same security level as RSA-3072.
Performance	RSA operations (encryption, decryption, signing, and verification) tend to be computationally more expensive, especially with larger key sizes. Performance can be a concern in resource-constrained environments.	ECC is more efficient and faster than RSA, especially for operations like signing and verification. ECC is well-suited for environments with limited computational resources, such as mobile devices and IoT devices.
Space Efficiency	RSA requires more storage space for keys compared to ECC due to the larger key sizes.	ECC keys are smaller in size, making it more space-efficient, which is beneficial for memory-limited devices and storage-constrained systems.
Security Margin	RSA relies on the difficulty of factoring large composite numbers. As computational power advances, the security margin of RSA may decrease with the same key size.	ECC is based on the difficulty of the elliptic curve discrete logarithm problem. Due to the mathematical properties of elliptic curves, ECC provides a higher security margin with smaller key sizes.
Adoption and Compatibility	RSA has been widely adopted and supported by various cryptographic libraries and standards for a long time.	ECC is gaining popularity, and its support is becoming more widespread. However, the adoption rate might be lower in some legacy systems or applications.

Differences and Considerations

RSA and ECC are both widely used public-key cryptographic systems, but they have fundamental differences. Table 4.2 explores the main differences between RSA and ECC and when to use one over the other:

When to use each algorithm:

- RSA is still a valid choice, especially when compatibility with older systems or specific cryptographic standards is required. It remains widely used and well-tested.
- ECC is increasingly becoming the preferred choice for modern cryptographic applications, especially in resource-constrained environments (e.g., IoT devices) and applications where performance and smaller key sizes are critical. ECC's security advantages and efficiency make it a compelling choice for many applications.

In summary, RSA and ECC are both strong cryptographic systems, but ECC offers significant advantages in terms of performance, space efficiency, and security with smaller key sizes. If you have the flexibility to choose newer cryptographic algorithms and libraries that support ECC, it is often a better choice, especially for modern cryptographic applications. However, if you are bound by compatibility or specific requirements, RSA remains a reliable option.

Symmetric Cryptography

Symmetric key algorithms use a single secret key for both encryption and decryption. While not as prevalent in blockchain networks, they are occasionally used in specific contexts, such as encrypting data stored off-chain or within private networks. Figure 4.2 illustrates the symmetric encryption/decryption flows, as described below:

1. **Key Generation**: A shared secret key is generated by the sender and securely shared with the recipient. Both parties keep this key confidential.
2. **Encryption Process**: The sender uses the shared key to encrypt the plaintext data. The encryption algorithm transforms the data into ciphertext. Only someone with the same key can decrypt the ciphertext back to plaintext.
3. **Decryption Process**: The recipient uses the same secret key to decrypt the ciphertext. The decryption algorithm reverses the encryption process, revealing the original data.

Common symmetric key algorithms include **Advanced Encryption Standard (AES)** and **Triple Data Encryption Standard (3DES)**.

Advanced Encryption Standard (AES)

The Advanced Encryption Standard (AES), also known as Rijndael after its creator, is a symmetric-key algorithm used for secure data transmission. It supports key sizes of 128, 192, or 256 bits and ensures confidentiality through multiple rounds of substitution, transposition, and mixing.

A full implementation using the **AesCryptoServiceProvider** class in C# is available in the open GitHub repository associated with this book: https://github.com/stefanotempesta/Application-Architecture-Patterns-Web3-Book.

In this example, we use the AesCryptoServiceProvider class from the System.Security.Cryptography namespace for AES encryption and decryption. The Encrypt method takes the

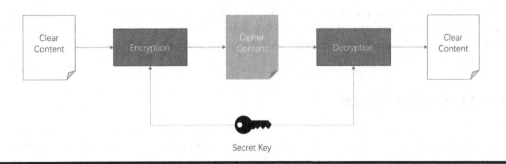

Figure 4.2 Symmetric cryptography flow

plaintext, AES key, and initialization vector (IV) as input and returns the encrypted data as a byte array. The Decrypt method takes the encrypted data, AES key, and IV as input and returns the decrypted plaintext as a string. In the Main method, we generate a random AES key and IV using AesCryptoServiceProvider. We then encrypt the original message and decrypt it back to verify the correctness of the AES encryption and decryption process.

Triple Data Encryption Standard (3DES)

Triple DES, officially the Triple Data Encryption Algorithm, is a symmetric-key block cipher that applies the DES cipher algorithm three times to each data block. It enhances security by using multiple encryption passes, compensating for DES's inadequate key size.

An example of 3DES implementation using the **TripleDESCryptoServiceProvider** class in C# is available in the GitHub repository mentioned above. In this example, we use the TripleDESCryptoServiceProvider class from the System.Security.Cryptography namespace for Triple DES encryption and decryption. The Encrypt method takes the plaintext, 3DES key, and initialization vector (IV) as input and returns the encrypted data as a byte array. The Decrypt method takes the encrypted data, 3DES key, and IV as input and returns the decrypted plaintext as a string. In the Main method, we generate a random 3DES key and IV using TripleDESCryptoServiceProvider. We then encrypt the original message and decrypt it back to verify the correctness of the 3DES encryption and decryption process.

Differences and Considerations

AES and 3DES are both symmetric key block ciphers used for encryption and decryption. While they both provide strong security, there are significant differences between them. Table 4.3 explores the main differences and when to use one over the other:

When to use each algorithm:

- AES is the recommended choice for most applications due to its higher security, better performance, and support for larger key sizes. It is suitable for modern cryptographic needs, such as data encryption, securing communications, and data protection.
- 3DES is still used in some legacy systems or where AES compatibility is not available. However, for new applications, it is generally better to use AES because of its superior security and performance.

In summary, AES is the more modern and secure option, while 3DES is primarily used in legacy systems or where AES support is not available. If you have the choice, prefer AES for most cryptographic purposes. However, if you're working with existing systems that only support 3DES, ensure proper security configurations and consider transitioning to AES when possible.

Key Derivation Functions

Key derivation functions are used to derive keys from other keys or passwords. In Web3 applications and wallets, these functions are used to derive private keys from mnemonic phrases or user passwords. Figure 4.3 describes a typical key derivation flow:

Table 4.3 Key differences between AES and 3DES algorithms

Attribute	AES	3DES
Key Size	AES supports key sizes of 128, 192, and 256 bits.	3DES uses a key size of 168 bits (three 56-bit keys), but only 112 bits are effectively used for encryption.
Performance	Due to its larger block size and efficient implementation on modern hardware, AES generally offers better performance than 3DES for most applications.	The triple encryption and decryption process in 3DES can make it slower compared to AES, especially for large datasets.
Space Efficiency	AES operates on 128-bit blocks, making it more efficient for modern hardware and software implementations.	3DES operates on 64-bit blocks, which can be slower for large amounts of data.
Security Margin	AES is considered more secure than 3DES due to its larger key sizes and block size, making it more resistant to brute-force attacks and other cryptanalytic techniques.	While 3DES is still considered secure, its security level is lower compared to AES, especially with advances in computing power.
Adoption and Compatibility	AES is a relatively newer encryption standard, and some legacy systems might not support it.	3DES has been around for a longer time and is more widely supported in older systems.

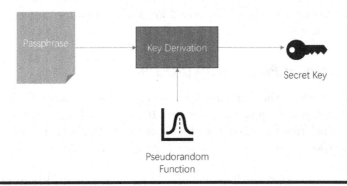

Figure 4.3 Key derivation flow

The key derivation function (KDF) flows as follows:

1. The KDF derives one or more secret keys from an original input (e.g., a master key, password, or passphrase).
2. It uses a pseudorandom function, often based on cryptographic hash functions or block ciphers.
3. KFDs enhance key security by transforming inputs into longer, more random, and harder-to-guess values.

Examples of key derivation functions include **PBKDF2 (Password-Based Key Derivation Function 2)** and **BIP39 (Bitcoin Improvement Proposal 39)**.

Password-Based Key Derivation Function 2 (PBKDF2)

PBKDF2 is a widely used cryptographic algorithm that generates a secure and unpredictable key from a password or passphrase. It finds applications in password-based encryption, secure key generation, and authentication.

Below is an example of PBKDF2 implementation in C#:

```
public class PBKDF2Example
{
    public static byte[] GeneratePBKDF2Key(string password, byte[]
        salt, int iterations, int keyLength)
    {
        using var pbkdf2 = new Rfc2898DeriveBytes(password, salt,
            iterations);
        return pbkdf2.GetBytes(keyLength);
    }
}
```

In this example, we use the **Rfc2898DeriveBytes** class from the System.Security.Cryptography namespace for PBKDF2 key derivation. The GeneratePBKDF2Key method takes the password, salt, number of iterations, and the desired key length as inputs and returns the derived key as a byte array. The salt is a random value that should be unique for each user and stored along with the derived key. The number of iterations should be chosen to provide a balance between security and performance, considering that a higher number of iterations increases security but also increases the time required to derive the key. The derived key can be used for various purposes, such as encrypting sensitive data or as a secure cryptographic key.

Bitcoin Improvement Proposal 39 (BIP39)

BIP39, or Bitcoin Improvement Proposal 39, is a widely adopted standard for mnemonic phrases used to back up and recover cryptocurrency wallets. It defines a way to represent binary data (such as private keys) in the form of a human-readable list of words. This mnemonic phrase, also known as a seed phrase, makes it easier for users to write down and store their wallet's backup information securely.

To implement BIP39 in C#, you'll need to use a library that supports BIP39. One such popular library is the NBitcoin library, which is commonly used for Bitcoin and cryptocurrency-related tasks in C#. Here's an example of how to use NBitcoin to generate a BIP39 mnemonic phrase and its corresponding seed:

First, you need to install the NBitcoin NuGet package:

```
Install-Package NBitcoin
```

Now, here's the C# code. In the line where a Mnemonic instance is created, you may change the value of WordCount to adjust the number of words in the mnemonic phrase. Replace "your passphrase" in the DeriveSeed function with your own passphrase.

```
using NBitcoin;

public class BIP39Example
{
    public static void GenerateBIP39Mnemonic()
    {
        Mnemonic mnemonic = new Mnemonic(Wordlist.English,
            WordCount.Twelve);

        Console.WriteLine("Mnemonic Phrase: " + mnemonic.
            ToString());
        Console.WriteLine("Seed: " + mnemonic.DeriveSeed("your
            passphrase"));
    }
}
```

In this example, we use the **Mnemonic** class from the NBitcoin library to generate a BIP39 mnemonic phrase with 12 words. As mentioned, you can adjust the WordCount parameter to generate different word lengths (e.g., 24 words for a stronger backup). The mnemonic phrase represents the seed from which all your private keys are derived. Make sure to securely store the mnemonic phrase and an optional passphrase (known only to you) to protect your cryptocurrency wallet. Losing the mnemonic phrase can result in permanent loss of access to your funds.

Differences and Considerations

PBKDF2 and BIP39 are both key derivation functions, but they serve different purposes and have distinct characteristics. Table 4.4 explores the main differences between PBKDF2 and BIP39 and when to use one over the other one.

When to use each function:

- Use PBKDF2 when you need a general-purpose key derivation function to derive cryptographic keys from passwords or passphrases for encryption, authentication, or other cryptographic applications.
- Use BIP39 when you are working with cryptocurrency wallets and want to provide users with a user-friendly backup mechanism using a mnemonic phrase. BIP39 ensures that users can easily restore their wallets and access their funds if needed.

In summary, PBKDF2 is a versatile key derivation function for general cryptographic purposes, whereas BIP39 is a specific key derivation scheme tailored for cryptocurrency wallets to enable easy backup and recovery of wallet information. Choose the appropriate function based on the specific requirements of your application and the context in which the key derivation is needed.

Signature Algorithms

Signature algorithms are used to verify the authenticity and integrity of data in blockchain networks and Web3 applications. A cryptographic signature proves ownership of an Ethereum address, for example, allowing users to control their digital identity and interact securely on the blockchain.

Table 4.4   Key differences between PBKDF2 and BIP39 functions

Property	PBKDF2	BIP39
Purpose	PBKDF2 is a general-purpose key derivation function designed to derive cryptographic keys from passwords or passphrases. It is commonly used to securely derive encryption keys for data protection, user authentication, and similar applications.	BIP39 is a specific key derivation scheme designed for cryptocurrency wallets. It generates a mnemonic (a list of words) from which a deterministic hierarchical wallet can derive private keys and addresses. BIP39 is primarily used in the context of cryptocurrency wallets for backup and recovery purposes.
Input	PBKDF2 takes a password, a salt (to increase security), and an iteration count as input to derive the key. The iteration count determines the computational effort, making it more resilient against brute-force attacks.	BIP39 takes entropy (usually generated randomly) as input to create a mnemonic phrase. This entropy is later used to generate the hierarchical deterministic wallet's master seed and private keys.
Output	PBKDF2 produces a fixed-size output key.	BIP39 generates a mnemonic phrase (a list of words) that is human-readable and used to recover the master seed and private keys.
Application	PBKDF2 is suitable for general cryptographic key derivation scenarios, such as password-based encryption, securing user passwords, and generating cryptographic keys from user passwords.	BIP39 is specifically tailored for cryptocurrency wallets, where users need a human-readable backup of their wallet's recovery information. It ensures users can easily restore their wallets and funds using the mnemonic phrase.
Security and Use Case	PBKDF2 is a secure key derivation function suitable for various cryptographic applications. It is used to securely derive keys that can protect data or authenticate users.	BIP39 is used in cryptocurrency wallets to provide a user-friendly backup and recovery mechanism. It is not meant to replace general-purpose key derivation functions for other cryptographic purposes.

A digital signature is a unique identifier attached to a message or document, providing authenticity, integrity, and non-repudiation. Its key components are illustrated in Figure 4.4 and described as follows:

- **Private Key**: Owned by the signer, it remains confidential.
- **Public Key**: Shared with others, it verifies the signature.
- **Message**: The content to be signed.
- **Signature Generation**: The signer applies a trapdoor function (often based on hash functions) to the message using their private key. The outcome is the digital signature. The signature uniquely represents the message and the signer.

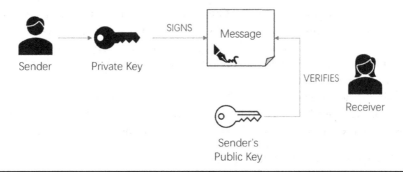

Figure 4.4   Key components of a digital signature

■ **Signature Verification**: Anyone with access to the public key can verify the signature. The verifier applies the same trapdoor function to the message using the public key. If the computed signature matches the received signature, the message is authentic.

Some commonly used signature algorithms include:

■ **Elliptic Curve Digital Signature Algorithm (ECDSA)**: Based on ECC, ECDSA is widely used for digital signatures in many blockchain networks, including Bitcoin and Ethereum.
■ **Edwards-curve Digital Signature Algorithm (EdDSA)**: EdDSA is another signature algorithm based on elliptic curves. It offers improved performance and security compared to ECDSA.

Elliptic Curve Digital Signature Algorithm (ECDSA)

ECDSA (Elliptic Curve Digital Signature Algorithm) is a digital signature algorithm that utilizes elliptic curve cryptography keys. It's an efficient equation based on cryptography with public keys and is widely used in security systems, encrypted messaging apps, and as the foundation for Bitcoin security.

Below is an example of ECDSA (Elliptic Curve Digital Signature Algorithm) implementation in C#:

```
public class ECDSAExample
{
    public static byte[] SignData(byte[] data, CngKey privateKey)
    {
        using var ecdsa = new ECDsaCng(privateKey);
        return ecdsa.SignData(data);
    }

    public static bool VerifyData(byte[] data, byte[] signature,
        CngKey publicKey)
    {
        using var ecdsa = new ECDsaCng(publicKey);
        return ecdsa.VerifyData(data, signature);
    }
}
```

In this example, we use the **ECDsaCng** class from the System.Security.Cryptography namespace for ECDSA signing and verification. The SignData method takes the data and the ECDSA private key as inputs and returns the signature as a byte array. The VerifyData method takes the data, signature, and ECDSA public key as inputs and returns a boolean indicating whether the signature is valid or not.

In the Main method, we generate an ECDSA key pair using the CngKey.Create method with the CngAlgorithm.ECDsaP256 algorithm, which represents the P-256 elliptic curve. We then sign the data using the private key and verify the signature using the corresponding public key.

```
string message = "Hello, ECDSA!";
byte[] data = Encoding.UTF8.GetBytes(message);

// Generate ECDSA key pair
using CngKey privateKey = CngKey.Create(CngAlgorithm.ECDsaP256);
CngKey publicKey = privateKey.Export(CngKeyBlobFormat.EccPublicBlob);

// Sign the data using the private key
byte[] signature = ECDSAExample.SignData(data, privateKey);

// Verify the signature using the public key
bool isSignatureValid = ECDSAExample.VerifyData(data, signature,
    publicKey);
```

As with any digital signature scheme, make sure to keep the private key secure and protect it from unauthorized access.

EEdwards-curve Digital Signature Algorithm (EdDSA)

EdDSA (Edwards-curve Digital Signature Algorithm) is a digital signature scheme based on the EdDSA family of Edwards curves. It is designed to be secure, efficient, and resistant to various cryptographic attacks. Unlike ECDSA, EdDSA provides built-in protection against certain implementation vulnerabilities like side-channel attacks. It is becoming increasingly popular in modern cryptographic applications.

Unfortunately, the .NET Framework does not natively support EdDSA. However, you can use third-party libraries like libsodium-net to implement EdDSA in C#. The libsodium-net library provides bindings to the Sodium cryptographic library, which includes support for EdDSA and other cryptographic primitives.

First, install the libsodium-net NuGet package:

```
Install-Package libsodium-net
```

The following C# code shows how to generate and verify EdDSA signatures:

```
using Sodium;

public class EdDSAExample
{
    public static byte[] GenerateEdDSAPrivateKey() => PublicKeyAuth.
        GenerateKeyPair().PrivateKey;

    public static byte[] GenerateEdDSAPublicKey(byte[] privateKey) =>
        PublicKeyAuth.ExtractEd25519PublicKey(privateKey);
```

```
    public static byte[] SignData(byte[] data, byte[] privateKey) =>
        PublicKeyAuth.SignDetached(data, privateKey);

    public static bool VerifyData(byte[] data, byte[] signature, byte[]
        publicKey) => PublicKeyAuth.VerifyDetached(signature, data,
        publicKey);
}
```

In this example, we use the libsodium-net library to generate **EdDSA** key pairs, sign data using the private key, and verify the signature using the corresponding public key.

```
string message = "Hello, EdDSA!";
byte[] data = Encoding.UTF8.GetBytes(message);

// Generate EdDSA key pair
byte[] privateKey = EdDSAExample.GenerateEdDSAPrivateKey();
byte[] publicKey = EdDSAExample.GenerateEdDSAPublicKey(privateKey);

// Sign the data using the private key
byte[] signature = EdDSAExample.SignData(data, privateKey);

// Verify the signature using the public key
bool isSignatureValid = EdDSAExample.VerifyData(data, signature,
    publicKey);
```

Differences and Considerations

ECDSA and EdDSA are both digital signature schemes based on elliptic curve cryptography, but they have some key differences. Table 4.5 explores the main differences between these signature algorithms and when to use one over the other.

When to use each algorithm:

- ECDSA: If you are working in an environment with well-established support for ECDSA and traditional elliptic curves (e.g., P-256), ECDSA is a valid choice. It has a long history of use and has proven to be secure when implemented correctly.
- EdDSA: If you have the flexibility to choose newer cryptographic algorithms and libraries that support EdDSA (e.g., Ed25519), EdDSA may offer better performance and security advantages. It is particularly well-suited for scenarios where efficiency and protection against certain implementation vulnerabilities are crucial.

Overall, both ECDSA and EdDSA are strong digital signature algorithms, but EdDSA tends to offer better performance and security features, making it a compelling choice for new applications. If possible, consider using EdDSA, especially in modern cryptographic systems. However, if you are bound by legacy systems or specific standard requirements, ECDSA remains a reliable option. As always, consult with cryptographic experts and follow best practices when selecting and implementing digital signature schemes.

Zero-Knowledge Proofs

Zero-knowledge proofs (ZKP) allow a party to prove knowledge of certain information without revealing the information itself. They are used for privacy-preserving transactions and

Table 4.5   Key differences between ECSDA and EdDSA algorithms

Property	ECDSA	EdDSA
Key Generation	ECDSA requires two keys for signing and verification – a private key and a public key. Key generation involves selecting a random private key and deriving the corresponding public key from it.	EdDSA uses a single key for both signing and verification, known as the seed. The public key is derived directly from the seed without the need for separate private and public key pairs.
Efficiency and Security	EdDSA is generally more efficient than ECDSA in terms of both signing and verification. It provides built-in protection against certain side-channel attacks, making it more secure in certain implementation scenarios.	While ECDSA is also secure, EdDSA is considered more secure against certain implementation vulnerabilities due to its design.
Performance	EdDSA is often faster than ECDSA for both key generation and signature verification, especially for certain curve types like Ed25519.	ECDSA can be slower than EdDSA, especially for certain curve types, but the performance difference may vary depending on the curve used and the specific implementation.
Curve Choices	EdDSA primarily uses Edwards curves, such as Ed25519 (based on the Ed25519 curve).	ECDSA can be used with various elliptic curves, such as NIST curves (e.g., P-256, P-384) and other standardized curves.
Adoption	ECDSA has been widely adopted and is supported by many cryptographic libraries and standards.	EdDSA is gaining popularity and is becoming more widely supported, especially for newer applications and systems.

authentication in blockchain networks. In a nutshell, the goal of ZKPs is for an entity (the *verifier*) to accept that an unknown and untrusted party (the *prover*) knows a secret parameter (the *witness*), which satisfies a relation, without revealing the witness to the verifier or any other party.

Figure 4.5 illustrates at high level the exchange between the prover and the verifier entities.

Examples include **zk-SNARK (Zero-Knowledge Succinct Non-Interactive Argument of Knowledge)** and **zk-STARK (Zero-Knowledge Scalable Transparent Arguments of Knowledge)**.

These are some of the common algorithms used for cryptography in blockchain networks, Web3 dApps, and wallets. It's important to note that the specific algorithms and cryptographic techniques employed may vary depending on the blockchain platform, application requirements, and security considerations.

zk-SNARK

Zero-Knowledge Succinct Non-Interactive Argument of Knowledge (zk-SNARK) is a fascinating cryptographic protocol that allows one party (the prover) to prove to another party (the verifier)

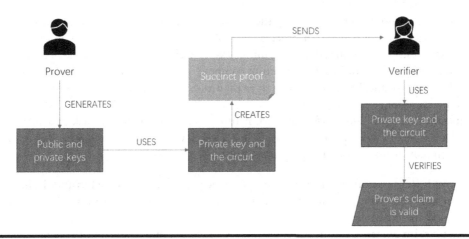

Figure 4.5 Zero Knowledge Proof flow

that a statement is true without revealing any information about the statement itself. zk-SNARKs are widely used in blockchain technologies and privacy-preserving applications.

Imagine you want to prove a statement to someone, but you don't want to disclose any additional details. For instance, Alice has more than $100,000 in her bank account, or proving that two DNA samples match without revealing the full DNA sequences. zk-SNARKs allow you to create succinct proofs that something is true without revealing the underlying data. It works in this way:

1. **Setup**: A trusted party generates public parameters and shares them with everyone.
2. **Prover**: The party who wants to prove a statement constructs a proof using their private data and the public parameters.
3. **Verifier**: Another party (the verifier) checks the proof against the public parameters without interacting with the prover.
4. **Zero-Knowledge Property**: The verifier learns nothing beyond the truth of the statement.

There is some mathematical *magic* in zk-SNARKs in using elliptic curve cryptography, cryptographic commitments, and polynomial equations. The prover constructs a succinct proof (a polynomial) that encapsulates the statement, and the verifier checks the proof using the public parameters. The magic lies in the fact that the verifier doesn't need to know the actual data; they only verify the correctness of the proof.

Implementing a full zk-SNARK system from scratch is beyond the scope of a simple example. Libsnark is a popular C++ library for building zk-SNARKs. Please note that implementing zk-SNARKs correctly and securely requires a deep understanding of cryptography and security concepts. It is highly recommended to use well-established libraries like libsnark and consult with cryptographic experts when working with zk-SNARKs in real-world applications.

zk-STARK

Zero-Knowledge Scalable Transparent ARguments of Knowledge (zk-STARK) is another cryptographic protocol, like zk-SNARK, that enables one party (the prover) to prove the correctness of a computation to another party (the verifier) without revealing any details of the computation itself.

zk-STARKs are non-interactive, meaning they do not require interaction between the prover and verifier during the proof generation process. zk-STARKs leverage leaner cryptography, particularly collision-resistant hash functions, and unlike zk-SNARKs, they eliminate the need for an initial trusted setup and are resistant to quantum computer attacks. However, zk-STARKs generate proofs that are typically 10 to 100 times larger than zk-SNARKs, making them more expensive and less practical for certain applications.

Implementing a full zk-STARK algorithm from scratch is a complex task and beyond the scope of a simple example. To provide a high-level overview of the steps required, this is a list of the key components of the zk-STARK protocol:

1. **Circuit Representation**: The computation to be proved is represented as an arithmetic circuit with input wires, output wires, and intermediate wires. Each gate in the circuit performs an arithmetic operation.
2. **Constraint System**: The arithmetic circuit is converted into a constraint system. Each gate in the circuit becomes a constraint equation involving the input, output, and intermediate wires.
3. **Encoding and Polynomialization**: The constraint system is encoded into a set of low-degree polynomials using techniques like Reed-Solomon codes and Fast Fourier Transform (FFT). These polynomials represent the constraints.
4. **Public Parameters Generation**: A setup phase generates public parameters, including the random coefficients for the polynomial constraints. This setup phase is typically non-interactive and requires a trusted setup.
5. **Prover's Computation**: The prover evaluates the polynomials and constructs a proof containing evaluations of these polynomials. This process involves solving the encoded constraints using specific mathematical techniques.
6. **Proof Verification**: The verifier receives the proof from the prover and checks whether the polynomial evaluations satisfy the constraints. Verification involves using a few polynomial evaluations to determine the correctness of the proof.

Note that zk-STARKs involve many mathematical and cryptographic techniques, including advanced coding theory, fast polynomial evaluation, and error correction codes. Implementing zk-STARKs requires a deep understanding of these concepts and their efficient implementation. For practical applications of zk-STARKs, it is recommended to use established libraries like libSTARK, which provides tools and utilities for zk-STARK constructions. libSTARK is developed by StarkWare (https://starkware.co/), a leading company in zk-STARK technology.

Differences and Considerations

zk-STARKs and zk-SNARKs have some similarities, such as the zero-knowledge property and the ability to prove complex computations in a succinct manner. However, they have several key differences, as described in Table 4.6.

Choosing between zk-STARK and zk-SNARK depends on the specific requirements and constraints of the application. Here are some considerations for when to use zk-STARK over zk-SNARK:

1. **Non-interactivity**: If your application requires a non-interactive proof generation process, zk-STARK is a better choice. Unlike zk-SNARK, zk-STARKs do not require interaction between the prover and verifier during the proof generation process, making them suitable for scenarios where interaction is not feasible or desirable.

Table 4.6   Key differences between zk-SNARK and zk-STARK

Property	zk-SNARK	zk-STARK
Proving and Verification	zk-SNARKs use polynomial commitments and arithmetic circuits to generate and verify proofs. The verification process is more computationally efficient, but the prover must generate the proof interactively with the verifier.	zk-STARKs use low-degree polynomials and Fourier transforms for proof generation and verification. The verification process is more resource-intensive and requires more computational power, but the prover can generate the proof non-interactively, making it more scalable.
Interactivity	zk-SNARKs are interactive protocols, meaning the prover and verifier need to exchange messages during the proof generation process.	zk-STARKs are non-interactive protocols, meaning the prover can generate the proof without any interaction with the verifier.
Scalability	zk-SNARKs are generally more efficient and faster than zk-STARKs for smaller computations and lower security levels.	zk-STARKs offer better scalability for larger computations and higher security levels. They can handle more complex computations at the cost of higher computational overhead during verification.
Trusted Setup	zk-SNARKs require a trusted setup phase to generate cryptographic parameters. The security of zk-SNARKs depends on the proper generation and disposal of these parameters.	zk-STARKs do not require a trusted setup, making them more appealing for applications where a trusted setup is a concern.

2. **Scalability**: zk-STARKs offer better scalability for larger computations compared to zk-SNARKs. They are designed to handle complex computations efficiently, making them well-suited for applications with extensive computations or large batch operations.

3. **No Trusted Setup**: If avoiding a trusted setup is a priority for your application, zk-STARK is a preferred option. zk-SNARKs require a trusted setup phase to generate cryptographic parameters, which might be a concern in some scenarios. zk-STARKs do not have this requirement, making them more appealing for trustless environments.

4. **Performance Overhead**: zk-STARKs generally have higher computational overhead during the verification process compared to zk-SNARKs. However, the gap is closing with advancements in zk-STARK research and implementations. If the computational overhead of zk-STARK is acceptable for your application's requirements, it might be a suitable choice.

5. **Decentralized and Trustless Environments**: In decentralized and trustless environments like blockchain applications, where the trusted setup and interactivity are concerns, zk-STARKs might be preferable. They provide strong security guarantees without relying on any trusted parties.

6. **Cryptographic Assumptions**: zk-STARKs are built on different cryptographic assumptions than zk-SNARKs. If you have specific concerns or preferences regarding the cryptographic assumptions used in the proof system, consider the assumptions and security models of both zk-STARK and zk-SNARK.

zk-STARKs excel in applications requiring the proof of large computations, especially in decentralized and trustless environments where a trusted setup may be challenging. For example, zk-STARKs can be used in blockchain applications to verify large computations, such as verifying smart contracts and validating batched transactions.

It is worth noting that zk-STARKs are relatively more complex to implement and use compared to zk-SNARKs, and they often require more computation during the verification process. As with any cryptographic protocol, it is essential to carefully consider the specific requirements and constraints of your application before choosing between zk-STARK and zk-SNARK.

It is also important to note that zk-STARKs are relatively newer and less mature than zk-SNARKs. While zk-STARKs offer unique advantages, they also come with additional complexity and challenges in implementation and use. zk-SNARKs are more widely adopted and supported, making them a more practical choice for some applications.

In summary, use zk-STARK when non-interactivity, scalability, absence of a trusted setup, or specific cryptographic assumptions are critical requirements for your application. Otherwise, zk-SNARK remains a solid and well-established choice for many cryptographic applications. As with any cryptographic protocol, consulting with experts and conducting a thorough analysis of your application's requirements is essential to making the right choice.

Homomorphic Encryption

Homomorphic encryption is a cryptographic technique that allows computations to be performed on encrypted data without decrypting it. In other words, it enables computations on encrypted data, yielding an encrypted result that can be decrypted to obtain the same result as if the computations were performed on the plaintext data. This property of homomorphic encryption preserves the privacy and security of the data throughout the computation process.

Homomorphic encryption can be beneficial for protecting Web3 applications in several ways:

1. **Secure Data Processing**: Web3 applications often handle sensitive user data, such as personal information or financial transactions. Homomorphic encryption enables secure data processing by allowing computations to be performed on encrypted data without exposing the underlying plaintext. This preserves the privacy and confidentiality of user data, even during computations executed on public or untrusted systems.
2. **Privacy-Preserving Smart Contracts**: Homomorphic encryption can be used in smart contracts to preserve privacy. For example, sensitive inputs or computations can be encrypted, and the contract can perform computations on the encrypted data while keeping the inputs hidden. This is particularly relevant for use cases such as decentralized finance (DeFi), where preserving privacy while executing financial operations is essential.
3. **Encrypted Voting and Auctions**: Web3 applications often involve voting systems or auctions where privacy and integrity are critical. Homomorphic encryption allows for secure voting and auction protocols by encrypting votes or bids and computing results without revealing the individual choices or bids until the final decryption stage. This ensures privacy while maintaining the integrity of the process.
4. **Secure Computation Outsourcing**: In Web3 applications, there might be scenarios where computation tasks need to be outsourced to external entities while preserving the confidentiality of the data. Homomorphic encryption enables secure computation outsourcing,

as the data can be encrypted before handing it over to the external party, who can perform computations on the encrypted data without accessing the sensitive information.

5. **Secure Data Sharing and Collaboration**: Web3 applications often involve data sharing and collaboration among multiple parties. Homomorphic encryption enables secure sharing of encrypted data, allowing authorized parties to perform computations on the encrypted data without the need to decrypt it. This maintains data confidentiality and privacy, even in collaborative environments.

It is worth mentioning that while homomorphic encryption provides powerful privacy-preserving capabilities, it also introduces additional computational overhead and complexity compared to traditional encryption methods. Implementing homomorphic encryption in Web3 applications requires careful consideration of the specific use cases, performance requirements, and the cryptographic libraries or frameworks available for the chosen encryption scheme.

There are different types of homomorphism, such as **partially homomorphic encryption** (PHE) and **fully homomorphic encryption** (FHE). FHE enables arbitrary computations on encrypted data, while PHE allows specific types of computations.

Differences and Considerations

PHE and FHE are two categories of homomorphic encryption schemes, each with distinct capabilities and use cases. Here are the main differences between FHE and PHE (Table 4.7):

When to use PHE over FHE: PHE can be advantageous in scenarios where you only need to perform specific types of homomorphic operations, and FHE's universal computation capabilities are not required. In such cases, PHE might offer a more straightforward and efficient solution.

When to use FHE over PHE: FHE is preferred when you need to perform arbitrary computations on encrypted data without the need for decryption. It allows for more advanced privacy-preserving applications, such as secure outsourcing of computations or secure multiparty computation. FHE is especially valuable in situations where the data must remain encrypted at all times, even during computation, and you want to delegate computation to untrusted parties while preserving data privacy.

Consider that, at the time of writing, fully homomorphic encryption is still an active area of research, and practical FHE schemes might have certain limitations, such as higher computational overhead and more complex key management. As a result, FHE might be more suitable for specialized use cases where its unique capabilities provide significant benefits, while PHE remains a practical choice for simpler homomorphic computations.

Confidential Computing

Confidential computing is a concept that aims at protecting sensitive data and computations (that is, algorithms) even when they are being processed in untrusted environments. It ensures that data remains encrypted and confidential throughout its lifecycle, including during computation, storage, and transmission. Data protection is achieved through hardware-powered encryption, and the creation of *secure enclaves* of memory that are accessible only by the CPU or GPU, where the encryption key is wired, and are completely opaque to the hypervisor and the operating system. This makes data and code running inside an enclave inaccessible by the virtual machine's

Table 4.7   Key differences between Partially Homomorphic (PHE) and Fully Homomorphic (PHE) encryption

Property	PHE	FHE
Homomorphic Operations	Partially Homomorphic Encryption supports only one type of homomorphic operation, either addition or multiplication, but not both. For example, a PHE scheme might allow homomorphic addition but not homomorphic multiplication, or vice versa.	Fully Homomorphic Encryption, on the other hand, supports both homomorphic addition and homomorphic multiplication, enabling arbitrary computations on encrypted data. In an FHE scheme, you can perform any sequence of additions and multiplications on encrypted data without the need for decryption.
Homomorphic Capability	Partially Homomorphic Encryption has limited computational capabilities due to supporting only one type of homomorphic operation. It can still be useful for specific applications, such as computing sums or products of encrypted data.	Fully Homomorphic Encryption is much more powerful and flexible as it allows for universal computation. FHE schemes are capable of evaluating any function on encrypted data, which makes them extremely versatile for performing complex computations without revealing the underlying data.
Complexity	Partially Homomorphic Encryption tends to be simpler to implement and more efficient in terms of computational overhead compared to FHE. It requires fewer mathematical operations to perform homomorphic operations, leading to better performance in certain scenarios.	Fully Homomorphic Encryption is more complex to implement and comes with higher computational overhead compared to PHE. The ability to perform universal computations on encrypted data introduces additional challenges in terms of performance and efficiency.

administrator, and even by the cloud hosting provider. Figure 4.6 shows the isolation between hardware-protected secure enclaves and the rest of the components in a cloud host stack. Code running in an enclave communicates directly with the host's hardware, bypassing all levels of virtualization in the stack. As a result of this isolation, the memory space where the enclave resides is not addressable by the operating system, making any attempt to tamper with the OS irrelevant from a security perspective for the security of applications and data running inside an enclave.

Confidential computing can be beneficial for protecting Web3 applications in the following ways:

1. **Secure Smart Contract Execution**: Web3 applications rely on smart contracts for executing code on the blockchain. Confidential computing allows the execution of smart contracts in a secure and confidential environment. It ensures that the contract's code and data remain encrypted during execution, protecting sensitive information and preventing unauthorized access or tampering.

Figure 4.6 Secure enclave stack

2. **Privacy-Preserving Computation**: Confidential computing enables privacy-preserving computations in Web3 applications. Sensitive data can be encrypted and processed within a secure enclave or trusted execution environment (TEE) without exposing the plaintext data to the external environment. This is particularly useful in scenarios where multiple parties need to collaborate on computations while preserving data privacy.

3. **Secure Data Sharing and Collaboration**: Web3 applications often involve data sharing and collaboration among multiple parties. Confidential computing allows encrypted data to be securely shared and processed in trusted environments. Authorized parties can perform computations on the encrypted data without having access to the underlying sensitive information, ensuring data confidentiality and privacy.

4. **Encrypted Data Storage and Processing**: Confidential computing protects data both at rest and in transit. It ensures that data stored in decentralized storage systems or off-chain databases remains encrypted, mitigating the risk of unauthorized access or data breaches. Additionally, confidential computing can be utilized for secure and encrypted processing of sensitive data stored in decentralized networks.

5. **Secure Oracles and External Data Processing**: Web3 applications often rely on oracles or external data sources for obtaining off-chain information. Confidential computing enables the secure processing of data received from these sources, protecting the integrity and confidentiality of the data while performing computations or validations on it.

To leverage confidential computing in Web3 applications, developers need to utilize secure enclaves, also known as **trusted execution environments** (TEEs), which provide isolated and secure execution environments for sensitive computations. Examples of TEEs include Intel SGX (Software Guard Extensions) and AMD SEV (Secure Encrypted Virtualization). These technologies provide hardware-backed security measures to ensure the confidentiality and integrity of data and code within the enclave.

For as much as it may sound promising, it is important to note that confidential computing is not a silver bullet and has its own set of considerations, such as enclave management, and secure enclave attestation. Nevertheless, it offers valuable capabilities for protecting sensitive data and computations in Web3 (and not only) applications and contributes to a more secure and privacy-preserving ecosystem.

Technology Availability

Intel, AMD, and NVIDIA are market leaders in offering CPUs and GPUs that boast secure extensions used in enabling confidential computing. Often, the choice of one technology over the other is dictated by the availability of a relevant offering by your preferred public cloud provider. Where Azure, GCP, and IBM Cloud offer confidential virtual machines and containers, notably AWS lacks an offering in this space. In addition to the hardware-related differences, there are decisions to be made on the software side, as applications running in a trusted execution environment would need to communicate with the hardware directly, using special libraries. This is certainly the case for confidential resources based on Intel SGX technology. Alternative and less invasive approaches exist, as described below:

- **Intel SGX** (Software Guard Extensions) provides a hardware-based mechanism for creating secure enclaves where code and data can be executed in a protected and isolated environment. SGX focuses on protecting specific portions of an application's code and data from unauthorized access, even in the presence of a compromised system.
- **Intel TDX** (Total Memory Encryption Extensions) is designed to provide system-wide memory encryption, ensuring that all data in memory, including RAM and memory caches, remains encrypted. It aims to protect against physical memory attacks and certain hypervisor attacks.
- **AMD SEV-SNP** (Secure Nested Paging) is a technology developed by AMD that enhances the security features of AMD SEV. SEV-SNP builds upon the foundation of SEV and introduces additional security enhancements to protect virtual machines (VMs) and sensitive data in cloud and virtualized environments.

While Intel and AMD have made significant strides in confidential computing with their CPU-based technologies, NVIDIA has also entered the arena by collaborating with Microsoft to bring GPU-accelerated confidential computing for cutting-edge AI workloads.

- **Ampere Protected Memory** (APM): NVIDIA A100 Tensor Core GPUs support APM, enabling organizations to use sensitive datasets for training and deploying more accurate AI models.
- The way it works is that the GPU is paired with a TEE on the host CPU. The GPU includes a **hardware root-of-trust** (HRoT), provisioned with a unique identity and a corresponding certificate during manufacturing.
- Data gets **encrypted between the CPU and GPU** across the PCI bus using securely exchanged encryption keys. This approach ensures that AI computations benefit from GPU acceleration while maintaining data privacy and security.

It is worth noting that these technologies have different underlying architectures and design considerations. They are complementary in enhancing security and can be used together to achieve stronger protection in confidential computing scenarios.

Frameworks and Libraries

There are several libraries and frameworks available that support confidential computing and help developers build secure applications. Here is a list of some popular libraries and frameworks:

1. **Open Enclave**: Open Enclave (https://openenclave.io/) is an open-source framework developed by Microsoft that enables developers to build secure and confidential computing applications. It provides a hardware-agnostic platform for creating trusted execution environments (TEEs) using technologies like Intel SGX and ARM TrustZone.
2. **Confidential Consortium Framework**: The Confidential Consortium Framework (CCF – https://ccf.microsoft.com/) is an open-source framework developed by Microsoft Research that enables the development of confidential, decentralized, and high-performance applications. CCF builds on top of Microsoft Open Enclave and Azure Confidential Computing to provide a secure and scalable platform for building confidential applications.
3. **Gramine**: Initially developed by Intel, Gramine (https://gramineproject.io/) is a library OS, that runs inside a guest OS in an Intel SGX-powered virtual machine or Docker container.
4. **Google Asylo**: Asylo (https://asylo.dev/) is an open-source framework developed by Google that simplifies the development of confidential computing applications across various TEEs, including Intel SGX and others.
5. **Enarx**: Enarx (https://enarx.dev/) is an open-source project that aims to provide hardware-agnostic TEEs. It supports various backends, including Intel SGX and AMD SEV, and allows for running applications securely in untrusted environments.
6. **Fortanix Runtime Encryption**: Fortanix provides a Runtime Encryption platform (https://www.fortanix.com/resources/datasheets/runtime-encryption-platform) that leverages Intel SGX to secure applications, data, and keys. It supports secure enclaves and allows developers to build and deploy confidential computing solutions.

Additional frameworks are referenced on the Confidential Computing Consortium (CCC) website https://confidentialcomputing.io/.

It is essential to choose the library or framework that best suits your requirements, taking into consideration factors such as hardware support, programming language compatibility, performance, and the level of trust required for your confidential computing application. Additionally, since the field of confidential computing is rapidly evolving, new libraries and improvements to existing ones may become available over time.

Differences and Considerations

Intel, AMD, and NVIDIA aim to provide hardware-based security features to protect sensitive data and computations. Table 4.8 makes a comparison of the key features of the most popular confidential computing technologies.

Intel SGX focuses on protecting specific parts of an application's code and data in isolated enclaves. It provides secure execution environments for sensitive computations, safeguarding data and code even in the presence of a potentially compromised system.

Intel TDX, instead, provides system-wide memory encryption. It primarily protects against physical memory attacks and certain hypervisor attacks. Intel SGX, on the other hand, defends against threats posed by the entire system, including malicious software, untrusted operating systems, and compromised hypervisors.

AMD SEV-SNP focuses on enhancing VM memory isolation and protecting nested VMs in multi-tenant cloud environments. It ensures that nested VMs remain secure even if the hypervisor

Table 4.8   Feature comparison of the key technologies for confidential computing

Technology	Feature Comparison
INTEL SGX	• Architecture: Process-based confidential computing environment. • Security model: Enclaves rely on firmware and microcode security. • Memory limitations: Important memory constraints. • Programming model: Peculiar programming model, slow legacy software porting. • Future outlook: Unclear; Intel discontinuing support on consumer platforms.
INTEL TDX	• Architecture: Virtualization-based confidential computing environment. • Security model: Depends on virtualized OS security and firmware. • Memory limitations: Fewer limitations compared to SGX. • Legacy applications: Allows trivial deployment of legacy apps. • Programming model: No need to change programming model.
AMD SEV-SNP	• Architecture: VM-based confidential computing. • Security boundary: More restricted than Intel SGX. • Memory isolation: Protects memory spaces inside VMs. • Ease of deployment: Well-suited for cloud environments.
NVIDIA AMP	• Collaboration: NVIDIA and Microsoft partnership. • GPU-accelerated: Combines GPU power with security. • Azure integration: Supports AI workloads with hardware-protected VMs. • Security boundary: Relies on virtualized OS security and firmware.

is compromised. AMD SEV-SNP primarily addresses security in virtualized environments, while Intel SGX is more focused on securing sensitive code and data within applications.

The NVIDIA AMP approach is to combine the computational power of its GPUs with the enclave protection of CPUs. Confidential machine learning workloads, where data used for training the ML models is kept private, are the most suited use cases for this kind of technology.

Note that technological advancements and the capabilities of Intel, AMD, and NVIDIA for confidential computing are evolving rapidly. For the latest information, always refer to official documentation and announcements.

Chapter 5

Decentralized Digital Identity

In an increasingly interconnected and digitized world, the need for secure and trustworthy digital identity solutions has become paramount. As individuals, we find ourselves navigating an ever-expanding online landscape, accessing services, conducting transactions, and interacting with others across numerous platforms. However, this convenience comes at a cost – our personal data often resides in centralized databases, making it vulnerable to breaches and misuse.

Decentralized Digital Identity (DID) emerges as a groundbreaking solution to these pressing concerns. By leveraging the power of distributed ledger technology, such as blockchain, DID offers individuals unprecedented control over their digital identities, fostering a more secure, privacy-centric, and user-centric approach to identity management.

At its essence, DID represents a paradigm shift from the traditional model, where centralized authorities and intermediaries validate and store personal information on our behalf. Instead, it empowers individuals with the ability to control their identity attributes, choose who gains access to which information, and participate in a self-sovereign manner within the digital realm.

This chapter explores the intricacies and potential of Decentralized Digital Identity, delving into its underlying principles, mechanisms, and benefits. As we venture into the core components of DID, we will shed light on the cryptographic techniques, consensus algorithms, and data structures that underpin its robustness and resilience against tampering and unauthorized access.

Furthermore, we will delve into the real-world applications of Decentralized Digital Identity, examining how this transformative technology is already revolutionizing industries like finance, healthcare, supply chain management, and beyond. From facilitating frictionless and trustless identity verification processes to enhancing data privacy and streamlining KYC (Know Your Customer) procedures, the versatile applications of DID continue to garner attention and adoption across various sectors.

However, as we embrace the potential of this groundbreaking technology, it is imperative to address the challenges and considerations that come hand-in-hand with its implementation. Scalability, interoperability, standardization, and ensuring inclusive access for all individuals remain critical factors that demand innovative solutions as we shape the future of digital identity.

By fostering a comprehensive understanding of DID, this chapter aims to contribute to the ongoing discourse surrounding the evolution of identity management in the digital age. As technology continues to advance, we stand on the precipice of a new era – one where individuals can reclaim control over their digital presence, while safeguarding their privacy and autonomy.

Together, we embark on a journey of exploration, paving the way toward a more secure, equitable, and empowering digital future through DID.

The Need for Decentralized Identity

Over 1 billion people worldwide are unable to prove their identity through any recognized means. As such, they are without the protection of law, are unable to access basic services, education, employment, participate as a citizen, or transact in the modern economy. Most of those affected are children, and many are refugees, forcibly displaced, or stateless persons.

Source: "The global identification challenge: Who are the 1 billion people without proof of identity?", World Bank Blogs, https://blogs.worldbank.org/voices/global-identification-challenge-who-are-1-billion-people-without-proof-identity

This figure itself should convince all of us of the importance of having a system of identification that is reliable and trustworthy. **The ability to prove one's identity is a fundamental and universal human right** [...] but systems of identification are archaic, insecure, and lack adequate privacy protection. A new form of identity is needed, one that weaves together technologies and standards to deliver key identity attributes, such as **self-ownership and censorship resistance**.

Source: "The Quest for Owning your Digital Identity", "Humans of IT" blog by Microsoft, https://techcommunity.microsoft.com/t5/humans-of-it-blog/guest-blog-the-quest-for-owning-your-digital-identity/ba-p/1616652

DIDs are user-generated, self-owned, globally unique identifiers rooted in decentralized systems. They possess unique characteristics, like greater assurance of immutability, censorship resistance, and tamper evasiveness. These are critical attributes for any ID system that is intended to provide self-ownership and user control.

Decentralized Identity Foundation

The **Decentralized Identity Foundation** (DIF – https://identity.foundation/) plays a pivotal role in advancing the adoption and standardization of DID solutions. Founded in 2017, DIF is a collaborative effort comprising industry leaders, technology experts, non-profit organizations, and governments, all united in their mission to empower individuals with control over their digital identities.

The primary objectives of the Decentralized Identity Foundation are illustrated in Figure 5.1 and described as follows.

■ **Developing Open Standards**: DIF is committed to creating and promoting open standards and specifications for decentralized identity technologies. By fostering a collaborative environment, DIF enables stakeholders to collectively work on interoperable and compatible solutions. These standards form the building blocks of DID ecosystems, ensuring that different platforms and applications can seamlessly interact with each other.

Figure 5.1   Objectives of the Decentralized Identity Foundation

- **Facilitating Interoperability**: Interoperability is a key aspect of DID adoption. DIF seeks to establish a unified framework that allows various DID implementations to interoperate harmoniously. By encouraging compatibility and adherence to common protocols, DIF aims to prevent fragmented identity solutions and foster a cohesive ecosystem that benefits users and service providers alike.
- **Promoting Self-Sovereign Identity (SSI)**: Self-sovereign identity is a fundamental principle underlying DID. DIF advocates for SSI, where individuals have full ownership and control over their identity attributes, granting them the ability to selectively share information with others. DIF actively encourages the development of tools, technologies, and best practices that reinforce this vision of user-centric identity management.
- **Ensuring Privacy and Security**: DIF places a strong emphasis on the privacy and security aspects of DID. As digital identity solutions handle sensitive personal data, ensuring robust privacy measures and secure data handling practices are crucial. DIF supports research and development in the areas of cryptographic techniques, zero-knowledge proofs, and secure data storage to build a trust layer into DID ecosystems.
- **Engaging in Collaborative Initiatives**: DIF fosters a collaborative ecosystem by bringing together individuals, organizations, and projects from diverse backgrounds. Through collaborative initiatives, working groups, and open-source projects, DIF enables cross-industry cooperation to address challenges and explore innovative solutions in the field of decentralized identity.
- **Educational Outreach**: DIF serves as an educational hub, providing resources, documentation, and best practices to help individuals and organizations understand and implement Decentralized Digital Identity. By raising awareness and promoting the benefits of DID, DIF aims to accelerate the adoption of user-centric identity solutions globally.

Through its inclusive and open approach, the DIF has emerged as a driving force behind the widespread acceptance and implementation of DID. As the world increasingly embraces the potential of DID, DIF's contributions in setting standards, fostering collaboration, and upholding the principles of privacy and self-sovereignty continue to shape the landscape of digital identity management for the better.

European Digital Identity Wallet

In the "How DIF Members Contribute to the Development of a Seamless and Secure European Digital Identity Wallet" post published on the DIF's blog website (https://blog.identity.foundation/) on July 2023, the author explores the role of DIF in advancing the **European Digital**

Identity Wallet and examine the various activities undertaken by its members in support of this crucial project.

In Europe, the **eIDAS regulation**, electronic Identification, Authentication, and Trust Services, an EU regulation on electronic identification and trust services for electronic transactions in the European Single Market (https://www.eid.as/), has set the stage for the creation of a European Digital Identity Wallet, a secure means for citizens to access online services throughout the EU. DIF members have been addressing key challenges in developing a secure European Digital Identity Wallet, including hardware binding and wallet attestation.

The full article is available at: https://blog.identity.foundation/how-dif-members-contribute-to-the-development-of-a-seamless-and-secure-european-digital-identity-wallet/.

In summary, DIF envisions a future where individuals have greater control over their personal data and can interact with others in a more secure and privacy-preserving manner. To achieve this vision, DIF focuses on creating open standards, protocols, and providing tools for developers to build DID solutions. The eIDAS regulation aims to establish a single framework for secure and seamless digital services across the European Union, and it does so through the European Digital Identity Wallet, a software application that enables citizens and organizations to manage verifiable identity information and access online services seamlessly.

DIF and its members actively support the European Digital Identity Wallet initiative through various activities:

- **Large-Scale Pilots**: DIF participates in large-scale pilots across the EU, providing real-world experience and feedback.
- **Concepts and Prototypes**: DIF members work on concepts and prototypes related to hardware binding and wallet attestation.
- **Hardware Binding**: They explore secure ways to bind the wallet to the user's device using techniques like secure hardware modules and cryptographic methods.
- **Collaborative Ecosystem**: This collaborative ecosystem is essential for driving the adoption of Decentralized Identity technologies and ensuring their long-term success.

DIF's active involvement in advancing the European Digital Identity Wallet underscores its commitment to empowering individuals with secure, decentralized control over their digital identities.

W3C Identifiers

The **World Wide Web Consortium** (W3C) plays a significant role in the development and standardization of **Decentralized Identifiers** through its working group called the "Decentralized Identifier Working Group" (https://www.w3.org/2019/did-wg/). W3C is a global community that develops open standards to ensure the long-term growth and accessibility of the World Wide Web. Its involvement in the field of DIDs underscores the importance of interoperability, security, and user-centricity in the evolving landscape of digital identity.

The role of W3C in the context of Decentralized Identifiers includes the objectives summarized in Figure 5.2 and described as follows. As you can notice, W3C's objectives align with DIF's ones.

- **Standardization and Specification**: W3C facilitates the creation of formal specifications for DIDs and related technologies. The Decentralized Identifier Working Group collaborates with experts and stakeholders to develop open and consensus-driven standards. By setting these standards, W3C ensures that different implementations of DIDs can interoperate seamlessly across various platforms and systems.

Figure 5.2   Objectives of the W3C for Decentralized Identifiers

- **Interoperability**: Interoperability is crucial for the widespread adoption of decentralized identity solutions. W3C's involvement ensures that DIDs adhere to common protocols, enabling different systems to recognize and interact with each other using a shared framework. This fosters a cohesive and interoperable ecosystem for DIDs, where users can leverage their identities across diverse applications and services.
- **Privacy and Security**: W3C emphasizes the importance of privacy and security in the development of DIDs. By leveraging its expertise in web standards, W3C works to ensure that DIDs incorporate robust cryptographic mechanisms and privacy-preserving techniques. This ensures that individuals have control over their identity attributes and can securely manage the sharing of their personal data with others.
- **Community collaboration**: W3C provides a platform for collaboration among stakeholders in the decentralized identity space. Through working groups and community engagement, different individuals, organizations, and projects can come together to contribute to the development of DIDs and related technologies. This collaborative approach fosters a diverse range of perspectives and helps address various use cases and challenges in the field.

W3C Identifiers, also known as "Decentralized Identifiers" (also DID in this context), are a foundational concept in the realm of decentralized digital identity. A DID is a unique identifier that represents a self-sovereign, decentralized identity. Unlike traditional identifiers, such as usernames or email addresses, DIDs are not tied to a centralized authority or service provider. Instead, they are designed to be globally unique and cryptographically verifiable.

The structure of a DID typically follows the `did` method syntax, which indicates the method or system used to create and manage the identifier. For example, a typical DID might look like:

```
did:method-name:identifier-specific-string
```

Here:

- `did` stands for decentralized identifier.
- `method-name` represents the specific method or technology used to generate the DID (e.g., ethr for the Ethereum blockchain or web for decentralized identifiers on the web).
- `identifier-specific-string` is a unique string that identifies the specific entity associated with the DID.

DIDs serve as the foundation for decentralized identity systems, providing individuals with the means to control their digital identities, selectively share personal information, and maintain privacy while engaging in various online activities. By leveraging DIDs, users can assert ownership over their digital presence, establish trust with other parties, and participate in secure and privacy-preserving interactions across the internet.

Identity Hubs

Identity Hubs are an essential component of the Decentralized Digital Identity ecosystem. They serve as secure and user-centric data stores, enabling individuals to control their identity-related information in a decentralized manner. The concept of Identity Hubs aligns with the principles of self-sovereign identity, empowering users to manage their digital identities independently and selectively share information as needed.

Identity Hubs are used in DID for data storage and governance, and specifically for:

1. **Data Control and Ownership**: Identity Hubs put users in control of their identity data. Instead of relying on centralized databases or third-party providers to store personal information, individuals can choose to store their data in their Identity Hubs. This ensures that users maintain ownership of their identity attributes, and no central authority can access or manipulate their data without their consent.

2. **Selective Disclosure**: With Identity Hubs, users can exercise granular control over which identity attributes they share and with whom. Instead of providing all personal data to every service or application, users can selectively disclose only the relevant information required for a specific transaction or interaction. This enhances privacy and reduces the risk of unnecessary exposure of sensitive data.

3. **Decentralization and Interoperability**: Identity Hubs are designed to be decentralized and interoperable. They can work with different DID methods and networks, allowing users to use their DIDs across various platforms and services. This interoperability ensures that users are not locked into specific identity providers or systems, promoting a diverse and open identity ecosystem.

4. **Secure Data Sharing**: Identity Hubs employ strong encryption and cryptographic mechanisms to protect users' data. Data shared with other parties is encrypted, and only authorized recipients with the corresponding decryption keys can access and verify the information. This ensures that even if the data is transmitted over public networks, it remains secure and tamper-proof.

5. **Consent Management**: Identity Hubs facilitate consent management, ensuring that users explicitly grant permission before sharing their data. Users have full visibility and control over which parties have access to their data and can revoke access at any time if they no longer wish to engage with a specific service or organization.

6. **Personalization and Portability**: Identity Hubs offer a personalized identity experience for users. Users can customize their identity attributes, update information, and manage their digital personas according to their preferences. Additionally, Identity Hubs make it easier to port identity data from one service or application to another, promoting data portability and avoiding vendor lock-in.

Figure 5.3 shows the role of Identity Hubs in securing educational credentials for students. With digital identities that they own across multiple educational institutes, students have a single,

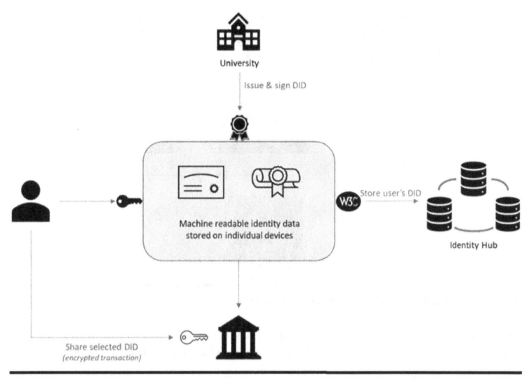

Figure 5.3   Decentralized verifiable credentials for high education

immutable, and verifiable curriculum of study. Digital signatures can be applied to certificates of attendance, exam completions, and diplomas. This eliminates the issues of counterfeit certifications, degree factories, and doctored documents. For instance, students who are seeking further education, employment, or immigration often need to demonstrate their academic level or language proficiency. Now, recruiters, employers, governments, and universities can swiftly validate a student's qualifications in mere minutes, bypassing needless middlemen. This also circumvents the need to depend on central authorities that may be delayed by weeks or even months due to a backlog of requests.

By shifting control and custody of identity-related information in the hands of individuals, Identity Hubs promote a user-centric approach to digital identity management. They align with the principles of self-sovereign identity, fostering a more secure, private, and empowering environment where individuals can interact with confidence in the digital world. As the adoption of Decentralized Digital Identity continues to grow, Identity Hubs play a pivotal role in reshaping the landscape of online identity management and authentication.

Identity Verifiers

Identity Verifiers are entities or services responsible for verifying the authenticity and accuracy of identity-related information provided by individuals or entities. In the context of Decentralized Digital Identity, Identity Verifiers play a crucial role in establishing trust and ensuring the validity of the claims made by the subjects holding DIDs.

The verification process in Figure 5.4 starts with an individual who wants to establish or update their digital identity. They may submit identity-related information, such as name, date of

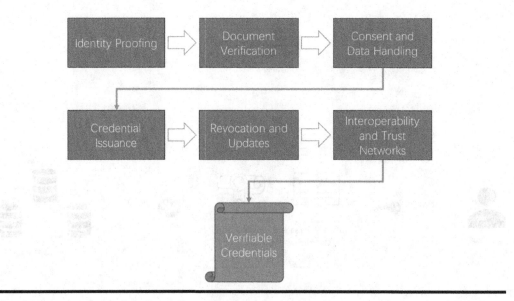

Figure 5.4   Identity and credentials verification process

birth, address, or official documents, to an Identity Verifier. The Identity Verifier then performs a verification process to validate the accuracy and legitimacy of the provided information.

1. **Identity Proofing**: Identity Verifiers often conduct identity proofing to ensure that the individual is who they claim to be. This process may involve verifying government-issued IDs, conducting background checks, or using biometric authentication methods to confirm the person's identity.
2. **Document Verification**: In cases where official documents are submitted, Identity Verifiers may check the authenticity of these documents to prevent the submission of forged or fraudulent information.
3. **Consent and Data Handling**: Identity Verifiers must obtain the individual's consent to access and verify their identity data. They must also adhere to strict data handling practices, ensuring that the individual's sensitive information is treated with confidentiality and stored securely.
4. **Credential Issuance:** Upon successful verification, Identity Verifiers can issue verifiable credentials or attestations that confirm the validity of specific identity attributes. These credentials are cryptographically signed to ensure tamper-resistance and are associated with the individual's DID.
5. **Revocation and Updates:** Identity Verifiers are responsible for managing the revocation of issued credentials in case of data changes or loss of trust. They may also update the credentials when the verified information needs to be renewed or modified.
6. **Interoperability and Trust Networks**: In a decentralized identity ecosystem, Identity Verifiers may be part of a trust network or consortium, where trust is established through network consensus or reputation systems. The more reputable an Identity Verifier is within the network, the more trust is placed in their verified credentials.
7. **Verifiable Credentials**: The credentials issued by Identity Verifiers are verifiable. This means that when an individual presents a verifiable credential to a relying party (e.g., an online service provider), the relying party can cryptographically verify the authenticity of the credential and the Identity Verifier's signature, without needing to contact the verifier directly.

By employing Identity Verifiers, the DID ecosystem ensures that individuals can confidently and securely use their digital identities across various services and applications. Identity Verifiers play a critical role in reducing identity fraud, enhancing privacy, and fostering a user-centric approach to identity management in the digital age.

Below is a simple example of an Identity Verifier implemented in Python. This example demonstrates a basic verification process for a person's age by checking if they are above 18 years old. Note that this is a simplified illustration and does not cover the complexities of real-world identity verification processes. Real-world implementations would involve more sophisticated mechanisms, such as connecting to external databases, verifying documents, and employing more robust cryptographic techniques.

```python
from datetime import date

class IdentityVerifier:
    def __init__(self):
        pass

    def verify_age(self, name, date_of_birth):
        current_date = date.today()
        birth_year, birth_month, birth_day = map(int, date_of_birth.
            split('-'))
        age = current_date.year - birth_year - ((current_date.month,
            current_date.day) < (birth_month, birth_day))

        if age >= 18:
            print(f"Identity of {name} verified. Age: {age} years.
                Age verification passed.")
            return True
        else:
            print(f"Identity of {name} verified. Age: {age} years.
                Age verification failed.")
            return False

# Example usage
if __name__ == "__main__":
        verifier = IdentityVerifier()
        person_name = "John Doe"
        person_date_of_birth = "1990-01-15" # Format: YYYY-MM-DD

        verification_result = verifier.verify_age(person_name,
            person_date_of_birth)
        if verification_result:
            print("Access granted. User is above 18 years old.")
        else:
            print("Access denied. User is under 18 years old.")
```

In this example, we create an **IdentityVerifier** class with a method verify_age. The verify_age method takes the person's name and date of birth as input. It calculates the age based on the current date and compares it to 18 years to determine if the person is above the legal age limit.

Again, this is a basic example to illustrate the concept of an Identity Verifier. In practice, Identity Verifiers would be much more sophisticated and would involve more comprehensive identity verification processes, including validating official documents and interacting with external services or databases.

Microsoft Entra Verified ID

Microsoft has been actively exploring and contributing to the development of decentralized identity solutions. Microsoft is one of the founding members of the Decentralized Identity Foundation.

One of Microsoft's significant contributions to the DID ecosystem is the development of the Microsoft Identity platform with support for decentralized identity standards. Microsoft's decentralized identity solution leverages open standards, such as the W3C DID standard and Verifiable Credentials Data Model (VC-DM), to enable users to control and manage their digital identities securely.

The relevance of Microsoft's involvement in DID lies in the potential to provide users with more control over their identity data while ensuring privacy, security, and interoperability. With decentralized identity solutions, users can manage their identity attributes, selectively share information with third parties, and reduce the dependency on central identity providers.

Moreover, Microsoft's involvement in DID aligns with the broader industry efforts toward creating a user-centric approach to identity management. Decentralized identity solutions can potentially transform how individuals interact with online services, reducing the need to create multiple accounts and sharing personal information with various platforms.

It is essential to note that the field of decentralized identity is rapidly evolving, and various companies, including Microsoft, are continually exploring and developing solutions to enhance digital identity management for users. With **Microsoft Entra Verified ID**, users and organizations can easily issue, request, and verify credentials to represent proof of employment, education, or any other claim.

More details about Microsoft's solution for decentralized identity management can be found here: https://learn.microsoft.com/en-us/azure/active-directory/verifiable-credentials/.

Digital Signatures

A **digital signature** is a cryptographic technique used to verify the authenticity and integrity of digital messages or documents. It is akin to a handwritten signature in the physical world, but in the digital realm, it provides an additional layer of security and non-repudiation, ensuring that the message's sender cannot deny having sent it.

In a digital signature, a mathematical algorithm is applied to the content of a message or document, generating a unique digital fingerprint or **hash**. This hash is then encrypted using the sender's private key, resulting in the digital signature. The signature, along with the original message, can be shared with recipients.

Digital signatures provide the following key properties:

▪ **Authentication**: The recipient can verify the identity of the sender, as the signature can only be generated using the sender's private key.
▪ **Integrity:** Any changes to the message or document will result in a different hash value, rendering the signature invalid.
▪ **Non-repudiation**: The sender cannot deny having sent the message, as their private key is required to generate the signature.

The typical patterns of implementing digital signatures involve the following steps, as shown in Figure 5.5.

Figure 5.5 Digital signature process

1. **Hashing the Message**: The first step is to create a unique digital fingerprint or hash of the message or document. Hash functions are cryptographic algorithms that take an input of any length and produce a fixed-size output (the hash value), which is unique to the specific input.
2. **Signing the Hash**: The sender uses their private key to encrypt the hash value, generating the digital signature. The private key is a closely guarded secret and is known only to the sender.
3. **Sending the Message and Signature**: The original message, along with the digital signature, is sent to the recipient. Both the message and the signature can be freely shared without compromising the security of the private key.
4. **Verifying the Signature**: Upon receiving the message and the signature, the recipient can use the sender's public key (which is associated with the private key used to create the signature) to decrypt the signature and obtain the original hash value.
5. **Comparing Hashes**: The recipient then computes the hash of the received message and compares it with the decrypted hash from the signature. If the two hashes match, it confirms that the message has not been altered in transit and that the signature is valid. If the hashes differ, the message may have been tampered with or the signature is not valid.

Digital signatures are widely used in various applications, including secure communication, digital contracts, software distribution, and financial transactions, to ensure the authenticity and integrity of digital data.

Cryptography is at the heart of digital signatures, providing the mathematical foundation for their security and non-repudiation properties. To understand the details of cryptography for digital signatures, we need to explore two fundamental components: hash functions and asymmetric (or public key) cryptography.

Hash Functions

A hash function is a one-way mathematical algorithm that takes an input (message, document, or data) of arbitrary size and produces a fixed-size output, known as the hash value or digest. The critical properties of hash functions in the context of digital signatures are:

- **Deterministic**: For the same input, the hash function always produces the same hash value. This ensures that identical messages result in identical hashes.
- **Pre-image Resistance**: Given a hash value, it is computationally infeasible to reverse the process and find the original input (pre-image).
- **Collision Resistance**: It is computationally infeasible to find two different inputs that produce the same hash value (collision).
- **Avalanche Effect**: A small change in the input results in a significantly different hash value.

Hash functions, such as SHA-256 (part of the SHA-2 family) and SHA-3, are commonly used in digital signatures.

Asymmetric (Public Key) Cryptography

Asymmetric cryptography involves a pair of cryptographic keys: a public key and a private key. These keys are mathematically related but have distinct functionalities:

- **Public Key**: The public key is used for encryption and can be freely shared with others. It is typically used to encrypt data or verify digital signatures.
- **Private Key**: The private key is kept secret and is used for decryption or generating digital signatures. Only the owner of the private key should have access to it.

The process of generating and verifying digital signatures using asymmetric cryptography involves the following steps:

1. **Signature generation**:
   a. The sender creates a hash of the message using a hash function.
   b. The sender uses their private key to encrypt the hash, creating the digital signature.
2. **Signature verification**:
   a. The recipient receives the message and the digital signature.
   b. The recipient uses the sender's public key to decrypt the signature, obtaining the hash value.
   c. The recipient independently computes the hash of the received message using the same hash function.
   d. If the computed hash matches the decrypted hash, the signature is valid, indicating that the message has not been altered in transit and was indeed sent by the holder of the corresponding private key.

The security of digital signatures relies on the computational infeasibility of finding a private key given its associated public key, as well as the strength of the underlying hash function. As long as these cryptographic components remain secure, digital signatures provide a robust mechanism for ensuring the authenticity and integrity of digital data, enabling secure communications and digital transactions in various domains.

Content Management System Integration

Integration of digital signature solutions in Content Management Systems (CMS) enhances the security and authenticity of documents, ensuring that they cannot be tampered with and can be attributed to specific users or organizations. Table 5.1 lists a few examples of how digital signature solutions can be integrated into a CMS.

These examples illustrate how digital signature solutions can enhance security, streamline workflows, and boost trustworthiness within Content Management Systems. By providing strong cryptographic assurances and facilitating secure interactions, digital signatures add value to a wide range of CMS applications across various industries.

Digital Port of Trust

CB Digital Port of Trust by Connecting Software is a solution developed by Connecting Software (https://www.connecting-software.com/) that focuses on digital trust and security. It is designed

Table 5.1   Examples of integration of digital signature in a Content Management System

Scenario	Description
Document Versioning and Approval	In a CMS, when documents undergo changes or updates, integrating a digital signature solution can ensure that each version is digitally signed and time-stamped. This allows users to verify the authenticity of each version and track the approval process. For example, when an important document is ready for review, the CMS can prompt the responsible party to digitally sign and approve it before it becomes available to others.
User Authentication and Authorization	CMS platforms can use digital signatures to authenticate users and manage their permissions. For instance, users can sign in using their digital signatures, proving their identity without relying on traditional passwords. Moreover, digital signatures can be used to authorize specific actions within the CMS, ensuring that only authorized users can perform critical tasks such as publishing or deleting content.
Secure Document Sharing and Collaboration	Digital signatures can enable secure document sharing and collaboration within a CMS. Users can sign documents to indicate their approval or ownership, making it easier to identify the origin of any changes or additions. This enhances accountability and minimizes the risk of unauthorized modifications.
Document Integrity Verification	By integrating a digital signature solution, a CMS can automatically verify the integrity of documents when they are accessed or modified. The CMS can compare the digital signature of the current document with the previously signed version to ensure that it has not been altered or corrupted
Regulatory Compliance and Audit Trail	For organizations operating in regulated industries, integrating digital signatures in a CMS can facilitate compliance with legal requirements. Signed documents can be stored securely with audit trails, demonstrating a clear chain of custody and providing evidence of authorized interactions with sensitive data.
Electronic Forms and Contracts	In CMS systems that handle electronic forms or contracts, digital signatures can be incorporated to ensure the authenticity and non-repudiation of user-submitted data. This is especially relevant for e-commerce platforms or applications where legally binding agreements are involved.
Document Archiving and Preservation	Digital signatures contribute to the long-term authenticity and preservation of archived documents in a CMS. When documents are digitally signed, they remain verifiable even after years of storage, assuring their integrity and reliability over time.

to enhance the authenticity, integrity, and non-repudiation of digital documents and transactions, making it a valuable tool for businesses and organizations seeking to establish trust in their digital interactions.

Key features and functionalities of CB Digital Port of Trust are listed in Figure 5.6 and described as follows:

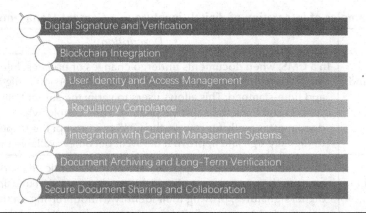

Figure 5.6 Key features of CB Digital Port of Trust by Connecting Software

- **Digital Signature and Verification**: The product generates digital signatures, enabling users to sign digital documents securely. The digital signatures generated by CB Digital Port of Trust can be verified to ensure the authenticity and integrity of the signed content.
- **Blockchain Integration**: The platform leverages blockchain technology to provide an immutable and tamper-resistant record of digital signatures and document transactions. Integrating blockchain can enhance the trustworthiness of the signed data and establish a transparent audit trail.
- **User Identity and Access Management**: CB Digital Port of Trust includes user authentication mechanisms to ensure that only authorized users can access and sign documents. It also offers access controls to manage permissions and user roles.
- **Regulatory Compliance**: Compliance with industry-specific regulations and legal requirements related to digital signatures and document authenticity is a focus of CB Digital Port of Trust. The solution assists organizations in meeting compliance standards and maintaining auditable records.
- **Integration with Content Management Systems (CMS)**: CB Digital Port of Trust integrates with various Content Management Systems, allowing organizations to incorporate digital signatures and trust mechanisms seamlessly into their existing workflows.
- **Document Archiving and Long-Term Verification**: The product provides mechanisms for archiving signed documents and ensuring their long-term verifiability, ensuring the integrity of stored data over extended periods.
- **Secure Document Sharing and Collaboration**: CB Digital Port of Trust enables secure sharing and collaboration on digital documents, with a focus on maintaining document integrity and user accountability.

The author is not affiliated with Connecting Software, currently, but has worked with the CB Port of Trust application in the past, hence the desire to share its capability in this chapter, as an example of a software solution to the CMS digital signature. As with any software, it is essential to refer to the official website and documentation for more detailed information about its specific features, benefits, and use cases. For inquiries or demonstrations, it is advisable to contact Connecting Software directly to better understand how the solution can address your organization's needs for digital trust and security. More details can be found here: https://www.connecting-software.com /cb-digital-port-of-trust/.

Blockchain and the Identity and Credentials Economy

The industrial organization of the identity and credentials economy has been relatively stable for a very long period. For hundreds of years, it has been a quasi-institutional monopoly centered around governments and universities, and with relatively little change and innovation. But recently, this industry has begun to be disrupted by several epochal forces. One force is the globalization of higher education and labor markets, requiring credentials to work over a much larger scale.

The other one is increasing the need for access to digital services, which require multiple forms of digital identity, for digital wallets, online banking, social media accounts, etc. These forms of digital ID allow us to travel, conduct business, access financial and health records, and stay connected. Digital ID offers access to vital social services and would enable everybody to exercise their rights as citizens and participate in the modern economy. But it also carries significant risk, if not thoughtfully designed and carefully implemented. Large-scale data breaches affecting millions of people have been the consequence of the use of archaic and insecure tools, along with the lack of appropriate privacy protection.

A new form of identity is needed, one that weaves together technologies and standards to deliver key identity attributes, such as self-ownership and censorship resistance, that are difficult to achieve with existing systems. Cryptographically secure, decentralized identity systems could provide greater privacy protection for users, while also allowing for portability and verifiability. These twin forces are significantly changing the economics of education, job markets, identity management, and data ownership. Blockchain technology is at the vanguard of this development.

Self-Sovereign Identity

Blockchain, and more broadly digital ledger technology (DLT), fits in the **self-sovereign identity** (SSI) framework of issuer–holder–verifier process. But they all must solve the problem in the *trust triangle* in which the verifier (who might be a potential employer) needs some way to trust the issuer of the credential (who might be a university or a company) that has been given them by the holder of the credential (e.g., a student or prospective employee). This trust triangle is illustrated in Figure 5.7.

The parties in the trust triangle rely on using a decentralized digital ledger to record credentials (onchain effectively tokenized credentials) and to provide a trust layer for the identification of issuers and credentials. The onchain data model is technically efficient but presents significant privacy and security risks. These can be overcome by only storing hashed and encrypted data (e.g., Blockcerts, or uPort, built on Ethereum). However, there are some instances where credentials could and perhaps should be written to DLT structures, such as organizational confirmation of

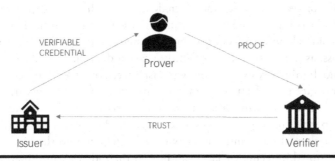

Figure 5.7 The trust triangle in decentralized digital identity

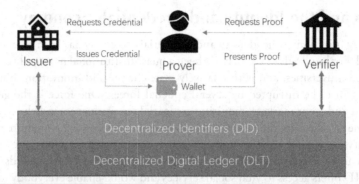

Figure 5.8   Credential verification flow leveraging decentralized technology

compliance to regulations that demand deep transparency and immutability (relating to modern slavery bills, etc.). Figure 5.8 shows the communication flow among the issuer of credentials, the prover, or holder of such credentials in their digital wallet, and the verifying authority that receives the proof of validity of the credential.

The general principle is that the holder of the credential (the person or organization who has been issued the credential) should be able to choose where they store their credential (including self-custody) without reducing or affecting the trustworthiness of the credential. The role of the DLT is to facilitate that trustworthiness while lowering the transaction costs, and possibly increasing the functional properties, of issuing, using (holding), and verifying a credential.

Confidential identity hubs, hosted on confidential computing infrastructure in multiple *hubs* around the world, can create the necessary distributed network for storing and securing identity elements at scale. Security of sensitive data is ensured by the redundancy of the distributed network, and governance remains decentralized by removing sole ownership of the provided infrastructure.

Public cloud providers will have identity hubs in multiple regions, with no technology and vendor lock-in for identity and credential issuers and verifiers. The opportunity for cloud providers is to be in the vanguard of technology offering for distributed identity hubs, which are secure and confidential, and provide "Identity & Verifiable Credentials as a Service" offerings.

Decentralized Trust

Decentralized digital identity is not about removing authorities. We obviously need governments to issue passports, universities for education diplomas, etc. The goal of DID is to offer a decentralized system of storage and verification of credentials which is not dependent on centralized systems, which can be compromised or not be in business after some time. For example, digitally signed PDFs are valid as long as that company is in business. Once gone, for any reason, all signed PDFs are worthless, as they cannot be verified. Education diplomas are likewise valid and verifiable until that school/university exists, otherwise just a piece of paper. Not to mention the risk of photoshopping or degree mills. Refugees and large immigration movements are tangible examples of how a self-sovereign identity can address this humanitarian challenge. Hundreds of thousands, if not millions, of people crossing country borders without documents, with little likelihood that they will ever go back to their country. How will they integrate into the new place with no ID? Digital credentials stored in secure enclaves can protect their identity information and have them verified anywhere in the world.

DID is not about removing governments or any other form of authorities. **DID is about helping governments focus on what they should do better**, which is issuing and verifying identity and credentials, and not storing and securing it. Technology providers will store and secure it, and ideally deliver this capability "as a service" to governments and credential issuers.

In conclusion, decentralization reduces system risk in two key ways: by changing the attack surface for hackers from a few highly valuable targets with large collections of data to many targets with little data; and by removing single points of failure. The combination of confidential infrastructure and decentralized ledger, along with cryptographic signature, is the foundation of a secure and scalable digital identity service.

Conclusion

Credentials technology has for centuries been low-tech in its substrate – written documents, on parchment or paper, stored in filing systems – with elaborate and costly provenance and security systems to verify and validate authenticity. These include witnessed wet signatures, centralized and secure record repositories, cross-checks on documents, tamper-resistant materials, multistage and socially sanctioned verification by professional notaries. All of these features add cost and slow down the process. Verifying a credential might cost some multiple of an hourly wage, and take days to weeks.

The evolution of credentials technology has followed a path of digitization. This occurs at two distinct levels: (1) digitization of the storage and record – the database or ledgers for the credentials, including indexing and search; and (2) digitization of the security and control of the credentials. The difference between these two phases relates to the evolution of the architecture of credentials. The first phase – digitization of paper records – replicates the existing centralized administrative structure. Paper-based files are transferred to PDFs and put into digital databases. This enables a larger scale, but the retrieval and processing operations remain fundamentally the same, and ownership of the digital signature/verification capability resides in the power of a few businesses offering a proprietary service.

Blockchain technology enables a second phase in the digital transformation of credentials by enabling a distributed architecture for verification. A credential in this sense is a non-fungible signed token (the token is a secure information container). In addition, the ownership of a credential cannot be traded in the context of education or personal identity management, unlike digital art or cryptocurrency.

The evolution of digital credentials has lowered the costs of verification on some margins, but the same technologies have also advanced the scope for fraud itself. As such, credentials are often excessively trusted, which is what creates opportunities for fraud and misuse. Blockchain technologies show promise of improving the effectiveness of credentials infrastructure and use by lowering the cost of verification without raising the unit cost of issuance.

Recommendation 1: Credentials Infrastructure Should Adopt Privacy-by-Design Principles

Credentials are a tool for selectively sharing private or closely held information, specifically in relation to an individual's skills, capabilities, experience, and knowledge, but also in relation to sensitive health data (e.g., vaccination certificates) or financial data (e.g., credit scoring), and which is inherently and intimately linked to identity information. A credentials infrastructure is therefore a privacy hazard. A poorly designed credentials infrastructure will leak private information, and thus its use will be perceived as risky or potentially costly by at least one party to the transaction (or a liability hazard by the counterparty). Therefore, in order to ensure wide adoption and use, it is imperative that effective privacy considerations are built into digital credentials infrastructure. Confidential computing provides hardware-based encryption of data being processed, helping with protection from rogue administrators and cloud provider personnel.

Recommendation 2: Support Self-Sovereign Data Architecture and Decentralization

Multiple countries have introduced Consumer Data Right regulations aimed at providing consumers with greater access to and control over their data. Self-sovereign data architecture and decentralization are significant contributors to taking Consumer Data Right beyond its current implementation into new sectors and new capabilities. Self-sovereign data architectures empower users, enable new markets, and reduce risk, complexity, and administration burdens for issuing organizations who no longer need to support authentication requests and consent management from receiving parties and users.

Decentralization reduces system risk in two key ways: by changing the attack surface for hackers from a few highly valuable targets with large collections of data to many targets with little data, and by removing single points of failure.

Case Study: Credentials for Social Good

The potential for verifiable digital credentials to create social good is immense. Whether it be enabling safer and more effective deployment of humanitarian aid, facilitating a fluid volunteering workforce or rapidly identifying people in times of need; the ability to quickly identify who someone is, or what skills and experience they might have, while at the same time preserving dignity, safety, and privacy is truly transformative, particularly for those who are experiencing, or are at risk of, vulnerability.

In 2018, Australian Red Cross embarked on a project to improve the motivation, engagement, and retention of volunteers across the sector to enable increased participation and effectiveness. The Australian Red Cross recognized the opportunity that decentralized ledger technology presented to not only improve the safety and security of individuals' data but put them completely in control, choosing what data to share and with whom they want to share it. For organizations, blockchain technology and digital credentials presented an opportunity to reduce the cost of verification and administration enabling more efficient and effective deployment of an increasingly mobile volunteer workforce.

The verifiable digital credentialing platform "Traverse" was developed in response to this opportunity with a focus on first helping volunteer-involving organizations start the verifiable credentialing journey within their own organizations. The potential for verifiable credentials and blockchain to facilitate the movement of volunteers between branches or depots or even between states quickly and safely, particularly in times of crisis, is significant. And while the portability of credentials between organizations is the goal, there have already been over 700 credentials issued via Traverse since launch.

In order to support the portability of the credentials and solve the issue of digital coordination and cooperation the Trust Alliance was established in June 2019. The Trust Alliance is a growing multi-sector collaboration that brings together private, public, and for-purpose stakeholders to develop the shared trust standards and design principles, as well as the trusted technology ecosystem, that are needed to enable portable credentials. While focused on volunteering credentials at present, the Trust Alliance organizations see this opportunity as a promising pathway to build an open and equitable digital credential ecosystem. The goal is to have organizations creating, sharing, and accepting trusted credentials within the Trust Alliance ecosystem, with more pilots and members in the pipeline, in 2021.

Chapter 6

The Token Economy: Digital Assets on the Blocks

In the ever-evolving landscape of the digital age, the emergence of blockchain technology has paved the way for revolutionary concepts that challenge conventional economic models. At the forefront of this digital transformation lies the captivating world of the token economy – an ecosystem that has redefined the way we perceive, create, and transact with assets in both the virtual and real realms.

In this groundbreaking era, the token economy has breathed new life into the concept of digital asset tokenization, unlocking immense opportunities for creators, investors, and enthusiasts alike. From the exhilarating realm of non-fungible tokens (NFTs) and vibrant marketplaces to the convergence of art, fandom, and finance, this article embarks on an exploration of the multifaceted facets that compose the very essence of the token economy.

Digital Asset Tokenization: A Paradigm Shift in Ownership

In the traditional financial world, ownership and trading of assets were often restricted by geographical barriers, complex intermediaries, and tedious paperwork. However, the token economy introduces a refreshing paradigm shift by enabling asset tokenization on the blockchain – the process of representing real-world assets digitally through unique tokens.

Whether it be real estate, precious metals, intellectual property, or even rare collectibles, the blockchain's immutable ledger ensures secure ownership records, making fractional ownership a tangible reality. This democratization of ownership not only empowers smaller investors with access to previously unattainable markets but also enhances liquidity and transparency, laying the groundwork for a more inclusive global economy.

DOI: 10.4324/9781003491934-6

The NFT Renaissance: Minting and Monetizing Digital Collectibles

At the heart of the token economy lies the meteoric rise of non-fungible tokens (NFTs). These one-of-a-kind cryptographic tokens serve as digital certificates of authenticity, verifiably representing ownership of unique items, artwork, music, and even virtual real estate within the metaverse.

NFT minting has opened doors for artists, musicians, and creators to monetize their digital masterpieces in unprecedented ways. By tokenizing their creations, they can reach a global audience, receive direct support from fans and collectors, and engage in royalty mechanisms that ensure long-term incentives for their creative endeavors.

Various token formats are used to represent different types of assets and functionalities. When it comes to non-fungible tokens (NFTs) and similar token formats, the following are the most common ones.

ERC-721 Tokens (Ethereum)

ERC-721 is a widely adopted standard on the Ethereum blockchain for creating NFTs. Each ERC-721 token is unique and non-interchangeable, making it ideal for representing individual digital assets such as collectibles, artworks, and virtual real estate. The standard allows for metadata storage, which contains additional information about the NFT, such as its name, description, and image.

ERC-1155 Tokens (Ethereum)

ERC-1155 is another popular token standard on Ethereum that supports both fungible (identical and interchangeable) and non-fungible assets within a single contract. This flexibility makes ERC-1155 suitable for representing a combination of NFTs and fungible tokens. It is often used for in-game items and digital collectibles in decentralized gaming platforms.

BEP-721 and BEP-1155 Tokens (Binance Smart Chain)

Binance Smart Chain (BSC) offers similar token standards to Ethereum's ERC-721 and ERC-1155. BEP-721 is used for NFTs, while BEP-1155 allows for the issuance of both fungible and non-fungible assets within a single contract.

TRC-721 and TRC-1155 Tokens (TRON)

The TRON blockchain also supports NFTs through TRC-721, and it offers the TRC-1155 standard for mixed fungible and non-fungible tokens, much like ERC-1155 on Ethereum.

Flow's NFT Standard (Flow Blockchain)

Flow is a blockchain designed for high-throughput and scalability, and it has its native NFT standard. It is used for creating unique digital assets on the Flow network, supporting various use cases, including digital art, collectibles, and gaming items.

Polygon (Matic) NFTs

The Polygon (formerly Matic) network, a Layer 2 solution for Ethereum, also supports NFTs using the ERC-721 and ERC-1155 standards. It provides lower transaction costs and faster confirmation times compared to the Ethereum mainnet.

These token formats serve as the backbone of the NFT ecosystem, enabling the representation and ownership of unique digital assets on different blockchain networks. NFTs have found applications in various industries, including art, gaming, music, sports, virtual real estate, and more, where ownership, authenticity, and scarcity are crucial factors for value and engagement.

Marketplaces of Tomorrow: Bridging the Gap between Artists and Collectors

In tandem with the NFT revolution, vibrant and decentralized marketplaces have emerged, acting as conduits connecting artists with eager collectors. These digital bazaars foster an environment of creativity, uniqueness, and accessibility, enabling users to discover and own a diverse array of digital assets across various platforms.

NFT marketplaces are platforms that facilitate the buying, selling, and trading of non-fungible tokens (NFTs). These marketplaces have become essential hubs for artists, creators, collectors, and investors to transact and discover unique digital assets. Here are some of the most common and popular NFT marketplaces.

OpenSea

OpenSea is one of the largest and most well-known NFT marketplaces. It supports a wide range of NFTs, including digital art, collectibles, virtual real estate, and more. OpenSea is built on the Ethereum blockchain and allows users to connect their wallets and seamlessly browse, list, and buy NFTs from various projects and artists.

Rarible

Rarible is a decentralized NFT marketplace that enables users to create, buy, and sell unique digital assets. It operates on the Ethereum blockchain and has its native governance token, RARI, which allows token holders to participate in platform decisions.

SuperRare

SuperRare is a platform focused on digital art NFTs. It curates high-quality and limited-edition digital art pieces created by artists from around the world. Each artwork on SuperRare is unique, making it a sought-after marketplace for collectors and art enthusiasts.

Foundation

Foundation is an exclusive NFT marketplace for digital creators and artists. It operates on the Ethereum blockchain and curates a select community of artists who can mint and sell NFTs. Foundation provides a platform for artists to showcase and monetize their digital creations.

Nifty Gateway

Nifty Gateway is a user-friendly NFT marketplace that offers a wide range of digital collectibles, art, and experiences. It is known for hosting regular drops and auctions featuring prominent artists, musicians, and celebrities.

NBA Top Shot

NBA Top Shot is an officially licensed NFT marketplace built on the Flow blockchain. It offers officially licensed NBA collectible highlights (moments) in the form of NFTs, allowing fans to own and trade iconic basketball moments.

Decentraland Marketplace

Decentraland is a virtual reality platform on the Ethereum blockchain, and its marketplace allows users to buy, sell, and lease virtual land and digital assets. Users can create and monetize experiences, content, and games within their virtual properties.

Enjin Marketplace

Enjin Marketplace is part of the Enjin ecosystem, which focuses on gaming and virtual items. It allows users to buy, sell, and trade blockchain-based gaming assets and virtual items, including NFTs created using the Enjin blockchain technology.

BakerySwap

BakerySwap is a decentralized NFT and DeFi marketplace on the Binance Smart Chain (BSC). It offers various NFT categories, including art, collectibles, and gaming items.

These NFT marketplaces serve as central hubs for NFT enthusiasts, providing them with access to a wide range of unique digital assets and opportunities for collecting, investing, and engaging with the growing NFT ecosystem. As the NFT space continues to expand, new marketplaces and platforms are likely to emerge, providing even more opportunities for creators and collectors to connect and transact.

Calculating Rarity

The *rarity* of an NFT refers to the level of uniqueness or scarcity of a specific token within a collection. In the context of NFTs, rarity is often associated with how rare or common a particular digital asset is compared to others in the same collection. The rarer an NFT is, the more valuable it might be in the marketplace.

Rarity in NFTs is determined by various factors, and the calculation can vary depending on the specific collection and project. Some common methods used to assess the rarity of an NFT are summarized in Figure 6.1 and described as follows:

1. **Edition Size**: The total number of tokens minted for a specific digital asset can influence its rarity. If only a limited number of tokens are created, the NFT is considered rarer. For example, an NFT from an edition of 10 is typically rarer than an NFT from an edition of 100.

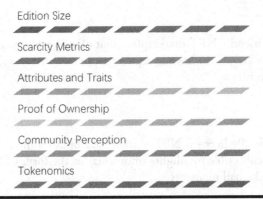

Figure 6.1   Common methods to calculate NFT rarity

2. **Scarcity Metrics:** Some collections use specific metrics to quantify the scarcity of each NFT. For example, an NFT representing a unique moment in time, a special event, or a rare character in a game might be considered rarer than others in the collection.

3. **Attributes and Traits:** In certain NFT collections, tokens may have different attributes or traits that contribute to their rarity. For example, a collectible card game NFT might have different levels of rarity based on the power, abilities, or characteristics of the card.

4. **Proof of Ownership:** In some cases, rarity might be determined based on the NFT holder's proof of ownership. For example, an NFT that was owned by a prominent artist or celebrity might be considered rarer and more valuable.

5. **Community Perception:** Rarity can also be influenced by the perception and demand from the NFT community. If a specific NFT becomes highly sought after, its rarity and value may increase due to increased demand.

6. **Tokenomics:** The tokenomics of the project, such as the distribution model or special rewards for early adopters, can also impact the rarity of NFTs within the collection.

Rarity is a significant factor in determining the value and desirability of NFTs in the marketplace. It adds an element of excitement and discovery for collectors and enthusiasts who are eager to acquire unique and scarce digital assets. Said that, it is important to note that rarity is a subjective and dynamic concept. What is considered rare in one context might not be the same in another. Additionally, as the NFT market evolves and new collections are introduced, the rarity of NFTs within existing collections may change over time based on factors like user demand and ongoing releases of new tokens.

Calculating the rarity of NFTs in a collection can be a complex process, as it depends on the specific attributes and characteristics of the NFTs within that collection. The following Python code snippet demonstrates how you can calculate the rarity based on the edition size of each NFT in the collection. For this example, let's assume the NFT collection has a fixed edition size for each token.

```
# Sample NFT Collection with edition sizes
nft_collection = {
    "NFT001": 100,
    "NFT002": 50,
    "NFT003": 10,
    "NFT004": 200,
    "NFT005": 5
}
```

```
# Function to calculate the rarity score of each NFT
def calculate_rarity(edition_size):
    # Rarity score formula: (1 / edition_size)
    return 1 / edition_size

# Dictionary to store the rarity score of each NFT
rarity_scores = {}

# Calculate the rarity score for each NFT in the collection
for nft_id, edition_size in nft_collection.items():
    rarity_score = calculate_rarity(edition_size)
    rarity_scores[nft_id] = rarity_score

# Sort NFTs by rarity in ascending order (from most rare to least rare)
sorted_rarity_scores = dict(sorted(rarity_scores.items(), key=lambda x:
    x[1], reverse=True))
```

In this example, the `nft _ collection` dictionary represents the NFTs in the collection, where the keys are the NFT IDs, and the values are their corresponding edition sizes. The calculate_rarity function takes the edition size as input and returns the rarity score based on a simple formula: `1 / edition _ size`. The rarity scores for each NFT are calculated and stored in the `rarity _ scores` dictionary. Finally, the NFTs are sorted based on their rarity scores in descending order, from most rare to least rare, and the results are displayed.

Keep in mind that this is a basic example, and in real-world scenarios, you might need to consider additional factors and more complex algorithms to determine the rarity of NFTs accurately, especially when attributes, traits, or community perceptions come into play.

Artwork, Fan Tokens, and Beyond: Nurturing the Power of Fandom

Beyond the realm of digital art, the token economy has taken fandom to a whole new level. Sports teams, entertainment franchises, and celebrities now have the ability to issue fan tokens, forging deeper connections with their audiences. Fan tokens provide holders with exclusive benefits, voting rights, and immersive experiences, thereby transforming passive supporters into active participants in the success of their favorite entities.

Walking between Worlds

Walking Between Worlds (WBW) is an ambitious, community-focused project that aims to provide a level playing field of opportunity for global indigenous artists and creatives to capitalize on the disruptive wave of the NFT revolution. The project is designed to empower global indigenous communities to take advantage of the growing NFT market. It is initially working with the oldest continuous, living culture in the world – the Australian Aboriginal and Torres Strait Island culture in its first art collections. The goal is to showcase the beauty of the Indigenous culture in Australia and create a playbook to capitalize on the journey of empowerment for global indigenous communities.

The project is led by founders Vanessa Lee-Ah Mat and Tim Lea. They aim to energize global indigenous communities to amplify First Nations voices through NFTs and narrow the digital divide between traditional and Western worlds. By doing so, indigenous communities across the globe can begin the long journey to greater empowerment and greater self-determination. WBW's website is https://www.walkingbetweenworlds.net/.

On a technical level, in this project there is a smart contract that implements a VIP list of users who can access the pre-minting of an NFT collection. Implementing a VIP list in a smart contract can be achieved using a mapping to keep track of the addresses of VIP users. The following is a simplified example of how you can create a smart contract with VIP list functionality for an NFT collection pre-minting.

```
contract NFTCollection {
    address public owner;
    mapping(address => bool) public isVIP;

    modifier onlyOwner() {
        require(msg.sender == owner, "Only the owner can call this
            function");
        _;
    }

    modifier onlyVIP() {
        require(isVIP[msg.sender], "Only VIP users can access this
            function");
        _;
    }

    constructor() {
        owner = msg.sender;
    }

    // Add an address to the VIP list
    function addVIP(address _user) external onlyOwner {
        isVIP[_user] = true;
    }

    // Remove an address from the VIP list
    function removeVIP(address _user) external onlyOwner {
        isVIP[_user] = false;
    }

    // Function to allow VIP users to pre-mint NFTs
    function preMintNFT(uint256 _tokenId) external onlyVIP {
        // Your pre-minting logic here
        // For example, minting an NFT with _tokenId and assigning
            it to msg.sender
        // This function can be customized based on your specific
            NFT implementation
    }
}
```

In this example, the **NFTCollection** contract has a mapping isVIP that tracks whether an address is a VIP user or not. The owner of the contract can add and remove addresses to/from the VIP list through the addVIP and removeVIP functions, respectively. The onlyOwner and only-VIP modifiers are used to restrict access to certain functions. The onlyOwner modifier allows only the contract owner (creator) to call certain functions, while the onlyVIP modifier allows only VIP users to call certain functions, such as the preMintNFT function.

The preMintNFT function is an example of how you can implement the pre-minting logic for VIP users. This function can be customized based on your specific NFT implementation, and it should handle the process of creating and assigning NFTs to VIP users.

Keep in mind that this is a simplified example to illustrate the concept of a VIP list in a smart contract. In a real-world scenario, you would need to consider security measures, handle edge cases, and implement additional features to make the contract production-ready. It is essential to thoroughly test and audit your smart contract before deploying it to the blockchain.

Leaguez

Leaguez is a revolutionary platform that brings the world of sports collectibles into the digital age. Leaguez is more than just a collection of digital items; it's the ultimate fan club for collecting, trading, and playing digital moments. These moments feature favorite players, games, and teams from both past and current seasons. Fans can collect and trade these moments while receiving exclusive experiences and rewards not otherwise available in the regular market for purchase.

In addition to the digital experience, fans can also engage in real-life events like meeting and training with their favorite players, or watching games courtside. The fun doesn't stop at collecting moments. Fans can interact with other fans by trading their player and moment cards, and playing online games to win prizes.

A smart contract for trading digital collectibles between two users would look like the following Solidity code. The contract assumes that the digital collectibles are represented as NFTs based on the ERC721 standard.

```
import "@openzeppelin/contracts/token/ERC721/ERC721.sol";

contract DigitalCollectibleMarket is ERC721 {
    struct Offer {
        uint256 tokenId;
        address payable seller;
        uint256 price;
    }

    mapping(uint256 => Offer) public tokenOffer;

    constructor() ERC721("DigitalCollectibleMarket", "DCM") {}

    function createCollectible(string memory tokenURI) public
        returns (uint256) {
        uint256 newTokenId = totalSupply();
        _mint(msg.sender, newTokenId);
        _setTokenURI(newTokenId, tokenURI);
        return newTokenId;
    }

    function setOffer(uint256 tokenId, uint256 price) public {
        require(msg.sender == ownerOf(tokenId), "Only the owner can
            set an offer");
        tokenOffer[tokenId] = Offer(tokenId, payable(msg.sender),
            price);
    }
```

```
function removeOffer(uint256 tokenId) public {
    require(msg.sender == tokenOffer[tokenId].seller, "Only the
        seller can remove an offer");
    delete tokenOffer[tokenId];
}

function buyCollectible(uint256 tokenId) public payable {
    require(msg.value == tokenOffer[tokenId].price, "The amount
        is incorrect");
    require(ownerOf(tokenId) == tokenOffer[tokenId].seller,
        "Token is not on sale");

    _transfer(tokenOffer[tokenId].seller, msg.sender, tokenId);
    tokenOffer[tokenId].seller.transfer(msg.value);
    delete tokenOffer[tokenId];
}
}
```

This contract allows users to create digital collectibles, set offers for their collectibles, remove offers, and buy collectibles from others. Note that this is a simplified example and a real-world contract would need additional checks and functionality. Always make sure to thoroughly test your smart contracts before deploying them. Also, consider getting them audited by professionals, especially when they involve financial transactions.

The Synergy between Digital and Physical Assets: A Bridge between Worlds

As the token economy continues to flourish, its impact extends beyond the boundaries of the virtual world. A fascinating convergence is taking place as digital assets find ways to interact with the physical realm. From tokenizing real-world assets like vintage cars or rare art pieces to creating hybrid experiences that blend virtual and physical realities, this synergy marks an innovative step towards a more interconnected and borderless economic landscape.

The synergy between digital and physical assets opens up exciting possibilities for various industries and use cases. Use cases of how the combination of digital and physical assets can create new opportunities and enhance existing experiences are flourishing, and include:

■ **Digital Art with Physical Tokens:** Artists can create digital art as NFTs, and each NFT can be associated with a physical representation, such as a limited-edition print or a physical collectible. Owning the NFT grants the owner access to exclusive digital content, while the physical token serves as a tangible keepsake or a certificate of ownership.

■ **Virtual Fashion and Wearable NFTs:** Fashion designers can create virtual clothing and accessories as NFTs. Users can then pretend to wear these virtual items in virtual reality (VR) or augmented reality (AR) experiences, enhancing their avatars' appearance. Some projects are even exploring ways to bring these virtual fashion pieces into the real world by producing limited-edition physical versions for collectors.

■ **Tokenized Real Estate:** Real estate properties can be tokenized as digital assets on the blockchain, allowing fractional ownership and easier transfer of ownership. Physical properties can be represented as NFTs, and token holders can receive rental income or participate in property value appreciation.

- **Smart Collectibles and Toys**: Physical collectibles, such as action figures, trading cards, or toys, can come with NFC or QR code tags that link to corresponding digital assets on the blockchain. These digital assets can hold additional content, provide exclusive experiences, or serve as proof of authenticity for the physical item.
- **Hybrid Gaming Experiences**: Gaming companies can offer hybrid gaming experiences where physical toys or cards can be scanned or connected to digital games. Players can unlock unique characters, abilities, or levels in the digital game by using physical components.
- **Blockchain-Backed Luxury Goods**: High-end luxury brands can use blockchain technology to verify the authenticity and provenance of luxury goods, such as designer handbags, high-end watches, or rare collectible items. NFTs can be associated with these physical items to ensure their genuineness.
- **Digital Tickets with Physical Souvenirs**: Event organizers can issue digital tickets as NFTs that grant access to concerts, sports events, or conventions. Attendees can receive physical souvenirs or merchandise associated with the event as a memorable keepsake.
- **IoT and Supply Chain Integration**: Internet of Things (IoT) devices can be used to track physical assets' location, temperature, or condition throughout the supply chain. Blockchain can then record this data and provide a transparent and tamper-proof audit trail for the asset's journey.
- **Tokenized Music and Vinyl Records**: Musicians and record labels can tokenize music albums or individual tracks as NFTs. The NFTs can grant access to exclusive content, behind-the-scenes footage, or special editions. For vinyl record collectors, NFTs can accompany the physical record with exclusive digital content.
- **Tokenized Sports Memorabilia**: Sports organizations can tokenize sports memorabilia, such as game-worn jerseys or autographed equipment, as NFTs. This allows fans to own digital representations of iconic physical items while maintaining their authenticity and provenance.

These examples demonstrate the potential of combining digital and physical assets to create unique and immersive experiences across various industries. The synergy between the two realms opens up new revenue streams, enhances user engagement, and provides exciting opportunities for collectors and enthusiasts alike.

Conclusion

The token economy has ushered in a new era of possibilities, revolutionizing the concept of ownership, creativity, and fan engagement. As the world embraces the boundless potential of blockchain technology, the journey toward a future where digital and physical assets seamlessly intertwine has just begun. This chapter aimed to shed light on the various components that make up this vibrant ecosystem, inviting readers to envision the limitless horizons of the token economy. Whether you are an artist, a collector, an investor, or simply an enthusiast, the token economy invites all to participate in shaping the dawn of a transformative economic era.

Chapter 7

Decentralized Gaming and Fan Clubs

In this follow-up chapter to the previous one, we dive deeper into the transformative potential of decentralized gaming and fan clubs, exploring the disruptive force they represent in the gaming and entertainment industries. Through an array of case studies, insights into token economics, and an examination of challenges and opportunities, readers will gain a comprehensive understanding of this burgeoning sector and its promising future. Let's explore together the captivating world of decentralized gaming and fan clubs!

The Evolution of Gaming and Fan Clubs

The world of gaming and fan clubs has come a long way since their humble beginnings. Both gaming and fan clubs have traditionally thrived in centralized ecosystems, where publishers and organizers held significant control over content, access, and engagement. However, with the advent of blockchain technology and the rise of decentralized platforms, a new era of innovation has ushered in a profound transformation for both industries.

The Evolution of Gaming

Gaming has evolved from pixelated adventures on early consoles to sophisticated and immersive virtual worlds that push the boundaries of realism. In the early days, gaming was primarily a solitary experience, with players enjoying single-player campaigns or engaging in local multiplayer sessions. As technology advanced, online gaming communities emerged, enabling players from across the globe to connect and compete in virtual environments.

The introduction of microtransactions and downloadable content allowed game developers to extend the life of their creations, monetizing additional content and customizations. However, this centralized model often faced challenges such as opaque ownership rights and limited player control over in-game assets.

DOI: 10.4324/9781003491934-7

Enter Decentralization in Gaming

Decentralization has brought a paradigm shift to the gaming landscape, fueled by the transformative power of blockchain technology. Blockchain's core principles of transparency, immutability, and ownership have enabled the creation of decentralized gaming platforms, where players have true ownership of their in-game assets through non-fungible tokens (NFTs).

Decentralized gaming platforms not only ensure that players have verifiable ownership of their digital assets but also facilitate interoperability between games. Players can now seamlessly transfer their unique NFTs between different games, breaking down the barriers that previously confined in-game assets to individual titles.

The Play-to-Earn Revolution

One of the most revolutionary aspects of decentralized gaming is the "play-to-earn" model. In traditional gaming, players would invest time and effort without any direct monetary rewards. In contrast, decentralized games with blockchain-based economies offer players the opportunity to earn real-world value for their in-game achievements.

Through skillful gameplay, participation in in-game economies, and ownership of valuable NFTs, players can earn cryptocurrencies or other digital assets that hold value beyond the game. This innovative approach has transformed gaming from a recreational activity into a viable source of income for many enthusiasts, leading to the rise of a new breed of professional players and crypto-gamers.

The Evolution of Fan Clubs

Fan clubs have long been an integral part of entertainment and sports industries, providing dedicated followers with a sense of belonging and exclusive access to their favorite artists, celebrities, or sports teams. Traditionally, fan clubs were managed by central entities that dictated membership benefits, interactions, and fan engagement.

In the digital age, social media platforms have played a crucial role in fan club evolution. Celebrities and brands can now directly engage with their fan bases, fostering a more intimate connection and real-time communication. However, this model still involves centralized control and limited opportunities for fans to participate actively in the success of their idols.

The Decentralized Fan Club Revolution

Decentralization has unleashed the true potential of fan clubs, offering a revolutionary shift in how fans interact with their beloved artists, entertainers, and sports teams. Blockchain-powered fan club platforms leverage fan tokens, NFTs, and decentralized governance to redefine fan engagement.

Fan tokens, which grant exclusive benefits and voting rights to holders, allow fans to have a say in certain decisions related to their favorite entities. This not only enhances fan participation but also creates a new avenue for artists and sports teams to monetize their fan base and reward loyal supporters.

The Advent of NFT Collectibles

In addition to fan tokens, NFTs have transformed fan club experiences through unique collectibles and memorabilia. NFTs representing iconic moments, limited-edition artwork, or digital collectibles allow fans to own a piece of history and showcase their passion in the virtual realm.

The evolution of gaming and fan clubs has undergone a profound transformation, driven by the disruptive force of decentralization. From gaming's solitary beginnings to the play-to-earn revolution and fan clubs' transformation into decentralized communities, blockchain technology has reshaped these industries, empowering players and fans alike. As we explore the decentralized gaming and fan club landscape further, it becomes evident that we stand at the cusp of a thrilling future, where gamers and fans actively shape the worlds they love, and digital assets carry true value and ownership beyond the confines of virtual realms.

Understanding Decentralized Gaming

The intersection of blockchain and gaming has given birth to a revolutionary concept known as decentralized gaming. Combining the disruptive power of blockchain technology with the immersive world of gaming, decentralized gaming platforms offer players unprecedented ownership, transparency, and economic opportunities within virtual landscapes. This convergence has paved the way for a new era where players are no longer mere participants but active stakeholders in the games they love.

The Intersection of Blockchain and Gaming

At the heart of decentralized gaming lies the integration of blockchain technology and its distributed and immutable ledger, that underpins the creation of unique NFTs and smart contracts. This innovation has profoundly impacted the gaming landscape in several key areas:

- **True Ownership of In-Game Assets**: In traditional gaming, players invest time, effort, and money in acquiring in-game items, skins, and virtual assets. However, these assets are usually owned and controlled by the game developers or publishers. With blockchain and NFTs, players now have true ownership of their in-game assets. Each asset is tokenized as an NFT, providing a digital certificate of authenticity and verifiable ownership on the blockchain.
- **Interoperability between Games**: In decentralized gaming ecosystems, NFTs are not confined to a single game or platform. They can be transferred and used across multiple games that support the same blockchain standards. This interoperability breaks down the walled gardens that traditionally separated gaming ecosystems, creating a seamless experience for players across different titles.
- **Play-to-Earn Economy**: The play-to-earn model has emerged as a defining feature of decentralized gaming. Through blockchain-based economies, players can earn valuable cryptocurrencies or NFTs by participating in games, contributing to in-game ecosystems, or achieving specific milestones. This economic model has turned gaming into a potential source of income, particularly for skilled and dedicated players.
- **Transparent and Secure Transactions**: Blockchain technology ensures transparent and secure transactions within gaming ecosystems. All in-game transactions, such as buying,

selling, or trading NFTs, are recorded on the blockchain, providing an immutable audit trail and preventing fraudulent activities.

■ **Community-Driven Development**: Decentralized gaming platforms often embrace community-driven development. Players and community members have a say in the evolution of the game through decentralized governance mechanisms, such as voting on proposed changes or improvements. This level of engagement fosters a stronger sense of community ownership and alignment with the game's direction.

Despite the exciting potential of decentralized gaming, several challenges remain on the path to widespread adoption. Scalability, high transaction costs, and user experience are among the primary hurdles that developers and blockchain projects strive to overcome.

Nonetheless, the opportunities presented by the intersection of blockchain and gaming are immense. As decentralized gaming ecosystems continue to evolve, we can anticipate a flourishing landscape that offers players genuine ownership, economic empowerment, and unprecedented levels of engagement. Moreover, this convergence is not limited to traditional video games; it extends to virtual reality experiences, augmented reality applications, and the rapidly growing metaverse.

The intersection of blockchain and gaming represents a transformative shift in the gaming industry, redefining how players interact with virtual worlds. Decentralized gaming empowers players with true ownership of in-game assets, introduces innovative economic models, and fosters a community-driven approach to game development. As developers and blockchain projects address the challenges, the future of decentralized gaming holds the promise of creating a more immersive, inclusive, and player-centric gaming experience, where players become not just participants but active co-creators in the virtual realms they inhabit.

In-Game Asset Ownership and Interoperability

In traditional gaming, players invest time, effort, and sometimes real money into acquiring in-game assets, such as virtual items, skins, weapons, or characters. However, the ownership of these assets remains firmly in the hands of game developers or publishers, leaving players with little control and no verifiable proof of ownership.

Decentralized gaming disrupts this model by introducing the concept of true asset ownership through the use of NFTs. In decentralized gaming ecosystems, in-game assets are represented as unique and indivisible NFTs on the blockchain. Each NFT serves as a digital certificate of authenticity, providing players with undeniable ownership rights.

With NFT-based asset ownership, players have the freedom to buy, sell, trade, or even transfer their virtual assets outside of the game's ecosystem. This newfound ownership empowers players to treat their in-game assets as valuable digital properties, making them more invested in their virtual experiences.

Additionally, NFTs introduce scarcity and rarity to in-game assets, which can significantly impact their perceived value. Just as rare items or collectibles in the real world fetch high prices at auctions, rare NFTs in decentralized games can become highly sought after and valuable, creating unique economic opportunities for players.

Interoperability is all about breaking down gaming silos. Interoperability is a defining feature of decentralized gaming that breaks down the barriers between different gaming ecosystems. In traditional gaming, in-game assets and progress are confined to specific titles, preventing players from utilizing their virtual possessions outside of the game in which they were acquired.

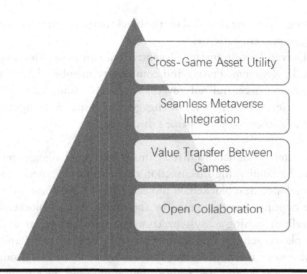

Figure 7.1 The pyramid of decentralized gaming interoperability

In contrast, decentralized gaming platforms embrace the standardization of blockchain protocols, enabling NFTs to be transferred and used across multiple games and applications that support the same standards. This interoperability unleashes a host of possibilities, as depicted in Figure 7.1 and described as follows:

- **Cross-Game Asset Utility**: NFTs gained in one game can be utilized in other games or virtual environments, granting players the ability to carry their prized possessions and achievements across different gaming experiences. For instance, a powerful sword earned in one fantasy game could be wielded in another game set in a similar genre, enriching the player's experience in each game.
- **Seamless Metaverse Integration**: As the concept of the metaverse gains traction, interoperability will become vital in creating a cohesive and interconnected virtual universe. A metaverse is a shared, persistent, and immersive digital space that integrates various virtual worlds, social platforms, and experiences. With interoperable NFTs, the metaverse can be seamlessly connected, providing players with a seamless and fluid experience as they traverse different virtual realms.
- **Value Transfer between Games**: Interoperability also enables value transfer between different gaming ecosystems. Players can sell or trade their NFTs acquired in one game to other players or collectors, potentially generating revenue that can be reinvested in other games or virtual assets.
- **Open Collaboration**: Interoperability encourages open collaboration between game developers and creators. By using standardized blockchain protocols, developers can create cross-game experiences, events, or quests that incentivize players to explore multiple games, fostering an interconnected gaming ecosystem.

In-game asset ownership and interoperability are two foundational pillars of decentralized gaming, redefining the relationship between players, virtual assets, and gaming ecosystems. With NFT-based asset ownership, players gain true ownership and control over their in-game possessions, creating a stronger sense of value and investment in their gaming experiences.

Meanwhile, interoperability breaks down the walls that have traditionally confined gaming experiences within isolated silos. By facilitating the seamless transfer and use of NFTs across different games and virtual realms, interoperability creates a dynamic and interconnected gaming landscape that enhances player agency, promotes collaboration, and nurtures the evolution of the metaverse.

As decentralized gaming continues to evolve, the fusion of asset ownership and interoperability will play a pivotal role in shaping a future where players are active participants in crafting their virtual destinies, and the boundaries between games and virtual experiences blur to create a unified and immersive gaming universe.

Play-to-Earn: Gaming as an Economic Opportunity

The traditional notion of gaming as a leisurely pastime has undergone a radical transformation in the world of decentralized gaming. With the advent of blockchain technology and the introduction of play-to-earn mechanics, gaming has transcended from being a recreational activity to a lucrative venture. Play-to-earn has revolutionized the way players engage with virtual worlds, offering them real-world economic opportunities and financial incentives for their skills, efforts, and contributions within decentralized gaming ecosystems.

Play-to-earn is a novel economic model that rewards players for their active participation and contributions in decentralized games. Unlike traditional games where players invest time and effort solely for entertainment, play-to-earn games introduce tokenized rewards, providing players with valuable cryptocurrencies or NFTs in exchange for their in-game achievements and actions.

So, how does play-to-earn work in simple terms? Figure 7.2 shows the three stages of play-to-earn: (i) Skillful gameplay, (ii) In-game contributions, and (iii) Ownership of in-game assets.

In play-to-earn games, players can earn rewards by showcasing their skills and expertise. This is what we call **Skillful Gameplay**. Achieving high scores, completing challenging quests, or excelling in competitive gameplay can trigger token rewards, offering a direct correlation between player performance and financial gains. With **In-Game Contributions**, players can contribute to the in-game economy by trading, crafting, or providing services to other players. This participation is incentivized through rewards, fostering a thriving virtual economy that drives engagement and interaction within the game. The **Ownership of In-Game Assets** as NFTs allows players to monetize their virtual possessions. Players can buy, sell, or rent their NFTs to others, creating opportunities for generating income within and beyond the game's ecosystem.

One of the most significant implications of play-to-earn gaming is its potential to empower players in emerging economies. In regions where access to traditional job opportunities is limited, decentralized gaming provides a means for players to earn a sustainable income by leveraging their gaming skills and dedicating time to the virtual worlds they inhabit.

Furthermore, play-to-earn models have the potential to combat issues of economic inequality and financial inclusion. By rewarding players with cryptocurrencies or valuable assets, play-to-earn gaming extends the benefits of blockchain technology beyond the realm of finance, enabling

Figure 7.2   The three stages of play-to-earn

individuals from diverse backgrounds to participate in the digital economy and gain financial independence.

While play-to-earn gaming offers exciting opportunities, it is not without challenges and considerations. As the popularity of these games grows, the influx of players seeking financial rewards may lead to increased competition and potential gaming addiction. Game developers and platform operators must strike a balance between rewarding players and ensuring sustainable gameplay experiences that prioritize player well-being.

Additionally, the volatility of cryptocurrency markets can impact the value of rewards earned in play-to-earn games. Players must be mindful of the risks involved and make informed decisions when managing their digital assets.

Play-to-earn has emerged as a groundbreaking model that transforms gaming into a viable source of income and economic empowerment. By integrating blockchain technology and NFTs into gaming ecosystems, play-to-earn offers players unprecedented ownership, financial incentives, and opportunities for economic mobility. As this innovative model gains traction, it has the potential to reshape the global gaming landscape, democratize access to financial opportunities, and redefine the boundaries of what it means to be a player in the digital age. However, it is essential to navigate the challenges responsibly and ethically, ensuring that play-to-earn gaming remains a sustainable and rewarding experience for all participants.

The Power of Decentralized Fan Clubs

Fan clubs have long served as a cornerstone of the entertainment and sports industries, fostering a sense of community, loyalty, and connection between fans and their favorite artists, celebrities, or sports teams. However, the traditional fan club model has often been limited by centralized control and restricted opportunities for active fan participation. Decentralized fan clubs, powered by blockchain technology, are revolutionizing fan engagement, offering a new paradigm that empowers fans with a deeper level of involvement and ownership within their beloved fandoms.

Decentraland (https://decentraland.org/) in Figure 7.3 is an example of a decentralized platform to "Make new friends, explore diverse events, and spark your creativity in a virtual world built and owned by its community".

Figure 7.3   Decentraland is an example of decentralized fan club

Reimagining Fan Engagement on the Blockchain

At the heart of decentralized fan clubs lies the concept of **fan tokens**. Fan tokens are blockchain-based assets that represent a stake in a particular fan community, artist, or sports team. Owning these tokens grants fans exclusive rights, access to unique benefits, and even a say in certain decision-making processes.

- **Enhanced Fan Involvement**: Fan tokens enable fans to actively engage with their favorite entities beyond passive support. By holding fan tokens, fans become active participants in the success of the community or team, creating a sense of collective ownership and shared responsibility.
- **Voting Rights and Influence**: Fan tokens often come with voting rights, allowing holders to participate in polls, surveys, and even crucial decisions that impact the direction of the fan club or team. This participatory governance model empowers fans to have a direct impact on matters they care about.
- **Exclusive Benefits and Rewards**: Fan token holders gain access to exclusive benefits, such as early access to event tickets, merchandise discounts, virtual meet-and-greets, and unique experiences that are not available to the general public. These rewards deepen fan loyalty and incentivize continued engagement.

Beyond fan tokens, decentralized fan clubs utilize NFTs to create exclusive and personalized experiences for fans. NFTs can represent digital collectibles, such as limited-edition artwork, iconic moments, or virtual memorabilia related to the fan club's subject. Owning these NFTs allows fans to showcase their fandom and establish a unique connection with the artist or team.

NFTs can unlock exclusive virtual experiences, such as virtual concerts, backstage access, or behind-the-scenes content. These immersive experiences redefine fandom by bridging the gap between fans and their idols, bringing them closer together in virtual realms.

Blockchain technology brings a new level of transparency and trust to fan engagement. All fan token transactions, governance decisions, and NFT ownership records are recorded on the blockchain, ensuring an immutable and auditable history of interactions between fans and the fan club.

Additionally, decentralized fan clubs remove the need for intermediaries, giving fans a direct and authentic relationship with the artists, celebrities, or sports teams they admire. This transparency fosters a deeper sense of trust and strengthens the bond between fans and their idols.

Decentralized fan clubs are reimagining fan engagement on the blockchain, offering fans unprecedented ownership, participation, and personalized experiences within their favorite fandoms. Through fan tokens, voting rights, exclusive benefits, and NFT collectibles, fans become active stakeholders, shaping the future of the fan club or team they support.

Moreover, the transparency and direct connection facilitated by blockchain technology fosters a deeper level of trust and engagement between fans and their idols. As decentralized fan clubs continue to evolve, they pave the way for a future where fan engagement is no longer limited by geographical boundaries or centralized control but instead thrives on inclusivity, community-driven decision-making, and the celebration of fandom in all its vibrant forms.

Fan tokens stand as a testament to the empowering potential of blockchain technology in redefining fan engagement. By granting fans ownership, decision-making power, and access to exclusive benefits, fan tokens transform fans into influential stakeholders, nurturing a more inclusive, participatory, and financially rewarding fandom experience. As decentralized fan clubs continue to evolve, the integration of fan tokens and blockchain technology is poised to shape a future where fandom is an immersive and interactive journey, creating a profound sense of community, connection, and celebration around the entities fans hold dear.

NFT Collectibles and Exclusive Fan Experiences

NFT collectibles and exclusive fan experiences are two powerful components of decentralized fan clubs that leverage blockchain technology to redefine how fans connect with their favorite artists, celebrities, and sports teams. Through NFTs, fans can obtain unique and limited-edition digital collectibles, while exclusive experiences offer personalized interactions and virtual encounters with their idols, creating a new era of engagement and fandom.

NFTs serve as digital certificates of authenticity, ensuring the uniqueness and scarcity of digital assets. In the context of decentralized fan clubs, NFT collectibles represent exclusive digital memorabilia, artwork, or moments associated with the fan community, artist, or team. These NFTs often carry emotional significance, representing cherished memories, iconic performances, or special events that hold profound value for fans.

The use cases are varied. Figure 7.4 lists a few of the most common, then described as follows:

Digital Art: Artists and creators within fan clubs can mint their artwork as NFTs, providing fans with the opportunity to own digital masterpieces that commemorate their favorite idols. Each NFT is one-of-a-kind, ensuring that fans possess a truly unique piece of art with verifiable ownership on the blockchain.

Virtual Memorabilia: NFTs can also represent virtual memorabilia associated with fan clubs or sports teams. From limited-edition jerseys and badges to unique in-game items or virtual concert tickets, these digital collectibles carry nostalgic and sentimental value for fans, creating a bridge between the virtual and real worlds.

Collectible Series: Fan clubs can curate collectible series, each comprising a set of themed NFTs. Collectible series introduce an element of discovery and excitement, encouraging fans to collect and complete entire sets, fostering engagement and loyalty.

Exclusive fan experiences go beyond traditional interactions, allowing fans to bridge the gap between the virtual and physical realms. These experiences enable a more personal and immersive connection with idols, breaking down barriers and fostering a stronger emotional bond between fans and the entities they support.

Virtual Concerts and Meet-and-Greets: Through virtual reality or augmented reality platforms, fan clubs can host exclusive virtual concerts and meet-and-greets. Fans gain the opportunity

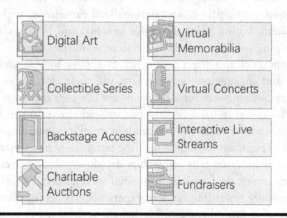

Figure 7.4   Common use cases for exclusive fan experiences using fan tokens

to attend intimate performances or interact with their idols in immersive digital environments, transcending geographical boundaries.

Backstage Access and Behind-the-Scenes Content: NFTs can unlock backstage access or exclusive behind-the-scenes content, giving fans a glimpse into the private lives and creative processes of their favorite artists, celebrities, or sports teams.

Interactive Live Streams: Fan clubs can organize interactive live streams, allowing fans to directly engage with their idols through Q&A sessions, interactive games, and personalized shout-outs. These live experiences make fans feel like an integral part of the event and create memorable moments.

Charitable Auctions and Fundraisers: Fan clubs can utilize NFTs for charitable purposes, organizing auctions or fundraisers where fans can bid on exclusive experiences or rare collectibles. These initiatives not only create a sense of community around a shared cause but also empower fans to contribute to meaningful social impact.

NFT collectibles and exclusive fan experiences are powerful tools that drive engagement, loyalty, and emotional connection within decentralized fan clubs. Through NFT collectibles, fans gain a sense of ownership and value as they acquire unique digital assets tied to their beloved fandoms. Meanwhile, exclusive fan experiences offer unprecedented opportunities for fans to engage with their idols, blurring the line between the virtual and real worlds.

As blockchain technology continues to evolve, NFT collectibles and exclusive experiences are poised to transform fan engagement, creating a dynamic and immersive fan culture that celebrates uniqueness, inclusivity, and the shared passion that unites fans and their idols in a new era of fandom.

Building Inclusivity and Diversity in Fan Clubs

Building inclusivity and diversity in fan clubs is essential for creating a welcoming and supportive community that celebrates individuality and embraces fans from diverse backgrounds. In addition to the general importance of inclusivity and diversity, there are specific actions and approaches that fan clubs can take to foster a more inclusive and diverse environment:

- **Representation Matters**: Fan clubs can actively promote diversity by ensuring representation in their leadership, management, and content creation teams. Having a diverse group of individuals in these roles helps in understanding and addressing the needs and interests of a broader range of fans.
- **Diverse Fan Engagement**: Encourage fan engagement that celebrates different cultures, languages, and perspectives. Embrace various fan expressions, including fan art, fanfiction, and other creative works that highlight the diversity within the community.
- **Cultivate a Safe Space**: Fan clubs should establish clear guidelines and policies to maintain a safe and respectful space for all members. Address and prevent harassment or discrimination, and foster an atmosphere where fans feel comfortable expressing themselves without fear of judgment.
- **Celebrate Identity and Intersectionality**: Recognize and celebrate the intersectionality of fans' identities, acknowledging that individuals may have multiple aspects to their identity, such as race, gender, sexual orientation, and disability.
- **Translation and Accessibility**: Provide translation services for content and interactions to accommodate fans who may speak different languages. Ensure that the fan club's content and events are accessible to all, including those with disabilities.

- **Collaborate with Diverse Communities**: Collaborate with other fan clubs, organizations, or communities that promote diversity and inclusivity. Engaging in joint initiatives can create opportunities for cross-cultural exchanges and increase the visibility of marginalized voices.
- **Address Cultural Sensitivity**: Be mindful of cultural sensitivity and avoid appropriating or misrepresenting cultural elements in fan club activities. Respectfully engage with cultures outside the dominant cultural norms to foster understanding and appreciation.
- **Outreach and Recruitment**: Actively seek to recruit and include fans from underrepresented communities. Outreach efforts can involve partnering with organizations, influencers, or advocates who champion diversity and inclusion.
- **Amplify Diverse Voices**: Provide platforms for fans from diverse backgrounds to share their experiences and perspectives. Amplify their voices through interviews, guest posts, or spotlight features.
- **Charitable Initiatives**: Support charitable causes that promote diversity, equity, and inclusion. Collaborate with fan club members to contribute to charitable organizations working towards social justice and equality.

Walking Between Worlds (https://www.walkingbetweenworlds.net/) is a community-focused project that brings a level playing field of opportunity for global indigenous artists and creatives to capitalize on the NFT revolution. This project is not only showcasing the beauty of the Aboriginal culture in Australia but also defining a journey of empowerment for indigenous communities around the world.

Building inclusivity and diversity in fan clubs is a continuous and ongoing effort. By implementing these specific actions and approaches, fan clubs can create a more welcoming, respectful, and enriching community that celebrates the uniqueness of each member. Embracing diversity not only enhances the fan club experience but also contributes to a more profound sense of belonging and unity among fans with different backgrounds, fostering a stronger and more compassionate fan community.

Tokenomics and the Economics of Decentralized Gaming

Tokenomics is a term derived from the words *token* and *economics*. It refers to the economic principles and mechanics behind the creation, distribution, and management of digital tokens, typically within a blockchain-based ecosystem or cryptocurrency network. Tokenomics plays a crucial role in shaping the behavior and value of tokens within these systems.

Tokenomics aims to create a sustainable and balanced economic model that incentivizes participation, encourages network growth, and maintains the stability and value of the token within the blockchain ecosystem. It is a critical aspect of designing and understanding the functioning of various blockchain-based projects and cryptocurrencies. This section explores how tokenomics applies to the gaming industry.

Token Utility and Value Proposition

Token utility refers to the various functions and use cases of the native cryptocurrency or digital asset within a decentralized gaming ecosystem. In decentralized gaming, these tokens play a central role in facilitating in-game transactions, rewarding players, enabling play-to-earn mechanisms, and creating a thriving virtual economy. The design and implementation of token utility are crucial in incentivizing active participation, fostering economic growth, and driving the overall success of the gaming platform.

Key aspects of token utility in decentralized gaming include:

- **In-Game Currency**: Tokens serve as the primary currency within the game, enabling players to buy, sell, and trade in-game items, assets, and virtual goods. This creates a seamless and decentralized in-game economy, where players can transact directly with one another without the need for intermediaries.
- **Play-to-Earn Mechanism**: Token utility enables the play-to-earn model, where players receive rewards in the form of tokens for their in-game achievements, contributions to the virtual world, or participation in events and challenges.
- **Asset Backing**: Some decentralized gaming platforms use tokens that are backed by scarce or valuable digital assets, such as NFTs. These tokens represent ownership or a stake in the underlying assets, providing additional value and utility to token holders.
- **Governance and Decision-Making**: In certain gaming ecosystems, holding tokens may grant users voting rights, allowing them to participate in governance and decision-making processes related to the game's development, updates, and future initiatives.
- **Staking and Yield Farming**: Some decentralized gaming platforms support staking mechanisms, where users lock their tokens to earn additional rewards or participate in yield farming to farm additional tokens by providing liquidity to the platform.

The token value proposition refers to the inherent value and benefits that owning and utilizing the native token brings to players, investors, and participants in the decentralized gaming ecosystem. The token's value proposition is instrumental in attracting users, increasing demand, and ensuring the long-term sustainability of the gaming platform.

The key factors that define value of tokens in decentralized gaming can be summarized as:

- **Scarcity and Limited Supply**: Tokens with a limited supply or controlled inflation mechanisms can gain value through scarcity. As demand for the token increases, its limited availability can drive up its price.
- **Play-to-Earn Incentive**: The play-to-earn model is a significant value proposition for players. The ability to earn tokens while playing the game incentivizes more users to join the platform and actively engage in gaming activities.
- **Real-World Value**: Tokens that can be easily converted into fiat currency or valuable assets, such as NFTs, provide real-world value to players, making them more attractive and sought-after.
- **Utility in the Ecosystem**: Tokens with multiple and diverse use cases within the gaming ecosystem enhance their value proposition. A token that serves as both an in-game currency and a governance tool holds more significance to users.
- **Platform Growth and Adoption**: A thriving gaming platform with a large user base and active community increases the utility and demand for its native token, creating a positive feedback loop for its value proposition.
- **Token Burning and Deflationary Mechanisms**: Some gaming platforms employ token burning or deflationary mechanisms, where a portion of the tokens used in transactions is permanently removed from circulation. This reduces the token supply over time, potentially increasing its value.

Token utility and the value proposition play a critical role in shaping the economics of decentralized gaming. By providing tangible benefits, rewards, and incentives to players and participants, the native token becomes the driving force behind a vibrant and sustainable virtual economy. Careful consideration of tokenomics ensures that the decentralized gaming platform attracts and retains users, fosters engagement and economic growth, and creates a thriving ecosystem where players can enjoy meaningful play-to-earn opportunities and a genuine sense of ownership in the virtual world.

Staking and Yield Farming in Gaming

In the context of gaming and decentralized gaming platforms, staking and yield farming are mechanisms that leverage cryptocurrency tokens to incentivize and reward participants for their contributions and commitment to the ecosystem. These mechanisms not only enhance user engagement but also contribute to the overall economic growth and sustainability of the gaming platform.

Staking involves locking up a certain amount of cryptocurrency tokens to support the operations and security of the decentralized gaming network. In return for staking their tokens, participants may earn rewards in the form of additional tokens or other benefits. The process of staking helps to validate transactions and secure the blockchain network, enhancing its integrity and reliability.

In the context of gaming, staking can take on various forms:

▪ **Proof-of-Stake (PoS) Consensus**: Some decentralized gaming platforms utilize the PoS consensus mechanism, where participants (known as validators) are chosen to create new blocks and validate transactions based on the number of tokens they have staked. Validators are rewarded with transaction fees or newly minted tokens.
▪ **Governance Voting**: Holding and staking tokens may grant participants voting rights in the decentralized governance of the gaming platform. This allows stakeholders to participate in decision-making processes, such as protocol upgrades, fee adjustments, or game feature proposals.
▪ **Staking Rewards**: Gaming platforms may offer staking rewards to incentivize users to lock up their tokens. These rewards can be in the form of additional tokens or other in-game benefits, encouraging long-term commitment and engagement.

Yield farming involves providing liquidity to decentralized finance (DeFi) protocols or decentralized exchanges (DEXs) by depositing cryptocurrency tokens into liquidity pools. In return for providing liquidity, participants receive rewards in the form of additional tokens, often as an incentive to attract liquidity to the platform.

In the context of gaming, yield farming can be integrated as an additional mechanism to incentivize liquidity provision and enhance the token economy. Figure 7.5 summarizes these concepts visually.

▪ **Liquidity for Virtual Assets:** Players may provide liquidity to liquidity pools that involve in-game assets or NFTs. This helps to facilitate trading and exchange of virtual assets within the gaming platform, enhancing liquidity and the overall user experience.

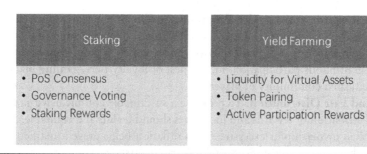

Figure 7.5 Staking and yield farming

- **Token Pairing**: Yield farming can involve pairing the gaming platform's native token with other popular tokens or stablecoins, encouraging participants to contribute liquidity to the designated pools.
- **Rewards for Active Participation**: Yield farming can reward players who actively engage in gaming activities or contribute to the in-game economy. The more active the player's participation, the higher their potential rewards from yield farming.

Staking and yield farming are innovative mechanisms that leverage blockchain technology to incentivize and reward participants within decentralized gaming platforms. These mechanisms promote engagement, liquidity, and economic growth within the gaming ecosystem, creating a dynamic and sustainable environment where players can actively participate, earn rewards, and contribute to the success of the platform.

Sustainable Incentive Models for Long-Term Growth

In the rapidly evolving world of decentralized gaming, sustainable incentive models are crucial for ensuring the long-term growth and success of gaming platforms. These models aim to strike a delicate balance between rewarding and incentivizing users while maintaining the economic stability and viability of the gaming ecosystem. By designing effective and sustainable incentive models, gaming platforms can attract and retain a loyal user base, foster engagement, and create a thriving virtual economy that benefits both players and the platform itself.

Putting in place sustainable incentive models requires the implementation of key components, such as:

- **Play-to-Earn Mechanisms**: Play-to-earn models form a fundamental pillar of sustainable incentive models in decentralized gaming. By offering players the opportunity to earn valuable rewards, such as cryptocurrencies or NFTs, for their in-game achievements and contributions, gaming platforms motivate users to actively participate in the virtual world. This not only enhances user engagement but also ensures that players see tangible benefits for their time and effort spent in the game.
- **Tokenomics and Token Utility**: A well-designed tokenomics system is essential for sustainable incentive models. The native cryptocurrency or digital asset of the gaming platform should have clear and diverse utility, serving as the primary in-game currency and offering various benefits, such as governance rights or staking opportunities. By ensuring that the token has real-world value and meaningful use cases, the platform can attract demand and maintain a healthy ecosystem.

- **Long-Term Rewards and Loyalty Programs**: Sustainable incentive models consider the long-term engagement of players. Long-term rewards and loyalty programs encourage players to stay committed to the platform over an extended period. By offering progressive rewards for continuous participation, milestones, or loyalty tiers, gaming platforms build a loyal and dedicated community of players.
- **Inclusive and Fair Distribution**: To promote a sustainable and inclusive gaming environment, the distribution of rewards and incentives should be fair and equitable. Avoiding concentrated token ownership or excessive token inflation helps prevent market manipulation and ensures that rewards are accessible to all participants.
- **Deflationary Mechanisms and Token Burns**: Some gaming platforms implement deflationary mechanisms, such as token burns or buybacks, to reduce the token supply over time. These mechanisms can create scarcity, increasing the value of the token and offering long-term benefits to token holders.
- **Community Governance**: Decentralized gaming platforms often involve community-driven governance models where users have a say in the decision-making process. Sustainable incentive models include mechanisms for community voting on important matters, fostering a sense of ownership and empowerment among players.
- **Dynamic and Evolving Rewards**: Sustainable incentive models should be flexible and adapt to the changing needs and dynamics of the gaming platform. Regular assessments of the effectiveness of incentive programs allow for adjustments and improvements to ensure ongoing engagement and growth.

The benefits of such sustainable incentive models include **long-term engagements**, when players are more likely to stay committed to a platform with sustainable incentives, leading to long-term engagement and retention. They also encourage a **healthy virtual economy**: A well-balanced incentive model promotes economic growth and stability within the virtual world, benefiting both players and the platform. Sustainable incentive models are **attractive to new users**, encouraging them to join the gaming community and contribute to its growth. All this brings to **token value appreciation**: By creating scarcity and real-world utility, sustainable incentive models can drive the appreciation of the native token's value, rewarding early adopters and loyal participants.

Sustainable incentive models play a crucial role in driving the long-term growth and success of decentralized gaming platforms. By offering meaningful rewards, fostering engagement, and maintaining a healthy token economy, these models create a thriving ecosystem that benefits players and the platform alike. The careful design and implementation of sustainable incentive models ensure that decentralized gaming continues to evolve and innovate, providing players with exciting opportunities and experiences in the dynamic world of blockchain-based gaming.

Case Studies: Decentralized Gaming and Fan Clubs in Action

Pioneering and success stories in fan club engagement on blockchain and decentralized platforms are an exciting and evolving aspect of the technology's potential. As more fan clubs, sports teams, and entertainment projects explore blockchain-based solutions, they can enhance fan engagement, provide unique rewards and experiences, and deepen the connection between artists, athletes, or clubs and their dedicated fan communities. These success stories highlight the opportunities for fan clubs to leverage blockchain to create innovative and rewarding experiences for their fans, transforming traditional fan engagement into more immersive and interactive experiences.

Pioneering Decentralized Gaming Projects

In the world of blockchain technology, several pioneering decentralized gaming projects have emerged to showcase the potential of merging gaming and blockchain ecosystems. These projects have been at the forefront of innovation, introducing unique gaming experiences and novel incentive models that have garnered significant attention from the gaming and blockchain communities alike. Let's explore some notable examples of pioneering decentralized gaming projects:

CryptoKitties (https://www.cryptokitties.co/), launched in 2017 by Canadian blockchain development studio Axiom Zen, is widely regarded as one of the first successful decentralized gaming projects on the Ethereum blockchain. CryptoKitties introduced the concept of non-fungible tokens (NFTs) to the mainstream by allowing users to collect, breed, and trade virtual cats. Each CryptoKitty is represented as a unique NFT, making them scarce and collectible.

CryptoKitties gained massive popularity and, at its peak, caused significant congestion on the Ethereum network due to its high transaction volume. The project demonstrated how NFTs could be used to create individual, provably scarce digital assets and laid the foundation for the NFT boom that followed.

Axie Infinity (https://axieinfinity.com/), developed by Sky Mavis, is a blockchain-based game that combines elements of gaming, collectibles, and play-to-earn. Players collect and breed fantasy creatures called Axies, each represented as an NFT. These Axies can be used in battles against other players, and players can earn rewards in the form of cryptocurrency tokens for their victories.

Axie Infinity gained popularity for its play-to-earn model, where players in some regions, particularly in the Philippines, have been able to earn a living by participating actively in the game. The project demonstrated the potential of blockchain-based gaming to provide economic opportunities and empower players through ownership of virtual assets.

The already mentioned **Decentraland** (https://decentraland.org/) is a virtual reality platform built on the Ethereum blockchain. It allows users to create, own, and monetize digital assets in the form of virtual land, represented as NFTs. Users can build and develop unique experiences and structures on their land, effectively owning virtual real estate in a decentralized metaverse.

Decentraland showcases the potential of blockchain technology to create immersive and user-driven virtual worlds, where ownership and creativity are rewarded. It has become a prominent example of how blockchain can revolutionize the concept of virtual property ownership and digital economies.

Sorare (https://sorare.com/) is a fantasy soccer game where players collect and manage virtual trading cards representing real-life soccer players. These player cards are tokenized as NFTs on the Ethereum blockchain. Users can assemble teams and compete against each other, with the performance of real players in real-world matches influencing the game's outcomes.

Sorare has gained popularity among sports fans and blockchain enthusiasts alike. It exemplifies how blockchain-based gaming can merge with traditional sports, creating a unique experience for soccer fans while providing true ownership of virtual collectibles.

These pioneering decentralized gaming projects have played a crucial role in shaping the landscape of blockchain-based gaming. They have demonstrated the potential of blockchain technology to revolutionize the gaming industry by introducing ownership, scarcity, and economic opportunities for players. These projects continue to inspire and influence the development of new decentralized gaming initiatives, paving the way for a future where blockchain and gaming converge to create more inclusive, rewarding, and immersive gaming experiences for players worldwide.

Success Stories in Fan Club Engagement

Success stories in fan club engagement within the context of blockchain and decentralized platforms are still emerging as the technology is relatively new. However, there are some notable examples of fan clubs and entertainment projects that have leveraged blockchain and tokenization to create engaging and rewarding experiences for their fans. Let's explore a couple of these success stories:

Paris Saint-Germain (PSG) Fan Tokens (https://en.psg.fr/fans/psg-fan-token). Paris Saint-Germain, one of the most popular soccer clubs globally, launched its own fan token called "PSG Fan Token" in partnership with Socios. Socios is a blockchain-based platform that enables sports clubs to tokenize fan engagement and decision-making. PSG fans can purchase PSG Fan Tokens, which grant them voting rights in certain club-related decisions and access to exclusive content and experiences.

The PSG Fan Token sale was a massive success, with millions of tokens sold in a matter of hours. The tokens provide a new way for fans to interact with the club, fostering a deeper sense of engagement and loyalty among supporters. This initiative showcases how fan tokens can enhance fan-club relationships, enabling fans to have a direct say in the club's initiatives and creating a sense of community ownership.

BLINK Fan Community (https://weverse.io/blackpink/) is the official fan community of the popular South Korean girl group BLACKPINK. It is powered by the blockchain-based platform Klaytn, developed by Ground X, a subsidiary of Kakao Corporation. BLINK members can access exclusive content, participate in fan-voting events, and earn BLINK Points by engaging with the community.

BLINK Points can be redeemed for various rewards, including limited-edition merchandise, concert tickets, and virtual experiences with the members of BLACKPINK. The platform's gamified features and the use of blockchain technology have contributed to a vibrant and active fan community. It has also provided new ways for fans to interact with their favorite artists beyond traditional social media platforms.

Atari X (https://atari.com/pages/atari-x), a legendary video game company, has ventured into the blockchain space with the launch of the Atari Token and Atari NFTs (rebranded as Atari X after the initial launch). The Atari Token is used as the native currency on the Atari blockchain, powering in-game purchases and transactions within the Atari ecosystem. Additionally, Atari has released NFTs representing classic Atari games and collectible items that fans can own and trade.

By leveraging blockchain technology, Atari has offered a new level of ownership and scarcity to its fan base. The Atari NFTs have become sought-after digital collectibles, while the Atari Token facilitates seamless transactions and economic opportunities within the gaming community.

The concept of fan tokens has resonated well with sports fans, as evidenced by the overwhelming demand during token sales and the rapid growth of the platform's user base. The sales of fan tokens have generated significant revenue for the partnered clubs and expanded the fan base's global reach.

The success and adoption of fan tokens highlights the immense potential of blockchain technology in transforming fan engagement and loyalty programs for sports clubs and entertainment franchises.

Lessons Learned and Best Practices

In the rapidly evolving landscape of blockchain-based fan engagement and decentralized gaming, there are several important lessons learned and best practices that can guide the development and implementation of successful projects. Table 7.1 summarizes some key lessons and practices to consider.

Table 7.1 Best practices for online communities and games built on decentralized technologies

Best Practice	Description
Community-Centric Approach	Prioritize building a strong and engaged community of users. Listen to their feedback, address their concerns, and involve them in decision-making processes. An active and passionate community is the backbone of a successful decentralized gaming or fan engagement platform.
User-Friendly Interfaces	Create intuitive and user-friendly interfaces that make it easy for users to navigate and interact with the platform. Blockchain technology can be complex, so ensuring a smooth user experience is crucial for broader adoption.
Scalability Planning	Consider scalability from the outset of the project. With the potential for rapid growth, ensure that the underlying blockchain infrastructure and smart contracts can handle increased transaction volumes without compromising performance.
Interoperability	Explore interoperability solutions to connect with other blockchains and decentralized applications. This can expand the platform's capabilities, user base, and utility, making it more attractive to users and partners.
Security and Auditing	Prioritize security measures and undergo regular third-party security audits to identify and address potential vulnerabilities. User trust is paramount in the blockchain space, and maintaining a secure platform is essential.
Regulatory Compliance	Stay informed about the regulatory landscape in the jurisdictions where the platform operates. Comply with relevant laws and regulations to mitigate potential legal risks and build trust with users and investors.
Token Utility and Value	Ensure that the platform's native token has clear utility and value within the ecosystem. A robust tokenomics model with diverse use cases can incentivize user participation and investment.
Transparent Governance	If the platform involves community governance, maintain transparency in decision-making processes. Clearly communicate the criteria for voting and involve the community in important decisions that affect the platform's direction.
Education and Outreach	Educate users about the benefits of blockchain technology and how to interact with the platform effectively. Outreach efforts can drive user adoption and foster a more informed and engaged community.
Partnerships and Collaborations	Forge strategic partnerships with other projects, sports clubs, or entertainment entities to expand the platform's reach and offerings. Collaborations can lead to mutually beneficial opportunities and increased exposure.
Sustainable Incentives	Design incentive models that strike a balance between rewarding users and maintaining the long-term sustainability of the platform. Sustainable incentives contribute to user retention and economic growth.
Embrace Feedback and Iterate	Be open to feedback and iterate on the platform's features and functionalities based on user preferences and market demands. Continuous improvement is essential for staying relevant and competitive.

Lessons learned and best practices in the blockchain-based fan engagement and decentralized gaming space are continually evolving. By embracing community feedback, prioritizing user experience and security, and staying adaptable to changing market dynamics, projects can position themselves for success in this exciting and dynamic industry. Remember that user engagement, trust, and innovation are at the heart of building a thriving and sustainable decentralized gaming or fan engagement platform.

Innovation and Technological Advancements

The future landscape of blockchain-based fan engagement and decentralized gaming is filled with potential for innovation and technological advancements. As the industry continues to evolve, several trends and predictions are shaping the direction of this sector:

- **Metaverse Integration**: The concept of the metaverse, a shared and interconnected virtual reality space, is gaining traction. Decentralized gaming platforms may increasingly integrate with the metaverse, allowing players to seamlessly transition between different virtual worlds and experiences.
- **Cross-Platform Interoperability**: Interoperability will become crucial as the number of decentralized gaming platforms and fan engagement projects grows. Players and fans may demand the ability to transfer virtual assets and tokens across different platforms and games.
- **Enhanced User Experience**: Improvements in blockchain technology and scalability solutions will lead to faster and more efficient transactions, resulting in a smoother and enhanced user experience. This will be particularly vital for real-time gaming experiences.
- **Tokenization of Real-World Assets**: Beyond virtual assets, the tokenization of real-world assets, such as sports memorabilia or concert tickets, may become more prevalent. Blockchain can offer a secure and transparent way to verify the authenticity and ownership of physical assets.
- **Play-to-Earn Ecosystems**: Play-to-earn models are expected to continue to evolve, providing players with more diverse and lucrative opportunities to earn rewards and income through gaming activities.
- **Non-fungible Tokens (NFTs) Expansion**: NFTs will continue to expand beyond gaming and digital art, finding applications in various industries, including music, sports, and entertainment. NFTs will serve as unique collectibles and representations of ownership for exclusive experiences.
- **Virtual Reality and Augmented Reality Integration**: As virtual reality (VR) and augmented reality (AR) technologies advance, they may be integrated into decentralized gaming platforms, creating more immersive and interactive experiences for players.
- **Decentralized Autonomous Organizations (DAOs)**: Fan clubs and gaming communities may embrace DAOs for governance and decision-making. DAOs enable community-driven initiatives and foster a sense of ownership and participation.
- **Sustainability and Green Initiatives**: With increasing concerns about the environmental impact of blockchain technology, gaming platforms may adopt more sustainable and eco-friendly protocols to mitigate their carbon footprint.
- **Mass Adoption and Mainstream Recognition**: As decentralized gaming and fan engagement platforms mature, they are likely to gain broader recognition and mainstream adoption. This could attract more traditional sports teams, artists, and entertainment entities into the blockchain space.

The future landscape of blockchain-based fan engagement and decentralized gaming is full of exciting possibilities. As technology advances, user demands evolve, and regulatory frameworks mature, these innovative platforms are poised to revolutionize fan-club relationships, transform gaming experiences, and create more inclusive and rewarding ecosystems for users worldwide. Through constant innovation, collaboration, and adaptation to market trends, the blockchain gaming and fan engagement sector will continue to shape the future of entertainment and digital interaction.

The Fusion of Gaming and Metaverse

The fusion of gaming and the metaverse is already becoming a real thing, and it is expected to continue growing in the future. The metaverse is a shared, interconnected virtual reality space where users can interact, socialize, and engage in various activities. It encompasses a wide range of digital experiences, including virtual worlds, social platforms, gaming environments, and more.

Gaming has been a significant driver of the metaverse's development and popularity. Many existing virtual worlds and social platforms within the metaverse have integrated gaming elements, such as interactive experiences, games, and virtual economies. At the same time, gaming platforms are increasingly exploring the possibilities of expanding their offerings to incorporate the metaverse concept.

Several trends contribute to the fusion of gaming and the metaverse:

- **Virtual Reality (VR) and Augmented Reality (AR) Advancements**: VR and AR technologies are evolving rapidly, enabling more immersive and realistic gaming experiences within the metaverse. These technologies facilitate the seamless integration of gaming activities into virtual worlds, blurring the lines between the two concepts.
- **Cross-Platform Interoperability**: Interoperability between different virtual worlds and gaming platforms is becoming a focus, allowing users to carry their virtual assets and identities across various metaverse experiences and games.
- **Play-to-Earn Models**: Play-to-earn gaming, which is prevalent in the metaverse, incentivizes players to engage in various gaming activities to earn valuable rewards, including cryptocurrencies and NFTs. This economic model enhances the connection between gaming and virtual economies in the metaverse.
- **NFT Integration**: NFTs are being used to represent ownership of in-game assets, characters, and virtual land. The use of NFTs in gaming aligns with the principles of digital ownership within the metaverse.
- **Collaborative Projects**: Gaming companies and metaverse platforms are increasingly collaborating to create integrated experiences. These partnerships aim to provide players with more seamless transitions between gaming environments and the broader metaverse.
- **User Demand and Engagement**: Players and users are increasingly seeking more interconnected and immersive experiences. The fusion of gaming and the metaverse addresses this demand by offering a more comprehensive and multifaceted digital experience.

The fusion of gaming and the metaverse is an exciting and rapidly evolving trend. As virtual reality, blockchain technology, and gaming innovation progress, the integration of gaming experiences within the metaverse will become even more prevalent. This convergence promises to provide users with unprecedented levels of immersion, social interaction, and economic opportunities within the digital realm, blurring the lines between gaming and virtual experiences.

Mainstream Adoption and Global Impact

To achieve mainstream adoption and global impact, the decentralized gaming and blockchain-based fan engagement sectors need to take strategic steps that address key challenges and capitalize on emerging opportunities. Here are some crucial next steps:

- **Usability and Accessibility**: Improve user interfaces and overall usability to make blockchain-based platforms more user-friendly and accessible to individuals with varying levels of technical expertise. Streamlining the onboarding process and minimizing friction in interactions will attract a broader user base.
- **Scalability Solutions**: Continue investing in and implementing scalability solutions to handle higher transaction volumes without compromising performance. Scalability is crucial for accommodating mainstream adoption and ensuring a smooth user experience.
- **Cross-Platform Integration**: Promote cross-platform integration and interoperability to allow users to seamlessly transfer assets and tokens between different decentralized gaming platforms and fan engagement projects. Interconnected experiences will enhance engagement and utility for users.
- **Regulatory Compliance**: Work closely with regulatory bodies to ensure compliance with evolving legal frameworks. Proactively addressing regulatory concerns will foster trust among users, investors, and potential partners.
- **Partnerships with Established Brands**: Forge strategic partnerships with established sports teams, entertainment entities, and celebrities to gain recognition and credibility. Collaborations with mainstream brands can introduce blockchain-based experiences to a wider audience.
- **Education and Outreach**: Conduct extensive education and outreach efforts to raise awareness about the benefits and potential of decentralized gaming and blockchain-based fan engagement. Target both existing crypto enthusiasts and mainstream audiences to expand the user base.
- **Enhanced Security**: Maintain a strong focus on security measures, including regular audits and vulnerability assessments, to protect user data and assets. A robust security framework will build confidence and attract risk-averse users.
- **Real-World Use Cases**: Demonstrate real-world use cases beyond gaming and entertainment to showcase the versatility and practicality of blockchain technology. Use cases in industries such as finance, supply chain, and digital identity can enhance the technology's credibility.
- **User Incentives and Rewards**: Develop compelling and sustainable incentive models that motivate users to actively participate and engage with the platform. Rewarding users for their contributions will foster loyalty and drive user retention.
- **Global Reach and Localization**: Tailor platforms and experiences to appeal to diverse global audiences. Localization efforts, including language support and cultural adaptation, will facilitate international expansion.
- **Transparent Governance**: Implement transparent and decentralized governance mechanisms, such as DAOs, to give users a sense of ownership and participation in platform decisions.
- **Environmental Sustainability**: Address environmental concerns associated with blockchain technology by adopting eco-friendly consensus mechanisms and supporting initiatives for a greener blockchain ecosystem.

Mainstream adoption and global impact require a concerted effort from the decentralized gaming and blockchain-based fan engagement sectors. By focusing on usability, scalability, regulatory compliance, security, and user incentives while fostering partnerships and outreach, these industries can overcome barriers and unlock their potential to revolutionize entertainment and fan engagement worldwide. Emphasizing innovation, education, and user-centricity will ultimately drive these sectors to become integral components of the digital landscape.

Chapter 8

KYC and KYB for Blockchain Operators

The blockchain industry has witnessed remarkable growth and disruptive potential over the years, revolutionizing various sectors through its decentralized and transparent nature. However, with increased adoption comes the need for regulatory compliance and enhanced security measures. This chapter focuses on the critical aspects of Know Your Customer (**KYC**) and Know Your Business (**KYB**) within the blockchain ecosystem. It explores how these processes can effectively address the challenges of identity verification and anti-money laundering (**AML**) while bolstering trust and legitimacy for all stakeholders involved.

Understanding KYC and KYB

In the blockchain industry, a problem to resolve revolves around ensuring compliance with regulatory requirements and preventing illicit activities. KYC and KYB are crucial processes implemented by blockchain companies to verify the identities of their customers and businesses. The anonymity and decentralization inherent in blockchain technology can be exploited by bad actors for money laundering, terrorist financing, or other illicit purposes. Therefore, implementing robust KYC and KYB procedures becomes essential to establish trust, maintain transparency, and mitigate the risks associated with financial crimes in the blockchain industry. These processes aim to validate the identity, background, and legitimacy of individuals and businesses engaging in blockchain-related transactions or services, ultimately promoting a safer and more secure environment for all participants.

Definition and Principles of KYC

KYC and KYB are important concepts in the realm of blockchain operators and financial institutions. KYC refers to the process through which businesses verify and collect information about their customers in order to assess their identity, integrity, and potential risks involved in a business relationship. It is a critical component of AML and counter-terrorism financing (CTF) efforts, as well as general risk management practices.

DOI: 10.4324/9781003491934-8

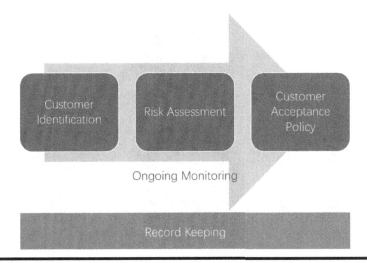

Figure 8.1   Core principles of KYC

The core principles of KYC are illustrated in Figure 8.1 and defined as follows:

- **Customer Identification**: This principle involves verifying the customer's identity using reliable and independent documents, data, or information. It typically includes obtaining personal details such as name, address, date of birth, and official identification documents.
- **Risk Assessment**: KYC requires assessing the potential risks associated with each customer to determine the level of due diligence required. This involves evaluating factors such as the customer's background, reputation, transaction patterns, and the nature of their business activities.
- **Customer Acceptance Policy**: Establishing a clear and comprehensive customer acceptance policy is crucial. This policy should outline the criteria for accepting or rejecting customers based on their risk profiles. It helps ensure that businesses only engage with customers who meet their predetermined risk tolerance.
- **Ongoing Monitoring**: KYC is not a one-time process; it requires continuous monitoring of customer activities to identify and report any suspicious transactions or behaviors. Regular updates of customer information, periodic reviews, and risk reassessments should be conducted based on risk levels and regulatory requirements.
- **Record Keeping**: Businesses must maintain comprehensive records of all customer identification and transactional data. These records should be securely stored and made available to regulatory authorities, if requested, to aid in investigations or audits.

Definition and Principles of KYB

KYB stands for "Know Your Business" and, although it is a similar concept, it is a separate process from KYC. KYB refers to the process of verifying the identity and assessing the risk associated with a business entity, typically within a business-to-business (B2B) context. It involves gathering information about the legal structure, ownership, and operations of the business to evaluate its legitimacy, integrity, and potential risks.

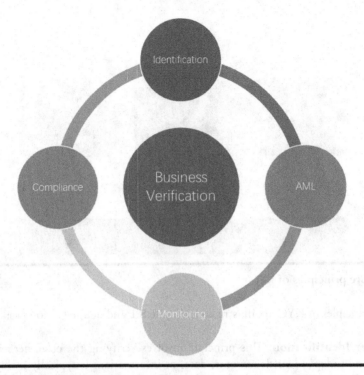

Figure 8.2 Core principles of KYB

The core principles of KYB, with business verification at the core of it, are visualized in Figure 8.2 and described as follows:

■ **Business Verification**: KYB requires verifying the legal existence and authenticity of the business. This involves obtaining valid registration documents, business licenses, tax identification numbers, and any other relevant legal documentation to ensure the business is legitimate.

■ **Ownership and Control Identification**: It is essential to identify the individuals or entities that own and control the business. This includes understanding the ownership structure, such as shareholders, partners, or members, and determining the ultimate beneficial owners (UBOs) who have significant control or influence over the business.

■ **Anti-Money Laundering (AML) Due Diligence**: KYB necessitates conducting due diligence to assess the business risk of being involved in money laundering or other illicit activities. This involves evaluating the industry sector, transaction patterns, geographic location, and the reputation of the owners or key personnel.

■ **Business Relationship Monitoring**: Similar to KYC, ongoing monitoring is crucial in KYB to identify any changes in the business structure, ownership, or activities that may affect the risk profile. Regular updates and reviews of the business information help ensure ongoing compliance with regulations and mitigate potential risks.

■ **Compliance with Regulatory Requirements**: KYB should align with the regulatory requirements specific to the industry and jurisdiction in which the business operates. Compliance obligations may vary, but KYB practices aim to ensure adherence to applicable laws, regulations, and industry standards.

By implementing effective KYB processes, businesses can mitigate risks associated with fraudulent entities, money laundering, and other illicit activities within their business relationships. KYB helps establish trust, transparency, and compliance in B2B interactions, allowing organizations to make informed decisions when entering into business partnerships or transactions.

Key Differences and Similarities between KYC and KYB

KYC and KYB are related concepts that serve different purposes within the realm of financial compliance and risk management. There are some important differences between the two processes, which are summarized in Table 8.1.

Table 8.1   Key differences between KYC and KYB processes

	KYC	*KYB*
Focus	KYC primarily focuses on verifying the identity and assessing the risk associated with individual customers. It aims to establish the identity, integrity, and potential risks of individuals engaging in financial transactions.	KYB, on the other hand, centers around understanding and evaluating the legitimacy, ownership, and risk profile of a business entity. It is concerned with gathering information about the legal structure, beneficial owners, and operations of a business.
Scope	KYC processes are designed to assess individual customers, irrespective of the type of business or industry they are associated with. It applies to both individuals and entities.	KYB specifically focuses on verifying and evaluating the legitimacy and risk associated with business entities. It is particularly relevant in business-to-business (B2B) relationships and aims to understand the entities' ownership structure and associated risks.
Data Collection	KYC involves collecting personal information about individual customers, such as name, address, identification documents, and financial information.	KYB entails gathering information about the legal structure of the business, registration documents, ownership details, and other relevant business-related information.
Purpose	The purpose of KYC is to prevent identity theft, fraud, money laundering, terrorist financing, and other illicit activities. It helps financial institutions assess the risk associated with individual customers and ensure compliance with regulatory requirements.	KYB aims to verify the legitimacy of businesses, identify their beneficial owners, and assess the risks associated with engaging in business relationships. It helps prevent fraud, money laundering, and other illicit activities within B2B transactions.
Relationship	KYC focuses on understanding and assessing the individual customer's risk profile and potential illicit activities.	KYB focuses on understanding the legitimacy, ownership, and associated risks of the business entity itself.

Despite these differences, KYC and KYB also share some similarities. Both KYC and KYB are crucial components of compliance and risk management practices in the financial industry. Both involve the collection and verification of information about customers/entities to establish their legitimacy and assess potential risks. Both require ongoing monitoring to detect any changes or suspicious activities.

Overall, while KYC focuses on individual customers, KYB concentrates on business entities, addressing different aspects of compliance and risk management in the financial sector.

Importance of KYC/KYB in the Blockchain Industry

KYC and KYB play a vital role in the blockchain industry, where trust, transparency, and regulatory compliance are crucial. Companies operating in the Web3 space are looking at implementing KYC/KYB for a variety of reasons. Let's now understand the most common and significant use cases for knowing more about your customers and businesses.

Mitigating Risks: KYC/KYB processes help blockchain operators mitigate various risks associated with money laundering, terrorist financing, fraud, and other illicit activities. By verifying the identities of customers and assessing the legitimacy of businesses, blockchain operators can better understand the risk profiles of their users and business partners.

Regulatory Compliance: The blockchain industry is subject to increasing regulatory scrutiny and evolving compliance requirements. KYC/KYB practices enable blockchain operators to fulfill their obligations by adhering to AML, CTF, and other regulatory frameworks. It helps prevent non-compliance penalties and legal consequences.

Anti-Money Laundering (AML) Measures: KYC/KYB processes are integral to implementing effective AML measures within the blockchain industry. By verifying the identities of customers and the legitimacy of business entities, blockchain operators can identify and report suspicious activities, detect patterns of money laundering, and support AML efforts.

Trust and Transparency: Blockchain technology aims to provide decentralized and transparent systems. Implementing robust KYC/KYB processes enhances trust among participants by ensuring that only legitimate and verified individuals and businesses can participate. It helps create a safer and more transparent ecosystem for transactions and interactions.

Reputation Management: Effective KYC/KYB practices contribute to maintaining the reputation of blockchain operators and the overall industry. By conducting due diligence and verifying customers and business entities, operators can identify and avoid engaging with individuals or entities involved in illicit or fraudulent activities. This helps protect the integrity and reputation of the platform and the broader blockchain ecosystem.

Investor Protection: KYC/KYB measures are crucial for investor protection in the blockchain industry. By verifying the identities and legitimacy of businesses, potential investors can have increased confidence in the projects and reduce the risk of falling victim to scams or fraudulent schemes.

Compliance with Global Standards: KYC/KYB processes align with international standards and recommendations set forth by organizations like the Financial Action Task Force (FATF). Compliance with these standards enhances the credibility and acceptance of the blockchain industry on a global scale.

Overall, KYC/KYB in the blockchain industry promotes a safer, compliant, and transparent ecosystem. It helps mitigate risks, adhere to regulatory requirements, foster trust, and protect the reputation of blockchain operators, all while contributing to the broader goals of the industry.

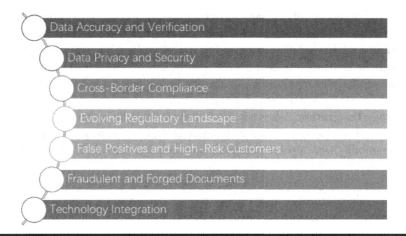

Figure 8.3   Common challenges for KYC and KYB

KYC and KYB Challenges

Implementing KYC and KYB processes can present several challenges for businesses. One of the first challenges is about **customer experience**: KYC processes often involve requesting extensive information and documentation from customers, which can lead to a cumbersome and time-consuming onboarding experience. Striking a balance between compliance requirements and providing a smooth and efficient customer experience is a challenge for businesses. Implementing robust KYC and KYB processes is not that simple, either, and it does require dedicated resources, including personnel, technology, and infrastructure. This can pose challenges for smaller businesses with limited resources, potentially leading to **higher costs and operational burdens**. Figure 8.3 illustrates additional common challenges associated with KYC and KYB, which are described as follows:

- **Data Accuracy and Verification**: One of the primary challenges is ensuring the accuracy and reliability of customer and business data. Verifying identities, ownership structures, and beneficial owners can be complex, especially when dealing with international entities. The availability and authenticity of provided documents can also pose challenges.
- **Data Privacy and Security**: KYC and KYB involve collecting and storing sensitive customer and business information. Safeguarding this data from unauthorized access, breaches, or misuse is crucial. Businesses must comply with data protection regulations and implement robust security measures to mitigate risks.
- **Cross-Border Compliance**: Dealing with customers and businesses across multiple jurisdictions adds complexity to KYC and KYB processes. Different countries may have distinct regulatory frameworks and compliance requirements, making it challenging to maintain consistent practices across borders.
- **Evolving Regulatory Landscape**: Regulatory requirements related to KYC and KYB are subject to constant change and updates. Staying abreast of evolving regulations, interpreting their implications, and implementing necessary changes in a timely manner can be challenging for businesses, especially in fast-paced industries like blockchain.
- **False Positives and High-Risk Customers**: KYC and KYB processes may generate false positives, flagging legitimate customers or businesses as high risk. This can lead to additional

scrutiny and delays in onboarding, impacting customer experience. Striking the right balance between risk mitigation and avoiding unnecessary barriers is crucial.

■ **Fraudulent and Forged Documents**: Determining the authenticity of submitted documents can be challenging, as fraudsters continually innovate and develop sophisticated techniques to forge or manipulate documents. Employing advanced document verification methods and staying vigilant is necessary.

■ **Technology Integration**: Adopting and integrating suitable technology solutions for KYC and KYB can be a challenge. Ensuring seamless integration with existing systems, scalability, and compatibility with regulatory requirements requires careful planning and investment.

Overcoming these challenges requires a proactive approach, robust internal controls, investments in technology, collaboration with regulatory authorities, and ongoing monitoring and training to adapt to the evolving landscape of KYC and KYB compliance.

Blockchain Solutions for KYC and KYB

Blockchain technology has the potential to improve KYC and KYB processes in several ways. In this context, risk management and fraud prevention are crucial aspects of maintaining the integrity and security of the blockchain industry.

Fraud prevention in the blockchain industry, specifically, involves implementing two key measures to detect and mitigate fraudulent activities:

1. **Identity Verification**: Implementing robust KYC and KYB procedures to verify the identity and legitimacy of users and businesses. This helps prevent identity theft, account takeovers, and unauthorized access to blockchain platforms.

2. **Anti-Money Laundering (AML)**: Implementing AML procedures and monitoring transactions for suspicious patterns or activities that may indicate money laundering or other financial crimes. This includes monitoring transaction volumes, identifying high-risk transactions, and reporting suspicious activities to the relevant authorities.

Smart contracts and decentralized identifiers can streamline the collection and validation of business registration documents, ownership structures, and beneficial ownership information. This enhances transparency and reduces the risk of fraudulent or shell businesses.

Verified entities, such as government agencies or trusted third-party providers, can attest to the accuracy and authenticity of customer data, which is recorded on the blockchain. This reduces the need for repetitive verification and increases trust among different parties in the ecosystem.

Blockchain's immutability ensures the integrity of KYC/KYB data. Once information is recorded on the blockchain, it cannot be altered or deleted without consensus. This feature provides a trustworthy audit trail and allows regulators and auditors to verify the authenticity and accuracy of the data, enhancing transparency and compliance.

Blockchain's decentralized and immutable nature can enhance the security of sensitive customer and business data. KYC/KYB information can be stored on the blockchain, encrypted, and distributed across nodes, reducing the risk of data breaches or unauthorized access. Blockchain's cryptographic features provide robust protection against tampering and unauthorized modifications.

Last but not the least, blockchain enables the concept of self-sovereign identity, where individuals have full control over their identity data. Users can maintain their personal information

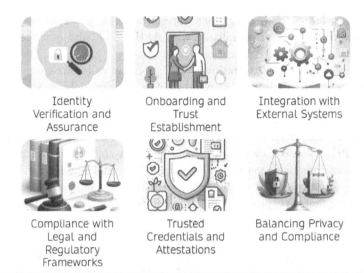

| Identity Verification and Assurance | Onboarding and Trust Establishment | Integration with External Systems |
| Compliance with Legal and Regulatory Frameworks | Trusted Credentials and Attestations | Balancing Privacy and Compliance |

Figure 8.4 Key impact areas of KYC on SSI

in a digital wallet on the blockchain and grant access to specific attributes when needed, reducing the reliance on centralized identity providers. SSI empowers individuals with privacy, control, and portability of their identity, aligning with KYC principles.

Decentralized Identity Solutions and Self-Sovereign Identity

Elaborating on this last point, KYC processes have a significant impact on decentralized identity solutions, including self-sovereign identity (SSI). Key impact areas of KYC on SSI are illustrated in Figure 8.4 and summarized as follows:

- **Identity Verification and Assurance**: KYC plays a crucial role in establishing the initial identity verification and assurance within decentralized identity solutions. Traditional KYC processes involve verifying the identity of individuals through documentation, verification procedures, and identity checks. This initial verification process provides a foundation for creating trusted and verified digital identities within decentralized identity solutions.
- **Onboarding and Trust Establishment**: KYC processes are often required for onboarding users onto decentralized identity platforms. By verifying the identity and establishing trust through KYC, decentralized identity solutions can ensure that only legitimate and verified individuals are granted access to the platform. This helps establish trust among participants and reduces the risk of fraudulent or malicious activities.
- **Integration with External Systems**: KYC requirements imposed by regulatory bodies often necessitate the integration of decentralized identity solutions with external systems. These external systems may include identity verification providers, government databases, or other trusted sources of identity information. KYC compliance ensures that the decentralized identity solution aligns with regulatory requirements and facilitates interoperability with existing identity infrastructure.
- **Compliance with Legal and Regulatory Frameworks**: Many decentralized identity solutions aim to give individuals greater control over their personal data and provide self-sovereign identity capabilities. However, these solutions must also adhere to legal and regulatory

frameworks, including KYC obligations. Integrating KYC processes within decentralized identity solutions allows for compliance with AML, CTF, and other regulatory requirements related to identity verification.

■ **Trusted Credentials and Attestations**: KYC processes can issue trusted credentials and attestations that verify the authenticity and validity of individuals' identity attributes. These credentials can be stored on a decentralized identity platform, allowing users to selectively share their verified identity information with service providers or other entities. KYC-enabled credentials enhance the trustworthiness and reliability of decentralized identity solutions.

■ **Balancing Privacy and Compliance**: KYC processes collect sensitive personal information, which can potentially conflict with the privacy principles of decentralized identity and self-sovereign identity. Balancing privacy concerns with compliance requirements is a challenge. Ensuring that KYC processes collect and handle only necessary data while protecting individuals' privacy rights is crucial to aligning KYC with decentralized identity solutions.

It's important to note that the implementation of KYC within decentralized identity solutions requires careful consideration of privacy, consent management, and user control. Striking the right balance between compliance, identity verification, and individual privacy is essential to harness the benefits of both KYC and decentralized identity solutions while ensuring regulatory compliance and user empowerment.

Smart Contracts for Secure and Automated Verification

Smart contracts can be utilized for secure and automated verification of customer and business identities in multiple ways. First of all, smart contracts can enable customers or businesses to submit their identity information directly to the blockchain. This is called a **self-verification** process: Information can include personal or business details, identification documents, and other relevant data. The smart contract can perform automated checks to ensure the completeness and accuracy of the provided information.

Smart contracts can **integrate with external identity verification services**, such as government databases or trusted third-party providers. A smart contract can trigger requests to these services via an *oracle*, and automatically verify the authenticity and validity of the submitted identity information. The verification results can be recorded on the blockchain for transparency and auditability. The following example in Solidity programming language shows how a trusted oracle would call the verifyUser function on the smart contract when it has verified a user's identity.

```
contract IdentityVerification {
    // Oracle address
    address private oracle;

    // Mapping of user addresses to verification status
    mapping(address => bool) private verifiedUsers;

    // Event that will be emitted when a user is verified
    event UserVerified(address user);

    constructor(address _oracle) {
        oracle = _oracle;
    }
```

```
function verifyUser(address user) external {
    // Only the oracle can verify users
    require(msg.sender == oracle, "Only the oracle can verify users");

    // Verify the user
    verifiedUsers[user] = true;

    // Emit the UserVerified event
    emit UserVerified(user);
}
function isUserVerified(address user) external view returns
    (bool) {
    return verifiedUsers[user];
}
}
}
```

Smart contracts can utilize a **consensus mechanism** to ensure the validity of identity information. Through consensus algorithms like Proof-of-Stake (PoS) or Proof-of-Authority (PoA), validators or designated entities can collectively verify and validate the identity information provided by customers or businesses. Consensus-based verification adds an additional layer of trust and security to the identity verification process.

Smart contracts record identity verification results on the blockchain, creating an **immutable record of the verified identities**. This ensures transparency, auditability, and tamper resistance, as the verification results cannot be altered once recorded. This feature enhances the integrity and reliability of the identity verification process.

Smart contracts can incorporate access control mechanisms to **allow only authorized entities** to access and view identity information. Customers or businesses can grant specific permissions to service providers or regulatory authorities, ensuring privacy and data protection while complying with regulatory requirements. Extending on the oracle example before, where only the oracle is allowed to verify the user's identity, more generally speaking, the following example shows a smart contract that implements an access control mechanism. The oracle or the user themselves can access the user's identity information by calling the getIdentityInformation function. Other entities are not allowed to access this information. The require statements are used to enforce these access control rules.

```
contract IdentityAccessControl {
    // Oracle address
    address private oracle;

    // Mapping of user addresses to verification status
    mapping(address => bool) private verifiedUsers;

    // Mapping of user addresses to identity information
    mapping(address => string) private identityInformation;

    // Event that will be emitted when a user is verified
    event UserVerified(address user);

    constructor(address _oracle) {
        oracle = _oracle;
    }

    function verifyUser(address user, string memory info) external {
        // Only the oracle can verify users
        require(msg.sender == oracle, "Only the oracle can verify
            users");
```

```
        // Verify the user and store their identity information
        verifiedUsers[user] = true;
        identityInformation[user] = info;

        // Emit the UserVerified event
        emit UserVerified(user);
    }

    function getIdentityInformation(address user) external view
        returns (string memory) {
        // Only the oracle or the user themselves can access the
            identity information
        require(msg.sender == oracle || msg.sender == user, "Only
            the oracle or the user themselves can access the identity
            information");

        // Check if the user is verified
        require(verifiedUsers[user], "The user is not verified");

        // Return the identity information
        return identityInformation[user];
    }
}
```

In conclusion, by leveraging smart contracts, businesses can establish secure, automated, and trustless processes for verifying customer and business identities. This not only enhances the efficiency of identity verification but also strengthens the security and reliability of the overall identity management ecosystem.

Data Privacy and Consent Management on the Blockchain

Managing data privacy and consent management on the blockchain requires careful consideration of privacy-enhancing techniques and the implementation of appropriate protocols. Table 8.2 lists key aspects to consider for managing data privacy correctly on the blockchain.

It's important to note that while blockchain can provide enhanced data privacy features, it's not a silver bullet. Careful consideration of privacy-enhancing techniques, legal compliance, and user-centric design is necessary to strike a balance between privacy and the transparent nature of the blockchain.

Identity Verification and Authentication Issues

Web3, which refers to the next generation of the internet built on decentralized technologies like blockchain, presents unique challenges and considerations for identity verification and authentication. Addressing these challenges requires a combination of technological innovation, industry collaboration, and adherence to evolving standards and best practices. The development of robust identity management protocols, secure and user-centric authentication mechanisms, and privacy-preserving solutions will be key in advancing identity verification and authentication in the Web3 landscape.

In the previous section, we have already touched on the aspects of **pseudonymity and privacy**, which allow users to interact with decentralized applications (dApps) without revealing their real-world identities. Balancing the need for privacy with compliance requirements for identity verification poses a challenge, especially in cases where regulatory obligations, such as KYC, exist.

Table 8.2 Key considerations for data privacy on blockchain

Key Aspect	Description
Pseudonymity and Encryption	Blockchain networks typically provide pseudonymity, allowing participants to transact without revealing their real-world identities. This pseudonymous approach can help protect privacy. Additionally, employing encryption techniques for sensitive data stored on the blockchain can provide an additional layer of security.
Off-Chain Data Storage	Storing all data on-chain may not be necessary or practical for privacy reasons. Off-chain storage solutions, such as encrypted distributed file systems or off-chain databases, can be utilized to store sensitive data separately from the blockchain while maintaining references or hashes on-chain for data integrity purposes.
Selective Data Sharing	Blockchain-based systems can allow individuals to selectively share their personal data with specific entities or for specific purposes. Through the use of smart contracts and user-controlled permissions, individuals can grant consent for data access on a granular level, ensuring that only authorized parties can access their data.
Privacy-Enhancing Technologies	Various privacy-enhancing technologies can be employed in conjunction with blockchain. Techniques such as zero-knowledge proofs, ring signatures, and secure multi-party computation can enable data verification and computations without revealing the underlying data, thereby preserving privacy.
Regulatory Compliance	Compliance with data protection regulations, such as the General Data Protection Regulation (GDPR), is crucial. Blockchain-based systems need to align with these regulations by ensuring that personal data is processed lawfully, collected for specific purposes, and retained for a defined period. Compliance with data subject rights, such as the right to access, rectify, and erase personal data, should also be ensured.
Transparent Consent Management	Implementing transparent consent management mechanisms on the blockchain helps individuals maintain control over their data. Smart contracts can facilitate the recording and enforcement of consent agreements, providing individuals with a clear understanding of how their data will be used and by whom.

Web3, notably, aims at enabling **self-sovereign identity**, where individuals have full control over their identity information. Implementing secure and reliable SSI solutions that allow users to manage and control their identity data while ensuring its integrity and authenticity is a significant challenge, as already discussed in *Chapter 6*.

In addition to the mentioned security concerns, Web3 platforms may face challenges in verifying the uniqueness and authenticity of users due to the potential for **sybil attacks**, where an entity creates multiple fake identities. Implementing effective identity verification mechanisms to mitigate sybil attacks while maintaining user privacy is a challenge.

At a high level, the following decentralized application (dApp) implements a mechanism to mitigate sybil attacks. One common approach to mitigate sybil attacks in dApps is to use a **Proof**

of Humanity system. This system requires users to verify their uniqueness through a vouching process and video submission. Once verified, the user's Ethereum address is added to a registry of verified humans. The following code snippet is a simplified example of how this might look in Solidity.

```
contract ProofOfHumanity {
    mapping(address => bool) public isHuman;

    function verify(address _address) external {
        // In a real-world scenario, there would be additional
            checks here
        // For example, a requirement that the caller is a trusted
        third party
        // And a process to verify the video submission
        isHuman[_address] = true;
    }
}
```

In this contract, once an address is verified as human, the isHuman mapping is updated. This provides a simple way for other contracts to check if an address has been verified as unique.

But exactly, what is a sybil attack? A sybil attack in the context of a blockchain network could involve an attacker creating many different addresses and pretending to be multiple nodes. This could allow the attacker to disproportionately influence the network, for example, by controlling a majority of voting power in a Decentralized Autonomous Organization (DAO). Have a look at the following smart contract.

```
contract VotingDAO {
    mapping(address => uint256) public votes;

    function vote(uint256 _votes) external {
        // In a real-world scenario, there would be additional
        checks here
        // For example, a requirement that the caller has sufficient
            tokens to vote
        votes[msg.sender] += _votes;
    }
}
```

In this contract, an attacker could call the vote function from many different addresses, potentially swaying the vote in their favor. Note that these are simplified examples and real-world implementations would be more complex. Also, it's important to note that while smart contracts can help mitigate sybil attacks, they can't completely prevent them. Additional off-chain measures may also be necessary.

Scalability Concerns

Scalability is a significant consideration in blockchain technology. Blockchain networks, especially public ones, often face scalability challenges related to transaction throughput. Traditional blockchain architectures, like Bitcoin and Ethereum, have limitations in processing a high volume of transactions per second, resulting in slower confirmation times and increased fees.

As blockchain networks gain popularity and usage increases, network congestion becomes a scalability concern. High demand for transactions can lead to delays, increased transaction

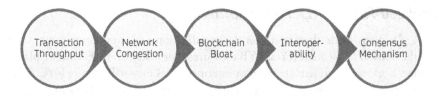

Figure 8.5   Scalability concerns for blockchain networks

costs, and reduced overall network efficiency. This becomes so critical, at times, that some blockchains may experience scalability issues due to the continuous growth of the blockchain's size over time. As more transactions are added to the blockchain, the storage and processing requirements increase, potentially leading to slower node synchronization and higher resource demands.

Figure 8.5 highlights the most common scalability concerns in blockchain. In addition to what already mentioned, two more challenges may arise, when trying to achieve interoperability between different blockchains, and on the choice of the consensus mechanism. For example, Proof-of-Work (PoW) algorithms, while secure, often suffer from scalability issues due to resource-intensive mining processes. Exploring alternative consensus mechanisms, such as Proof-of-Stake (PoS) or sharding, aims to enhance scalability without compromising security.

Addressing scalability concerns requires continuous research, technological advancements, and innovation. Solutions such as layer 2 scaling solutions, sharding, state channels, and hybrid blockchain models are being explored to tackle these challenges while maintaining the security, decentralization, and trust that blockchain technology offers.

Case Studies

There are many applications of KYC and KYB across industries. Here we want to identify a few real-world examples of how KYC/KYB is implemented specifically in solutions that have blockchain technology at their core.

Cryptocurrency Exchanges

Cryptocurrency exchanges are one of the primary entry points for users to buy, sell, and trade digital assets. To comply with regulatory requirements and prevent illicit activities, most reputable exchanges implement strict KYC procedures. When users sign up for an account, they are typically required to provide personal identification documents, such as government-issued IDs, proof of address, and sometimes even a selfie to verify their identity. This process helps the exchange know their customers better and ensures that only legitimate users are using their platform.

Initial Coin Offerings (ICOs) and Token Sales

During ICOs and token sales, blockchain projects raise funds by selling their native tokens to investors. To maintain transparency and compliance, many projects enforce KYC procedures for participants. Potential investors are required to submit their identification documents and other relevant information to verify their identity and eligibility to participate. This helps prevent money laundering and ensures that the project adheres to the regulations of the jurisdictions in which they operate.

Decentralized Finance (DeFi) Platforms

While DeFi platforms pride themselves on decentralization and autonomy, some projects have recognized the need to implement KYC/KYB measures. For instance, DeFi lending platforms that aim to connect borrowers and lenders without intermediaries may still require KYC for users who wish to access larger loan amounts. This ensures that participants on the platform are not engaging in fraudulent or illegal activities and can provide some level of protection to lenders.

Security Token Offerings (STOs)

STOs are token sales that represent ownership of real-world assets, such as real estate or company shares. Because they deal with regulated assets, STOs often incorporate robust KYC/KYB processes. Investors seeking to participate in an STO are required to provide detailed information about their identity, financial status, and sometimes even their investment experience. This helps issuers comply with securities laws and gives confidence to potential investors that the project is legitimate.

Enterprise Blockchain Solutions

In the context of enterprise blockchain solutions, companies that implement blockchain technology for supply chain management or record-keeping may conduct KYB checks. Businesses interacting with each other on a blockchain network may need to verify the legal status, ownership structure, and beneficial ownership of other participating businesses. This helps maintain trust and transparency within the network and reduces the risk of fraudulent or unauthorized access to sensitive data.

Remember that KYC and KYB practices may vary depending on local regulations and the specific use case of the blockchain platform. While these examples highlight how KYC/KYB is often implemented in the blockchain industry, it's essential for operators to stay updated on the latest compliance requirements and best practices to ensure their operations remain secure and compliant.

Best Practices

Implementing KYC and KYB in a blockchain solution requires careful planning and adherence to regulatory guidelines. Here are some best practices to consider when incorporating KYC/KYB into your blockchain platform.

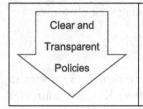

| Clear and Transparent Policies | Clearly communicate your KYC/KYB policies to users and businesses interacting with your blockchain solution. Provide detailed information about the type of data collected, how it will be used, and the purposes behind the verification process. Transparency builds trust among participants and helps them understand the importance of compliance. |

Risk-Based Approach	Adopt a risk-based approach to KYC/KYB. Assign different levels of scrutiny based on risk profiles, transaction volumes, and user activities. High-risk customers or businesses should undergo more rigorous verification procedures to mitigate potential risks associated with their participation in the blockchain ecosystem.
Data Security and Privacy	Ensure that all personal and business data collected during the KYC/KYB process is stored securely and protected from unauthorized access. Implement robust encryption techniques, access controls, and data segregation to safeguard sensitive information.
Automated Verification	Leverage technological solutions for automated verification of identity and business information. Utilize AI-powered tools that can validate identification documents, cross-check against databases, and detect potential fraud patterns efficiently.
User-Friendly Experience	Although KYC/KYB is essential for compliance, it should not deter users from joining the blockchain platform. Design the verification process to be user-friendly, straightforward, and quick. Minimize the number of steps required and provide clear instructions throughout the process.
Regular Updates and Reviews	Stay updated with the latest regulatory requirements and industry best practices. Review and update your KYC/KYB procedures regularly to adapt to changing compliance standards and emerging risks.
Third-Party KYC Services	Consider partnering with reputable third-party KYC service providers. These services specialize in identity verification and background checks, ensuring a more robust and comprehensive KYC/KYB process for your platform.
Audit and Compliance Reports	Maintain detailed records of the KYC/KYB process and have a comprehensive audit trail. This documentation can serve as evidence of compliance in case of regulatory inquiries or investigations.

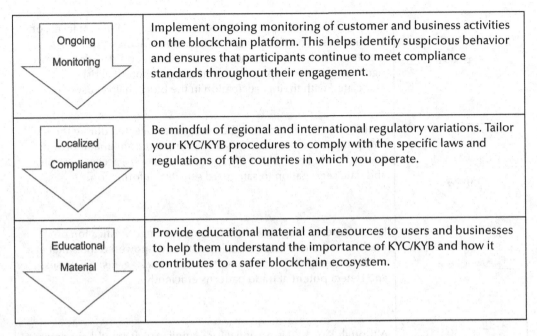

Ongoing Monitoring	Implement ongoing monitoring of customer and business activities on the blockchain platform. This helps identify suspicious behavior and ensures that participants continue to meet compliance standards throughout their engagement.
Localized Compliance	Be mindful of regional and international regulatory variations. Tailor your KYC/KYB procedures to comply with the specific laws and regulations of the countries in which you operate.
Educational Material	Provide educational material and resources to users and businesses to help them understand the importance of KYC/KYB and how it contributes to a safer blockchain ecosystem.

By following these best practices, you can strengthen the security and integrity of your blockchain solution, build trust among participants, and ensure compliance with applicable laws and regulations.

Future Directions and Recommendations

Blockchain technology has the potential to revolutionize the way KYC and KYB processes are conducted, making them more efficient, secure, and user-centric. There are multiple advancements in KYC/KYB that can be impacted by the use of blockchain technology, including decentralized identity solutions (**DID**) and self-sovereign identity (**SSI**).

Blockchain can facilitate the development of DID solutions, where individuals and businesses can have ownership and control over their identity information. Users can store their verified identity data on the blockchain, and service providers can request access to specific attributes for KYC/KYB purposes without the need to store the entire dataset centrally. SSI takes decentralization further by enabling users to manage their identities without relying on centralized authorities. It allows users to present verifiable credentials directly from their blockchain wallet to prove their identity, reducing the need for multiple KYC verifications across different platforms.

Advancements in interoperability protocols will allow different blockchain networks to communicate and share verified identity data securely. This will streamline KYC/KYB processes across various blockchain-based services and reduce redundancy in identity verification. Not only cross-blockchain communication can be addressed with more mature integration protocols, but also **cross-border compliance** can be met. Blockchain-based KYC/KYB solutions can streamline cross-border transactions by allowing for seamless identity verification across different jurisdictions. This can simplify compliance processes for businesses operating internationally. Smart contracts can be integrated into the KYC/KYB process to automatically enforce compliance rules and requirements. They can trigger alerts or restrict certain actions based on predefined compliance criteria.

Blockchain can enable granular consent management, where users can control which specific attributes of their identity are shared with whom. Service providers can request access to certain information only when necessary, reducing the exposure of sensitive data. Zero-knowledge proofs (ZKP) offer a way to prove the validity of information without revealing the actual data. ZKPs can be applied to verify identity attributes without exposing private details, **ensuring privacy** during KYC/KYB processes.

In addition to the anonymity of data, blockchain's immutable nature ensures that all KYC/KYB-related actions and updates are recorded in an unchangeable ledger. This creates a transparent and **tamper-proof audit trail**, enhancing compliance and accountability. With blockchain, the verification data can be cryptographically hashed and stored on the blockchain, providing a tamper-resistant record of the verification process. This **instils trust** in the accuracy and authenticity of the KYC/KYB data.

Lastly, blockchain analytics tools can be employed to identify and track suspicious activities, aiding anti-money laundering (**AML**) and countering the financing of terrorism (**CFT**) efforts.

While these advancements hold great promise, it's essential to address privacy concerns and ensure that appropriate security measures are in place to protect sensitive identity data. Additionally, collaboration among regulatory bodies, businesses, and technology providers will be critical to establish global standards and facilitate the adoption of blockchain-based KYC/KYB solutions on a broader scale.

Recommended Approach to KYC/KYB

A balanced approach to KYC and KYB is essential to ensure that regulatory objectives are met without unduly burdening businesses and customers. Best practices for achieving a balanced approach to KYC/KYB are listed in Figure 8.6 and described as follows:

Risk-Based Approach: Adopt a risk-based approach to KYC/KYB, where the level of scrutiny and verification requirements are commensurate with the risk posed by the customer or business. High-risk entities, such as those involved in cross-border transactions or dealing with large volumes of funds, may require more thorough verification, while low-risk entities may undergo a simplified process.

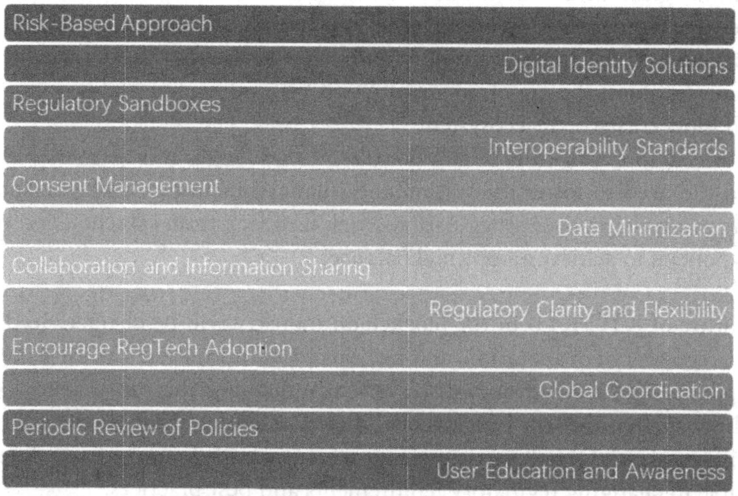

Figure 8.6   Best practices for a balanced approach to KYC/KYB

Digital Identity Solutions: Promote the development and adoption of secure and privacy-preserving digital identity solutions based on blockchain and decentralized technologies. Encouraging the use of self-sovereign identity (SSI) and verifiable credentials can reduce the need for repetitive KYC checks across different services.

Regulatory Sandboxes: Establish regulatory sandboxes or controlled testing environments where innovative KYC/KYB solutions can be piloted under limited regulatory oversight. This allows for the evaluation of new technologies and approaches while ensuring consumer protection and compliance.

Interoperability Standards: Encourage the development of interoperability standards for KYC/KYB data sharing across different platforms and industries. This can reduce redundancy in verification processes and enhance the efficiency of compliance procedures.

Consent Management: Emphasize the importance of consent management, where customers have control over the sharing of their identity data and are aware of how it will be used. Implement clear and transparent consent mechanisms to empower users to make informed decisions about data sharing.

Data Minimization: Advocate for the principle of data minimization, where only essential information required for KYC/KYB purposes is collected and retained. Avoid unnecessary data storage to reduce privacy risks.

Collaboration and Information Sharing: Encourage collaboration between industry stakeholders and regulatory bodies to share insights, best practices, and emerging risks. This cooperation can lead to more effective and informed policy decisions.

Regulatory Clarity and Flexibility: Provide clear and unambiguous regulatory guidelines on KYC/KYB requirements, while allowing for flexibility to adapt to technological advancements and changing business models.

Encourage RegTech Adoption: Support the adoption of RegTech solutions that leverage blockchain, AI, and other technologies to streamline KYC/KYB processes, enhance accuracy, and reduce costs for businesses.

Global Coordination: Foster international cooperation and coordination among regulators to establish harmonized KYC/KYB standards and cross-border data sharing mechanisms. A unified approach can facilitate compliance for businesses operating globally.

Periodic Review of Policies: Regularly review and update KYC/KYB policies to keep pace with technological advancements and changing risk landscapes. Periodic assessments can help fine-tune regulations and ensure their effectiveness.

User Education and Awareness: Invest in public awareness campaigns to educate customers and businesses about the importance of KYC/KYB, its benefits, and how it contributes to a safer and more trustworthy ecosystem.

A balanced approach to KYC/KYB strikes a middle ground between regulatory objectives and the need to foster innovation and financial inclusion. Policymakers should continuously assess the impact of regulations, seek feedback from stakeholders, and be open to refining policies to achieve an optimal balance.

Overall, the future of KYC/KYB in the blockchain industry will be characterized by a push for user-centricity, regulatory collaboration, and technological innovation. Striking the right balance between compliance and innovation will be key to unlocking the full potential of blockchain technology while safeguarding the interests of all stakeholders involved. As the industry continues to evolve, it will be essential for all participants to stay informed about the latest developments and remain adaptable to changing regulatory requirements and best practices.

Chapter 9

Blockchain for Good

In an era marked by global interconnectedness and technological innovation, the quest for improving the human condition has taken on unprecedented dimensions. With each passing day, new challenges arise, necessitating novel solutions that transcend traditional boundaries. In this pursuit, blockchain technology has emerged as a revolutionary force with immense potential to reshape the landscape of humanitarian efforts.

Originally conceptualized as the underlying technology supporting the cryptocurrency phenomenon, blockchain has swiftly evolved into a versatile tool with applications that transcend the financial realm. Its decentralized and immutable nature has captured the attention of visionaries, technologists, and humanitarians alike, who recognize its power to foster transparency, accountability, and efficiency in humanitarian endeavors.

At its core, humanitarian work is focused on addressing the needs of vulnerable populations, providing aid during crises, and empowering communities to thrive. However, despite the noble intentions behind these initiatives, traditional systems often grapple with challenges such as corruption, bureaucratic inefficiencies, and difficulties in tracking the flow of resources. It is within this context that blockchain technology offers a beacon of hope, promising a transformative shift towards a more equitable and impactful approach to humanitarian aid.

This chapter delves into the dynamic landscape of blockchain technology and explores its potential applications in the realm of humanitarianism. From disaster response and refugee assistance to ensuring fair aid distribution and fostering trust among stakeholders, blockchain's unique attributes hold the promise of overcoming long-standing obstacles in the humanitarian sector.

In this chapter, we will examine the fundamental principles that underpin blockchain technology, highlighting its features that make it a game-changer for humanitarian purposes. Furthermore, we will explore real-world use cases where blockchain has already made significant strides in improving the effectiveness and accountability of humanitarian initiatives. By analyzing these successes, we will uncover the potential hurdles that must be navigated to maximize the benefits of blockchain technology in this arena.

The use cases analyzed are **Land Registry** and **Culture Protection**.

As we embark on this exploration of blockchain's utilization for good humanitarian purposes, it is crucial to maintain a balanced perspective, acknowledging both its transformative capabilities and inherent limitations. While blockchain technology is not a panacea for all humanitarian

DOI: 10.4324/9781003491934-9

challenges, it undoubtedly represents an innovative approach that, when applied judiciously, can revolutionize the way we deliver assistance and support to those most in need.

Ultimately, this chapter seeks to ignite a dialogue surrounding the fusion of cutting-edge technology and compassionate altruism. By understanding how blockchain can serve as an enabler of positive change, we aspire to inspire future generations of innovators, humanitarians, and policymakers to collaborate toward a world where the full potential of technology is harnessed for the greater good of humanity.

Land Registry

Land registry is one of the areas that can greatly benefit from the application of blockchain technology for good humanitarian purposes. Blockchain has the potential to revolutionize traditional land registries, making them more secure, transparent, and efficient. The author has worked on relevant projects for the Australian Government. From direct experience, the following are the significant ways in which blockchain can bring positive impact to land registry systems:

- **Immutable Record Keeping**: Blockchain's inherent immutability ensures that once a land transaction or record is added to the blockchain, it cannot be altered or deleted. This helps prevent fraudulent activities and enhances the trustworthiness of land records.
- **Transparency and Traceability**: Blockchain's transparent and distributed nature allows all stakeholders, including government authorities, landowners, and the public, to access and verify land records in real-time. This increased transparency can reduce disputes and conflicts over land ownership.
- **Decentralization and Trust**: By eliminating the need for a central authority to manage transactions and payments for land records, blockchain-based land registries can reduce bureaucracy and corruption. The decentralized nature of blockchain instills trust in the system, as multiple nodes validate and maintain the records.
- **Smart Contracts for Automated Transactions**: Smart contracts, which are self-executing agreements on the blockchain, can be used to automate land transactions. This can streamline the process of buying, selling, or leasing land, reducing paperwork and processing times.
- **Improved Security**: Blockchain's cryptographic mechanisms ensure that land records are secured with strong encryption, safeguarding sensitive data from unauthorized access and tampering.
- **Disaster Recovery and Resilience**: Blockchain's distributed nature makes it resilient to single points of failure, making it suitable for disaster-prone regions where physical infrastructure may be at risk.
- **Inclusion of Informal Settlements**: Blockchain can enable the inclusion of informal settlements and undocumented landowners by providing a secure and accessible digital platform for land registration.
- **Efficiency and Cost Savings**: Blockchain's automation and elimination of intermediaries can streamline the land registration process, reducing administrative costs and delays.
- **Global Accessibility**: Blockchain-based land registries can be accessed and updated from anywhere with an internet connection, making land information available globally and facilitating cross-border investments and development.

Many countries and organizations are already exploring or implementing blockchain-based land registries as a way to address existing challenges in traditional land registration systems. However, it is essential to carefully consider the specific context and challenges of each region and to ensure proper governance, privacy protections, and community engagement in the implementation process. When applied thoughtfully, blockchain can indeed play a crucial role in transforming land registries for the better, leading to more secure and equitable land rights, improved land governance, and sustainable socioeconomic development.

Immutable Record-Keeping

Immutable record-keeping, in technical terms, refers to the characteristic of data being stored in a way that prohibits any alterations or deletions once the data is recorded. In the context of blockchain, immutability is a fundamental property achieved through the cryptographic hashing of data and the decentralized nature of the network.

Implementation of Immutable Record-Keeping

To demonstrate immutable record-keeping in a land registry solution built on blockchain technology, we will use the popular Python library called *pycryptodome* to perform cryptographic hashing. For the blockchain implementation, we will use a simplified version of a blockchain using a list as the chain. In real-world scenarios, blockchain implementations would involve more sophisticated data structures and consensus mechanisms. The entire source code is available online in the GitHub repository associated with this book. The following code snippet is a short representation of two classes: LandRegistryBlock and LandRegistryBlockchain.

```
class LandRegistryBlock:
    def calculate_hash(self):

class LandRegistryBlockchain:
    def create_genesis_block(self):

    def get_last_block(self):

    def add_block(self, new_block):
```

In this example, we have implemented a simple blockchain for the land registry. Each block contains the land registration data (land_id, owner, location) along with an index, timestamp, previous hash, and current hash. The blocks are linked through their cryptographic hashes, creating an immutable chain. Attempting to modify the data in any block will lead to a mismatch in the hash links, exposing the tampering.

In real-world scenarios, blockchain implementations would use more sophisticated data structures and may include consensus algorithms to reach agreement on the validity of new blocks. Additionally, a distributed network of nodes would be used to maintain the blockchain, further enhancing its security and resilience.

Transparency and Traceability

Transparency and traceability are important aspects of a land registry solution built on blockchain technology. They provide the ability to track and verify the history of land transactions and ownership changes, enabling increased trust among stakeholders and reducing disputes. The practical implementation that follows explores how transparency and traceability can be coded in a Python-based land registry solution using blockchain.

Implementation of Transparency and Traceability

To achieve transparency and traceability, we can enhance blockchain implementation by adding functionalities to retrieve and verify the history of land transactions and ownership changes.

```python
class LandRegistryBlockchain:
    def __init__(self):
        self.land_ownership = {} # Store land ownership history

    def get_land_ownership_history(self, land_id):
        return self.land_ownership.get(land_id, [])
```

In this enhanced implementation of the LandRegistryBlockchain class, we have introduced the concept of land _ ownership, which stores the history of ownership changes for each land based on its unique land _ id. Whenever a new block is added to the blockchain with land registration data, the ownership change is recorded in the land _ ownership dictionary.

With this approach, it becomes possible to retrieve the land ownership history for a specific land by querying its land _ id. The history will include all past transactions related to ownership changes, along with the associated timestamps and owners.

```python
land_registry = LandRegistryBlockchain()

# Get the land ownership history for a specific land
land_id_to_query = "12345"
ownership_history = land_registry.get_land_ownership_history(land_
    id_to_query)
```

This level of transparency and traceability empowers stakeholders to validate land ownership records and understand the entire history of land transactions, enhancing trust in the land registry system and reducing the likelihood of disputes. Additionally, the blockchain's immutable nature ensures that this ownership history cannot be tampered with, further strengthening its integrity and reliability.

Smart Contracts for Automated Transactions

In the context of a land registry solution, smart contracts can be used to automate land transactions, such as the transfer of ownership, rental agreements, or lease contracts. Below is an example of a simple smart contract for automating the process of transferring land ownership between two parties on a blockchain-based land registry.

For this example, we will use the Ethereum blockchain and Solidity programming language. Keep in mind that this is a simplified example for illustrative purposes, and in real-world scenarios, additional security measures and validations would be necessary.

```solidity
contract LandRegistry {
    struct Land {
        address owner;
        string location;
    }
```

```
        mapping(uint256 => Land) public lands;

        event LandOwnershipTransferred(...);

        function registerLand(uint256 landId, string memory location) public
        function transferOwnership(uint256 landId, address newOwner) public
        function getLandOwner(uint256 landId) public view
}
```

In this smart contract, we have a `LandRegistry` contract with two main functions:

1. **registerLand**: This function allows landowners to register their land on the blockchain by providing the land ID and location. When a land is registered, the owner's Ethereum address and the location are stored in the lands mapping.
2. **transferOwnership**: This function allows the current owner of the land to transfer ownership to another address. The function requires that the land has already been registered and that the sender is the current owner of the land. Upon successful transfer, the smart contract emits the `LandOwnershipTransferred` event to record the ownership change.

In this example, the smart contract handles the automated transfer of land ownership. By executing the `transferOwnership` function with the appropriate parameters, landowners can transfer ownership of their land to other Ethereum addresses directly on the blockchain, without the need for intermediaries.

In a real-world implementation, additional features, such as contract approval mechanisms, payment handling, and legal validation, would be added to create a more comprehensive and secure land registry solution. Furthermore, it is essential to consider proper governance and regulatory compliance to ensure that the smart contracts adhere to local laws and regulations governing land transactions.

Improved Security

Improved security in the context of a land registry solution refers to the implementation of robust security measures to protect the integrity, confidentiality, and authenticity of land-related data and transactions. Blockchain technology itself provides inherent security through its cryptographic mechanisms and decentralized nature. However, additional security measures can be applied to enhance the overall security of the land registry system. Let's now explore some specific security best practices and potential code examples.

Access Control and Permissions

In a land registry system, certain operations, such as land registration and ownership transfer, should be restricted to authorized users. Access control mechanisms can be implemented to define different user roles and permissions.

The following example using Solidity implements a simple access control modifier in a smart contract.

```
contract LandRegistry {
    address public admin; // The address of the contract admin
```

```
modifier onlyAdmin() {
    require(msg.sender == admin, "Only the admin can perform this
        operation");
    _;
}

constructor() {
    admin = msg.sender;
}
// Rest of the contract code...
}
```

Data Encryption

Sensitive data related to landowners or land details can be encrypted to protect it from unauthorized access.

The following example uses Python to encrypt landowner data with the *cryptography* library, using the Fernet symmetric encryption algorithm.

```
from cryptography.fernet import Fernet

# Generate a random encryption key
key = Fernet.generate_key()
fernet = Fernet(key)

# Landowner data to encrypt
landowner_data = {"name": "John Doe", "address": "123 Main St"}

# Encrypt the data
encrypted_data = fernet.encrypt(str(landowner_data).encode())

# Decrypt the data
decrypted_data = fernet.decrypt(encrypted_data).decode()
```

Audit Trails and Logging

Implementing logging and audit trails can help track actions and changes made to the land registry, enhancing accountability and traceability.

The following example uses Python to log land registration events to a file.

```
import logging

logging.basicConfig(filename="land_registry.log", level=logging.INFO)

# Example land registration event
land_id = "12345"
owner = "John Doe"
location = "City X"
logging.info(f"Land {land_id} registered by {owner} at {location}")
```

It is important to note that security measures should be adapted and implemented according to the specific requirements and threat landscape of the land registry system. Additionally, security is an ongoing process, and regular security audits and updates are necessary to maintain the integrity and protection of the land registry solution.

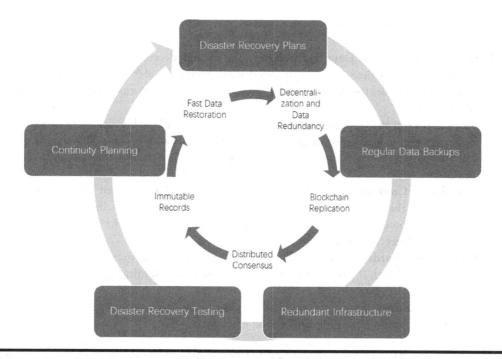

Figure 9.1   Best practices for disaster recovery and resilience

Disaster Recovery and Resilience

Disaster recovery and resilience are critical considerations for any land registry system, ensuring that the system can quickly recover from unexpected events, such as data loss, hardware failures, or natural disasters. Blockchain technology, with its distributed and immutable nature, provides a solid foundation for disaster recovery and resilience, which can be achieved by implementing the best practices in Figure 9.1, and described as follows.

Best practices for disaster recovery and resilience of software solutions:

- **Disaster Recovery Plans**: Having well-defined disaster recovery plans in place helps the land registry system recover from various types of disasters effectively. These plans include procedures for data restoration, failover mechanisms, and continuity of operations.
- **Regular Data Backups:** Despite the immutability of the blockchain, other data related to the land registry system, such as user information or metadata, may need regular backups to prevent data loss. These backups can be stored securely off-site or on redundant storage systems.
- **Redundant Infrastructure**: Using redundant infrastructure, such as redundant servers, networks, and power sources, improves the overall resilience of the land registry system.
- **Disaster Recovery Testing**: Regularly testing disaster recovery procedures and failover mechanisms helps identify potential issues and weaknesses in the system, allowing for improvements and better preparedness.
- **Continuity Planning**: Creating continuity plans that outline critical functions and priorities during disasters ensures that essential land registry services continue with minimal disruption.

Blockchain-specific best practices:

- **Decentralization and Data Redundancy**: The use of a decentralized blockchain network ensures that land registry data is distributed across multiple nodes. In case of a failure or loss of data in one node, the data can be retrieved from other nodes, ensuring data redundancy and availability.
- **Blockchain Replication**: Maintaining multiple instances of the blockchain network in different geographic locations enhances resilience. If one instance becomes unavailable due to a disaster, other instances can continue to operate, ensuring the continuity of land registry services.
- **Distributed Consensus**: The distributed consensus mechanism used in the blockchain ensures that the system continues to operate even if some nodes become unavailable. Consensus protocols, such as Proof of Work (PoW) or Proof of Stake (PoS), maintain the blockchain's integrity and operation.
- **Immutable Records**: The immutability of blockchain records ensures that once land transactions are recorded, they cannot be altered or deleted, safeguarding against data tampering and ensuring data integrity.
- **Fast Data Restoration**: In the event of data loss, blockchain nodes can synchronize with other nodes to restore the data quickly and efficiently.

By leveraging the inherent features of blockchain technology and implementing robust disaster recovery and resilience strategies, a land registry system can effectively withstand unforeseen events and ensure the availability and reliability of land-related data and services. These measures are essential for instilling confidence among stakeholders and maintaining the integrity of the land registry system even in challenging circumstances.

Inclusion of Informal Settlements

Inclusion of informal settlements refers to the process of integrating and recognizing informal or undocumented settlements into the formal land registry system. Informal settlements, also known as slums, shantytowns, or squatter settlements, are residential areas that have developed without proper legal recognition or formal land tenure rights. These settlements often lack basic infrastructure and services, and their residents may face significant challenges in accessing essential amenities and social services.

The inclusion of informal settlements in the land registry system aims to address the key objectives listed in Table 9.1.

Incorporating informal settlements into the land registry system is a complex and multi-faceted process. It requires collaboration between various stakeholders, including governments, local authorities, community representatives, and non-governmental organizations (NGOs). Community engagement and participation are crucial to ensure that the rights and needs of informal settlement residents are adequately addressed.

Technology, particularly blockchain-based land registries, can play a role in facilitating the formalization process. The transparency and tamper-resistance of blockchain can help build trust and accountability in the land registration process. Additionally, digital records can reduce paperwork and streamline the registration of informal settlements, making the process more accessible and efficient.

Table 9.1   Key objectives for land rgsettlements

Key Objective	Description
Formalizing Land Tenure	By integrating informal settlements into the formal land registry, residents can be granted legal recognition and tenure rights over the land they occupy. This formalization can provide them with greater security, protection against forced evictions, and the ability to invest in their homes and communities.
Access to Services and Development	Recognizing informal settlements allows local governments and authorities to plan and provide basic services and infrastructure to these areas. Access to water, sanitation, electricity, schools, and healthcare services can improve the living conditions of residents.
Reducing Vulnerability	Inclusion in the formal land registry can reduce the vulnerability of informal settlement residents to exploitation, land grabbing, and displacement. It also enables them to access financial services and credit opportunities, promoting economic empowerment.
Data Collection and Planning	Formalizing informal settlements helps governments collect accurate data about the population and living conditions in these areas. This data can inform urban planning, development, and policy decisions to improve the overall urban landscape.
Social Integration	By recognizing informal settlements, there is an opportunity to foster social integration and promote a sense of belonging among residents. It can also encourage community involvement in local governance and decision-making processes.

However, it is essential to approach the inclusion of informal settlements with sensitivity to the unique social, economic, and cultural aspects of each settlement. Customized solutions that consider the specific challenges and aspirations of the residents are more likely to lead to successful outcomes and positive social impact.

The concept of including informal settlements into the formal land registry is a complex process that involves legal, social, and administrative considerations. It requires collaboration with various stakeholders, and its implementation varies significantly depending on the specific context and legal framework of each region. As a result, there is no one-size-fits-all solution that can capture the entire process.

The following simplified example demonstrates how a blockchain-based land registry smart contract in Solidity could potentially be used to register land ownership for informal settlements. Keep in mind that this is a basic and generalized example, and in a real-world scenario, the actual implementation would be more comprehensive and tailored to specific requirements and legal frameworks.

```
contract LandRegistry {
    struct Land {
        address owner;
        string location;
        bool isFormalized;
    }
```

```
mapping(uint256 => Land) public lands;

event LandOwnershipTransferred(...);
event LandFormalized(...);

function registerLand(uint256 landId, string memory location)
function transferOwnership(uint256 landId, address newOwner)
function formalizeLand(uint256 landId
function isLandFormalized(uint256 landId
}
```

In this simplified smart contract, we have added a boolean variable `isFormalized` to the `Land` struct to indicate whether the land ownership has been formally recognized. The contract includes two additional functions: `formalizeLand` and `isLandFormalized`. The `formalizeLand` function allows the owner of the land to formally recognize their ownership. The `isLandFormalized` function allows anyone to check whether a specific land is formally recognized in the registry.

Again, this is a basic example, and the actual implementation of including informal settlements into the formal land registry would involve a much more extensive and customized process that addresses legal and social complexities. The involvement of legal experts, community representatives, and other stakeholders is crucial in such implementations.

Global Accessibility

Global accessibility in the context of a land registry solution refers to the ability of individuals from various regions, including remote or underserved areas, to access and participate in the land registry system. Achieving global accessibility involves overcoming barriers such as language differences, digital literacy, internet connectivity, and legal recognition. Here are some key technical details and considerations to meet the requirement of global accessibility in a land registry solution.

Multilingual Support

The user interface and documentation of the land registry system should be available in multiple languages to accommodate users from different linguistic backgrounds. Providing multilingual support improves user experience and ensures that language barriers do not prevent individuals from accessing the system.

User-Friendly Interface

The land registry platform should have an intuitive and user-friendly interface, even for individuals with limited digital literacy. Clear instructions, simple navigation, and user assistance features can help users interact with the system effectively.

Offline Capability

Global accessibility may require consideration for areas with limited or unreliable internet connectivity. Implementing an offline capability in the land registry application allows users to perform essential functions without a continuous internet connection and synchronize data when connectivity is available.

Mobile Accessibility

Emphasizing mobile accessibility enables users to access the land registry system through smartphones and feature phones, which are prevalent in regions with limited access to desktop computers.

Government Partnerships

Collaborating with local governments and authorities in different regions can facilitate the integration of land registry data into national systems and enable seamless data sharing between the land registry and other government services.

Lightweight Data Formats

To optimize performance in regions with limited internet bandwidth, the land registry system should use lightweight data formats for communication and data storage.

By using JSON or other lightweight data formats such as protobuf, we can minimize the amount of data transmitted and stored, reducing bandwidth and storage requirements. This is particularly beneficial in scenarios where network connectivity and resources are limited, enabling efficient communication and interaction with the land registry system. In more sophisticated implementations, other compact data formats or binary serialization methods can be explored to further optimize data representation.

Scalability and Performance

Ensuring the land registry system's scalability and performance is crucial to handle a potentially large user base spread across different regions. Implementing efficient data storage, caching, and load-balancing mechanisms can contribute to improved performance.

Offline Data Synchronization

Users in remote areas may face challenges with real-time synchronization. Implementing offline data synchronization mechanisms allows users to make changes locally and synchronize the data once they regain internet connectivity.

Offline data synchronization in a land registry solution involves enabling users to perform actions and update data while offline and then synchronizing those changes with the central database or blockchain once the internet connection is restored.

Accessible Documentation and Training

Providing comprehensive and accessible documentation, tutorials, and training materials can assist users in learning how to navigate and utilize the land registry system effectively.

Compliance with Local Regulations

Ensuring compliance with local land laws and regulations is essential to gain legal recognition and acceptance in different regions. Collaborating with local legal experts and authorities can help address legal requirements and nuances.

Addressing global accessibility in a land registry solution requires a user-centric approach, focusing on the needs and limitations of users from diverse backgrounds. Embracing technological innovations and partnerships with local stakeholders can play a vital role in creating an inclusive land registry system that is accessible and beneficial to individuals worldwide, regardless of their location or circumstances.

Culture Protection

The application of blockchain technology for culture protection is a fascinating and relevant area. Cultural heritage is of immense value to communities and societies, and preserving it is crucial for future generations. Blockchain technology offers unique features that can significantly contribute to culture protection efforts. In this section, we will explore some thoughts on how blockchain can be applied in this context.

Provenance and Authenticity

Blockchain's immutable nature can be used to establish the provenance and authenticity of cultural artifacts, artworks, or historical documents. By recording information about the origin, ownership, and historical transactions on the blockchain, we can create a reliable and transparent chain of custody, ensuring that cultural artifacts are genuine and preserving their value.

Digital Archives and Preservation

Blockchain can facilitate the creation of decentralized digital archives for cultural heritage, ensuring long-term preservation and accessibility. Digital content, such as historical documents, photographs, audio recordings, and videos, can be stored on the blockchain, guaranteeing data integrity and protection against tampering.

Intellectual Property Rights

Blockchain-based smart contracts can be utilized to manage intellectual property rights for cultural creations. Artists, authors, and creators can register their works on the blockchain, enabling transparent and automated royalty distribution and licensing while protecting their rights from infringement.

Fighting Illicit Trade and Looting

Blockchain can help combat the illegal trade and looting of cultural artifacts by providing an immutable record of ownership history. This transparency can deter potential buyers from engaging in illicit transactions and make it easier to identify stolen artifacts.

Cultural Funding and Donations

Blockchain-based crowdfunding platforms can support cultural projects and initiatives. By leveraging cryptocurrencies and smart contracts, these platforms can provide transparent funding mechanisms, enabling donors to see how their contributions are used for culture protection efforts.

Language and Cultural Preservation

Blockchain can contribute to language and cultural preservation by providing a secure and decentralized platform for storing and sharing indigenous languages, traditions, and customs. It can support collaborative efforts to document and revitalize endangered cultural practices.

Interoperability and Collaboration

Interoperable blockchain networks can facilitate collaboration between different cultural institutions, governments, and communities. This cooperation can lead to more comprehensive cultural preservation strategies and efficient data sharing while respecting the autonomy and identity of each participant.

Digital Identity for Cultural Artifacts

Blockchain-based digital identities can be assigned to cultural artifacts, which include detailed information about the object's historical significance, cultural context, and preservation status. This information can be easily accessible and verifiable, aiding in research and cultural exchange.

Disaster Recovery for Cultural Assets

Blockchain technology can play a role in tracking and recovering cultural assets after natural disasters or conflicts. The tamper-resistant nature of the blockchain can provide critical evidence of provenance to aid in recovery and restoration efforts.

While the application of blockchain technology for culture protection holds great potential, it is essential to approach such initiatives with sensitivity to cultural diversity, ethical considerations, and the involvement of local communities and stakeholders. Collaborative efforts, combining technological innovations with traditional cultural practices, can ensure that blockchain's application aligns with the unique needs and aspirations of each cultural context.

Provenance and Authenticity

Implementing provenance and authenticity using a blockchain platform involves leveraging the blockchain's immutable and transparent nature to create a reliable record of an artifact's origin, ownership, and transaction history. Technical details on how this can be achieved include:

- **Unique Identifiers (Tokens)**: Each cultural artifact can be represented as a unique digital token on the blockchain. These tokens serve as a digital representation of the physical artifact and include metadata such as a description, provenance, and historical data.
- **Token Creation and Minting**: When a new cultural artifact is discovered or registered, a corresponding token is created on the blockchain. This process is often referred to as *minting* the token. Metadata about the artifact is associated with the token, including details about its provenance and authenticity.
- **Ownership Transfer (Token Transfer)**: When the artifact changes ownership, a token transfer occurs on the blockchain, indicating the new owner. This transfer is recorded as a transaction on the blockchain and is immutable, providing a clear chain of custody.

- **Digital Signatures and Verification**: Stakeholders involved in the transfer or registration of cultural artifacts can use digital signatures to validate their actions. Digital signatures ensure the authenticity of the transactions and prevent unauthorized changes to the token's information.

- **Decentralized Storage of Artifact Information**: Metadata, images, and information about the cultural artifact can be stored either directly on the blockchain or better in off-chain decentralized storage systems (such as IPFS). This ensures that the data is not only tamper-resistant but also accessible without relying on a single centralized authority.

- **Timestamps and Audit Trail**: Each transaction on the blockchain is timestamped and linked to the previous transaction, forming an unalterable audit trail. This ensures the historical accuracy and integrity of the artifact's provenance and transaction history.

- **Consensus Mechanisms**: The chosen consensus mechanism (e.g., Proof of Work, Proof of Stake) ensures that all participants in the blockchain network agree on the validity of transactions. This consensus mechanism maintains the integrity of the provenance and authenticity records.

- **Interoperability with Existing Systems**: To achieve broader adoption, the blockchain solution should be designed to integrate with existing cultural heritage databases and systems. APIs and smart contracts can facilitate data exchange between the blockchain and other platforms.

- **Access Controls and Permissions**: Access controls and permissions mechanisms can be implemented to ensure that only authorized parties can update or view specific artifact information. This prevents unauthorized modifications and protects sensitive data.

- **Public and Private Blockchain Considerations**: Depending on the requirements, a public blockchain (e.g., Ethereum) or a private/permissioned blockchain (e.g., Kaleido, Hyperledger Fabric) may be chosen. Public blockchains offer transparency, while private blockchains provide more control over network participants and data access.

- **Off-Chain Verification Sources**: External verification sources, such as historical records, experts, or cultural institutions, can be linked to the blockchain to provide additional evidence of an artifact's provenance and authenticity. These verifications can be stored as off-chain data but linked to the blockchain for reference.

- **Metadata Standards**: Defining standardized metadata formats is essential to ensure consistency and interoperability across various cultural artifacts. Adopting metadata standards helps in the seamless exchange of information between different blockchain networks or databases.

By leveraging blockchain technology and these technical aspects, the provenance and authenticity of cultural artifacts can be better preserved and shared with the broader public, researchers, and enthusiasts. This approach ensures that historical and cultural information is verifiable, transparent, and protected against unauthorized alterations, thereby fostering a greater sense of trust and confidence in the preservation of cultural heritage.

Below is a simplified example of a smart contract in Solidity representing the provenance and authenticity of cultural artifacts. This smart contract enables the minting of tokens representing unique artifacts and tracks ownership transfers through blockchain transactions.

```
contract CulturalArtifactRegistry {
    address public owner;

    struct Artifact {
        string name;
        string provenance;
        uint256 tokenId;
        address currentOwner;
        uint256 transferTimestamp;
    }

    mapping(uint256 => Artifact) public artifacts;
    uint256 public totalArtifacts;

    event ArtifactMinted(...);
    event ArtifactTransferred(...);

    function mintArtifact(string memory name, string memory provenance)
        public
    function transferArtifact(uint256 tokenId, address newOwner) public
}
```

In this smart contract, we have a `CulturalArtifactRegistry` contract that allows the minting and transfer of cultural artifact tokens. Each token (representing a cultural artifact) is created with specific metadata, including its name, provenance, and an identifier (`tokenId`). When a new artifact is minted, it is assigned a unique tokenId, and the ownership is set to the contract deployer (owner).

The `mintArtifact` function enables the owner to create a new cultural artifact with a given name and provenance. The `transferArtifact` function allows the current owner to transfer the ownership of an artifact (specified by tokenId) to a new owner. The transfer is recorded as a transaction on the blockchain, capturing the previous and new owners' addresses and the timestamp of the transfer.

This is a basic example to illustrate the concept of provenance and authenticity using a smart contract. In a real-world implementation, additional functionality, access controls, and integration with other systems would be required for a more comprehensive and secure cultural artifact registry.

Digital Archives and Preservation

Creating a digital archives and preservation system using blockchain involves securely storing and preserving digital cultural content, such as historical documents, photos, audio, and videos. Here are some technical details and a code example of how such a system can be implemented using IPFS (InterPlanetary File System) for decentralized storage and a smart contract on Ethereum for the metadata and ownership tracking.

Technical components of the digital archive solution include:

- **IPFS for Decentralized Storage**: IPFS is used to store the actual digital content (files) of cultural artifacts in a distributed and decentralized manner. IPFS hashes are recorded on a smart contract to establish a link between the blockchain and the off-chain content.
- **Smart Contract for Metadata and Ownership Tracking**: Smart contracts store metadata related to each cultural artifact, including its name, description, creator, timestamps, and

the IPFS hash representing the location of the digital file. Smart contracts also track ownership transfers when artifacts are bought, sold, or donated.

■ **Access Control Mechanisms**: Access control mechanisms can be implemented in smart contracts to manage who can upload, update, or view the digital content and metadata. This ensures that only authorized individuals can contribute to the archive.

■ **Decentralized Governance**: Smart contracts can be designed to include decentralized governance mechanisms, allowing the community to collectively decide which artifacts to add or remove from the archive.

Code Example

Below is a simplified example of a smart contract in Solidity representing a digital archives and preservation system.

```
contract DigitalArchives {
    address public owner;
    IPFSStorage public ipfsStorage;

    struct Artifact {
        string name;
        string description;
        address creator;
        uint256 timestamp;
        bytes32 ipfsHash;
        address currentOwner;
    }

    mapping(uint256 => Artifact) public artifacts;
    uint256 public totalArtifacts;

    event ArtifactAdded(...);
    event ArtifactTransferred(...);

    function addArtifact(string memory name, string memory description,
        bytes32 ipfsHash) public
    function transferArtifact(uint256 artifactId, address newOwner) public
}
```

In this example, we have a `DigitalArchives` contract representing the smart contract for the digital archives. The contract allows users to add new artifacts with a name, description, and IPFS hash representing the digital content's location. The `IPFSStorage` contract (not shown in detail) is a separate contract responsible for storing the actual content on IPFS and returns a success flag upon successful storage.

When an artifact is added, its metadata is recorded on the blockchain, and the IPFS hash is stored. This link between the blockchain and IPFS ensures that the metadata is accessible on-chain while the actual content is stored off-chain in a decentralized manner. The smart contract also allows ownership transfers between users, ensuring proper tracking of artifact ownership.

Note that this is a simplified example, and a complete implementation would require additional features, security considerations, and access controls. Additionally, the `IPFSStorage` contract's implementation would involve integrating with the actual IPFS storage system or another decentralized storage solution.

Intellectual Property Rights

Implementing intellectual property rights (IPR) using blockchain involves creating a system that allows artists, authors, and creators to register and protect their intellectual property, manage licensing agreements, and receive royalties transparently. Below are technical details and a code example of how IPR can be implemented using a smart contract on Ethereum. Technical details of an IPR solution include:

- **IPR Registration Smart Contract**: A smart contract on Ethereum can be designed to facilitate the registration of intellectual property, such as artworks, literary works, or music compositions. Creators can submit their work's details and metadata to the smart contract.
- **Digital Signature and Verification**: Creators' submissions can be digitally signed to verify the authenticity of their claims and establish a link between the creator's Ethereum address and their intellectual property.
- **License Agreements as Smart Contracts**: Smart contracts can be used to create licensing agreements between creators and users interested in using their intellectual property. These agreements can include terms, conditions, and royalties.
- **Royalty Distribution**: When users utilize the licensed intellectual property, the smart contract can automatically trigger royalty payments to the creator's Ethereum address based on predefined conditions.
- **Access Control and Permissions**: Access controls and permissions mechanisms can be implemented in the smart contract to ensure that only authorized users can interact with specific intellectual property registrations or licensing agreements.
- **Interoperability with IPFS or Off-Chain Storage**: For storing intellectual property content (e.g., digital files), the IPFS or other off-chain storage can be used, and the corresponding IPFS hash can be recorded on the smart contract.

Code Example

Below is a simplified example of a smart contract in Solidity representing an IPR management system.

```
contract IPRManagement {
    address public owner;

    struct IntellectualProperty {
        string title;
        string description;
        address creator;
        bytes32 contentHash; // IPFS hash of the content
        uint256 registrationTimestamp;
    }

    mapping(uint256 => IntellectualProperty) public intellectualProperties;
    uint256 public totalProperties;

    event IntellectualPropertyRegistered(...);

    function registerIntellectualProperty(string memory title, string
        memory description, bytes32 contentHash) public
}
```

In this example, we have an `IPRManagement` contract representing the smart contract for IPR management. Creators can register their intellectual property by providing a title, description, and the IPFS hash of the content (e.g., digital file) they wish to protect. The contract records the metadata and content hash on the blockchain, establishing a link between the creator and their intellectual property.

This is a basic example to illustrate the concept of IPR management using a smart contract. In a real-world implementation, additional features like licensing agreements, royalty distribution, and access controls would be added for a complete IPR management system. Furthermore, additional verification mechanisms can be integrated to ensure the authenticity of the creator's claims, such as digital signatures or integration with external registration authorities.

Fighting Illicit Trade and Looting

Fighting illicit trade and looting using blockchain involves establishing an immutable and transparent record of ownership for cultural artifacts. By creating a blockchain-based registry of artifacts and their ownership history, it becomes more challenging for illicit actors to trade or sell stolen cultural items without raising suspicion. Below are technical details and a code example of how this can be achieved using a blockchain smart contract and IPFS for content storage.

- **Artifacts Registry Smart Contract**: The smart contract maintains a registry of all cultural artifacts, including their unique identifiers, metadata, and ownership history.
- **Unique Identifiers (Tokens)**: Each cultural artifact is represented as a unique digital token on the blockchain. These tokens link to metadata and IPFS hashes representing the content.
- **Ownership Transfer (Token Transfer)**: Whenever an artifact changes ownership, a token transfer occurs on the blockchain, updating the current owner information in the smart contract.
- **Public and Private Access**: The registry can be designed with different access levels, allowing the public to view the artifact information while restricting certain actions (e.g., transfer) to authorized users.
- **Interoperability with External Databases**: To enhance security and traceability, the smart contract can integrate with external databases (e.g., national cultural heritage authorities) to verify and validate artifact data.

Code Example

Below is a simplified example of a smart contract in Solidity representing a cultural artifact registry to fight illicit trade and looting.

```
contract ArtifactRegistry {
    address public owner;
    IPFSStorage public ipfsStorage;

    struct Artifact {
        string name;
        string description;
        address currentOwner;
        uint256 tokenId;
        uint256 transferTimestamp;
    }
```

```
mapping(uint256 => Artifact) public artifacts;
uint256 public totalArtifacts;

event ArtifactMinted(...);
event ArtifactTransferred(...);

function mintArtifact(string memory name, string memory description,
    bytes32 contentHash) public
function transferArtifact(uint256 tokenId, address newOwner) public
}
```

In this example, we have an `ArtifactRegistry` contract representing the smart contract for the cultural artifact registry. When a new artifact is minted, it is assigned a unique tokenId, and the ownership is set to the contract deployer (owner). The content of the artifact can be stored on IPFS (not shown in detail) and linked to the smart contract using its IPFS hash.

Whenever an artifact changes ownership, a token transfer occurs on the blockchain, updating the current owner information in the smart contract. This creates a transparent and immutable record of ownership history, making it more difficult for illicit trade and looting of cultural artifacts.

Note that this is a simplified example to illustrate the concept of fighting illicit trade and looting using a smart contract-based artifact registry. In a real-world implementation, additional features, access controls, and integration with external databases or authorities would be required for a more comprehensive and secure solution.

Cultural Funding and Donations

Implementing cultural funding and donations using blockchain involves creating a transparent and auditable platform for crowdfunding cultural projects and accepting donations. Blockchain can provide an immutable record of contributions and ensure that funds are used as intended. Below are technical details and a code example of how this can be achieved using a blockchain-based smart contract.

- **Crowdfunding Smart Contract**: The smart contract acts as a crowdfunding platform, allowing cultural projects to create funding campaigns and receive donations from contributors.
- **Project Registration and Details**: Cultural projects can register on the platform by providing details such as project title, description, funding goal, and duration of the campaign.
- **Donation Mechanism**: Contributors can donate funds to support a specific project by sending their donations to the smart contract address.
- **Funds Disbursement**: Upon reaching the funding goal or the campaign end date, the smart contract can automatically disburse the funds to the project creator, ensuring that funds are released only when the campaign is successful.
- **Transparency and Auditability**: Contributions and disbursements are recorded on the blockchain, providing transparency and allowing stakeholders to audit the flow of funds.
- **Refund Mechanism** (optional): If the funding goal is not met within the campaign duration, the smart contract can allow contributors to reclaim their donations through a refund mechanism.

Code Example

Below is a simplified example of a crowdfunding smart contract in Solidity representing cultural funding and donations.

```
contract CulturalFunding {
    address public owner;

    struct Project {
        string title;
        string description;
        address creator;
        uint256 fundingGoal;
        uint256 deadline;
        uint256 totalFunds;
        bool campaignClosed;
    }

    mapping(uint256 => Project) public projects;
    uint256 public totalProjects;

    event ProjectCreated(...);
    event DonationReceived(...);
    event FundsDisbursed(...);

    function createProject(string memory title, string memory
        description, uint256 fundingGoal, uint256 deadline) public
    function donate(uint256 projectId) public payable
    function closeCampaign(uint256 projectId) public onlyOwner
}
```

In this example, we have a `CulturalFunding` contract representing the smart contract for cultural funding and donations. Cultural projects can be registered by creators using the `createProject` function, specifying the title, description, funding goal, and deadline for the campaign. Contributors can donate funds to a specific project using the `donate` function, which is marked as payable because it accepts payments. Once the campaign deadline has passed, the project owner (or contract owner) can close the campaign using the `closeCampaign` function. If the funding goal is met, the contract disburses the funds to the project creator; otherwise, it returns the funds to the donors.

This is a basic example to illustrate the concept of cultural funding and donations using a crowdfunding smart contract. In practice, additional features like monitoring and reporting mechanisms, access controls, and security measures would be required for a more comprehensive and secure funding platform.

Language and Cultural Preservation

Implementing language and cultural preservation using blockchain involves creating a decentralized platform for preserving and promoting languages and cultural heritage. Blockchain can help maintain immutable records of cultural content, provide incentives for contributions, and ensure access to cultural resources. Below are technical details and a code example of how this can be achieved using a blockchain-based smart contract and IPFS for content storage.

- **Cultural Content Registry Smart Contract**: The smart contract acts as a registry for storing cultural content, such as texts, audio, video, and other artifacts related to language and cultural preservation.
- **Metadata and Content Storage**: The smart contract records metadata (e.g., title, description, author, language, and timestamp) along with the IPFS hash of the content, which is stored off-chain on IPFS.
- **Content Verification and Authenticity**: Creators and contributors can digitally sign their contributions to verify the authenticity and authorship of the content.
- **Incentives for Contributors**: Incentive mechanisms, such as reward tokens or reputation systems, can be integrated into the smart contract to encourage contributors to share their cultural knowledge.
- **Decentralized Governance**: Community members can participate in governance decisions, such as content curation, addition, or removal.
- **Access Control and Copyright Protection**: Access controls can be implemented in the smart contract to manage content visibility and ensure compliance with copyright and IPR.

Code Example

Below is a simplified example of a smart contract in Solidity representing a language and cultural preservation platform.

```
contract CulturalContentRegistry {
    address public owner;
    IPFSStorage public ipfsStorage;

    struct CulturalContent {
        string title;
        string description;
        string language;
        address author;
        bytes32 contentHash; // IPFS hash of the content
        uint256 timestamp;
    }

    mapping(uint256 => CulturalContent) public contentRegistry;
    uint256 public totalContent;

    event ContentAdded(...);

    function addContent(string memory title, string memory description,
        string memory language, bytes32 contentHash) public
}
```

In this example, we have a `CulturalContentRegistry` contract representing the smart contract for preserving cultural content. When new content is added, it is assigned a unique contentId, and the metadata, along with the IPFS hash representing the content, is stored on the blockchain. The actual content is stored off-chain on IPFS.

Contributors can add cultural content using the `addContent` function, providing details such as title, description, language, and the IPFS hash of the content. Digital signatures or authentication mechanisms can be integrated to verify the authenticity of the content and its author.

Note that this is a simplified example to illustrate the concept of language and cultural preservation using a smart contract-based content registry. In a real-world implementation, additional features, access controls, content curation mechanisms, and governance systems would be required to create a comprehensive platform for preserving and promoting languages and cultural heritage. Additionally, the `IPFSStorage` contract's implementation would involve integrating with the actual IPFS storage system or another decentralized storage solution.

More details can be found in this article by the Coin Telegraph, which describes how researchers have developed a blockchain-based verification service for cultural artifacts. The solution represents a combination of human expertise, NFTs, and blockchain technology to help humanity protect its priceless artifacts from theft and looting: https://cointelegraph.com/news/researchers-develop-blockchain-verification-service-for-cultural-artifacts.

Digital Identity for Cultural Artifacts

Implementing digital identity for cultural artifacts using blockchain involves creating a decentralized and tamper-proof system to establish the provenance and authenticity of cultural artifacts. By assigning a unique digital identity to each artifact and recording its history on the blockchain, stakeholders can verify its origin, ownership, and historical significance. Below are technical details and a code example of how this can be achieved using a blockchain-based smart contract and IPFS for content storage.

- **Digital Identity Smart Contract**: The smart contract serves as a digital identity registry for cultural artifacts. Each artifact is assigned a unique identifier (token) representing its digital identity on the blockchain.
- **Provenance and Ownership History**: The smart contract maintains a record of each artifact's provenance and ownership history, including information about previous owners and transactions.
- **Metadata and Content Storage**: The contract records metadata (e.g., title, description, age, culture, historical context) and the IPFS hash representing the content (e.g., images, documents) of each artifact.
- **Digital Signature and Verification**: Authenticity and provenance claims can be verified through digital signatures from trusted authorities, museums, or experts.
- **Access Control and Privacy**: Access controls can be implemented to manage data visibility, ensuring that sensitive information is accessible only to authorized users or institutions.
- **Interoperability and Collaboration**: The system can facilitate collaboration between cultural institutions, researchers, and experts, allowing them to contribute to the identification and verification process.

Code Example

Below is a simplified example of a smart contract in Solidity representing a digital identity registry for cultural artifacts.

```
contract ArtifactIdentityRegistry {
    address public owner;

    struct ArtifactIdentity {
        string title;
        string description;
```

```
        string culture;
        address currentOwner;
        bytes32 contentHash; // IPFS hash of the content
        uint256 timestamp;
    }

    mapping(uint256 => ArtifactIdentity) public artifacts;
    uint256 public totalArtifacts;

    event ArtifactRegistered(...);

    function registerArtifact(string memory title, string memory
        description, string memory culture, bytes32 contentHash) public
}
```

In this example, we have an `ArtifactIdentityRegistry` contract representing the smart contract for digital identity and provenance tracking of cultural artifacts. Each cultural artefact is assigned a unique artifactId, and the metadata, including title, description, culture, and the IPFS hash representing the content, is stored on the blockchain. The actual content (e.g., images, documents) is stored off-chain on IPFS, and its IPFS hash is recorded on the smart contract.

Cultural institutions, experts, or owners can register artifacts using the `registerArtifact` function, providing relevant details and the IPFS hash representing the artifact's content.

Note that this is a simplified example to illustrate the concept of digital identity for cultural artifacts using a smart contract-based identity registry. In a real-world implementation, additional features like digital signature verification, access controls, interoperability mechanisms, and collaboration features would be required for a more comprehensive and secure system for managing and verifying the identities of cultural artifacts. Additionally, the `IPFSStorage` contract's implementation would involve integrating with the actual IPFS storage system or another decentralized storage solution.

Disaster Recovery for Cultural Assets

Implementing disaster recovery for cultural assets using blockchain involves creating a resilient and distributed system to safeguard cultural assets and information in the event of natural disasters or emergencies. By leveraging blockchain's immutability and decentralized nature, critical cultural data can be stored securely and redundantly, ensuring its preservation and accessibility even during catastrophic events. Below are technical details and a code example of how this can be achieved using a blockchain-based smart contract and IPFS for content storage.

- **Disaster-Resilient Data Storage Smart Contract**: The smart contract serves as a disaster-resilient data storage platform for cultural assets. It ensures data redundancy and integrity across multiple nodes in the network.
- **Data Replication and Backup**: Data, such as digital representations of artifacts, historical documents, or cultural information, can be replicated and backed up across multiple IPFS nodes to ensure availability even if some nodes are affected by disasters.
- **Decentralized Network of Nodes**: IPFS provides a decentralized network of nodes that store and distribute data. Cultural assets can be stored across multiple nodes to prevent data loss due to a single point of failure.
- **Time-Stamped Records**: The smart contract records time-stamped information about data updates and backups, enabling the recovery of historical versions of cultural assets.

■ **Community Participation**: Cultural institutions, experts, and stakeholders can actively participate in data verification and recovery efforts, ensuring accurate and reliable information.

■ **Public and Private Access**: The smart contract can have public access for viewing publicly available cultural data and private access controls for sensitive or restricted data.

Code Example

Below is a simplified example of a smart contract in Solidity representing a disaster-resilient data storage platform for cultural assets.

```
contract CulturalDataStorage {
    address public owner;
    IPFSStorage public ipfsStorage;

    struct CulturalAsset {
        string title;
        string description;
        bytes32 contentHash; // IPFS hash of the content
        uint256 timestamp;
    }

    mapping(uint256 => CulturalAsset) public culturalAssets;
    uint256 public totalCulturalAssets;

    event AssetStored(...);

    function storeCulturalAsset(string memory title, string memory
        description, bytes32 contentHash) public
}
```

In this example, we have a `CulturalDataStorage` contract representing the smart contract for disaster-resilient data storage of cultural assets. Cultural assets, such as digital representations of artifacts or historical documents, can be registered using the `storeCulturalAsset` function, providing relevant details and the IPFS hash representing the asset's content. The actual content is stored off-chain on IPFS, and its IPFS hash is recorded on the smart contract.

Note that this is a simplified example to illustrate the concept of disaster recovery for cultural assets using a smart contract-based data storage platform. In a real-world implementation, additional features like data replication, access controls, data versioning, community participation mechanisms, and integration with disaster recovery protocols would be required to create a comprehensive and resilient system for safeguarding cultural assets during emergencies. Additionally, the `IPFSStorage` contract's implementation would involve integrating with the actual IPFS storage system or another decentralized storage solution.

Chapter 10

Decentralized Finance (DeFi)

Decentralized Finance, popularly known as DeFi, represents a fundamental shift in the world of finance, effectively challenging the traditional financial systems by leveraging blockchain technology. It is an innovative system where financial products become universally accessible, regardless of one's geographic location, and without the need for intermediaries such as banks or brokers.

At its core, DeFi embodies a financial system by the people, for the people, and of the people, unbound by the conventional barriers of geography, bureaucracy, and socioeconomic status. It seeks to transform the age-old financial system into a permissionless, open-source, and transparent ecosystem that operates without any central authority.

DeFi applications are primarily built on top of blockchain platforms, with Ethereum being the most prominent one due to its smart contract capabilities. These applications offer services like lending and borrowing, stablecoins, decentralized exchanges (DEXs), derivatives, payments, and more. All these are traditionally provided by banks or financial institutions, but with DeFi, they are programmatically run through smart contracts.

What truly sets DeFi apart is its potential to democratize finance. It can eliminate barriers to financial services, enabling anyone with a smartphone and an internet connection to access financial services. Furthermore, its transparent and open nature has the potential to enhance financial inclusion and equality. However, it's not without risks and challenges, such as regulatory scrutiny, security vulnerabilities, and scalability issues, which need to be addressed for it to achieve its full potential.

Overall, Decentralized Finance is at the forefront of the blockchain revolution, promising to redefine our financial systems with increased accessibility, efficiency, and transparency.

Definition of Decentralized Finance (DeFi)

Decentralized Finance, or DeFi from now on, is a term that embodies a variety of financial applications based on cryptocurrency or blockchain technology geared toward disrupting traditional financial intermediaries. The term "decentralized" refers to the system not being controlled or governed by a single entity or authority such as banks, governments, or financial institutions. Instead, the control is distributed across the network, which is typically powered by blockchain technology.

DOI: 10.4324/9781003491934-10

DeFi aims to build a new financial system that is open to everyone and does not require intermediaries like banks or brokers. This new system is typically built on public blockchains, the most common of which is Ethereum, due to its advanced smart contract capabilities that automate the execution of financial transactions.

Financial services like lending, borrowing, trading in derivative products, insurance, and more, traditionally provided by centralized financial institutions, are offered in a decentralized manner on the blockchain through DeFi applications. These applications run on smart contracts, which are self-executing contracts with the terms of the agreement written into code.

This means that financial transactions, agreements, and contracts can be automatically validated, executed, and enforced on the blockchain, with no need for intermediaries, leading to cheaper, faster, and more efficient financial services. Furthermore, since the system is decentralized, it is theoretically resistant to censorship and has the potential to be more secure and resilient than traditional financial systems.

It's important to note that while DeFi has the potential to revolutionize the financial industry, it is still a nascent field with various technical and regulatory challenges that need to be overcome. However, its promise of a more inclusive, efficient, and transparent financial system makes it a fascinating area of innovation in the blockchain space.

DeFi vs Traditional Finance

Table 10.1 offers a comparison between traditional finance and DeFi on several key parameters.

While DeFi offers numerous advantages over traditional finance, it's important to remember that it's still in its early stages, with many risks and uncertainties. It also needs to overcome significant barriers, including regulatory acceptance and the general wariness of people towards new financial systems. But with its potential for democratizing access to finance, DeFi could play a transformative role in the global economy.

History and Evolution of DeFi

The evolution of DeFi has its roots in the invention of Bitcoin, the first-ever cryptocurrency, and blockchain technology by Satoshi Nakamoto in 2008. Bitcoin introduced the world to a decentralized and secure form of digital money, thus sowing the seeds for the development of DeFi.

However, the real evolution of DeFi can be traced back to the development of Ethereum, the second-largest cryptocurrency by market capitalization. In 2015, Ethereum introduced smart contracts, self-executing contracts with the terms of the agreement directly written into code, onto its blockchain. This innovation was pivotal as it opened the door for developers to create decentralized applications (dApps) that could automate financial transactions, leading to the beginning of DeFi.

Figure 10.1 shows the key milestones in DeFi's evolution.

Chronologically, the significant milestones in DeFi's evolution are:

1. **MakerDAO and DAI (2015):** MakerDAO was one of the first projects in the DeFi space. It introduced DAI, a stablecoin pegged to the US dollar, which could be loaned out with interest.

Table 10.1 Key differences between traditional and decentralized finance

Parameter	Traditional Finance	Decentralized Finance
Centralization vs. Decentralization	Traditional finance operates on a centralized model, meaning transactions have to go through intermediaries such as banks, brokers, or regulatory bodies.	DeFi operates on a decentralized model where transactions happen peer-to-peer, eliminating the need for intermediaries.
Access and Inclusion	Traditional finance systems often exclude a significant portion of the global population that do not have access to basic banking facilities.	DeFi aims to promote "financial inclusion", providing anyone with an internet connection access to financial services.
Transparency	Traditional finance systems are often criticized for their opaque nature. The inner workings of transactions and decision-making processes are usually not public knowledge.	DeFi operates on blockchain technology, which by its nature is open and transparent. Anyone can verify the transactions and the protocols' codes.
Speed and Availability	Traditional financial systems often involve time-consuming processes and paperwork, and services might not be available 24/7.	In contrast, DeFi applications run on the blockchain are available round the clock without any downtime.
Ownership	In traditional finance, your assets are held by a third party like a bank, and you are essentially entrusting them with your money.	In the DeFi world, you have complete control over your assets. Thanks to cryptographic security, only the holder of the private key has access to the assets.
Interoperability	Traditional finance DeFi lacks a level of easy interoperability between banks and products within an institute, for the exception of international circuits like SWIFT and IBAN for international payments.	DeFi platforms are built on blockchain standards that make them interoperable, meaning one DeFi application can easily interact with another. This interoperability allows for the creation of complex financial instruments.
Regulation	Traditional financial systems are heavily regulated with a clear framework in place to protect consumers from scams, fraud, and market manipulation.	DeFi is still in a regulatory grey area. While this provides greater freedom, it also exposes users to more risk.

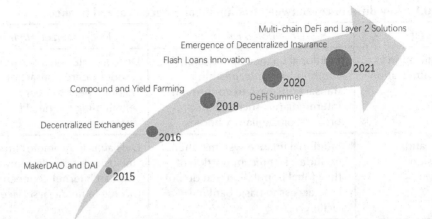

Figure 10.1 DeFi's evolution timeline

2. **Decentralized Exchanges (2016)**: EtherDelta, launched in 2016, was one of the first decentralized exchanges (DEX), allowing users to trade Ethereum tokens directly with one another. Later, Uniswap and Sushiswap improved upon this model and are now among the most prominent DEXs.

3. **Compound and Yield Farming (2018)**: Compound introduced an algorithmic, autonomous interest rate protocol, which lets users earn interest on and borrow Ethereum tokens. The practice of "yield farming" – earning yield on crypto assets that are lent out on DeFi platforms – started gaining traction around this time.

4. **DeFi Summer (2020)**: DeFi truly entered the mainstream in the summer of 2020, with the total value locked (TVL) in DeFi protocols surging from around $1 billion in June 2020 to over $40 billion by the end of the year. Yield farming and the introduction of governance tokens were significant drivers of this growth.

5. **Flash Loans Innovation (2020)**: DeFi protocols introduced flash loans, an innovation that allows borrowers to take out loans without collateral, provided the loan is repaid within the same transaction block. This allows for arbitrage opportunities and other complex financial maneuvers.

6. **Emergence of Decentralized Insurance (2020–2021)**: The emergence of decentralized insurance platforms like Nexus Mutual represented another step in the maturation of the DeFi space. These platforms allow users to hedge against risks in the DeFi space, including smart contract bugs and other technical risks.

7. **Multi-chain DeFi and Layer 2 Solutions (2021 onwards)**: To mitigate issues with scalability and high transaction fees on Ethereum, DeFi started to expand to other blockchains like Binance Smart Chain (BSC), Polkadot, and Layer 2 solutions like Polygon.

The evolution of DeFi is ongoing and fast-paced, with new protocols and platforms being developed constantly. The field is ripe with innovation as it seeks to redefine our financial systems, promising to make them more inclusive, efficient, and transparent. However, it's not without its challenges, including regulatory scrutiny, scalability issues, and security vulnerabilities, which the DeFi community continues to work on.

These milestones illustrate the rapid growth and innovation in the DeFi space. While it is still relatively young, DeFi's impact on the financial world has already been substantial, and its potential for future development is enormous.

Technical Foundation of DeFi

The technical foundations of DeFi are deeply intertwined with blockchain technology, particularly smart contracts, which are fundamental to most DeFi applications. The technology pyramid in Figure 10.2 shows the dependencies of key technical components in a DeFi platform, starting with the foundational blockchain, all the way up to dApps and wallets.

At its core, DeFi is built on **blockchain** technology. As a decentralized ledger of all transactions across a peer-to-peer network, a blockchain network such as Bitcoin or Ethereum allows participants to confirm transactions without the need for central authority. Blockchain technology is transparent, immutable, and provides security against fraud, making it ideal for financial transactions.

Smart contracts are self-executing contracts with the terms of the agreement between buyer and seller being directly written into lines of code. In the context of DeFi, smart contracts automate financial transactions and agreements, reducing the need for intermediaries and making the process more efficient. Ethereum was the first blockchain to incorporate smart contracts and remains the leading platform for DeFi applications.

DeFi relies on **cryptocurrency tokens**, which represent certain values or rights within a given ecosystem. In Ethereum's DeFi ecosystem, the ERC-20 standard is used for fungible tokens, and ERC-721 is used for non-fungible tokens (NFT). These standards ensure that different tokens can interact in a predictable way, creating a unified environment.

Decentralized applications (**dApp**) are applications that run on a decentralized network, typically a blockchain and are governed by smart contracts. Most DeFi services are dApps that allow users to perform financial activities like lending, borrowing, or trading assets.

Decentralized exchanges (**DEX**) are platforms that allow peer-to-peer trades of digital assets using smart contracts. They represent a key component of the DeFi ecosystem, enabling users to maintain control over their assets rather than entrusting them to a centralized entity.

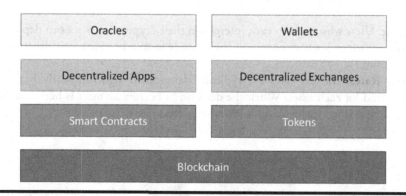

Figure 10.2 Technology components of a DeFi platform

In DeFi, smart contracts often need to access real-world data, which is not natively available on the blockchain. This is provided by **oracles**, which are third-party services that send data to smart contracts. Reliable oracles are critical for many DeFi applications, including those involving derivatives, loans, and prediction markets.

To interact with DeFi applications, users need **wallets** that can interact with smart contracts. MetaMask, for instance, is a popular Ethereum wallet that is used to interact with the various DeFi dApps on the Ethereum blockchain.

These technical foundations allow DeFi to function as a decentralized, open, and efficient financial system. It's these elements that are fueling the ongoing innovation and development within the DeFi sector.

Financial Components of the DeFi Ecosystem

The DeFi ecosystem is composed of the various technical components described in the previous sections, each serving a critical role in building a decentralized, open, and efficient financial system. These components work together to create an open and permissionless financial system that anyone with an internet connection can access. They enable the creation of financial products and services that are more transparent, efficient, and inclusive than those in the traditional financial system.

In this section, we are going to look at the financial components that represent the ecosystem of applications with which users interact and transact. These components provide user interfaces, often as a mobile app, and implement sophisticated algorithms for the several financial products that the DeFi platform makes available to its customers.

Lending and Borrowing

Lending and borrowing products are a fundamental part of the DeFi ecosystem. These products allow users to lend and borrow cryptocurrencies directly on the blockchain, bypassing traditional intermediaries like banks. These apps use smart contracts to create a decentralized marketplace where lenders and borrowers can interact directly. Figure 10.3 shows how these apps generally work.

The process can be summarized as follows:

1. **Lending**: Users who want to earn interest on their cryptocurrencies can deposit them into a lending platform's smart contract. These funds form a liquidity pool that borrowers can borrow from.
2. **Interest Rates**: Interest rates are typically determined algorithmically based on supply and demand for each asset. When the demand to borrow an asset is high, the interest rate increases, and when the demand is low, the interest rate decreases.

Figure 10.3   Lending and borrowing process

3. **Borrowing**: Borrowers can take out a loan by providing collateral, usually in another cryptocurrency, to the smart contract. The collateral is usually over-collateralized, meaning it is worth more than the loan, to protect lenders in case the borrower fails to repay.

Liquidation: If the value of the collateral falls below a certain threshold, due to market fluctuations, the smart contract can automatically liquidate it to repay the lenders. This mechanism protects the lenders' interests.

There are a few key players in this space that are worth attention. To be clear, this is not an invite to make any form of investment with any of these platforms. The list that follows is purely illustrative of some of the DeFi platforms that are available in the market. Any potential decision to sign up and transact on these systems is entirely personal.

Aave (https://aave.com/) is a decentralized non-custodial money market protocol where users can participate as depositors (lenders) or borrowers. Depositors provide liquidity to the market to earn a passive income, while borrowers can borrow in an over-collified or under-collateralized way. Aave also introduces features like flash loans.

Compound (https://compound.finance/) is an algorithmic, autonomous interest rate protocol, allowing users to supply and borrow cryptocurrencies. Users can earn COMP tokens, the platform's native governance token, for interacting with the platform, influencing the protocol's governance.

MakerDAO's DAI stablecoin system (https://makerdao.com/) allows users to lock in collateral like ETH, and generate DAI, a stablecoin pegged to the US dollar. This is effectively a loan. The system maintains the peg through a system of incentives and autonomous feedback mechanisms.

While not solely a lending platform, **Yearn** (https://yearn.fi/) automates yield farming strategies by shifting pooled funds between different lending platforms like Aave and Compound to maximize returns.

These platforms represent a new paradigm in lending and borrowing, enabling anyone in the world with an internet connection to earn interest or take out a loan. They offer open, permissionless, and transparent alternatives to traditional financial systems.

Creating a lending and borrowing algorithm for a DeFi application involves interacting with the smart contracts of a DeFi protocol using a library such as web3.py. However, actual lending and borrowing involve real financial transactions on the blockchain, which could incur costs and involve risks.

For safety and practical reasons, let's create a simplified example that demonstrates how an algorithm for lending and borrowing could be structured in Python.

This will be a basic demonstration and will not interact with the blockchain. It won't take into account important real-world factors such as interest rate calculations, collateral management, and risk assessments.

```python
class Account:
    def __init__(self, name):
        self.name = name
        self.balance = 0

    def deposit(self, amount):
        self.balance += amount
        return self.balance
```

```
    def withdraw(self, amount):
        if amount > self.balance:
            return "Insufficient balance"
        else:
            self.balance -= amount
            return self.balance

class DeFiPlatform:
    def __init__(self):
        self.accounts = []
        self.loans = {}

    def create_account(self, name):
        account = Account(name)
        self.accounts.append(account)
        return account

    def lend(self, lender_name, amount):
        lender = next(account for account in self.accounts if account.
            name == lender_name)
        if amount > lender.balance:
            return "Insufficient balance for lending"
        else:
            lender.balance -= amount
            self.loans[lender_name] = amount
            return f"{lender_name} has lent {amount}"

    def borrow(self, borrower_name, lender_name, amount):
        if lender_name not in self.loans or self.loans[lender_name]
            < amount:
            return "Loan amount not available"
        else:
            borrower = next(account for account in self.accounts if
                account.name == borrower_name)
            borrower.balance += amount
            self.loans[lender_name] -= amount
            return f"{borrower_name} has borrowed {amount} from
                {lender_name}"
```

This example creates a basic DeFi lending platform with lend and borrow functions. Customers, represented as Account objects with a name and balance, can deposit funds, lend out funds, and can borrow these funds.

Remember, this example is vastly simplified. Real DeFi protocols use complex smart contracts on the Ethereum blockchain, or other blockchains, to handle lending and borrowing, including mechanisms to handle variable interest rates, collateral management, liquidation, etc. Developing such smart contracts requires a solid understanding of blockchain technology, and the Solidity programming language (for Ethereum-based contracts), and must be done with utmost care due to the financial and security implications involved.

Decentralized Exchanges (DEX)

Decentralized exchanges (DEX) are a critical component of the DeFi ecosystem. Unlike traditional centralized exchanges (CEX), which are managed by a single authority, DEXs operate on blockchain technology and allow for direct peer-to-peer trading without intermediaries. Here is an overview of their operation and some notable examples.

Working principles include:

- **Peer-to-Peer Trading**: DEXs allow users to trade cryptocurrencies directly with one another. This is made possible by smart contracts that facilitate and automate the trading process.
- **Liquidity Pools**: Rather than using an order book like traditional exchanges, most DEXs use a model called Automated Market Making (AMM). In AMM, liquidity is provided by users who deposit an equal value of two tokens in a pool. These pools are then used to facilitate trading between users.
- **Decentralization and Custody**: DEXs are decentralized and non-custodial, meaning users maintain control of their assets until the moment the trade is executed. This differs from CEXs where users have to deposit their assets into the exchange's custody to trade.
- **Interoperability**: As most DEXs are built on the same blockchain (like Ethereum), they can easily interact with one another and with other DeFi protocols, offering more complex financial services.

Examples of DEXs:

- **Uniswap** is one of the most popular DEXs. It introduced the concept of Automated Market Makers to DeFi. Anyone can provide liquidity by adding tokens to Uniswap's liquidity pools and earn fees from the trading activity.
- **SushiSwap** is a fork of Uniswap with additional features. Apart from providing liquidity, users can also stake their SUSHI tokens to participate in the platform's governance.
- **Balancer** generalizes the concept of an AMM. Instead of a 50/50 split, Balancer allows liquidity providers to create liquidity pools with up to 8 tokens in any ratio.
- **Curve Finance** is optimized for stablecoin and same-asset trading, offering users lower slippage and fees for these types of trades.
- **Kyber Network** is an on-chain liquidity protocol that allows decentralized token swaps to be integrated into any application. It aggregates liquidity from various sources to provide competitive rates.

DEXs represent a significant step towards a truly decentralized financial system, where intermediaries are removed, and users have full control over their assets. While they offer increased privacy and control, they also come with their own risks and complexities, such as smart contract vulnerabilities and high transaction fees, that users need to be aware of.

A DEX is composed of several technical components that work together to facilitate peer-to-peer trades in a decentralized and automated manner. The **blockchain** network obviously serves as the underlying infrastructure for a DEX. Most DEXs are built on the Ethereum blockchain due to its robust smart contract capabilities, but others exist on different blockchains like BSC, Polkadot, and Solana.

Smart contracts on a DEX are used to automate the trading process, facilitating trustless exchange of tokens, managing liquidity pools, and executing trades when certain conditions are met.

Many DEXs utilize the concept of **AMMs** instead of a traditional order book to enable liquidity provision and price determination. AMMs allow liquidity providers to pool their assets into a smart contract, and prices are determined based on the ratio of assets in the pool.

In an AMM-based DEX, **liquidity pools** are a collection of funds locked in a smart contract. They are used to facilitate trading by providing liquidity and are essential for the operation of the DEX. Liquidity providers (LPs) fund these pools with different tokens and receive LP tokens in return.

DEXs typically deal with a variety of **tokens**, including native platform tokens, governance tokens, LP tokens, and a wide range of traded tokens. These tokens are used for trading, providing liquidity, and participating in the protocol's governance.

Oracles are used to bring external price information into the DEX. They help provide price data for the traded assets, ensuring trades are made at fair and accurate prices. Some DEXs, however, rely on the ratios within their liquidity pools to determine prices, reducing reliance on oracles.

While not a blockchain component, the **user interface** is crucial for users to interact with the DEX. It communicates with the blockchain and the underlying smart contracts, allowing users to perform actions such as swapping tokens, adding or removing liquidity, or staking tokens.

DEXs interact with blockchain **wallets**, like MetaMask or Trust Wallet. These wallets are used to connect to the DEX, enabling users to trade directly from their personal wallets, providing a more secure, non-custodial trading experience.

It is important to remember that building and operating a DEX or any other DeFi application requires a deep understanding of both blockchain technology and financial markets, as it involves substantial risks, including smart contract vulnerabilities and regulatory challenges.

Automated Market Makers Smart Contract

Automated Market Makers (AMMs) are an integral part of many DeFi platforms and DEXs. In essence, AMMs utilize smart contracts to create a liquidity pool of tokens, which users can trade against, with prices set by a mathematical formula.

Let's try to build a simplified example of an AMM smart contract on the Ethereum blockchain, using the Solidity programming language. This example creates a basic AMM for two tokens, with the price determined by the ratio of the two tokens in the pool.

This is a highly simplified example that does not include many real-world considerations, such as fees, price slippage, or liquidity provider rewards. It should not be used for actual trading.

```
contract SimpleAMM {
    uint public reserve0; // reserve of token 0
    uint public reserve1; // reserve of token 1

    function getReserves() public view returns (uint _reserve0, uint
        _reserve1) {
        _reserve0 = reserve0;
        _reserve1 = reserve1;
    }

    function addLiquidity(uint _reserve0, uint _reserve1) public {
        reserve0 += _reserve0;
        reserve1 += _reserve1;
    }

    function getExchangeRate(uint _token0Amount, uint _token1Amount)
        public view returns (uint) {
        return _token0Amount / _token1Amount;
    }
```

```
function swap(uint _token0Amount, uint _token1Amount) public {
    require(_token0Amount <= reserve0 && _token1Amount <= reserve1,
        "Insufficient liquidity.");

    uint exchangeRate = getExchangeRate(_token0Amount, _token1Amount);

    reserve0 -= _token0Amount;
    reserve1 += _token0Amount / exchangeRate;
    }
}
```

In the above contract:

- reserve0 and reserve1 represent the quantity of two tokens in the liquidity pool.
- getReserves() returns the current reserves of both tokens.
- addLiquidity() allows a liquidity provider to add tokens to the pool.
- getExchangeRate() calculates the current exchange rate between the two tokens based on their reserves.
- swap() allows a user to trade _token0Amount of token 0 for an equivalent amount of token 1, based on the current exchange rate.

Again, remember that this is a highly simplified example that does not include many aspects of a real-world AMM. Developing an AMM for actual use would require a deep understanding of blockchain programming, financial math, and security considerations.

Liquidity Pools Smart Contract

Let's now expand on the previous example of the AMM and include liquidity providers who can add liquidity to the pool and receive LP tokens in return. As before, this is a highly simplified example that does not include many aspects of a real-world liquidity pool, such as fees, slippage control, or token price management. This should not be used for actual trading.

```
contract SimpleAMM {
    uint public reserve0; // reserve of token 0
    uint public reserve1; // reserve of token 1

    mapping(address => uint) public lpTokenBalance; // balance of LP
        tokens per address
    uint public totalLPTokens; // total supply of LP tokens

    function getReserves() public view
    function addLiquidity(uint _reserve0, uint _reserve1) public
    function getExchangeRate(uint _token0Amount, uint _token1Amount)
        public view
    function swap(uint _token0Amount, uint _token1Amount) public
}
```

In this contract:

- lpTokenBalance tracks the balance of LP tokens for each liquidity provider.
- totalLPTokens is the total supply of LP tokens.

- addLiquidity() now issues LP tokens to liquidity providers. The amount of LP tokens is the average number of token 0 and token 1 deposited (a simplification).
- removeLiquidity() allows a liquidity provider to burn LP tokens and withdraw their share of the reserves. Their share is determined by the percentage of total LP tokens they are burning.

This contract is still quite basic and does not handle the transfer of actual tokens; it does not implement fees or price controls and uses a simplistic and unrealistic formula for issuing LP tokens. It is also missing important safety checks, such as re-entrancy guards and safe math operations.

Building a production-ready AMM contract for a DeFi protocol requires a high level of expertise in blockchain development and security, as well as a deep understanding of the economic and game-theoretic principles involved. The strong recommendation is to work with experienced blockchain developers and to conduct thorough smart contract audits before deploying any DeFi protocol.

Stablecoins

Stablecoins are cryptocurrencies designed to minimize price volatility, with their value typically pegged to a stable asset or a group of assets. These assets could be other cryptocurrencies, fiat money, or commodities. Examples include Tether (USDT), USD Coin (USDC), and DAI.

Let's consider the simplest kind of stablecoin, which is backed 1:1 by a reserve of a certain asset (like the US dollar). For example, every USDT is supposed to be backed by one US dollar held in reserve by Tether Ltd.

This is an oversimplified Solidity smart contract example of such a stablecoin, a very basic version of an ERC20 token contract where the total supply is fixed at contract creation and all tokens are assigned to the creator. In a real-world scenario, the contract would need to manage reserves and handle deposits and withdrawals to issue and burn tokens.

```
contract SimpleStableCoin {
    string public name = "Simple Stable Coin";
    string public symbol = "SSC";
    uint8 public decimals = 18; // 18 is the most common number of
        decimal places
    uint public totalSupply;

    mapping(address => uint) public balanceOf;

    constructor(uint _initialSupply) {
        totalSupply = _initialSupply;
        balanceOf[msg.sender] = _initialSupply;
    }

    function transfer(address _to, uint _value) public returns (bool
        success) {
        require(balanceOf[msg.sender] >= _value, "Insufficient
balance.");

        balanceOf[msg.sender] -= _value;
        balanceOf[_to] += _value;

        return true;
    }
}
```

In this contract:

- name, symbol, and decimals are the standard ERC20 fields that provide basic information about the token.
- totalSupply is the total supply of the token.
- balanceOf` is a mapping that keeps track of the balance of each account.
- The constructor sets the total supply and assigns all tokens to the contract creator.
- transfer() allows a user to transfer tokens to another address.

Again, this is a simplified example. A real-world stablecoin contract would need to handle a wide range of additional concerns, such as:

- Minting and burning tokens as assets are deposited and withdrawn.
- Interacting with the reserve assets (whether that's other tokens on the Ethereum blockchain, or off-chain assets like US dollars).
- Implementing security measures to protect against attacks.
- Complying with regulatory requirements.

As with all smart contracts, building a stablecoin contract for actual use would require a high level of expertise in blockchain development and security, as well as a deep understanding of the underlying economic principles.

Yield Farming

Yield farming, also known as liquidity mining, is a way to generate rewards with cryptocurrency holdings. It is one of the newest and fastest-growing domains in the field of DeFi. In essence, it involves lending your assets to others by putting your trust in smart contracts.

Figure 10.4 shows the flow of how yield farming works, followed by a step-by-step explanation.

1. **Tokens and Liquidity Pools**: To begin yield farming, a user would typically need to have some cryptocurrency tokens (e.g., Ether or a stablecoin like DAI, USDC). These tokens can be supplied to a liquidity pool (LP), which is a smart contract that contains funds. In return for supplying these tokens to the pool, the user receives LP tokens. These LP tokens can be thought of as a receipt or claim for the funds deposited into the pool.

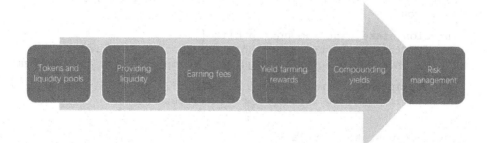

Figure 10.4   Yield farming flow

2. **Providing Liquidity**: The LP tokens are then used to provide liquidity in markets. For example, if you have ETH and DAI, you can supply both of these to a Uniswap DAI/ETH liquidity pool. Providing liquidity helps to stabilize the price of the assets and enables trades to happen even when there are large orders.

3. **Earning Fees**: By providing liquidity, you enable trades to take place. Traders pay a fee for this service, which is distributed to the liquidity providers according to their share of the liquidity pool. This is the first way to earn rewards through yield farming.

4. **Yield Farming Rewards**: But there is another layer in the reward system. To incentivize activity on their platform, many DeFi projects have their own tokens that they distribute as rewards to liquidity providers. These tokens are typically distributed to the LP token holders. This is the "yield farming" part – by providing liquidity, you are "farming" the platform's tokens.

5. **Compounding Yields**: Many yield farmers reinvest their earned tokens into the liquidity pool. This increases their potential returns over time, as they now have a larger share of the pool and can therefore earn a larger share of the fees. This process can be repeated to potentially compound the yield farmer's earnings.

6. **Risk Management**: It is important to note that yield farming is not without risks. Some of these include smart contract bugs, platform volatility, impermanent loss, and more. Therefore, it is crucial for users to understand the mechanics of the protocol they are using, and the risks associated with them.

It is also worth noting that yield farming has become a highly competitive and complex field, with various strategies and protocols being used. Many yield farmers use sophisticated strategies, automated tools, and constantly move their funds around to chase the highest returns. Some DeFi platforms offer yield farming "optimizers" that automatically switch users' funds between different pools to maximize returns.

Yield farming typically involves a combination of different smart contracts for handling different aspects such as governance tokens, liquidity pools, and reward distribution. Below is an extremely simplified example of a reward distribution contract that might be used in a yield farming scenario. This example uses the Solidity programming language for Ethereum smart contracts. In this contract, users can stake their LP tokens and earn reward tokens over time.

```
contract SimpleYieldFarm {
    mapping(address => uint) public stakingBalance;
    mapping(address => uint) public rewardBalance;
    mapping(address => uint) public stakingTime;

    uint public rewardRate = 1; // reward rate in reward tokens per
        second

    function stake(uint _amount) public {
        // Transfer LP tokens to this contract for staking
        // This would actually require a token contract and approval

        stakingBalance[msg.sender] += _amount;
        stakingTime[msg.sender] = block.timestamp;
    }

    function unstake() public {
        uint reward = calculateReward(msg.sender);
        rewardBalance[msg.sender] += reward;
```

```
        stakingBalance[msg.sender] = 0;
        stakingTime[msg.sender] = 0;

        // Transfer LP tokens back to the user
        // And send the reward tokens
    }
    function calculateReward(address _user) public view returns (uint) {
        uint stakingDuration = block.timestamp - stakingTime[_user];
        return stakingBalance[_user] * stakingDuration * rewardRate;
    }
}
```

In this contract:

- stakingBalance keeps track of how many LP tokens each user has staked.
- rewardBalance keeps track of how many reward tokens each user has earned but not yet claimed.
- stakingTime keeps track of when each user last staked or unstaked.
- rewardRate is the rate at which users earn reward tokens for each LP token staked per second.
- stake() allows a user to stake LP tokens.
- unstake() allows a user to unstake their LP tokens and collect their reward.
- calculateReward() calculates the current reward for a user based on the duration of staking and the reward rate.

Remember, this is a highly simplified example. In a real-world scenario, you would also have to interact with the token contracts, handle fractional amounts, prevent overflow and underflow errors, manage contract permissions, and more. The proposed example is also missing important safety checks, like re-entrancy guards.

Also note that the design of yield farming contracts can vary widely depending on the specific mechanics of the yield farming protocol, such as how rewards are distributed and what actions users need to take to earn rewards.

In all cases, designing and building smart contracts for yield farming or any other DeFi application requires a high level of expertise in both blockchain development and the specific economic and game-theoretic principles of the DeFi protocol. It is always recommended to conduct thorough testing and auditing before deploying any smart contracts.

Synthetic Assets

Synthetic assets in the context of DeFi are financial instruments in the form of tokens that represent real-world assets or other cryptocurrencies. These "synthetic" versions can track the price of virtually anything, including cryptocurrencies, traditional currencies, commodities, stocks, or even indices. The primary purpose of creating synthetic assets is to gain exposure to certain markets without having to hold the underlying asset. Let's take a look at some of the key characteristics and benefits of synthetic assets:

- **Permissionless Access**: Synthetic assets remove barriers to entry in certain markets. For instance, a user from a country where a particular asset, say a US stock, is not accessible can buy a synthetic version of that asset on the Ethereum blockchain.

- **24/7 Market Availability**: Traditional markets operate within regular business hours and are closed on weekends and holidays. On the contrary, synthetic assets on blockchain networks are available for trading 24/7.
- **Cost-Effective**: Synthetic assets can make it more cost-effective to trade certain kinds of assets. For instance, if a user wants to trade gold, instead of physically buying and storing it, they can trade a synthetic asset that tracks the price of gold.
- **Fractional Ownership**: Synthetic assets can be divided into smaller units, allowing for fractional ownership of expensive assets.
- **Interoperability**: Being on a blockchain network, synthetic assets can be easily integrated with other DeFi protocols for lending, borrowing, yield farming, and more.

One of the well-known projects in the DeFi space that allows the creation of synthetic assets is Synthetix (https://synthetix.io/). Users stake the Synthetix Network Token (SNX) or ETH as collateral to mint synthetic assets called Synths that follow the price of assets such as Bitcoin (sBTC), USD (sUSD), gold (sXAU), and many others.

However, it is important to note that synthetic assets come with their own set of risks, including smart contract vulnerabilities, collateralization risks, and liquidity concerns. Furthermore, they rely on oracles to track the price of the underlying asset, and any failure or manipulation of these price feeds can lead to issues. As always, due diligence and risk assessment are essential when dealing with complex financial products like synthetic assets.

Bitcoin or Ethereum for DeFi?

When it comes to DeFi, the majority of development and innovation has happened on the Ethereum blockchain. Ethereum is built-in support for smart contracts, which enable programmable and automatic execution of agreements, making it a more natural home for complex financial applications than Bitcoin.

While Bitcoin is the largest and most established cryptocurrency, its functionality for DeFi applications is limited compared to Ethereum due to its lack of built-in support for smart contracts. However, projects like RSK are bringing smart contract functionality to Bitcoin, and projects like Sovryn are building DeFi platforms on top of RSK. There are also protocols like Wrapped Bitcoin (WBTC) that make Bitcoin accessible on the Ethereum network by representing it as an ERC-20 token.

Creating a DeFi platform directly on Bitcoin can be challenging but not impossible. There are a few strategies that developers have used:

- **Sidechains**: Sidechains are separate blockchains that are pegged to Bitcoin and allow for more complex operations. An example of this is RSK (Rootstock), which is a smart contract platform that is a sidechain of Bitcoin. With RSK, you can create DeFi applications using Solidity, the same language used for Ethereum smart contracts. This allows for a more extensive range of DeFi applications to be built, as RSK is compatible with Ethereum's tooling and ecosystem.
- **Interoperability Protocols**: Interoperability protocols such as WBTC (Wrapped Bitcoin) allow Bitcoin to be used on other blockchains. WBTC is an ERC-20 token on the Ethereum blockchain that represents Bitcoin. This means that Bitcoin can be used directly in Ethereum's DeFi applications.

- **Layer 2 Solutions**: Layer 2 solutions, such as Lightning Network, provide faster and cheaper transactions than the Bitcoin network. They also offer more complex transaction types, which could potentially be used for certain types of DeFi applications.
- **Bitcoin Forks**: Creating a fork of Bitcoin specifically designed to support DeFi could be another approach. This would involve altering the Bitcoin codebase to add additional features required for DeFi, such as more advanced scripting or smart contract capabilities. This would be a complex and ambitious project, requiring significant development expertise and community support.

It is worth noting that building a DeFi platform, whether on Bitcoin, Ethereum, or any other blockchain, is a highly complex task that requires deep understanding of blockchain technology, financial systems, and security practices. It is not something to be undertaken lightly, and it is crucial to ensure any DeFi platform is thoroughly audited and tested before it's released to the public.

If you are interested in building DeFi applications and want to use Bitcoin as part of your platform, it may be more feasible to start by building on an existing smart contract platform (like Ethereum or Binance Smart Chain) and incorporate Bitcoin through a wrapped token (like WBTC) or a cross-chain bridge. This would allow you to leverage the established tooling and ecosystem of these platforms, while still enabling Bitcoin holders to participate in your application.

Binance Smart Chain

Binance Smart Chain (BSC) is a blockchain platform built for running smart contract-based applications. It was created by Binance, one of the world's largest cryptocurrency exchanges, to provide a more scalable and efficient alternative to Ethereum, which has been challenged by high fees and network congestion. Here are some key aspects of BSC:

- **Dual-Chain Architecture**: BSC operates alongside Binance Chain, Binance's original chain, allowing users to get the best of both worlds: the high transaction capacity of BC and the smart contract functionality of BSC. Furthermore, the dual-chain architecture lets users transfer assets from one blockchain to the other quickly and efficiently.
- **Ethereum Compatibility**: BSC is compatible with the Ethereum Virtual Machine (EVM), meaning it supports existing Ethereum smart contracts and is compatible with Ethereum tools like MetaMask and Truffle. This has made it easy for developers to port projects from Ethereum to BSC.
- **Fast and Low-Cost Transactions**: BSC boasts a block time of about 3 seconds and lower transaction fees compared to Ethereum, making it an attractive platform for DeFi projects and users.
- **Staking and Delegated Proof-of-Stake**: BSC uses a consensus model called Delegated Proof-of-Stake (DPoS). Binance Coin (BNB) holders can stake their coins to become validators or vote for validators on the network. Validators earn rewards for securing the network and processing transactions.
- **Vibrant DeFi Ecosystem**: Many DeFi projects have chosen to build on BSC due to its lower fees and faster transactions. Notable projects include PancakeSwap (a DEX similar to Uniswap), Venus (a lending and borrowing platform similar to Compound or Aave), and Beefy.Finance (a yield optimizer).
- **Binance Coin (BNB)**: BNB, originally created on the Binance Chain, serves as the native coin of the BSC. BNB is used for transaction fees, staking, and participating in token sales, among other uses.

However, while BSC has many advantages, it has also faced criticism for its level of centralization. The validators are selected through a process that favors BNB holdings, leading to a concentration of power within Binance and a few large holders. This is in contrast to more decentralized networks like Ethereum, where anyone can participate in network validation (through mining or, in Ethereum 2.0, staking). As with any blockchain platform, it is essential to do thorough research and understand the benefits and risks before developing on or using BSC.

PancakeSwap

Yes, one of the most well-known dApps that integrates with the BSC is called "pancake". Well, precisely PancakeSwap. PancakeSwap is a DEX built on BSC, which has gained popularity due to its fast transaction times and low fees compared to Ethereum-based DEXs like Uniswap or SushiSwap. A general outline of how a user might interact with PancakeSwap includes the following steps:

1. **Connect a Wallet**: First, the user connects a wallet that is compatible with BSC. This could be MetaMask (with the BSC network added), Trust Wallet, or several others. The wallet needs to contain BNB for transaction fees and any other tokens the user wants to trade.
2. **Swap Tokens**: The user can now trade (or "swap") one token for another directly on PancakeSwap's platform. The tokens they can trade include any BEP-20 tokens on BSC. The price of each token pair is determined by an automated market maker (AMM) system.
3. **Provide Liquidity**: If a user wants to contribute to the liquidity of a token pair, they can deposit an equal value of each token into the liquidity pool. In return, they receive LP (Liquidity Provider) tokens. The user earns a portion of the trading fees for that token pair proportional to their share of the liquidity pool.
4. **Farming and Staking**: PancakeSwap also offers yield farming and staking opportunities. Users can stake their LP tokens to earn CAKE, PancakeSwap's native token. They can also stake CAKE to earn other tokens.

Remember, while PancakeSwap and other dApps on BSC offer potential opportunities for earning, they also come with significant risk. The value of cryptocurrencies can be extremely volatile, and smart contracts may have vulnerabilities that could be exploited. As always, anyone considering using these platforms should do thorough research and consider consulting with a financial advisor.

The following example of a Node.js app shows how to integrate with the BSC using the web3.js library. This app retrieves the balance of a BSC account. Please install the necessary npm package by running `npm install web3` in your terminal before you start.

```
const Web3 = require('web3');

// BSC Testnet RPC
const rpcURL = 'https://data-seed-prebsc-1-s1.binance.org:8545/';

// Account on BSC
const account = "0xYourAccount";

// Connect to BSC
const web3 = new Web3(rpcURL);
```

```
// Get balance
web3.eth.getBalance(account, (err, wei) => {
    balance = web3.utils.fromWei(wei, 'ether');
});
```

Replace 0xYourAccount with the address of the account you want to check. This is a basic example. Real-world applications would require more complex interaction with smart contracts on the BSC, like sending transactions, calling contract functions, or listening for events.

Also be aware that interacting with real Ethereum accounts (which also applies to BSC, since it is an Ethereum fork) involves handling private keys, which can be used to control your account. They should be managed with extreme care, as losing them can lead to irreversible loss of assets, and if they are exposed or sent over an insecure connection, a malicious actor could use them to take control of your account. For real-world applications, consider using an Ethereum library designed for secure, user-friendly account management like ethers.js or a service like Infura.

Polkadot

Polkadot is an open-source project founded by the Web3 Foundation, created by Ethereum co-founder Dr. Gavin Wood. It is a multi-chain platform that enables various blockchains to interoperate in a scalable, secure environment. Unlike other blockchain networks, which operate largely in isolation, Polkadot allows different blockchains to communicate and share information. Here are some key aspects of Polkadot:

- **Relay Chain**: This is Polkadot's central chain, providing security and consensus for the network. All other chains (referred to as "parachains") connect to the Relay Chain.
- **Parachains**: Parachains are independent blockchains that run in parallel within the Polkadot ecosystem. They can have their own tokens, functionality, and consensus mechanisms, as long as they maintain a connection to the Relay Chain. This parallel structure is what allows Polkadot to process transactions from different chains simultaneously, greatly increasing its scalability.
- **Bridges**: Polkadot uses bridges to connect with blockchains outside its ecosystem, like Ethereum or Bitcoin. This enables these external chains to communicate with Polkadot's parachains.
- **Shared Security**: Parachains benefit from the shared security of the Relay Chain, meaning they don't need to bootstrap their own validator communities. This makes it easier and more efficient to create and launch a parachain.
- **Interoperability**: One of Polkadot's key advantages is its interoperability. Different parachains can exchange any type of data or asset, enabling a wide range of cross-chain functionality.
- **Polkadot's Native Token (DOT)**: DOT is the native token of Polkadot. It has three primary functions in the network: governance, where DOT holders have a voice in the network's future, staking (used to secure the network), and bonding, where new parachains are added by locking up DOT.
- **Governance**: Polkadot has a robust on-chain governance model that includes all stakeholders. DOT holders can vote on network upgrades and changes, creating a system where the network can evolve and adapt over time.

Polkadot has the potential to greatly expand the capabilities of the blockchain landscape, enabling diverse blockchains to work together seamlessly. However, like any technology, it is essential to keep in mind that Polkadot, while promising, is still a complex and evolving platform that comes with its own set of risks and challenges.

Below is an example of a simple Node.js application that connects to a Polkadot node using the @polkadot/api package. This application retrieves the latest block number. Firstly, install the necessary dependencies by running npm install @polkadot/api in your terminal.

```
const { ApiPromise, WsProvider } = require('@polkadot/api');
async function main() {
  // Connect to a Polkadot node
  const wsProvider = new WsProvider('wss://rpc.polkadot.io');
  const api = await ApiPromise.create({ provider: wsProvider });

  // Retrieve the latest block number
  const lastHeader = await api.rpc.chain.getHeader();
  console.log(`Last block number: ${lastHeader.number}`);
}
```

This is a simple example that only retrieves the latest block number. More complex applications might interact with the Polkadot network in various ways, such as submitting transactions, reading blockchain state, or interacting with smart contracts (on networks that support them, such as Polkadot's canary network Kusama).

Interacting with blockchain networks often involves handling sensitive information, such as private keys. Always ensure that your application handles such information securely, especially if it's a real-world application handling real value. If your application needs to sign transactions, consider using a secure solution for key management, such as a hardware wallet or a secure enclave.

Advantages and Opportunities of DeFi

Decentralized finance holds numerous advantages and opportunities for individuals and institutions. DeFi platforms operate on public blockchains, which means anyone with an internet connection and a digital wallet can access and use their services. This can be particularly beneficial for the unbanked or underbanked, who might lack access to traditional banking services. DeFi apps are built on shared standards, which means they can interact seamlessly. A user might deposit tokens in a lending protocol, use those as collateral for a loan on another platform, and then trade the loaned funds on a decentralized exchange, all without leaving the blockchain.

As all transactions and contracts on DeFi platforms are recorded on a public blockchain, anyone can audit them, providing a level of transparency rarely seen in traditional finance. In traditional finance, trusted intermediaries hold and control your assets. With DeFi, you have full control over your assets, reducing the risk of third-party failures.

DeFi offers potentially higher yields than traditional finance. Yield farming, for example, can generate returns far exceeding those of a standard savings account. DeFi has pioneered several new financial services that do not have traditional equivalents, such as flash loans (loans taken and repaid within a single blockchain transaction) and automated portfolio managers.

While the advantages of DeFi are compelling, it's crucial to also acknowledge the risks. DeFi is still a relatively new space, and there are uncertainties and potential pitfalls, including smart contract bugs, market volatility, and scalability issues. It is also less regulated than traditional finance, which can increase certain risks. As always, participants should carefully research and consider the risks before engaging in DeFi activities.

Financial Inclusion

Financial inclusion is a global initiative aimed at providing individuals and businesses with access to useful and affordable financial products and services that meet their needs. These needs can include transactions, payments, savings, credit, and insurance, and they should be delivered in a responsible and sustainable way.

Financial inclusion strives to address and offer solutions to the constraints that exclude people from participating in the financial sector. Globally, around 1.7 billion adults remain unbanked, yet two-thirds of them own a mobile phone that could help them access financial services.

But how can DeFi help drive financial inclusion? DeFi applications can provide basic financial services such as saving and lending to people in remote locations or those without access to traditional banking infrastructure. Since these applications are built on blockchain platforms, all you need to access them is an internet connection and a digital wallet.

Remittances are a crucial source of income for people in many developing countries. However, the cost of sending remittances is often high. DeFi can make these cross-border transfers more efficient and less costly, directly benefiting low-income people who rely on these funds.

Many people in developing countries are self-employed entrepreneurs who need loans to start or expand their small businesses. However, these people often lack the necessary collateral or credit history to obtain a loan from a traditional bank. DeFi lending platforms can potentially address this issue by providing collateral-free microloans.

Blockchain's immutable and transparent nature can help to create a decentralized, reliable source of identity, helping those who might not have government-issued IDs to access financial services. Similarly, decentralized credit scoring systems can offer fairer and more inclusive access to credit.

DeFi platforms often offer better returns on investments than traditional banks. This can benefit all savers but particularly those in developing countries, where interest rates are often low or even negative.

While the potential for DeFi to contribute to financial inclusion is significant, there are also substantial challenges to overcome, including legal and regulatory issues, scalability, privacy concerns, and the need for more user-friendly interfaces. The volatility and complexity of the crypto market can also pose significant risks to new users, underscoring the need for robust risk management and user education initiatives.

Interoperability and Composability

Interoperability and composability are two critical characteristics of DeFi that have contributed to its rapid growth and innovation. **Interoperability** refers to the ability of different systems to work together. In the context of DeFi, it means that various blockchain networks and the applications built on them can interact and communicate with each other. Interoperability can be facilitated through various mechanisms, including cross-chain bridges and protocols, and it allows for a more interconnected and efficient ecosystem.

For example, a DeFi app built on the Ethereum blockchain might leverage the interoperability to interact with another app built on the BSC, or even NFTs minted on the Flow blockchain. This kind of cross-chain interaction can open up new opportunities and functionalities for DeFi users.

Composability, also often referred to as "money legos", is a concept borrowed from software engineering that suggests that systems should be designed as a collection of interoperable parts that can be composed and re-used in different systems.

In the DeFi world, this concept means that each DeFi protocol can be stacked or interacted with another, allowing developers to build complex financial products by combining existing ones. An example of this would be a user who deposits DAI (a stablecoin) into a lending protocol like Aave to earn interest, then uses the interest-bearing aDAI tokens as collateral for a loan on a different platform.

Together, interoperability and composability allow for endless possibilities for building and interacting with financial products on the blockchain. However, they also come with challenges and risks, such as complex interdependencies and potential for cascading failures if one protocol suffers an exploit or issue. These are active areas of research and development in the DeFi space.

Ethereum–BSC Interoperability

Interoperability between Ethereum and BSC is a critical function that allows for tokens and other assets to move between these chains. The main method of achieving this interoperability is through the use of cross-chain bridges, which lock assets on one chain and mint equivalent assets on another chain.

Building a cross-chain bridge involves creating a series of smart contracts on both chains, as well as setting up an off-chain relayer network to monitor for events on both chains, and it's not something that can be easily condensed into a simple example of code. Moreover, due to the high value of assets that often get moved across chains and the complexity of the operations involved, bridge contracts are a prime target for hackers and require a high degree of security.

If you are interested in how bridges work, you might want to look at the code of some existing bridges. Both Binance and several other projects have open-source bridge solutions. For example, the **Peggy Bridge** developed by the Cosmos project, which uses Tendermint and Cosmos SDK, has open-source code available on GitHub (https://github.com/Sifchain/peggy), and the **PoA Bridge** developed by the PoA Network is also open-source (https://github.com/omni/poa -bridge).

Another example is the aptly named **London Bridge** (https://londonbridge.io/), a secure bridge between Algorand and Ethereum, developed by London, UK-based Applied Blockchain. What's unique about this bridge, and hence the "secure" attribute in its tagline, is that it's built on Intel SGX hardware secure enclave technology to verify each side of the blockchain. Transactions and keys are secured using attested (that is, verified) code tied to the bridge contracts. Keys are generated in a trusted execution environment (TEE) and never leave the enclave. This makes the keys inaccessible even to the bridge operator. The validation of the state of a chain is done directly in the TEE and this means the only way to move funds to the destination chain is to perform a transaction on the source chain. The logic is bound in encrypted hardware with the keys.

Remember, creating a secure bridge requires significant expertise in smart contract development and knowledge of both chains' specifics, and should not be undertaken lightly. For most purposes, it is best to use existing bridges that have been thoroughly audited and tested. For more specific functionalities like calling a smart contract on BSC from Ethereum or vice versa, an oracle solution like Chainlink could be used to pass data between chains, but this also does not constitute a full bridge solution and is subject to the limitations and requirements of the oracle system used.

Security and Smart Contract Risks

DeFi platforms rely heavily on smart contracts, self-executing contracts with the terms of the agreement directly written into code. While this offers many advantages, it also introduces specific risks and vulnerabilities that are unique to the blockchain and DeFi ecosystem:

- **Smart Contract Bugs**: Given their complexity and immutability, smart contracts are prone to bugs. Such bugs can result in the loss of funds or other unintended consequences. For instance, the DAO hack in 2016 was due to a bug in the smart contract code that allowed an attacker to siphon off one-third of the DAO's funds.
- **Reentrancy Attacks**: This type of attack, also exploited in the DAO hack, occurs when a called contract, often maliciously, calls back (re-enters) the calling contract before the first invocation of the function is finished. This can cause the different states, like the balance of an account, within a contract to get out of sync.
- **Oracles and Data Manipulation**: Many DeFi applications rely on oracles, which are trusted data feeds that bring off-chain data onto the blockchain. If an oracle is compromised or manipulated, it can impact the functioning of the DeFi application. For instance, if a price oracle is manipulated, it can lead to inaccurate loan collateralizations or incorrect trading.
- **Lack of Standardization**: In the absence of standardization, developers often have to write contract code from scratch, which increases the likelihood of bugs. There are efforts to standardize certain aspects of smart contract development (e.g., the ERC-20 standard for tokens on Ethereum), but many parts of a DeFi application will still require custom code.
- **Upgradability and Admin Keys**: Some smart contracts are designed to be upgradeable for fixing bugs and adding new features. However, this usually means that there is an admin key that can alter the contract. If these keys are compromised, or if the power of these keys is not limited appropriately, they can pose a central point of failure.
- **Flash Loan Attacks**: Flash loans allow users to borrow assets without collateral, provided that the loan is returned within a single transaction. Attackers can use flash loans to manipulate prices on a DEX and profit off these price discrepancies.

These risks highlight the importance of adequate testing, auditing, and monitoring of smart contracts. Many DeFi projects now employ formal verification, a mathematical approach to verify that a contract's code will behave as intended, and several organizations specialize in auditing the code of smart contracts before they go live. It is crucial to remember that even with these measures, there is no such thing as 100% security in DeFi or any other software application.

Scalability Issues

Scalability has been a significant concern for the DeFi sector, particularly for platforms built on the Ethereum blockchain, which hosts the majority of DeFi applications. There are a few key aspects to these issues:

- **Transaction Throughput**: The Ethereum blockchain, like many others, can only process a certain number of transactions per second (TPS). As of 2024, Ethereum's TPS is in the range of 10–15. This limit can lead to network congestion when the network is busy, leading to slow transaction times.

- **Gas Fees**: Transactions on Ethereum and some other blockchains require the payment of "gas fees", which compensate miners for validating transactions. When the network is congested, these fees can skyrocket, making it prohibitively expensive to perform transactions, especially smaller ones. This has been a significant barrier to user adoption and usability.
- **Data Storage**: Each transaction on the Ethereum blockchain adds to the total amount of data stored on the blockchain. As the blockchain grows, so does the computational expense of participating in the network. This can make it more challenging for individual users to run a node, contributing to network centralization.

Solutions to these scalability issues are being developed and fall into two main categories:

1. **Layer 2 Scaling Solutions**: These are protocols built on top of the Ethereum blockchain that take transactions off-chain, perform them more efficiently, and then record the results on the main blockchain. Examples include Optimism, zkSync, and Polygon.
2. **Ethereum 2.0**: Ethereum's developers have been working for years on a significant upgrade known as Ethereum 2.0, which has moved Ethereum from a Proof of Work to a Proof of Stake consensus mechanism. Ethereum 2.0 has introduced sharding, which distributes the computational and storage workload across many nodes. These changes are intended to significantly improve the scalability of the Ethereum network.

Remember, though, that each of these solutions comes with its own trade-offs in terms of security, decentralization, and compatibility. It is never a one-size-fits-all solution to the scalability issue.

Future of DeFi

The future of decentralized finance holds immense potential, promising to redefine the financial landscape by incorporating blockchain technology. What can we likely expect?

As DeFi continues to mature, we can expect to see increased adoption among both individual users and institutional investors. DeFi's promise of democratized access to financial services will continue to attract a wider user base globally, especially in unbanked or underbanked regions.

As multiple blockchain networks continue to develop and mature, there will likely be an increased focus on interoperability, i.e., the ability for different blockchains to communicate and interact with each other. This will enable cross-chain DeFi applications that can tap into liquidity and user bases across different networks, further expanding the DeFi landscape.

As DeFi grows, it will likely draw more attention from regulatory bodies. This could lead to a more defined legal and regulatory environment for DeFi, which could help reduce fraud and scams and protect consumers, but could also pose challenges for the open and permissionless nature of DeFi.

As DeFi continues to grow, so will the demand for faster, cheaper transactions. Layer 2 solutions and other scalability solutions like Ethereum 2.0 will likely become more prevalent and crucial for DeFi's continued growth.

With the increased adoption of DeFi protocols, we can expect to see more robust risk management practices, and DeFi insurance markets could see substantial growth. These products can help protect users from smart contract failures, price volatility, and other risks inherent in the DeFi ecosystem.

DeFi has already begun to innovate traditional financial products and services like lending, borrowing, and trading. In the future, we might see more complex financial instruments being decentralized, such as derivative products, options, and more.

As DeFi matures, there will likely be a greater emphasis on privacy-preserving DeFi applications. While blockchain networks like Ethereum are transparent, they are not private. Transactions can be traced, and while addresses may not be directly tied to identities, enough data can often de-anonymize users. Solutions that provide more privacy will likely be a focus.

Remember, though, that like any technology, the future of DeFi will be shaped by a wide range of factors, including technological advances, user adoption, regulatory developments, and macroeconomic trends. The journey of DeFi is just beginning, and its potential to revolutionize the world of finance makes it an exciting space to watch.

Chapter 11

Central Bank Digital Currency (CBDC)

In recent years, the world has seen a significant shift toward digital economies. Amidst this digital revolution, a particular financial innovation that has generated tremendous attention is the Central Bank Digital Currency (CBDC).

The CBDC is a type of digital currency issued and regulated by a country's central bank. It is considered a legal tender, just like physical money, and represents a digital form of a nation's fiat currency. However, unlike traditional forms of money, CBDCs exist entirely in the digital realm, offering new possibilities and challenges in the world of finance and beyond.

The advent of CBDCs was primarily spurred by advancements in blockchain technology, the very same technology that underpins cryptocurrencies like Bitcoin and Ethereum. However, it's essential to differentiate between CBDCs and cryptocurrencies. While both exist digitally, cryptocurrencies are decentralized and often not regulated, whereas CBDCs are a centralized form of digital money under the strict purview of a nation's central bank.

Implementing CBDCs could potentially revolutionize the current financial ecosystem in several ways. On the one hand, they promise increased efficiency in payment systems, decreased transaction costs, and enhanced financial inclusion, especially for those underserved by the current banking system. On the other hand, they pose challenges, including threats to financial stability and privacy concerns, which necessitate thorough investigation and careful policy design.

As we move further into the digital era, CBDCs are likely to be a crucial part of discussions surrounding monetary policy, financial stability, and the broader economy. Despite the associated complexities and risks, the potential benefits of CBDCs could be vast, propelling economies into a new phase of digital financial infrastructure.

Brief History of Money

To fully comprehend the significance of Central Bank Digital Currencies, we must first journey through the historical development of money itself. The evolution of money provides valuable

DOI: 10.4324/9781003491934-11

context for understanding why CBDCs could be the next significant milestone in the long time-line of economic exchange mediums.

Money, in its most basic definition, is anything widely accepted as a medium of exchange for goods and services. Historically, the physical form of money has evolved in accordance with the needs of society and the progress of technology, beginning from the barter system and culminating in the digital currencies we see today.

The earliest form of trade involved the **barter system** (6000 B.C.), which was a direct exchange of goods or services. However, the barter system had inherent limitations, such as the "double coincidence of wants" problem, where two parties each need to have what the other wants.

To overcome these limitations, societies gradually transitioned toward **commodity money** (3000 B.C.–1000 B.C.). This included any form of commodity that was widely accepted for trade, such as gold, silver, grains, or cattle. These commodities had intrinsic value and were relatively scarce, making them a more standardized and reliable store of value.

Over time, carrying and trading in commodities became cumbersome and impractical, leading to the introduction of **specie money** (600 B.C.), which was metal money in the form of coins. It was easier to carry, more durable than other commodities, and could be standardized in weight and purity. The first coins were minted in the kingdom of Lydia (now part of Turkey). These coins were made from electrum, a natural alloy of gold and silver.

With the rise of economies and growth in trade, **representative money** (17th century) emerged. This was a form of money where the face value represented a certain amount of a recognized standard like gold or silver. Paper bills started circulating as a more convenient form of money but were still linked to and could be exchanged for a fixed quantity of the precious metal.

The 20th century saw the shift toward **fiat money**, where currencies were no longer backed by a physical commodity like gold. The US dollar became a fiat currency after President Nixon ended its convertibility into gold in 1971 The value of fiat money is derived from the trust and confidence people have in the stability of their government. Fiat money is what most of us use daily, the coins and banknotes issued by the central bank of a country.

The advent of the internet ushered in a new era of **digital money** (1990s). Money became information, leading to electronic payment methods, online banking, and mobile wallets. However, this digital form of money still represents the traditional fiat currency managed by central banks and commercial banks.

In the past decade, we have seen the emergence of **cryptocurrencies** (2009), like Bitcoin, that operate on decentralized platforms. Now, CBDCs represent the latest evolution in this ongoing history of money. CBDCs aim to combine the advantages of digital forms of money with the regulated, secure nature of central bank money, potentially reshaping the future of our financial system.

Figure 11.1 shows the key milestones of money over the centuries.

The Emergence of Digital Currencies

As the digital revolution swept across the globe, it was only a matter of time before it reached the financial industry, disrupting traditional systems and ways of conducting transactions. In this new era, money took on a digital form, drastically transforming the landscape of payments, remittances, and cross-border transfers.

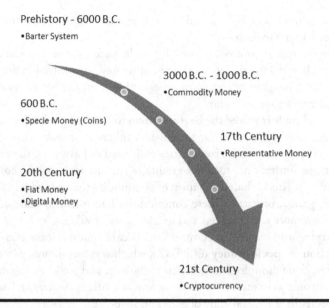

Prehistory - 6000 B.C.
•Barter System

3000 B.C. - 1000 B.C.
•Commodity Money

600 B.C.
•Specie Money (Coins)

17th Century
•Representative Money

20th Century
•Fiat Money
•Digital Money

21st Century
•Cryptocurrency

Figure 11.1   The timeline of money

The first significant wave of this revolution was the advent of digital payment systems. These systems allowed the transfer of fiat money in digital form. Services like online banking, credit card transactions, mobile payment apps, and digital wallets made it possible to store and transfer money digitally. However, these digital representations of money were still tightly linked to physical currency, requiring trust in the banking system and government backing.

The digital landscape further evolved with the arrival of cryptocurrencies, the most famous being **Bitcoin**, introduced by an anonymous entity known as Satoshi Nakamoto in 2008. Cryptocurrencies are a completely digital form of money that operate independently of a central bank. They are underpinned by blockchain technology, a type of distributed ledger system that ensures secure transactions through decentralization and cryptographic proof.

Cryptocurrencies presented a paradigm shift in the concept of money. They represented an innovative step toward "trustless" transactions, where transactions could be verified without the need for an intermediary like a bank. This offered benefits like reduced transaction fees and faster cross-border transfers. However, they also raised issues related to volatility, regulatory oversight, and illicit uses due to their decentralized nature and lack of control by any central authority.

In response to the rise of cryptocurrencies and to leverage the opportunities provided by digital currencies, central banks around the world began exploring the idea of **Central Bank Digital Currencies**. These are digital forms of fiat money, different from traditional reserves or settlement accounts. CBDCs aim to provide the best of both worlds – the convenience and security of digital forms of currency along with the regulated, risk-free environment of traditional banking systems.

The emergence of digital currencies represents a significant leap in the evolution of money, with potential to redefine the very foundation of the global financial system. As the world stands on the brink of this potential transformation, it is essential to understand the underlying concepts, benefits, and challenges of this innovation, especially in the case of CBDCs, the focus of this article.

Understanding Central Bank Digital Currency

A Central Bank Digital Currency is a type of digital currency that is issued and regulated by a country's central bank. CBDCs represent a digital form of a nation's fiat currency and are considered legal tender, which distinguishes them from other digital assets such as cryptocurrencies or e-money.

While CBDCs are entirely digital, they share many characteristics with traditional money. Like banknotes and coins, a CBDC carries the central bank's credibility and is recognized as a secure medium of exchange. It can be used to settle transactions, acts as a store of value, and can be used as a unit of account. Unlike private digital currencies and cryptocurrencies, the value of CBDCs does not fluctuate relative to the national currency, they are one and the same.

However, CBDCs also offer functionalities that traditional forms of money cannot. They are programmable, meaning that digital smart contracts could be utilized to automatically execute transactions under specific conditions. They can also be designed to be accessible to all citizens, even those who are currently unbanked or underbanked, potentially improving financial inclusion.

There are primarily two types of CBDCs – retail and wholesale. **Retail CBDCs** are intended for use by the general public for everyday transactions, much like physical cash. **Wholesale CBDCs**, on the other hand, are restricted for use by financial institutions for interbank payments and financial settlements.

In summary, a CBDC is a digital form of central bank money that offers the promise of improved functionality, increased efficiency, and wider accessibility compared to traditional money. The integration of modern technology with the trustworthiness of central bank regulation could make CBDCs a significant part of the future of the financial system.

Types of CBDC

CBDCs can be categorized into two main types, each with its specific use case and implications: retail CBDCs and wholesale CBDCs.

Retail CBDC

Retail CBDCs, also known as general purpose CBDCs, are intended for use by the general public in daily transactions. They serve as a digital complement or substitute for physical cash and deposits at commercial banks. Retail CBDCs would be issued and regulated by the central bank but could potentially be distributed through intermediaries like banks or other financial institutions.

The implementation of retail CBDCs has the potential to revolutionize everyday commerce by speeding up transactions, reducing costs, and enhancing financial inclusion. By providing a digital payment method that does not require a bank account, retail CBDCs could provide access to digital financial services for the unbanked or underbanked populations.

However, the widespread adoption of retail CBDCs also raises significant concerns. There could be implications for the current banking system, as the availability of CBDCs could lead to a transfer of deposits from commercial banks to the central bank, especially in times of financial stress. This could potentially destabilize the financial system, a phenomenon often referred to as a "digital bank run".

Wholesale CBDC

Wholesale CBDCs are a restricted form of digital currency, available only to financial institutions that hold reserve deposits with the central bank. They are primarily used for large-scale interbank payments and financial settlements.

The adoption of wholesale CBDCs could improve the efficiency, speed, and transparency of these transactions. They could also facilitate the implementation of innovative financial services like programmable money and smart contracts.

Given that wholesale CBDCs would be limited to regulated financial institutions, they present fewer risks regarding financial stability compared to retail CBDCs. However, they may have less impact on the general public, as their use is confined to the financial sector.

In conclusion, the decision to implement a retail or wholesale CBDC (or a hybrid of both) depends on a central bank's specific goals, the financial landscape, and the readiness of the economy for digital currency adoption. Both forms of CBDC offer distinct advantages but also present unique challenges that need to be carefully addressed.

Figure 11.2 summarizes the differences between retail and wholesale digital currencies, followed by a brief explanation of such differences.

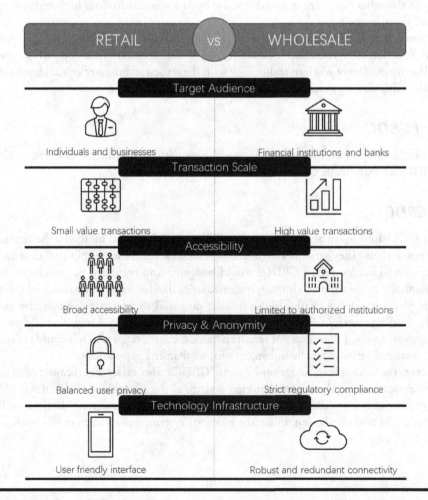

Figure 11.2 Retail vs wholesale CBDC

In summary, retail CBDCs, accessible to the general public, aim to enhance financial inclusion and consumer protection while facing challenges related to public education and adoption. Wholesale CBDCs, used by financial institutions, improve interbank settlements and financial system efficiency. The key differences lie in their target audience, transaction scale, and technology requirements, with each serving distinct roles in the economy.

CBDC and Cryptocurrency

CBDCs and cryptocurrencies represent two different manifestations of digital currency, but they have fundamental differences in terms of their structure, governance, and purpose.

Centralization vs Decentralization

The most significant difference between CBDCs and cryptocurrencies lies in their governance structure. CBDCs are centralized; they are issued and regulated by a country's central bank, which can control the supply of the digital currency, much like they do with physical cash.

On the other hand, cryptocurrencies like Bitcoin and Ethereum are decentralized. They operate on blockchain where transactions are verified and recorded by a network of computers (nodes) rather than a central authority. No single entity has control over the issuance or regulation of these currencies.

Legal Tender Status

CBDCs are considered legal tender in the country of issuance, meaning that they are recognized by the government as a valid form of monetary exchange for goods or services.

Cryptocurrencies, however, do not have legal tender status in most countries. They are considered assets rather than currencies, and their acceptance as a form of payment is at the discretion of individual businesses and entities.

Price Stability

CBDCs represent a digital form of a nation's fiat currency, maintaining parity with the value of a country's currency. Hence, they offer price stability relative to the national currency.

Cryptocurrencies, however, are known for their price volatility. Since their value is determined by supply and demand dynamics in the market, cryptocurrency prices can fluctuate wildly over short periods, making them riskier as a store of value.

Privacy and Anonymity

Cryptocurrencies, especially those like Bitcoin, initially became popular due to the anonymity they provided to users. However, complete anonymity can lead to potential misuse, including money laundering and funding illicit activities.

On the other hand, CBDCs are likely to offer less privacy than cash, given the traceability of digital transactions. Yet, the degree of privacy would depend on the design choices made by the central bank. Some degree of privacy can be achieved, but total anonymity is unlikely as that could hinder efforts to combat illicit activities.

Accessibility

CBDCs, particularly retail CBDCs, aim to be universally accessible to all residents of a country, improving financial inclusion.

Cryptocurrencies, while globally accessible to anyone with an internet connection, require a certain level of technical knowledge to use safely and effectively, potentially limiting their accessibility to the general public.

In conclusion, while both CBDCs and cryptocurrencies are forms of digital money, they represent very different concepts and have different implications for the future of finance and monetary policy. Understanding these differences is essential as digital currencies continue to evolve and impact the global financial landscape.

The Technology Behind CBDC

The precise technology that would underpin CBDCs is a topic of much research and debate, with various potential solutions proposed. However, it is widely recognized that Distributed Ledger Technology (DLT), including blockchain, could play a significant role.

Distributed Ledger Technology (DLT)

DLT allows for the recording, sharing, and synchronization of data across a decentralized network spread across multiple sites, countries, or institutions. This technology is best known for underpinning cryptocurrencies like Bitcoin, but its application to CBDCs would differ in significant ways.

For a CBDC, a central bank would maintain control over the currency's issuance and overall volume, contrasting with the decentralized control in cryptocurrencies. A DLT-based CBDC could operate on a permissioned network, where only authorized entities could validate transactions, unlike permissionless networks used by many cryptocurrencies.

Using DLT could improve security, transparency, and efficiency of transactions. The immutability of the ledger could prevent fraud, and transparency could assist in auditing and regulatory oversight. The distributed nature of the ledger could also increase resilience, as there isn't a single point of failure.

Blockchain Technology

Blockchain is a specific type of DLT where data is stored in blocks that are chronologically linked in a chain and additions to this chain are accepted by consensus of the participants. It could offer particular benefits for CBDCs, including smart contracts that automatically execute transactions when certain conditions are met, which could automate various financial operations.

Other Potential Technologies

However, DLT and blockchain are not the only potential technologies for CBDCs. Some propose that CBDCs could use more conventional centralized database systems, given that these systems have long been used for digital financial services. They might be less complex to implement and integrate with existing infrastructures.

Others propose a hybrid approach, where a DLT-based system is used in conjunction with a traditional centralized system. This could combine the advantages of both systems.

Security Considerations

Regardless of the specific technology used, the security of a CBDC would be of paramount importance. It would need to be resistant to cyber-attacks, fraud, and system failures. It would also need to protect users' privacy while complying with regulations against illicit activities.

In conclusion, the technology behind CBDCs is a complex subject with many potential solutions. The choice of technology would need to balance several factors, including security, efficiency, scalability, and integration with existing systems. As such, central banks around the world are investing heavily in research and pilot projects to explore these issues.

Build a CBDC

Developing a CBDC is a complex task that involves careful planning, extensive research, stakeholder engagement, technological development, and rigorous testing. Figure 11.3 depicts a broad guidance to develop a CBDC, though the precise steps may vary depending on the specific circumstances and objectives of the central bank.

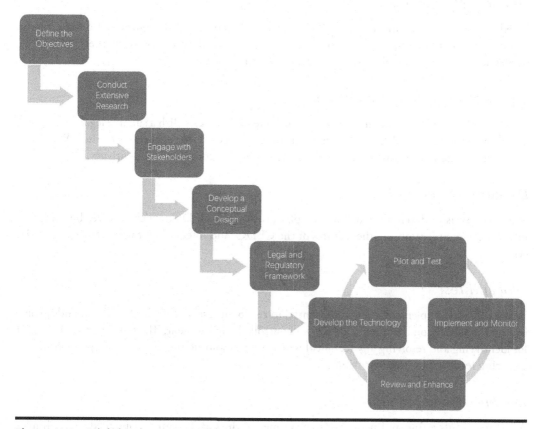

Figure 11.3   High-level steps to build a CBDC

Define the Objectives

The first step is to clearly define the objectives of the CBDC. What problems is it aiming to solve? How does it fit into the broader financial and monetary strategy of the central bank? Potential objectives could include improving payment efficiency, enhancing financial inclusion, maintaining monetary sovereignty in the face of digital currencies, etc.

Conduct Extensive Research

Once the objectives are defined, the next step is to conduct thorough research into all aspects of CBDCs. This could involve studying the experiences of other central banks, analyzing technological options, and understanding legal, economic, and social implications.

Engage with Stakeholders

It is crucial to engage with all relevant stakeholders throughout the CBDC development process. This includes the government, financial institutions, technology providers, businesses, and the public. Stakeholder engagement can help identify potential issues, gather feedback, and build support.

Develop a Conceptual Design

Based on the objectives and research, the central bank can develop a conceptual design for the CBDC. This should outline the fundamental features of the CBDC, such as whether it is retail or wholesale, the technology platform, the operating structure, etc.

Legal and Regulatory Framework

Parallel to the conceptual design, it is important to review and establish a suitable legal and regulatory framework for the CBDC. This should provide clarity on the legal status of the CBDC, the rights and obligations of parties involved, and the measures for security and privacy.

Develop the Technology

The next step is to develop the technology platform for the CBDC, which involves building the infrastructure, programming the features of the CBDC, and integrating it with existing financial systems.

Pilot and Test

Before full-scale implementation, it is essential to run pilot tests of the CBDC. This could involve issuing the CBDC on a limited scale or in a controlled environment. The testing phase is crucial for identifying and resolving any technical issues, understanding the real-world implications, and gathering feedback for improvements.

Implement and Monitor

After successful testing and necessary improvements, the CBDC can be launched. After implementation, it is important to continuously monitor the performance of the CBDC, ensure its stability and security, and make any required adjustments.

Review and Enhance

Developing a CBDC is not a one-time task, but an ongoing process. After implementation, the central bank should periodically review the CBDC's performance and impact, conduct research to keep up with technological advancements, and make enhancements as necessary.

Developing a CBDC is a major undertaking that could have significant implications for a country's financial system and economy. Therefore, it is essential to proceed with caution, ensuring every step is meticulously planned and executed.

Develop the Technology

The development of a CBDC hosted in a cloud environment involves several key technical components. Let's break them down:

- **Distributed Ledger Technology (DLT)/Blockchain Platform**: This forms the backbone of the CBDC system. DLT, including blockchain, allows for the secure, transparent, and decentralized recording of transactions. While a CBDC is a centralized currency, the use of DLT can help ensure security, transparency, and efficiency in transactions.
- **Node Infrastructure**: In the DLT environment, nodes are responsible for processing transactions and maintaining the distributed ledger. In a permissioned blockchain, which is likely for a CBDC, nodes would be controlled by known, trusted entities such as the central bank, financial institutions, or other authorized entities.
- **Smart Contracts**: Smart contracts are scripts that automatically execute transactions when certain conditions are met. They can enable programmable money and automate various operations, which can be a valuable feature of a CBDC.
- **Digital Identity Management**: A secure and reliable digital identity system is critical for a CBDC. This system needs to verify the identity of participants, prevent fraudulent activities, and ensure compliance with regulations, while also preserving user privacy to an appropriate extent.
- **Security Infrastructure**: Security is paramount for a CBDC. The system needs robust defenses against cyber threats, including encryption for data protection, firewalls to block unauthorized access, and intrusion detection systems to identify potential threats.
- **Transaction Processing System**: The CBDC system needs a reliable and efficient transaction processing mechanism, capable of handling potentially high volumes of transactions quickly and accurately.
- **Interoperability Components**: CBDC systems should ideally be interoperable with other payment systems, both domestically and internationally. This requires specific components that can translate and communicate transactions across different systems and standards.
- **Wallets and APIs**: Users and businesses will need digital wallets to hold and transact CBDCs. APIs will allow third-party developers to build applications that interact with the CBDC system, facilitating a range of services and uses.
- **Data Storage and Management**: The CBDC system will generate significant amounts of data, which needs to be securely stored, managed, and accessible for auditing or analytics. Cloud storage solutions provide scalable and efficient options for this.
- **Compliance Tools**: Compliance with regulations such as Anti-Money Laundering (AML) and Counter-Terrorist Financing (CTF) is crucial. The system will require built-in tools for monitoring transactions and reporting suspicious activities.

It is important to remember that developing a CBDC involves not just these technical components but also a range of non-technical considerations, such as regulatory compliance, economic impacts, and user education. Therefore, the successful deployment of a CBDC requires a holistic approach that combines technology with other aspects of policy and operations.

If you are interested in the underlying technology behind CBDC, you might explore blockchain development. For example, you could study the code of open source blockchain projects, such as Bitcoin or Ethereum, which are available on platforms like GitHub. But remember, these cryptocurrencies function very differently from what a CBDC would be, as they are decentralized and not controlled by any central authority.

Let's pretend for a moment that we have the capacity to create a CBDC for a bank. A first step into coding the digital currency would start from its smart contract. This contract would represent a very basic token system based on the Ethereum Request for Comment (ERC) number 20, one of the most significant smart contract standards on Ethereum, which has emerged as the technical standard used for all smart contracts on the Ethereum blockchain for fungible token implementations.

```
import "@openzeppelin/contracts/token/ERC20/ERC20.sol";

contract MyCBDCPrototype is ERC20 {
    constructor(uint256 initialSupply) ERC20("MyCBDCPrototype",
        "CBDCP") {
        _mint(msg.sender, initialSupply);
    }
}
```

In this contract, we are creating a new ERC20 token. The contract imports code from the OpenZeppelin library, which includes secure implementations of ERC20. The contract itself is very simple: when it is deployed, it mints a certain amount of the new token and assigns it to the sender.

Note that this is a vast oversimplification. A real CBDC would be far more complex and would likely involve many more features and controls to ensure security, privacy, regulatory compliance, and integration with existing financial systems. It is also crucial to note that the development and deployment of a CBDC are tasks that only a central bank or similar authority can undertake, due to legal, financial, and regulatory implications.

But, as mentioned, we are pretending to work for a central bank with the authority to emit currency, aren't we? Let's now enable transactions for our CBDC. We need to ensure the security and integrity of transactions, deal with delays in transaction verification, and manage the risk of lost or stolen identities and devices. Furthermore, designing and implementing this system in a user-friendly manner is crucial for user adoption and acceptance.

This system would also require a legal and regulatory framework to handle disputes and fraud. For instance, rules would need to be established for situations where a device is lost or stolen, or where there is a dispute between parties about a transaction.

It is worth noting that the basic principles and technologies involved – such as cryptographic signing of transactions, secure data storage, and synchronization with a central server – are well-established techniques for the implementation of transactions in a CBDC. What follows is a very simplified example of how a transaction might be recorded using cryptographic signing, implemented in Python.

```
def make_transaction(sender_wallet, receiver_wallet, amount):
    # Check if the sender has enough balance
    if sender_wallet["balance"] < amount:
        return "Insufficient balance"

    # Create the transaction record
    transaction = {
        "sender": sender_wallet["public_key"],
        "receiver": receiver_wallet["public_key"],
        "amount": amount,
        "time": str(datetime.datetime.now())
    }

    # Create a signature using the sender's private key
    transaction_string = str(transaction)
    signature = hashlib.sha256((transaction_string + sender_wallet
        ["private_key"]).encode()).hexdigest()

    # Attach the signature to the transaction
    transaction["signature"] = signature

    # Adjust the sender and receiver's balance
    sender_wallet["balance"] -= amount
    receiver_wallet["balance"] += amount

    return transaction

transaction = make_transaction(sender_wallet, receiver_wallet, 20)
```

Note that this example is very simplified and does not cover many of the complexities involved in a real CBDC system. For instance, it does not address the issues of storing and syncing offline transactions, checking signatures, preventing double-spending, or securing private keys. Also, this code uses SHA-256 for signing, whereas a real-world system would use a more secure and sophisticated method, such as the Elliptic Curve Digital Signature Algorithm (ECDSA).

Security Considerations

Security is a fundamental concern when developing a CBDC. A secure CBDC can promote trust and encourage adoption, while security breaches could undermine confidence and lead to significant financial and reputational damage. Here are some of the main security considerations that need to be addressed.

- **Cybersecurity**: Given that a CBDC is a digital currency, it would be a potential target for a range of cyber threats, including hacking, malware, phishing, and denial of service attacks. Defenses against such threats include strong encryption, firewalls, intrusion detection systems, and regular security audits.
- **Distributed Ledger Security**: If a CBDC uses a blockchain, specific security considerations arise. For instance, the system needs to guard against double spending, where someone spends the same digital currency unit twice, and ensure the integrity and immutability of the ledger. Security features inherent to DLT, like cryptographic hashing and consensus algorithms, can help address these concerns.
- **Digital Identity and Authentication**: A secure digital identity and authentication system is crucial for preventing fraud and ensuring that only authorized users can access and transact

the CBDC. This system could involve traditional methods like passwords, biometric methods like fingerprints, or more advanced methods like digital certificates.

■ **Privacy and Data Protection**: While a CBDC system needs to be transparent to prevent fraud and ensure compliance, it also needs to protect users' privacy and sensitive data. Techniques like pseudonymization, where users are identified by a pseudonym rather than their real name, or zero-knowledge proofs, where transactions can be verified without revealing all transaction details, could be used to balance these needs.

■ **Resilience and Recovery**: A CBDC system needs to be resilient to withstand various potential disruptions, ranging from technical failures to natural disasters. This includes having redundant systems, backup procedures, and a robust disaster recovery plan.

■ **Legal and Regulatory Compliance**: A CBDC system needs to comply with a range of legal and regulatory requirements, including financial regulations, data protection laws, and standards for IT systems. Compliance tools and procedures need to be built into the system.

■ **Monitoring and Incident Response**: Continuous monitoring is essential for detecting potential security incidents promptly. If an incident does occur, a well-planned and practiced incident response plan can help limit the damage and restore normal operations quickly.

■ **User Education and Awareness**: Even the most secure system can be undermined by user behavior. Therefore, educating users about safe practices, like protecting their digital wallets and being vigilant for phishing attempts, is crucial.

It is important to note that security is not a one-time task but a continuous process. The threat landscape evolves constantly, so the CBDC's security measures need to be reviewed and updated regularly. In addition, security needs to be built into the design of the CBDC system from the outset, rather than being added on later. This approach, known as "security by design", can help ensure that the CBDC system is as secure as possible.

Confidential Computing

Confidential computing is an emerging approach that can significantly enhance the security and privacy of sensitive data, making it a potentially valuable tool for a CBDC. It goes beyond traditional methods of data encryption that secure data at rest and in transit, by also securing data while it is being processed.

Confidential computing involves running applications within secure environments, known as **Trusted Execution Environments** (TEEs) or secure enclaves. These enclaves are isolated from other parts of the host system, including the operating system and hypervisor, which means that data within the enclave cannot be viewed or accessed by anything outside the enclave, even while it is being processed.

In the context of a CBDC, confidential computing could help protect the privacy of CBDC users by ensuring that transaction data is encrypted not just when it is stored or transmitted, but also when it is being processed. This could be particularly important for CBDC designs that aim to replicate the anonymity of cash transactions.

By isolating data during processing, confidential computing can help protect the CBDC system against a range of threats, including malicious insiders, sophisticated cyber-attacks, and vulnerabilities in other parts of the system.

Confidential computing could help a CBDC system comply with data protection regulations, as it provides a high level of protection for personal data. It can also aid in maintaining transparency and auditability without compromising privacy. By enhancing privacy and security, confidential computing could help build trust in the CBDC, which is crucial for widespread adoption.

However, while confidential computing has significant potential, it also has challenges and limitations. For instance, it requires specific hardware that supports TEEs, and managing these secure enclaves can be complex. Furthermore, like any security measure, it is not foolproof and needs to be part of a broader, multi-layered security strategy.

As with any technology, the decision to use confidential computing for a CBDC should be based on a thorough assessment of the benefits, costs, risks, and alternatives, as well as the specific objectives and requirements of the CBDC. Given the sensitive nature of CBDCs and the high stakes involved, it is crucial to ensure that any technology used is thoroughly tested, proven secure, and implemented correctly.

Homomorphic Encryption

Both homomorphic encryption and confidential computing are powerful techniques for enhancing the privacy and security of data processing, and each has its own strengths and potential applications. The decision to use one over the other – or even to use both in tandem – will depend on the specific requirements and constraints of the CBDC in question.

Homomorphic encryption is a form of encryption that allows computations to be performed on encrypted data, without needing to decrypt the data first. The results of the computation are then encrypted and can only be viewed by someone who holds the decryption key. This can enhance privacy and security, as sensitive data can remain encrypted at all times.

For a CBDC, homomorphic encryption could be particularly useful in scenarios where the central bank wants to perform computations on transaction data – for example, to calculate aggregate statistics or identify suspicious patterns – but does not want to expose individual transactions. This could help balance the need for privacy with the need for regulatory oversight and financial integrity.

However, homomorphic encryption is computationally intensive and currently much slower than standard methods of data processing. This could be a significant drawback for a CBDC, which might need to handle large volumes of transactions quickly.

Confidential computing instead involves running applications within secure enclaves that are isolated from other parts of the host system. Data within the enclave is encrypted directly by the CPU (no software libraries are used) and cannot be viewed or accessed by anything outside the enclave, even while it's being processed.

For a CBDC, confidential computing could help protect the privacy of transactions and secure the CBDC system against various threats. Unlike homomorphic encryption, confidential computing does not add significant computational overhead, so it could be more suitable for processing large volumes of transactions. However, confidential computing requires specific hardware that supports TEEs, and managing these secure enclaves can be complex.

In conclusion, both homomorphic encryption and confidential computing have potential uses for a CBDC, and the decision to use one or the other (or both) should be based on a detailed analysis of the CBDC's requirements, the potential benefits and drawbacks of each technique, and the overall security strategy. It is also important to remember that no single technology can provide complete security, and a robust CBDC system will need to use a range of security measures in combination.

The Architecture of a CBDC

Central banks are investigating the potential of CBDC to support them in protecting financial and monetary stability. Organizations need to understand the different technology requirements of a multi-functional digital currency, while also meeting current monetary requirements and taking advantage of data analytics and machine learning advancements. Central Banks solutions hosted in public clouds can help with these efforts by offering CBDC objectives and architectural considerations, technology options, performance criteria, and design implementation best practices and simulations.

The design of a CBDC depends on a variety of objectives. A common objective is to reduce dependency on traditional payment methods. This has the benefit of increasing competition, and encouraging innovation in a space that is notably very resistant to change. New digital economy services, such as programmable money, can enter the market and enable conditional payments and micro-payments. Others include increasing financial inclusion to the underbanked, improving transparency into and traceability of cross-border payments, and detecting and preventing unlawful activities.

Figure 11.4 gives an overview of possible architectures for CBDC. Customers interact with digital banks via their digital wallet and plastic cards, both offering payment services. All transactions are scrutinized for fraud and risk of money laundering. A central role in transaction management is identifying the parties involved. Knowing the customer (individual or business) identity, and in general account management, is essential to any monetary transaction that occurs on the digital platform.

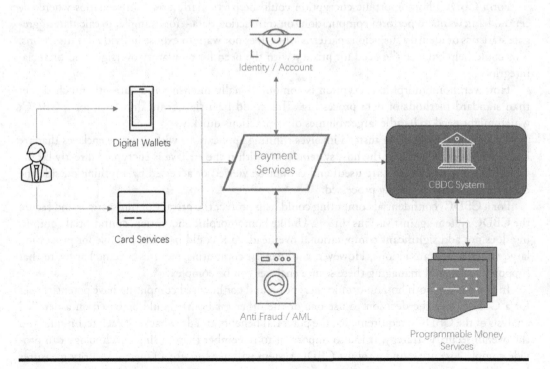

Figure 11.4   Architecture of CBDB

Programmable Money Services

Programmable money services refer to managing conditional payments, often by leveraging technologies such as digital ledgers and smart contracts. In general, with the expression "**programmable money**", we refer to digital currency that can be pre-programmed to follow certain rules or conditions. This capability allows for advanced financial functionalities and automation, for example:

- **Conditional payments** can be made only if certain conditions are met. A payment could be programmed to release funds only when goods are delivered and verified.
- **Micropayments** enable transactions of very small amounts, which can be useful for Internet of Things (IoT) applications and subscription-based services.
- Funds can be **programmed** to be **accessible** only during certain periods or by specific individuals or entities.

In addition to specific types of payments, compliance with **regulatory requirements** (such as KYC, AML) can be automated, reducing the need for manual intervention and increasing efficiency.

The Role of Distributed Ledger Technology

Distributed ledger technology (DLT) is a digital system for recording transactions where the details are recorded in multiple places at the same time. DLT is being used to support programmable money services in several ways, from enhancing security with decentralization and distribution in the system, to improving efficiency and interoperability. As an example, by eliminating the need for a central authority, DLT enhances security and reduces the risk of single points of failure. It allows for the secure execution of programmable money services in a decentralized manner. Not only that but also the cryptographic nature of DLT ensures that transactions and programmable money services are secure from tampering and fraud.

The distributed nature of DLT can streamline processes by automating them, reducing the need for manual oversight and the associated costs. This makes programmable money services more efficient. DLT can also facilitate interoperability between different systems and platforms, making it easier to implement and integrate programmable money services across various financial and non-financial ecosystems.

Example use cases are abundant in the financial world and include supply chain finance, government benefits, corporate governance, automated insurance payouts, and many others (Table 11.1).

In conclusion, programmable money services, enabled by CBDCs and supported by DLT, offer a range of innovative and efficient financial solutions. They provide a secure, transparent, and automated way to manage and execute transactions, reducing costs and increasing reliability.

The Potential Benefits of CBDC

One significant potential benefit of CBDCs is the opportunity to improve financial inclusion. For many people worldwide, particularly in developing economies, access to traditional banking

Table 11.1 Examples of use of distributed ledger technology for f

Use Case	Description
Supply Chain Finance	Payments can be automatically released when goods move through different stages of the supply chain, reducing delays and improving cash flow.
Government Benefits	Welfare payments or subsidies can be programmed to be spent only on specific goods or services, ensuring that funds are used as intended.
Corporate Governance	Automated execution of shareholder agreements and distribution of dividends based on predefined criteria.
Automated Insurance Payouts	Insurance claims can be settled automatically when certain conditions are met, such as flight delays or weather events.

services is limited or non-existent. A CBDC, accessible through simple mobile devices, could provide a form of banking to these unbanked populations.

CBDCs could streamline payments and remittances by reducing the need for intermediaries and allowing for faster, if not instant, transactions. This increased speed and efficiency could be particularly beneficial for cross-border payments, which are currently often slow and expensive.

If implemented effectively, CBDCs could provide a secure and trusted form of digital payment. Because they are backed by the central bank, CBDCs carry no risk of default, unlike private digital currencies.

CBDCs could provide central banks with a new tool for implementing monetary policy. For example, they could make it easier to implement negative interest rates or distribute "helicopter money" directly to citizens.

A CBDC could help reduce illegal activity, such as money laundering and the financing of terrorism, by providing a traceable digital payment method that can be monitored and controlled by the central bank. However, this benefit needs to be balanced against the need for privacy.

The development of a CBDC could spur innovation in the financial sector, by providing a new platform for developing and delivering financial services. This could lead to new business models and improved services for consumers.

At the end, CBDCs offer an opportunity for nations to maintain sovereignty over their monetary policy in an increasingly digital global economy. This is especially significant considering the rise of private cryptocurrencies and digital currencies proposed by tech giants, which could otherwise undermine national currencies.

It is worth noting that these potential benefits need to be weighed against potential risks and challenges, including issues related to privacy, security, financial stability, and the technological complexity of implementing a CBDC. The optimal design for a CBDC – for instance, whether it should be account-based or token-based, whether it should use blockchain or other technologies, how it should handle privacy – will depend on how a country chooses to balance these potential benefits and risks.

Fight Money Laundering

Money laundering is the process of making illegally gained proceeds (dirty money) appear legal, also known as "cleaning". It usually involves three steps: placement, layering, and integration.

With the digital revolution in the financial sector and the increasing use of cryptocurrencies, there has been a rise in the use of digital means to launder money. This underscores the need for effective AML technologies. An effective AML solution includes multiple technical components.

- **Customer Identification Program**: A crucial first step in any AML program is knowing your customers. KYC involves collecting and verifying customer's identification information to prevent identity theft, financial fraud, money laundering, and terrorist financing.
- **Customer due diligence** involves assessing the risk posed by a customer and categorizing them accordingly. Enhanced due diligence might be needed for high-risk customers.
- It is crucial to monitor transactions to **identify suspicious activities**. This could involve tracking large transactions, frequent transactions, transactions involving high-risk locations, or transactions that do not fit a customer's usual behavior. Artificial intelligence (AI) and machine learning (ML) algorithms can significantly improve the ability to detect anomalous patterns that might suggest money laundering.
- **Screening and sanctions checking** involves checking customers and transactions against national and international sanctions lists. This is crucial because doing business with a sanctioned individual or entity can lead to significant penalties.
- If a potentially **suspicious transaction** is detected, it must be reported to the relevant authorities. An effective AML solution should automate the reporting process to ensure reports are made promptly and accurately.
- **Data is key to AML**. AML solutions need effective data management systems, and increasingly, they are leveraging data analytics, AI, and ML to analyze patterns, identify risks, and detect suspicious activities more effectively and efficiently.

These components can be integrated into a single, comprehensive AML solution, which should be regularly updated to keep up with evolving regulations and threats. Also, the importance of training for staff involved in AML activities cannot be understated, to ensure they are equipped with the knowledge and skills needed to operate the AML solution effectively.

Build an AML Solution

It is hard to provide concrete source code examples for an AML solution, due to the proprietary nature of such solutions. Companies that provide these solutions closely guard their methods as they are integral to their business models and revealing them might compromise their efficiency and effectiveness.

Similarly, each AML solution is unique and tailored to the specific needs of an organization, its business model, the regulatory requirements it faces, and the specific risks it needs to mitigate. Therefore, it's difficult to provide a one-size-fits-all architecture diagram.

However, based on experiences working with clients that have implemented an AML solution, Figure 11.5 identifies a general conceptual framework for how such solution could be structured.

1. **Data Ingestion**: At this stage, raw data is collected from various internal and external sources. This could include transaction data, customer information, and data from external databases or watchlists. This data might need to be cleaned and formatted before it can be used.
2. **Risk Assessment and Profiling**: This module would typically use algorithms (including machine learning models) to assess the risk level of each customer, based on their behavior and other characteristics. This could form the basis for a risk-based approach to AML.

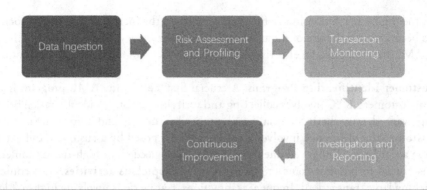

Figure 11.5   A framework for AML

3. **Transaction Monitoring**: This module would continuously monitor transactions in real-time, using algorithms to detect unusual patterns or suspicious activities. Alerts could be generated when potential issues are detected.
4. **Investigation and Reporting**: When a potential issue is detected, it would be investigated by human analysts. They might use a case management system to help track and document their investigations. If they confirm that suspicious activity has occurred, they will generate a report for the relevant authorities.
5. **Continuous Improvement**: The system should continuously learn and improve over time. This could involve using machine learning models that learn from past cases, or regularly reviewing and updating the rules and thresholds used to detect suspicious activity.

Remember that this is a simplified overview, and a real AML solution could be much more complex, depending on the needs of the organization and the specific regulatory requirements it faces. Moreover, any AML solution should be accompanied by comprehensive training for staff, as well as regular audits and reviews to ensure its effectiveness.

Risks and Opportunities Associated with CBDC

With any digital system, there are significant technological and security risks to consider. Ensuring the security, integrity, and reliability of a CBDC system would be a considerable challenge, requiring robust solutions for encryption, fraud detection, cyber defense, and more. Additionally, there is a risk of potential failures or glitches, which could disrupt the monetary system.

Balancing the need for transparency to prevent illicit activities, with the right to privacy, is a significant challenge. If not properly managed, a CBDC could lead to excessive surveillance and loss of privacy, which might be unacceptable in many societies.

Let's not underestimate that the introduction of a CBDC could potentially disrupt the traditional banking system. If people move their money from commercial banks to a CBDC, it could potentially destabilize banks and impact lending.

While CBDCs have the potential to enhance financial inclusion, there are also risks. Not everyone has access to the internet or digital technology, which could lead to a "digital divide" in access to money. It is crucial to ensure that a CBDC system is widely accessible.

The impact of a CBDC on monetary policy, financial stability, and the broader economy is uncertain and could be significant. For example, a CBDC could facilitate "bank runs" in times of crisis, if people rapidly switch their deposits to CBDC.

If a CBDC is used for cross-border payments, it could lead to challenges related to exchange rates, monetary sovereignty, and regulatory jurisdiction. Coordination and cooperation at the international level would likely be needed.

Implementing a CBDC would likely require substantial changes to legal and regulatory frameworks, to address issues such as consumer protection, dispute resolution, AML, and more. These changes could be complex and time-consuming.

Finally, the practical task of designing, developing, testing, and rolling out a CBDC would be a complex and challenging project, requiring significant resources and expertise.

These challenges and risks do not necessarily mean that a CBDC is a bad idea, but they underscore the importance of careful planning and risk management. Many central banks are currently conducting research and pilot projects to explore these issues and find ways to mitigate the risks associated with CBDC.

The Future of CBDC

As central banks around the world continue to explore and experiment with Central Bank Digital Currencies, there are several potential developments we can anticipate.

We are likely to see more central banks advancing from the exploration phase to the experimentation and implementation stages. This could result in an increase in pilot projects and potentially even full-scale launches of CBDCs in certain jurisdictions.

As with all areas of digital technology, we can expect ongoing innovation in the technologies used to implement CBDCs. This could involve developments in areas like distributed ledger technology, digital identity systems, cybersecurity, and privacy-enhancing technologies.

As CBDCs become more widespread, they could lead to significant changes in monetary and financial systems. This could involve shifts in the way monetary policy is implemented, changes in the role and operation of financial intermediaries, and the development of new financial products and services based around CBDCs.

The advent of CBDCs will likely necessitate the development of new regulatory frameworks, both at the national and international levels. These could cover a range of areas, from the operation of CBDC systems to their use in cross-border transactions.

As CBDCs become more prevalent in cross-border transactions, there will be an increasing need for international cooperation and standardization. This could involve the development of common standards for CBDC systems, as well as coordination on regulatory and policy matters.

As more CBDCs are implemented, there will be increasing opportunities for research and learning. This could help to improve our understanding of the impacts and potential benefits of CBDCs, and inform the design and implementation of future CBDC systems.

It is important to note that the future of CBDCs is still uncertain and will depend on a range of factors, including technological developments, policy decisions, regulatory responses, and the evolving needs and behaviors of businesses and consumers.

Chapter 12

Decentralized Autonomous Organizations (DAO)

In the ever-evolving realm of blockchain technology, one of the most intriguing concepts to emerge is that of the Decentralized Autonomous Organization (**DAO**). At its core, a DAO is an organization that operates based on predefined rules encoded as computer programs called smart contracts. Unlike traditional organizations, a DAO functions autonomously, without the need for centralized control, relying on the collective decision-making of its members.

The key characteristics are tied to the nature of blockchain: Decentralization and smart contracts. A DAO operates on a blockchain, ensuring transparency and eliminating the need for intermediaries. Automated, self-executing contracts with the agreement directly written into code facilitate, verify, and enforce the negotiation or performance of a contract, governing the operation of the DAO.

Rather than a hierarchical structure, DAOs often rely on a democratic or stake-weighted voting mechanism for decision-making. Token or coin holders typically have voting rights, making them active participants in the organization's governance. The idea behind DAOs is to create organizations where every operation and decision is rooted in transparency, resistant to censorship, and unaffected by external influences. They have the potential to reshape how organizations are structured and governed, with applications spanning from venture capital to community governance. However, DAOs are not without challenges, including security vulnerabilities and the need for scalable governance mechanisms, as we will understand in this chapter.

The Genesis of DAOs

At its most fundamental level, a DAO represents a new paradigm in organizational structure, one that leverages the power of blockchain technology. Traditional organizations, from corporations to non-profits, operate with centralized decision-making processes, often concentrated within a group of leaders or a singular entity. In contrast, a DAO is an organization where operational decisions are made autonomously or by consensus, driven by predefined rules embedded in smart contracts.

DOI: 10.4324/9781003491934-12

Structure and Functionality

A DAO's structural foundation is the blockchain, ensuring transparency, immutability, and, most importantly, decentralization. This decentralized nature allows for distributed governance, where decisions are made collectively by the members or stakeholders. The roles traditionally held by boards of directors, CEOs, and managers in conventional organizations are transformed into programmable code in a DAO. This code, or set of smart contracts, acts as an unbiased executor of the organization's directives.

Inherent Value Proposition

The allure of DAOs lies in their promise to minimize bureaucracy, enhance transparency, and reduce the potential for human error or manipulation. By removing intermediaries and placing power in the hands of the collective, DAOs can theoretically lead to more democratic, efficient, and fair organizations.

Tokenization and Incentive Mechanisms

A crucial component of many DAOs is their native token or cryptocurrency. These tokens can serve various purposes, including representing ownership, granting voting rights, or incentivizing certain behaviors within the organization. As members contribute to the DAO or make decisions beneficial to its objectives, they can be rewarded with these tokens, aligning individual incentives with the organization's broader goals.

A Paradigm Shift

In essence, DAOs offer a shift away from centralized control toward a model where every participant has a say, and every action is transparently recorded. They embody the broader move in the tech world toward decentralization, bringing democratic principles directly into the realm of organizational management.

Historical Context

Before the advent of DAOs, digital organizational models primarily focused on internet-based platforms and e-businesses, where the concept of decentralization was not yet a prominent factor. While these platforms offered digital interactions and operations, central authorities predominantly controlled them.

The seeds of DAOs were sown with the inception of blockchain technology. Satoshi Nakamoto's 2008 whitepaper on Bitcoin introduced the idea of a decentralized peer-to-peer electronic cash system. While Bitcoin itself is not a DAO, it introduced the underlying technology that would eventually enable DAOs. The blockchain, with its ability to run decentralized protocols on a network of computers, opened the door for more complex decentralized operations beyond just financial transactions.

In 2013, Vitalik Buterin proposed Ethereum, a new blockchain that would support more than just currency transactions. Ethereum introduced the idea of smart contracts, self-executing contracts where the terms of agreement or conditions are written into lines of code. With Ethereum, developers could now create decentralized applications, and it was not long before the concept of fully decentralized organizations was explored.

The DAO Experiment

In 2016, the Ethereum community witnessed the creation of "The DAO", a venture capital fund and the first significant experiment in decentralized autonomous organizations. Members would invest in Ether (Ethereum's native cryptocurrency) and get voting tokens in return. The DAO, as a decentralized venture capital fund built on the Ethereum platform, aimed to give token holders voting rights over which projects would receive funding. Within a short period, it raised over $150 million in Ether, making it the largest crowdfunded project at the time.

However, due to a vulnerability in its code, "The DAO" was hacked, leading to a significant portion of the invested funds being siphoned off. This incident was both a cautionary tale about the risks associated with such nascent technology and a testament to its potential, as the very nature of the hack revolved around the autonomous execution of a smart contract.

What happened exactly? In June 2016, an unknown attacker exploited a vulnerability in The DAO's smart contract, draining over 3.6 million Ether (equivalent to around $50 million at that time). The vulnerability was tied to a recursive call exploit in the contract's code, allowing the attacker to repeatedly withdraw Ether.

The Ethereum community faced a moral and technical dilemma: Let the attacker keep the funds, acknowledging the code's supremacy, or intervene to revert the theft. Eventually, the community chose to implement a hard fork to return the stolen funds to the original investors. This decision led to the split of Ethereum into two separate blockchains: Ethereum (ETH), the new hard fork, and Ethereum Classic (ETC), which kept the original chain.

The failure of "The DAO" did not deter the community. Instead, it led to introspection, better security practices, and the development of more sophisticated governance mechanisms. Since then, multiple other DAOs have been created, each with their unique purpose, governance model, and set of rules. From decentralized finance (DeFi) projects to content creation platforms, DAOs have gradually permeated various sectors.

Evolution of Organizational Structures

In the annals of human history, the earliest forms of organizations were tribal and clan based. Leadership typically revolved around the strongest, wisest, or most skilled individual or group within the tribe. Decisions were often made collectively, with an emphasis on the well-being and survival of the group. These were inherently decentralized structures, though limited by the constraints of communication and the scope of their objectives.

As societies grew in complexity, so did their organizational structures. The feudal system saw power centralized around monarchs and landowners. Decisions were top-down, with little to no input from the common populace. While efficient in terms of decision-making, these structures were often oppressive and lacked broad-based inclusivity.

The industrial revolution ushered in a significant shift. The rise of factories and mass production meant the creation of large corporations that required hierarchical management structures. The corporate model was primarily centralized, with decisions made by a select group of leaders or board members. This model promoted efficiency and scalability but often at the expense of individual agency among workers and stakeholders.

With the advent of the digital age, organizations began to adapt to the rapid flow of information. The late 20th century saw the emergence of networked organizations – structures that were more fluid, with decentralized decision-making processes. The emphasis was on collaboration, agility, and adaptability. The internet played a pivotal role, enabling real-time communication, reducing hierarchies, and fostering global collaborations.

The 21st century marked the rise of platform-based business models, where companies like Airbnb, Uber, and Alibaba acted as intermediaries, connecting service providers with consumers. While these models utilized technology to disrupt traditional industries, they remained centralized entities controlling the platform's rules, operations, and profit distribution.

Emergence of DAOs – The Next Evolution

DAOs can be seen as the next step on this evolutionary ladder. Drawing from the decentralized essence of tribal organizations and combining it with the technological prowess of the digital age, DAOs aim to create organizations where power is distributed, decisions are transparent, and operations are automated. They challenge the very notion of traditional centralized authority, advocating for a system where rules are predefined, and governance is in the hands of the collective.

The journey from early tribal structures to modern DAOs highlights humanity's continuous quest to find organizational models that balance efficiency, inclusivity, and adaptability. DAOs represent the convergence of historical decentralization ideals with cutting-edge technology, promising a future where organizations might operate in more democratic and transparent ways.

Key Characteristics of DAOs

As mentioned before, the key characteristics of a DAO are decentralization and the use of automated smart contracts running on a blockchain network. These two features define the rules for collective governance and member participation and provide an open, borderless, and secure platform to operate.

We will now enter each feature in more detail, and describe the typical patterns of technical implementation that define a DAO, starting with the core decentralization attributes in Figure 12.1.

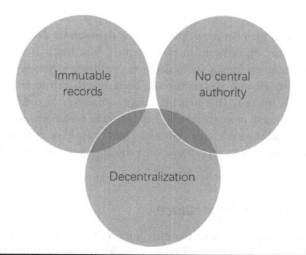

Figure 12.1   Key attributes of decentralization in a DAO

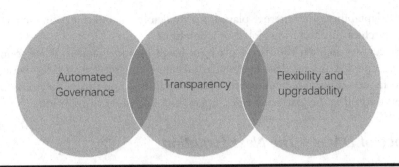

Figure 12.2   Core capabilities of smart contracts in a DAO

- **Decentralization**: At the heart of every DAO is the principle of decentralization. Unlike traditional organizations, which centralize decision-making and control, DAOs distribute these elements across the network.
- **Immutable Records**: The use of blockchain ensures that once decisions are made or transactions occur, they are recorded immutably. This transparency can foster trust among members and stakeholders.
- **No Central Authority**: DAOs operate without a single point of control or failure. This decentralization can lead to enhanced resilience against external threats and internal failures.

Similarly, smart contracts deliver core capabilities to a DAO, which are listed in Figure 12.2.

- **Automated Governance**: Smart contracts automate most of the processes in a DAO. From executing payments to enforcing decisions made by members, these contracts reduce the need for intermediaries and manual interventions.
- **Transparency**: Every rule and operation is visible on the blockchain. This transparency ensures that members can audit and verify operations, fostering trust and accountability.
- **Flexibility and Upgradability**: While smart contracts are immutable once deployed, many DAOs implement mechanisms to upgrade or modify them, allowing for adaptability and evolution.

Collective governance and member participation bring **democratic decision-making** in a DAO. Most DAOs operate based on some form of consensus, whether it is majority rule or a more complex mechanism, members have a say in decisions, ensuring a democratic approach. In many DAOs, governance rights are also tied to tokens. These tokens can represent voting power, and in some cases, economic interest. This structure aligns incentives, as those with a larger stake in the DAO's success often have more influence. Lastly, where traditional organizations have fixed hierarchies with clearly defined roles, in contrast, DAOs can have fluid structures where roles, influence, and responsibilities can shift based on various factors like expertise, contribution, or token ownership.

Decentralization and Its Importance

At its essence, decentralization refers to the distribution of functions, powers, people, or things away from a central authority. Instead of having a single point of control, authority, or decision-making, decentralized systems distribute these elements across multiple points or actors.

Human societies have often oscillated between centralized and decentralized structures. Ancient tribal societies operated on a decentralized model, with collective decision-making. However, as societies grew, centralization became more common for efficiency. Today, with advancements in technology, there is a renewed interest in decentralization, offering a balance between efficiency and individual empowerment.

Decentralization brings **enhanced security** with reduced single points of failure and an increased resistance to attacks. In a centralized system, if the central entity fails, the entire system can collapse. Decentralized systems, by distributing operations and authority, reduce the risks associated with a single point of failure. Decentralized systems can be more resilient to malicious attacks. An attacker would need to compromise a majority of the system to gain control, which is typically harder and costlier.

Transparency and trust are obtained with immutable records and verifiable operations. With the use of blockchain, decentralized systems ensure that records, once made, cannot be altered without consensus. This transparency can build trust among users or members. In decentralized systems, operations are visible and can be audited, ensuring accountability and reducing the chance of fraudulent activities. This focus on transparency makes censorship harder to apply. Decentralized systems, especially those built on blockchain, can be tough to censor or shut down. This is critical for ensuring freedom of speech, expression, and innovation in restrictive environments.

Speaking of **innovation and competition**, decentralized platforms often allow for open innovation, enabling individuals to create, modify, and improve without seeking permissions from a central authority. Diverse ideas are born, that can lead to a variety of solutions for a single problem, fostering competition and leading to optimized outcomes.

This is the perfect climate to foster **empowerment and inclusion** with democratized decision-making, and open participation to all members. The decentralized nature of DAOs can lead to more democratic decision-making processes, giving individuals a say in matters that affect them. Many decentralized systems are indeed open to anyone who wishes to participate, promoting a more inclusive environment.

For DAOs, decentralization is not just a technical feature; it is a foundational philosophy. The very essence of a DAO is to operate without a central authority, ensuring that decisions, operations, and benefits are distributed among its members or stakeholders. This decentralization promises more equitable, transparent, and resilient organizations.

The Role of Smart Contracts

Many DAOs use smart contracts to implement voting systems, decision-making processes, and governance rules. This ensures that governance is transparent, automated, and strictly follows the DAO's constitution. Figure 12.3 shows the three typical uses of smart contracts in DAOs.

DAOs often have native tokens that represent voting power, membership, or economic stake. Smart contracts manage these tokens' creation, distribution, and rules of operation.

Resource allocation, investment decisions, or funding of proposals within DAOs can be handled through smart contracts, ensuring that funds are used as the community directs without the risk of mismanagement or misappropriation.

While blockchain records are immutable, many DAOs use smart contracts that can be paused, upgraded, or replaced. This allows for adaptability and evolution while maintaining a record of all changes. The balance between enforcing governance by code on the one hand, and the need for flexibility poses frequent challenges:

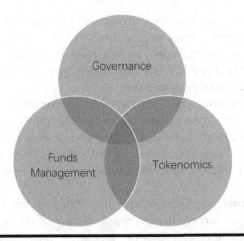

Figure 12.3 The "trinity" of use cases of smart contracts in DAOs

- **Code Is Law**: If there is a flaw or vulnerability in a smart contract, it can lead to undesired outcomes or exploitation. Notable incidents, like the DAO hack in 2016, have highlighted this risk.
- **Complexity and Scalability**: As DAOs and their associated operations grow in complexity, the underlying smart contracts can become more challenging to manage and maintain.
- **Interoperability**: Smart contracts on one blockchain platform may not seamlessly interact with those on another, creating potential silos.

Smart contracts are the backbone of DAOs, providing the infrastructure that automates and enforces the rules and operations of these decentralized organizations. While they offer numerous benefits in terms of efficiency, trust, and transparency, it is essential to approach their implementation with caution, ensuring they are robust, secure, and truly representative of the community's intent.

Collective Governance and Member Participation

Collective governance and member participation are foundational to the very essence of DAOs. Unlike traditional organizations, where decision-making may be vested in a few individuals or bodies, DAOs empower their broader membership to take active roles in various aspects of governance.

The philosophy of collective governance centers around **distributed power**, **inclusivity**, and **meritocracy**. By dispersing decision-making authority, DAOs prevent undue concentration of power, aiming for a more democratic and egalitarian structure. Collective governance emphasizes the participation of all stakeholders, ensuring that diverse perspectives are considered. In many DAOs, contributions, expertise, and engagement can lead to increased influence, fostering a merit-based system.

Typical mechanisms of member participation include **token-based voting systems**. Voting rights might be tied to token ownership, where the number of tokens one holds corresponds to their voting weight. Some DAOs might opt for equal voting rights regardless of token ownership to ensure equity, something referred to as "one member, one vote", as it happens in democratic societies irrespective of individual's wealth. Some DAOs use **reputation** as a metric, where members earn reputation based on contributions, and this can influence their governance power.

As in parliamentary-based societies, where representatives of the people are elected, DAOs may allow their members to delegate voting on matters of specific importance. This is often indicated as "**liquid democracy**": Members can choose to delegate their voting power to experts or trusted members, blending direct and representative democracy.

In summary, the benefits of collective governance can be listed as:

- **Wisdom of the Crowd**: Diverse inputs can lead to better decision-making, tapping into a broad base of knowledge and experience.
- **Transparency**: Open participation and collective decision-making ensure operations are transparent, fostering trust among members.
- **Alignment of Interests**: With members actively involved in governance, there's a stronger alignment between the DAO's direction and the collective interest.

Its challenges and considerations are mostly as follows:

- **Decision-Making Efficiency**: With many voices involved, decision-making can sometimes be slower, requiring mechanisms to strike a balance between participation and efficiency.
- **Low Voter Turnout**: Paradoxically, while DAOs enable widespread participation, many face challenges with low engagement in voting processes.
- **Sybil Attacks**: Where one user creates multiple identities to gain disproportionate influence. DAOs need mechanisms to prevent such attacks.
- **Plutocracy Concerns**: In token-weighted voting systems, there is a risk of wealthy members having excessive influence, detracting from the egalitarian spirit of DAOs.

Collective governance and member participation are central to the transformative potential of DAOs, offering a fresh approach to organizational decision-making. While the promise of a more democratic and inclusive governance model is compelling, DAOs must also navigate the complexities and challenges that come with such a system to ensure both efficiency and equity.

Technical Foundations of DAOs

Underlying Blockchain Platforms

DAOs require a technological framework to function. The foundational layer of this framework is the blockchain platform, which provides the infrastructure for creating, managing, and operating a DAO. The major blockchain platforms supporting DAOs are listed in Table 12.1, with their relevant core capabilities.

The underlying blockchain platform is the bedrock on which DAOs are built. While several platforms offer DAO-supporting features, the choice often boils down to the DAO's specific requirements, values, and long-term vision. As the blockchain landscape continues to evolve, DAOs will likely have even more sophisticated and tailored platforms to choose from.

Design and Implementation of Smart Contracts

Smart contracts are the lifeblood of a DAO, governing how it operates, manages funds, interacts with members, and makes decisions. Proper design and implementation are crucial to ensure the seamless functioning and security of a DAO.

Table 12.1 List of blockchain networks supporting DAO-based operations

Blockchain	DAO Features
Ethereum	• Smart Contract capabilities: Ethereum introduced the concept of smart contracts, self-executing contracts with the terms directly written into code. This innovation made it a natural choice for creating DAOs. • ERC standards: Protocols like ERC-20 (for fungible tokens) and ERC-721 (for non-fungible tokens) have been pivotal for DAO tokenomics and governance models. • dApps integration: Ethereum's ecosystem of decentralized applications (dApps) allows DAOs to integrate with various services and tools.
Binance Smart Chain (BSC)	• Compatibility with Ethereum: BSC is compatible with Ethereum's smart contract, allowing easy migration or cross-chain operations for DAOs. • Scalability and low fees: BSC provides faster transaction times and lower fees compared to Ethereum, which can be advantageous for DAO operations.
EOS	• DPoS consensus: EOS uses a Delegated Proof-of-Stake system, potentially offering quicker consensus and scalability. • Flexible Smart Contracts: EOS offers a more flexible approach to smart contract design, which can be appealing to some DAO structures.
Polkadot and Kusama	• Cross-chain compatibility: These platforms allow multiple blockchains to interoperate, potentially enabling DAOs to tap into resources and tools from various blockchain ecosystems. • Customizable DAO infrastructure: DAOs can build their custom parachains (blockchains) tailored to their needs.
Tezos	• On-chain governance: Tezos itself operates through on-chain governance, aligning with the DAO philosophy of decentralized decision-making. • Formal verification: Tezos emphasizes the mathematical accuracy of its smart contracts, aiming for a higher degree of security.

The design and implementation of smart contracts for a DAO are paramount to its success and security. While the allure of automating governance and operations is compelling, it comes with the responsibility of meticulous design, rigorous testing, and continuous oversight. As DAOs become more intricate and their role in the digital ecosystem grows, the emphasis on robust smart contract design will only intensify.

Below is a basic example of a DAO-specific smart contract written in Solidity. This example will depict a simple voting mechanism for a DAO. The SimpleDAOVoting contract implements:

■ A structure to hold the proposal details (what the proposal is about, the number of votes received, and whether the proposal is active or not).

■ A list of DAO members and a list of published proposals available for voting.

■ Two events to notify members when a new proposal is added, and when a vote is cast.

■ Methods to add members to the DAO, create a new proposal, vote for a proposal, deactivate a proposal (for example, after it is accepted or rejected), and a view method (that is, it does not change the state of the blockchain) to simply return the number of existing proposals in the DAO.

The full source code is available in the GitHub repository of the book.

```
contract SimpleDAOVoting {
    struct Proposal {
        string description;
        uint voteCount;
        bool active;
    }

    address public owner;
    mapping(address => bool) public members;
    Proposal[] public proposals;

    event ProposalAdded(uint proposalId, string description);
    event Voted(uint proposalId, address voter);

    function addMember(address _member) external {
    }

    function createProposal(string calldata _description) external
        onlyMember {
    }

    function vote(uint _proposalId) external onlyMember {
    }

    function deactivateProposal(uint _proposalId) external {
    }

    function getProposalsCount() external view returns (uint) {
    }
}
```

This is a basic demonstration, and real-world DAO contracts would be far more complex, incorporating additional features like:

■ Different types of voting mechanisms.
■ Delegation of votes.
■ Periodic intervals for proposals.
■ Handling of funds, payouts, or investments.
■ Advanced membership criteria and onboarding.

Always ensure that any smart contract meant for real-world deployment undergoes rigorous testing and auditing by experts to ensure its security and correctness.

Integration with Other Technologies

For DAOs to operate effectively and leverage the broader ecosystem's benefits, integration with other technologies is paramount. Two such essential integrations are with *oracles* (to fetch external data) and *dApps* (to interact with decentralized applications).

Oracles provide a bridge between the blockchain and the outside world. They fetch data from external sources and feed it into smart contracts, allowing these contracts to make decisions based on real-world data.

So why do DAOs need oracles? For proposals related to external events (e.g., the price of an asset, weather conditions, or other real-world metrics), DAOs need accurate and timely data. DAOs might also have contracts that execute under certain conditions, such as releasing funds if a specific real-world event occurs.

There are three types of oracles:

1. **Software Oracles**: Fetch and relay online data, such as website information or API data.
2. **Hardware Oracles**: Gather data from the physical world, e.g., IoT sensors.
3. **Consensus Oracles**: Aggregate data from multiple sources to determine the most accurate result.

Before using an oracle, it is important to make some considerations on its trustworthiness and decentralization. As a guarantee of data quality, we need to ensure that the chosen oracle is reliable and resistant to manipulation. Using decentralized oracles or multiple data sources can enhance accuracy and reduce manipulation risks.

Why do DAOs need to interface with dApps? DAOs can leverage dApps to extend their capabilities, like using a decentralized finance (DeFi) dApp for investment purposes. Some DAOs might be built around dApps like a game or a service, and need integration for governance and operations.

Financial dApps, for example, can be interfaced by DAOs for interacting with DeFi platforms for lending, borrowing, staking, or yield farming. Marketplaces provide DAOs related to arts or collectibles with a decentralized platform for buying/selling items. Or another example, decentralized storage dApps like Filecoin or IPFS are commonly used by DAOs for decentralized data storage.

Through considerations must be taken for DAO – dApp integration, especially for guaranteeing compatibility of smart contracts on different platforms and versions. DAO's contracts should effectively communicate and interact with the dApp's contracts. dApp interactions often incur transaction fees, which need to be factored into DAO operations. And on the security side, we need to ensure that any dApp the DAO interacts with follows best security practices to avoid risks by association.

Integration with other technologies like oracles and dApps not only enhances a DAO's capabilities but is often essential for its effective functioning. By fetching real-world data and interacting with a variety of decentralized applications, DAOs can remain dynamic, responsive, and effectively governed in a rapidly evolving digital ecosystem. As with all integrations, due diligence and security considerations must be paramount.

Below is a basic example of integrating an oracle into a smart contract. This will be a simplified example where a DAO needs to fetch the current USD price of ETH to make a decision. We will use the Chainlink oracle, one of the most popular decentralized oracle networks, for this demonstration.

```
contract DAOWithOracle {
    address public owner;
    AggregatorV3Interface internal priceFeed;
    int256 public latestEthUsdPrice;

    event PriceUpdated(int256 newPrice);

    constructor(address _priceFeed) {
        owner = msg.sender;
```

```
        // Initialize the Chainlink price feed contract
        priceFeed = AggregatorV3Interface(_priceFeed);
    }

    function getLatestEthUsdPrice() public returns (int256) {
    }

    function makeDecisionBasedOnPrice() external view returns (string
        memory) {
    }
}
```

Notes about this contract's code:

- The contract is using the AggregatorV3Interface Chainlink interface.
- The address (_priceFeed in the constructor) is the Chainlink price feed address for the desired data. Different networks (Mainnet, Kovan, etc.) and different data sources (ETH/USD, BTC/USD, etc.) will have different addresses.
- Two methods are defined, one to fetch the latest ETH/USD price from the Chainlink oracle (getLatestEthUsdPrice), and the other makeDecisionBasedOnPrice is just an example function where the DAO makes a decision based on the ETH price.

This is a basic integration. In more advanced scenarios, the contract could utilize more features from Chainlink, like Request & Receive data, Multi-Node consensus, and more. Always consider security best practices when implementing and deploying smart contracts. Chainlink is generally secure, but the way you handle data in your contract can introduce vulnerabilities. Remember, this example serves as a starting point. In real-world implementations, more complex logic, error handling, and integration methods would be required.

Applications of DAOs

Venture Capital and Fundraising

The disruptive nature of blockchain technology and the concept of DAOs has not only shifted how operations and governance are handled in digital realms but has also begun to reshape traditional industries. One such industry, fundamentally redefined by DAOs, is Venture Capital (VC) and fundraising.

Table 12.2 compares a traditional venture capital with a DAO-led venture capital model.

The DAO: A Case Study

Remember "The DAO" mentioned at the beginning of this chapter? The DAO was one of the earliest attempts to create a decentralized organization for investment purposes. Launched on the Ethereum blockchain in April 2016, it aimed to work as a venture capital fund for the crypto and decentralized space. The DAO is infamous for its fundraising success. Within a month, it raised over $150 million worth of ether, making it one of the largest crowdfunded projects at the time. People who sent their ether to The DAO received DAO tokens in return. These tokens represented voting rights in the organization. Projects could submit proposals to The DAO, and token holders

Table 12.2   Key differences between traditional and DAO-led venture capital businesses

Traditional Venture Capital	DAO-Led Venture Capital
Centralized decision-making: A select group or committee decides where funds are allocated.	Decentralized decision-making: All members (or those with tokens) can participate in decision-making.
Limited participation: Typically, only accredited investors or institutions can participate in early-stage investments.	Inclusive participation: Potentially open to anyone who can buy a token or meet the DAO's criteria.
Geographical constraints: Often restricted to specific regions or countries.	Global outreach: As it is on the blockchain, it can attract global investors and fund global projects.
Lengthy processes: Due diligence, legal work, and fund allocation can be time-consuming.	Streamlined processes: Smart contracts can automate many of the processes, making it faster and sometimes more transparent.

would vote on whether to grant funding. The proposal, voting, and fund release mechanisms were all coded into smart contracts.

In June 2016, a vulnerability in The DAO's code was exploited, resulting in the theft of around 3.6 million ether, roughly $50 million at the time. This led to a controversial decision to hard fork the Ethereum blockchain to recover the funds, resulting in the split between Ethereum and Ethereum Classic. The DAO's failure served as a valuable lesson about the importance of rigorous smart contract auditing and the challenges of decentralized governance. It highlighted the potential risks associated with complex smart contracts and large sums of money.

Post "The DAO incident", the crypto community has taken more precautions. Newer DAOs and decentralized funds often have more security measures, clearer governance structures, and sometimes even escape hatches to prevent significant losses. Several decentralized funds and investment DAOs have sprung up, aiming to fund projects in the crypto and decentralized space. These DAOs often combine traditional due diligence with decentralized voting.

The intersection of DAOs with VC and fundraising brings about **regulatory concerns**. Many jurisdictions are still grappling with how to categorize and regulate DAOs, especially those involved in investment. While DAOs promise a more democratized, transparent, and efficient model for venture capital and fundraising, they are not without challenges. Balancing the strengths of decentralization with the necessities of security, regulatory compliance, and effective governance is crucial. The DAO serves as both a testament to the potential of this new model and a cautionary tale of its pitfalls.

Build a Fundraising DAO

Below is a simple example of a fundraising DAO smart contract. This contract allows users to contribute funds and then vote on proposals. Each proposal can be for a specific amount of funding. The contract aims to demonstrate the core mechanics but is simplified for clarity.

```
contract FundraisingDAO {
    struct Proposal {
        address payable recipient;
        uint256 amount;
        uint256 votes;
        bool executed;
        mapping(address => bool) voters;
    }

    Proposal[] public proposals;
    mapping(address => uint256) public contributions;
    address public owner;
    uint256 public totalContributions;

    function contribute() external payable {
    }

    function createProposal(address payable _recipient, uint256 _
        amount) external onlyOwner {
    }

    function vote(uint256 proposalIndex) external {
    }

    function executeProposal(uint256 proposalIndex) external onlyOwner {
    }
}
```

Key functionalities of this contract's code are:

- **Contributions**: Users can contribute funds to the DAO. Their contribution serves as their voting power.
- **Proposal Creation**: The owner can create a funding proposal. In a more advanced system, any member might submit a proposal for consideration.
- **Voting**: Members can vote on proposals. Their vote weight is proportional to their contribution.
- **Proposal Execution**: If a proposal has more than 50% support (based on contributed funds), the owner can execute it, sending the requested funds to the proposal's recipient.

Important notes and security: This example is rudimentary and might contain vulnerabilities. A real-world DAO would need rigorous testing, auditing, and more features. Don't forget, also, that the voting mechanics can vary. This example uses a simple majority-based mechanism. Others might include quadratic voting, reputation-based voting, etc. Overall, many other functions and features would be required in practice, such as proposal expiration, fund withdrawal, more detailed voting dynamics, events, etc. Always consult with a blockchain development expert when creating and deploying smart contracts, especially those that handle funds.

Charitable Organizations and Non-profits

The charitable sector, like many others, has been exploring the advantages of blockchain technology, and by extension, DAOs, to tackle some of its intrinsic challenges. DAOs have the potential to redefine how charitable organizations and non-profits operate, making them more transparent, efficient, and inclusive.

Table 12.3   Key differences between traditional and DAO-led charities

Traditional Charitable Organizations	DAO-Led Charities
Opacity in fund allocation: There is often a lack of clarity about how donations are used, leading to trust issues.	Transparent fund allocation: Every transaction is recorded on the blockchain, allowing donors to see exactly where their funds go.
Administrative overhead: Significant funds can be consumed by administrative costs.	Reduced overhead: Automated processes via smart contracts can reduce administrative costs.
Limited engagement: Donors typically contribute and hope for the best without any real say in the organization's operations.	Active participation: Donors can become active participants in decision-making, choosing projects to fund or even proposing new initiatives.

Table 12.3 compares traditional charitable organizations with DAO-led charities. Which model do you prefer, and would you trust the most?

I don't know about you, but we can see several advantages of DAOs in charitable organizations:

■ **Trust through Transparency**: With every transaction being traceable on the blockchain, donors can see where their contributions are going, fostering trust.
■ **Direct Impact**: DAOs can minimize intermediaries, ensuring that a larger portion of donations directly impacts the intended cause.
■ **Engaged Donor Base**: By turning donors into active participants, a DAO can foster a more engaged and committed community.
■ **Global Outreach**: DAOs can operate without geographical boundaries, making it easier to address global challenges and gather international support.

Not all is gold, and potential challenges with regulation and adoption barriers may compromise the success of a DAO initiative. Being a relatively new concept, DAOs might face regulatory challenges in some jurisdictions when used for charitable purposes, and the public's unfamiliarity with blockchain and cryptocurrencies might deter some potential donors.

A simplified version of a CharityDAO smart contract may look like the following code snippet. This basic example allows users to donate to the DAO, propose charitable projects, and then fund these projects using the donated funds. This DAO ensures that no single project is overfunded.

```
contract CharityDAO {
    struct Project {
        string description;
        uint256 targetAmount;
        uint256 currentAmount;
        address payable beneficiary;
        bool funded;
    }

    Project[] public projects;
    mapping(address => uint256) public donations;

    function donate() external payable {
    }
```

```
function proposeProject(string memory _desc, uint256 _amount,
    address payable _beneficiary) external {
}

function fundProject(uint256 projectId) external {
}
}
```

Remember, this is a simplified model, and real-world applications would require a much more robust and secure system.

Challenges and Controversies

While DAOs offer transformative benefits, they are not without their challenges. DAOs, especially in their early stages, have experienced significant setbacks, some of which have led to substantial financial losses and heated debates in the crypto community. One of the most salient issues has been the vulnerabilities in smart contract codes, leading to notable failures and raising valid security concerns.

Security concerns in DAOs are brought from a variety of sources, as in Figure 12.4.

Crafting a secure and efficient **smart contract** is challenging due to its immutable nature. Making upgrades or changes to DAOs to rectify issues can be complex and controversial. Once deployed, any oversight or **vulnerability** in the code remains unless there is a community consensus to change it, often involving network-wide actions (like forks). The DAO incident is an example of a **re-entrancy attack** that occurred when an attacker could repeatedly call a function before the previous function call was completed.

DAOs, given their transparent and open-source nature, are prone to **external attacks**. Malicious actors continuously seek vulnerabilities in smart contract codes to exploit. As DAOs

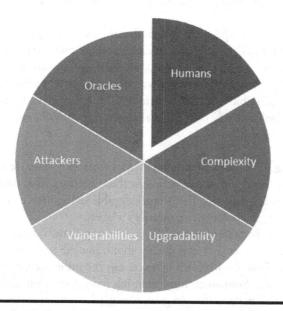

Figure 12.4   Sources of security concerns in DAOs

may rely on external data sources (**oracles**), there is a risk that these oracles can be tampered with, leading to flawed decision-making or exploitation.

And let's not forget: Even with the best intentions, **human errors** in code writing or under-standing the intricacies of the system can lead to significant losses. Mitigation strategies for such risks include thorough auditing of the code. Before deploying, smart contracts should undergo rigorous audits by multiple independent parties to ensure their security.

Organizations can incentivize the discovery of vulnerabilities by offering **bug bounties**, rewarding those who identify and report potential issues. Implementing **timelocks** (delays) before critical actions is also another mitigation strategy that can be executed to provide a window to catch and respond to suspicious activities.

In general, from an architecture perspective, the best approach is always designing smart con-tracts in a **modular fashion** which allows for easier upgrades and can isolate potential breaches.

Scalability of Governance Mechanisms

Decentralized governance, one of the cornerstone principles of DAOs, faces unique challenges when it comes to scalability. As DAOs grow in size and complexity, ensuring that every participant has a voice while also making timely and efficient decisions becomes increasingly challenging.

Challenges in scaling governance mechanisms are mostly related to decision-making ineffi-ciencies, which can be summarized as **low participation rates** and **decision gridlock**. As DAOs grow, not every member may participate in every vote, leading to decisions that might not rep-resent the majority's views. With an increasing number of participants, reaching consensus can become time-consuming and even lead to gridlocks where decisions are delayed or never made.

Large DAOs can have multiple proposals, discussions, and debates running concurrently. Parsing through all this information to make informed decisions can become overwhelming for members. If voting power is tied to token ownership, entities with significant holdings can dispro-portionately influence outcomes, leading to a **plutocratic system** rather than a truly democratic one. **Sybil attacks**, where one entity creates multiple identities to influence voting, can also distort governance.

As DAOs become more complex, the proposals can also become more technical or nuanced, requiring specialized knowledge. This can alienate average members who might not have the expertise to understand or vote on these matters. On some blockchain platforms, participating in governance (e.g., casting a vote) can incur transaction fees. As the **network becomes congested**, these costs can become prohibitive for some members, limiting participation.

DAO developers faced with any of these challenges may consider any of the following poten-tial solutions and innovations:

- **Delegate Voting or Liquid Democracy**: Members can delegate their voting rights to trusted entities or experts who can represent their interests. This combines direct and rep-resentative democracy, ensuring that knowledgeable individuals can handle complex issues while still reflecting the broader community's wishes.
- **Quadratic Voting**: Instead of one-token-one-vote systems, quadratic voting allows mem-bers to cast votes on issues they care deeply about, but the cost of casting multiple votes for an issue increases quadratically. This balances out the influence of large token holders.
- **Layer 2 Governance Solutions**: Implementing layer 2 solutions can help in reducing the costs associated with participating in governance, promoting more extensive participation.

- **Incentivized Participation**: DAOs can offer rewards or incentives for members to participate in governance processes, ensuring higher engagement.
- **Adaptive Quorum**: Adjusting the quorum requirements based on the importance of decisions or the number of active participants can help in mitigating decision gridlocks.
- **Time-Locked Voting**: To prevent sudden swings in decision-making, votes can be time-locked, requiring participants to lock their tokens for a certain period when voting, ensuring a degree of commitment and reducing the influence of short-term token holders.

The scalability of governance mechanisms remains one of the most intricate challenges for DAOs. Balancing inclusivity with efficiency requires innovative solutions that respect the decentralized ethos while ensuring that DAOs can function smoothly as they grow. As the space matures, it is likely that a combination of technological innovations and governance best practices will emerge to address these concerns effectively.

Ethical and Legal Considerations

The rise of DAOs has presented both novel ethical dilemmas and legal challenges. These organizations operate on the fringes of traditional legal frameworks, prompting discussions on their place in society and the broader implications for governance, rights, and responsibilities.

Ethical considerations span from **access and inclusivity** to the never-ending "**Transparency vs. Privacy**" debate. While DAOs champion decentralization, participation often requires technological know-how and sometimes financial resources (e.g., to buy tokens or pay transaction fees). This can exclude individuals without such capabilities or resources, raising concerns about true decentralization and inclusivity. While transparency is one of the cornerstones of DAOs, it can sometimes conflict with individual privacy, especially if all transactions and interactions are publicly viewable on the blockchain.

Another ethical aspect is connected to **fairness and equality of token distribution**. If voting power in a DAO is tied to token ownership, there are ethical concerns about fair token distribution. Those who acquire large amounts early on (or through substantial financial means) can have disproportionate influence, potentially leading to plutocracy. The principle of "**code is law**" can sometimes conflict with ethical considerations. If the code allows for actions that the community deems unethical, but no rule in the smart contract prohibits it, is it ethically permissible?

I am not a lawyer, and this question can open a bigger conversation, but what do you think are the legal considerations on the **legal status of DAOs**? Traditional legal systems often do not have provisions for recognizing DAOs. This raises questions about their legal status: Are they associations, partnerships, corporations, or something entirely new? With whom is the **liability and responsibility** of actions undertaken within a DAO? If a DAO's operation or decision leads to harm or losses, who is held liable? Without a central entity or clear leadership, assigning responsibility can be challenging.

Regulatory bodies worldwide are grappling with how to oversee and regulate DAOs, especially in areas like fundraising (akin to securities offerings) or governance. While smart contracts govern DAOs, they might not always be recognized as **legally binding contracts** in traditional courts. This poses challenges in disputes.

Cross-border operations may also need regulation. DAOs inherently operate on a global scale. Navigating the legal frameworks of multiple countries can be a daunting task, especially if there are conflicting regulations. This of how **intellectual property** rights (e.g., creations or inventions resulting from a DAO's collaborative efforts) are managed and attributed in a decentralized context, for example.

Balancing act and the way forward require a few critical actions. For DAOs to achieve mainstream adoption, legal systems might need to evolve to recognize and accommodate these novel structures. DAO communities might consider establishing ethical codes of conduct, ensuring that beyond just adhering to code, there is a commitment to broader ethical principles. Lastly, proactive engagement with regulators can help in shaping friendly regulations and providing clarity for DAO operations.

In conclusion, DAOs present a paradigm shift in organizational structures and governance, leading to uncharted territories in ethics and law. While they promise transformative potential, the path forward requires a delicate balance between leveraging their decentralized benefits and addressing the ethical and legal concerns that arise. As the DAO ecosystem matures, collaboration between the crypto community, legal experts, and regulators will be crucial in navigating these challenges.

The Future of DAOs

As the world becomes more digitally interconnected and the promise of decentralized governance gains traction, DAOs are poised to play a pivotal role in the next wave of organizational and societal evolution. Drawing from current trajectories and emerging technologies, we can anticipate several trends and developments in the DAO landscape.

- **Interoperability**: As more DAOs emerge with varied objectives, there will be a push for interoperability among them, allowing for more seamless interactions and collaborations.
- **Mergers**: Just as companies merge in traditional economies, DAOs might opt for mergers to pool resources, knowledge, and achieve shared objectives more efficiently.

AI-driven decision-making, integrating artificial intelligence into DAO governance, could help process vast amounts of data, propose optimal decisions, or even predict future trends to guide collective choices. As DAOs mature, their governance models will likely evolve based on feedback and experience, leading to more efficient and inclusive decision-making processes.

Predicted Trends and Developments

Mainstream adoption requires integration with traditional systems. As the benefits of DAOs become clearer, traditional organizations might adopt DAO-like structures or integrate with existing DAOs. Diversification is also key to broader adoption: Beyond finance and tech, DAOs will find applications in areas like supply chain management, healthcare, education, and even local governance.

But probably the most considerable evolution is **legal recognition** of DAOs. Given the challenges DAOs currently face with legal recognition, as identified in the previous section, it is plausible that jurisdictions will develop specific legal structures tailored to DAOs, much like corporations or partnerships in today's legal frameworks. As DAOs inherently operate beyond borders, there might be a push for international standards or regulations governing their operation.

DAO services and infrastructure will grow in multiple directions:

- **DAO-as-a-Service**: Companies and platforms might emerge that offer DAO creation and management as a service, simplifying the process for those wanting to establish a DAO without starting from scratch.
- **Infrastructure Enhancement**: Technologies supporting DAO operations, from voting mechanisms to communication platforms, will witness innovation and growth.
- **Identity Verification**: To combat sybil attacks and ensure genuine participation, DAOs might integrate with decentralized identity verification systems.
- **Reputation Systems**: As interactions within DAOs grow, there will be a need for trust mechanisms. Decentralized reputation systems can help members gauge the reliability and contribution history of other participants.

We can also expect a greater focus on ethical and environmental considerations:

- **Sustainable Operations**: As the broader tech community becomes more environmentally conscious, DAOs might emphasize more sustainable blockchain operations, perhaps favoring proof-of-stake or other energy-efficient consensus mechanisms over proof-of-work.
- **Ethical Mandates**: Future DAOs might have clear ethical guidelines or missions, ensuring that their operations and investments align with broader societal goals.

The future of DAOs is a mosaic of potentialities, promising to reshape how we think about organizations, governance, and collective decision-making. As with all disruptive innovations, challenges will emerge alongside opportunities. However, given the dynamism and adaptability inherent in the DAO model, it is a realm teeming with possibilities, set to redefine many facets of our societal structures in the coming years.

Conclusion

DAOs have the potential to redefine many facets of our global society. From altering economic power dynamics to influencing cultural and political structures, their impact can be both transformative and multifaceted. As with all innovations, the true potential of DAOs will unfold with time, shaped by both their inherent capabilities and how society chooses to leverage them. Adopting a proactive approach, which involves understanding, iterating, and refining DAO structures, can steer their impact in directions that foster a more inclusive, transparent, and collaborative global community.

Chapter 13

Carbon Tokenization

In the quest to tackle global climate change, humanity has sought to innovate across multiple sectors. As these efforts converge with advances in blockchain technology, a groundbreaking concept has emerged: **Carbon tokenization**. This introduction sets the stage for an in-depth exploration of carbon tokenization within the broader framework of blockchain technology.

Carbon Emissions and Climate Change

Human activities have dramatically increased the concentration of carbon dioxide (CO_2) and other greenhouse gases in the Earth's atmosphere. As these levels rise, they trap more heat, leading to a series of cascading environmental impacts collectively known as climate change. Mitigating these impacts requires a substantial decrease in carbon emissions.

The Role of Carbon Markets

One strategy to reduce emissions is through carbon markets, where carbon credits are traded. Historically, one credit might represent a metric ton of CO_2 equivalent (tCO_2e) reduced or offset. However, verifying, tracking, and ensuring the authenticity of these credits has been challenging. This is where blockchain, with its promise of transparency, traceability, and immutability, presents a solution.

Blockchain and Tokenization

At its core, blockchain is a decentralized ledger that chronologically records transactions across many computers. The process of converting rights to an asset into a digital token on a blockchain is known as tokenization. Tokenization ensures the asset's provenance, ownership, and authenticity can be tracked and verified without a central authority.

Merging Carbon Credits with Blockchain

Carbon tokenization is the process of converting carbon credits into digital tokens on a blockchain. This not only simplifies the trading of carbon credits but also ensures their provenance, traceability, and, most critically, their legitimacy.

DOI: 10.4324/9781003491934-13

Benefits of Carbon Tokenization

Benefits of carbon tokenization on a blockchain are aligned with the advantages that blockchain technology brings to the industry: transparency, trust, interoperability, etc. Speaking of **transparency and trust**, with each token representing a specific quantity of reduced or offset CO_2, stakeholders can easily verify the authenticity of carbon credits. The carbon market is largely based on volunteer measurement, and thus unregulated for the most part of it. Tokenizing carbon credits on a blockchain can introduce that level of transparency and trust that is needed before credits can be traded.

Trading of carbon credits can occur on entire units or on fractions of them. **Fractionalization** of tokenized carbon credits allows for the whole units of credits to be divided into smaller units, making carbon trading accessible to a broader audience (smaller units cost less to buy).

The other technical benefits of blockchain apply also to carbon tokenization system: **Interoperability** of digital tokens means that the carbon trading platforms can easily interact with other systems, enabling integration with other environmental and financial platforms. **Efficiency and speed** of execution is then gained at scale. The automation capabilities of blockchain streamline and expedite the carbon credit trading process all along its supply chain.

In the subsequent sections of this chapter, we will delve deeper into the technical nuances of carbon tokenization, explore its implications for the future of climate action, and discuss potential challenges and solutions. As you journey through, you will discover the transformative potential of merging two revolutionary concepts for the greater good of our planet.

Understanding Carbon Markets

Over the past century, the Earth's atmosphere has undergone significant alterations due to human activities. The most consequential of these changes has been the increased concentration of greenhouse gases (GHGs), especially carbon dioxide (CO_2). GHGs have the unique property of trapping heat from the sun, leading to a warming effect known as the greenhouse effect.

Natural amounts of GHGs have always been present in our atmosphere and have played a crucial role in keeping our planet warm enough to support life. However, since the industrial revolution, the burning of fossil fuels, deforestation, and other industrial processes have resulted in a rapid and unprecedented increase in the concentration of these gases. CO_2, in particular, has seen its levels rise from a pre-industrial value of approximately 280 parts per million (ppm) to over 410 ppm in recent years, the highest in at least 800,000 years. The repercussions of this increased GHG concentration are manifold:

- **Global Warming**: The Earth's average temperature has risen by approximately 1.2° C, or 34.16° F, since the late 19th century, with most of this warming occurring in the last 40 years. This might seem like a minor change, but even small shifts in global temperatures can result in dramatic ecological and climatic shifts.
- **Melting Ice and Rising Sea Levels**: The warming has led to the melting of glaciers and polar ice, resulting in rising sea levels. This puts coastal cities and island nations at risk, threatening to displace millions of people.
- **Extreme Weather Events**: The frequency and severity of extreme weather events, such as hurricanes, droughts, and heavy rainfall, have increased, leading to significant economic and human losses.

- **Ocean Acidification**: CO_2 is absorbed by the oceans, leading to acidification, which harms marine life, especially coral reefs and shelled organisms.
- **Biodiversity Loss**: Changes in temperature and habitat disruption have put many species at risk, leading to a rapid decline in biodiversity.

While natural processes can influence climate, the current rate and scale of change have been largely attributed to human activities. Factors such as the burning of coal, oil, and natural gas for energy; large-scale deforestation; and various industrial processes release vast amounts of CO_2 and other GHGs into the atmosphere.

The relationship between carbon emissions and climate change is inextricable. The choices we make today concerning energy consumption, land use, and industrial activities have long-term implications for our planet's health. Recognizing the role of human-induced carbon emissions in exacerbating climate change underscores the urgent need for innovative solutions to reduce our carbon footprint and move towards a more sustainable future.

The Need for a New Solution

As the aforementioned impacts of carbon emissions on our climate become increasingly evident, it is apparent that traditional methods of addressing the issue, while important, may not be enough. While efforts have been made on international, national, and local scales to curb emissions – ranging from global agreements like the Paris Agreement to technological advancements in renewable energy – the rate of progress is often outpaced by the growth in emissions from burgeoning economies and increasing global energy demands. Shortcomings of existing measures include:

- **Inconsistent Regulation**: Climate policies vary dramatically from one country to another. While some nations have made significant strides in reducing their carbon footprint, others lag behind. Without a unified global approach, the efforts of one nation can be negated by the inaction of another.
- **Verification and Transparency Issues**: Traditional carbon markets sometimes lack the transparency required to ensure that emission reductions are genuine. There have been instances where carbon credits have been sold for projects that did not result in genuine carbon reductions.
- **Economic Disincentives**: Fossil fuels, especially coal and natural gas, often remain cheaper than renewable alternatives. Without proper economic incentives, businesses and nations may opt for the less environmentally friendly option.
- **Technological Barriers**: Although technological advancements have been made in renewable energy, storage solutions, and carbon capture, these technologies still face challenges in scalability, efficiency, and costs.

Amidst these challenges, carbon tokenization emerges as a promising solution, particularly in addressing the transparency and verification concerns of traditional carbon markets. By utilizing the decentralized, transparent, and immutable nature of blockchain technology, carbon credits can be traced back to their origin, ensuring that every ton of CO_2 reduced or offset is accounted for and not double-counted. Parties can engage in carbon trading with greater confidence, knowing that the credits they purchase have a genuine impact. Tokenized carbon credits can be fractionalized, allowing a broader audience, including individuals and small businesses, to participate in the carbon market. This brings increased accessibility and democratization in the market, which, along with a global unification of carbon exchange platforms, that is, decentralized, universally accessible platforms, fosters a more cohesive global approach to carbon reduction.

The accelerating impacts of climate change underscore an urgent need to rethink and innovate our strategies. While existing measures have their merits, they also have significant gaps that need to be addressed. Carbon tokenization offers a fresh perspective, leveraging modern technology to address some of the most pressing challenges in the fight against climate change. As we move forward, embracing such novel solutions will be critical in our collective journey toward a sustainable future.

Challenges in Traditional Carbon Markets

Carbon markets emerged as a mechanism to address greenhouse gas emissions by assigning a monetary value to the cost of emitting carbon. The idea is simple: by creating a financial incentive for reducing emissions, businesses and nations would naturally work towards cleaner practices. However, while the premise is straightforward, its execution has proven to be riddled with challenges.

First, the market is facing a typical infancy problem: lack of standardization due to varied protocols. Different regions and organizations have their own standards and methodologies for measuring carbon reductions and issuing credits.

This leads to inconsistent pricing: The absence of a universal standard leads to varying prices for carbon credits, causing confusion and potential misuse. In addition, without a centralized, transparent system, the same carbon offset can be claimed and sold multiple times, leading to inflated emission reduction claims (the "double spending" problem of tokens on blockchains).

The lack of a system of verifiable carbon credits not only leads to inconsistent pricing, but also to inconsistent auditing. Ensuring that a project has genuinely reduced or offset the amount of carbon it claims is crucial. However, rigorous auditing is resource-intensive and sometimes lacks the necessary transparency.

The process is often opaque, causing transparency and trust deficits. The journey of a carbon credit from its origin to its final sale often lacks transparency, making it difficult for buyers to ascertain the legitimacy of their purchase. Some projects that receive credits, such as certain large hydroelectric projects or fast-growing plantations, might have detrimental environmental or social impacts that overshadow their carbon-reducing benefits.

Limited accessibility and lack of liquidity create high entry barriers. Traditional carbon markets often have high entry barriers, making it difficult for smaller businesses and individuals to participate. Trading carbon credits can sometimes be a lengthy process, reducing the incentive for businesses to engage in the market.

Regulatory and policy hurdles are caused by volatile policies. Political changes can lead to shifts in climate policies, impacting the stability and predictability of carbon markets. The divide between compliance markets (where entities are legally obligated to reduce emissions) and voluntary markets (where entities reduce emissions out of goodwill or for corporate social responsibility) can sometimes cause discrepancies in pricing and standards.

While traditional carbon markets have played a significant role in incentivizing emission reductions, they are not without their challenges. These issues not only hinder the effectiveness of carbon markets but also diminish trust in them. As the urgency to address climate change intensifies, refining these systems or finding innovative alternatives like carbon tokenization becomes paramount.

Introduction to Carbon Credits

At the intersection of environmental conservation and financial markets lies the concept of carbon credits. In essence, a **carbon credit** represents the reduction or offsetting of one metric ton of carbon dioxide equivalent (tCO_2e). By attributing a tangible value to the act of reducing greenhouse gas emissions, carbon credits aim to financially incentivize sustainable practices and promote a transition to a low-carbon economy.

The genesis of carbon credits can be traced back to international environmental agreements. The most notable among these is the Kyoto Protocol, adopted in 1997, which introduced market-based mechanisms to help countries achieve their emission reduction targets. Later on, the Paris Agreement in 2015 reinforced global commitment to climate action, further underlining the significance of carbon credits. There are four types of globally recognized carbon credits:

1. **Certified Emission Reduction (CER)**: Originating from the Kyoto Protocol's Clean Development Mechanism (CDM), a CER represents the reduction of one metric ton of CO_2 through sustainable development projects in developing countries.
2. **Emission Reduction Unit (ERU)**: Derived from the Joint Implementation (JI) mechanism of the Kyoto Protocol, an ERU represents emission reductions from projects in developed countries that exceed their emission commitments.
3. **Verified Emission Reduction (VER)**: Often used in the voluntary carbon market, VERs are not tied to any specific international treaty but are instead generated by projects that have undergone third-party verification against recognized standards.
4. **Removal Units (RMU)**: These are generated through activities that directly remove and store carbon dioxide, such as afforestation and reforestation.

How do carbon credits exactly work? Figure 13.1 shows the process for measuring and trading carbon credits. There is an initial phase of **project initiation**: An entity, say a company or a community, initiates a project intended to reduce or offset CO_2 emissions. This could be anything from planting trees to setting up a wind energy farm. Once the project is operational, its emission reductions are **measured and verified** by an accredited third party to ensure they meet specific standards.

Upon successful verification, the project is **awarded** a corresponding number of carbon credits. These credits can then be sold on carbon markets (**trading**). Entities that wish to offset their own emissions can purchase these credits, essentially compensating for their emissions by supporting emission-reducing projects elsewhere. Once a carbon credit is used to offset emissions, it is **retired** to prevent it from being used again.

Carbon credits have both an environmental and economic impact. At an **environmental** level, by incentivizing projects that reduce or offset emissions, they play a direct role in combatting climate change. From an **economic** consideration, they provide a source of revenue for sustainable

Figure 13.1 Carbon credit lifecycle

initiatives, especially in developing regions, promoting economic growth alongside environmental conservation.

Carbon credits are a testament to the power of merging financial mechanisms with environmental objectives. By translating emission reductions into a tradable commodity, they have brought about a unique approach to combatting climate change. As the world grapples with the climate crisis, understanding and optimizing the role of carbon credits becomes increasingly crucial.

Benefits of Carbon Tokenization

Before delving into the specific advantages of **carbon tokenization**, it is essential to grasp the broader concept of tokenization. In the realm of blockchain technology, tokenization refers to the representation of an asset or a right in the form of a digital token on a blockchain. These tokens can signify various assets, from real estate and stocks to intellectual property and, in our context, carbon credits.

Tokenized carbon credits benefit from enhanced transparency and trust. Blockchain, by its very nature, is immutable. Once a carbon credit is tokenized and recorded on the blockchain, it cannot be altered or deleted, ensuring its authenticity and integrity. With the entire lifecycle of a carbon credit – from project initiation to credit retirement – visible on the blockchain, all stakeholders can verify the carbon reduction's legitimacy.

Critical to trust in a carbon offsetting project is also the elimination of double counting by assigning a unique digital identity to a carbon credit. Basically, each tokenized carbon credit is given a distinct digital identity, making it impossible for the same credit to be sold or claimed multiple times. Blockchain's smart contracts can automate the retirement of used carbon credits, ensuring they are taken out of circulation once utilized.

Another key factor, increased accessibility and democratization of carbon credits, can be achieved by **fractionalization**. Tokenization allows for the division of a single carbon credit into smaller fractions, enabling smaller businesses and even individuals to invest in or offset their carbon footprint without the need to buy a whole credit. In addition, a decentralized carbon market on the blockchain allows participants from anywhere in the world to buy or sell tokenized carbon credits, fostering a truly global carbon market. This is a real 24/7 market, which, unlike traditional markets that have operating hours, operates round the clock, making it easier to trade carbon credits at any time. This enhanced liquidity increases participation: The combined benefits of transparency, accessibility, and efficiency can attract more participants to the carbon market, enhancing liquidity and price discovery.

Investors, in the end, want efficient and cost-effective transactions. Blockchain technology reduces the need for intermediaries. By streamlining the process of buying and selling carbon credits, blockchain can reduce the number of intermediaries, leading to faster and potentially cheaper transactions. Cost efficiencies are also brought in by automated compliance: Smart contracts can be programmed to ensure that trades and transfers of tokenized carbon credits comply with prevailing regulations and standards.

In conclusion, carbon tokenization, powered by blockchain technology, offers a transformative approach to addressing the challenges inherent in traditional carbon markets. By leveraging the unique capabilities of blockchain, carbon tokenization can rejuvenate the carbon market, making it more transparent, efficient, and accessible. As the world intensifies its efforts to combat climate change, such innovations will play a pivotal role in shaping a sustainable future.

Use Cases and Real-World Examples

Carbon Tokenization in Renewable Energy

Renewable energy stands at the forefront of global efforts to combat climate change. With advancements in blockchain technology, carbon tokenization has emerged as a promising tool to augment the renewable energy sector by seamlessly merging carbon credits with digital token systems.

Use Case 1: Solar Energy Projects

Solar energy projects can tokenize the carbon credits they earn by offsetting traditional energy sources. Investors can buy these tokens as a means of supporting solar initiatives and simultaneously offsetting their carbon footprint.

SolarCoin (https://solarcoin.org/) is a global rewards program for solar electricity generation. For every MWh of solar electricity produced, a solar panel owner receives one SolarCoin, serving both as an incentive to invest in solar panels and as a digital representation of the carbon savings generated by the project. According to its website, SolarCoin is an alternative digital currency that works like air miles for solar electricity generation. Anyone can invest in SolarCoin on any cryptocurrency exchange, which gives it similar attributes to Bitcoin. Still, the only way to receive SolarCoin for free is to go solar yourself and produce solar energy. This makes sense, as its purpose is to spread the adoption of solar energy being produced. This is akin to the idea of mining cryptocurrency. In this instance, you are "mining" energy.

Use Case 2: Wind Energy Farms

By transforming the carbon savings from wind farms into digital tokens, wind energy producers can attract investment and reward stakeholders for their green initiatives.

WePower (https://www.wepower.energy/) is a blockchain-based green energy trading platform that connects energy buyers directly with green energy producers. Through the platform, renewable energy producers can tokenize their future energy production and sell it upfront, providing them with the capital needed to develop their projects. WePower is basically a provider of blockchain-powered virtual power purchase agreements (PPA). A PPA is an agreement between one or more parties for the use of energy. For example, a PPA for renewable energy projects like wind and solar will incentivize the build of more farms, knowing they will have customers to service upon completion. So, in effect, these agreements help to drive the construction of more renewable energy facilities, thus helping carbon reduction.

Use Case 3: Biomass and Waste-to-Energy Projects

Biomass and waste-to-energy projects, which turn waste materials into energy, can tokenize the carbon emissions they prevent, offering an innovative solution for waste management and clean energy production.

BioCoin (https://biocoin.life/), an eco-cryptocurrency, rewards eco-friendly initiatives, including biomass projects. Businesses that reduce carbon emissions through waste-to-energy mechanisms can earn BioCoins, which can then be used within a dedicated eco-friendly ecosystem or traded in crypto exchanges.

Use Case 4: Integrating Grid Systems with Tokenized Energy

Tokenization can facilitate the creation of decentralized energy grids where users can trade tokenized renewable energy in real-time based on demand and supply.

decVolt (https://www.decvolt.com/) is a virtual power plant (VPP) enabler, a peer-to-peer energy trading platform on the blockchain. It enables consumers and businesses to sell their surplus renewable energy directly to their neighbors, using tokenized energy credits, enhancing grid efficiency, and promoting renewable sources. Simply put, a VPP is a network of solar power and battery systems installed at homes and businesses. The systems are coordinated by a central control software system run by the VPP operator that taps into the stored energy of the batteries during periods of peak demand to supply the mains grid.

By all these use cases, we can conclude that carbon tokenization in the renewable energy sector provides a fresh perspective on how we perceive and trade carbon credits. By offering tangible, tradable tokens that represent real-world carbon reductions, blockchain technology can foster a more dynamic and transparent renewable energy market. These use cases and real-world examples underscore the transformative potential of marrying blockchain technology with renewable energy initiatives.

Afforestation and Reforestation Projects

Forests play a pivotal role in maintaining the balance of our planet's ecosystems. Afforestation and reforestation are essential tools in the arsenal against climate change, not only for their carbon sequestration capacity but also for the myriads of ecological benefits they offer.

Afforestation refers to the process of planting trees on land that has not been forested for a minimum of 50 years. Essentially, it is about converting a barren or agricultural land into a forested area.

Reforestation involves replanting trees in areas where forests were removed due to logging, farming, or other reasons. Its primary purpose is to restore areas that were once forested.

Benefits and challenges of afforestation and reforestation are listed in Table 13.1.

Incorporating carbon tokenization can add value and foster investment in these projects. As these projects sequester carbon, they can earn carbon credits. By tokenizing these credits, projects can raise funds by selling tokens to investors or individuals looking to offset their carbon footprint.

Blockchain can offer transparent and immutable records of carbon sequestration rates, ensuring stakeholders that the projects are genuinely contributing to carbon reductions. Token incentives can encourage community involvement, ensuring that local communities benefit from reforestation and afforestation initiatives.

In summary, afforestation and reforestation stand as significant strategies to combat the adverse impacts of climate change and restore ecological balance. With the incorporation of modern tools like carbon tokenization, the potential to amplify the impact and reach of such projects is vast. In the interplay between nature and technology, the future of our planet's green cover can be promising and robust.

Aetlas Protocol

Aetlas Protocol (https://www.aetlas.xyz/), another example of a startup operating in this market, has embarked on creating a blockchain-based system to more accurately track how companies

Table 13.1   Key benefits and challenges of generating carbon dioxide with afforestation and reforestation approaches

Benefit	Challenge
Carbon sequestration: Trees absorb CO_2 from the atmosphere, converting it into biomass and storing carbon, thereby mitigating greenhouse gas concentrations.	**Land availability:** With increasing urbanization, privatization of land, and agricultural expansion, finding suitable land for large-scale afforestation or reforestation can be challenging.
Biodiversity conservation: Forests serve as habitats for countless species, and their regeneration can help preserve the planet's biodiversity. Forests also play a crucial role in regulating the water cycle, influencing precipitation patterns and groundwater recharge.	**Biodiversity concerns:** Incorrect tree species selection can disrupt local ecosystems and reduce biodiversity.
Soil conservation: Forests prevent soil erosion, maintain soil fertility, and promote the growth of beneficial microbial communities.	**Long-term maintenance:** Continuous care, protection against pests, and monitoring are essential to ensure the forest's sustainability.
Livelihoods and economy: Sustainable forestry can provide job opportunities, resources like timber, and non-timber forest products, promoting economic growth.	**Economic barriers:** Initial costs for planting and nurturing forests can be high, and return on investment may be slow, especially when prioritizing ecological over economic benefits.

offset their carbon footprints through access to certified carbon credit issuing projects. By tokenizing carbon offset credits, they aim to simplify the carbon accounting process and create a more transparent market.

Aetlas is taking the tokenized carbon credits even further, into the financial world. Not only they help green project developers and companies in need to buy carbon credits to meet and commit with digital agreements signed on a blockchain. The protocol also offers financial products such as digital offtakes and bonds that provide instant liquidity. Project developers can secure forward buying commitments from corporate buyers, and therefore unlock funds for future project financing and bond issuance. They then can issue green bonds to fund development for new carbon removal infrastructure, they can set the bond's coupon rate and maturity date and mitigate the risk profile with programmable pledges on future offtake revenue.

A **digital offtake agreement**, as illustrated in Figure 13.2, is an innovative financial product in the blockchain-based carbon removal market. The agreement represents a forward buying "promise" between a buyer and a supplier. The buyer, properly KYB-ed, signs a legally binding contract. The terms of the contract and its pricing structure are coded in a traditional contract, which is paired to its twin digital contract on the blockchain. Buyers (companies looking to offset their carbon footprint) and suppliers (green project developers) define the terms of the offtake agreement and sign a legal contract. The blockchain smart contract is used a payment escrow and for delivery of certified units of carbon credits.

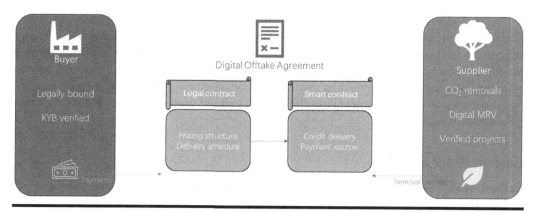

Figure 13.2   A digital offtake agreement

The structure of the smart contract, which supports credit and payment delivery, is listed below.

```
contract DigitalOfftakeAgreement {
    // State variables
    address public projectDeveloper;
    address public buyer;
    uint256 public creditAmount;
    uint256 public pricePerCredit;
    uint256 public totalPrice;
    uint256 public creditsTransferred;
    uint256 public balance;

    enum State { AWAITING_PAYMENT, AWAITING_DELIVERY, COMPLETE }
    State public currentState;

    // Events
    event PaymentDeposited(address indexed buyer, uint256 amount);
    event CreditsTransferred(address indexed developer, uint256 amount);
    event PaymentReleased(address indexed developer, uint256 amount);

    // Function for buyer to deposit payment
    function depositPayment() public payable onlyBuyer inState(State.
        AWAITING_PAYMENT) {
    }

    // Function for project developer to transfer carbon credits
    function transferCredits(uint256 _credits) public onlyProject
        Developer inState(State.AWAITING_DELIVERY) {
    }

    // Function to release payment to project developer
    function releasePayment() internal inState(State.COMPLETE) {
    }
}
```

This contract provides a basic implementation of an escrow mechanism for carbon credit transactions. You may need to extend it with additional features such as credit verification, dispute resolution mechanisms, or more complex state transitions based on your specific requirements.

We will observe more and more initiatives like Aetlas Protocol in the future. Aetlas, as a decentralized protocol focused on financing carbon removal infrastructure, is pioneering the convergence of the carbon credit market with green financial products, helping project developers secure non-dilutive funding. The protocol aims to simplify and accelerate the financing process for carbon removal projects, providing solutions for both engineered and nature-based initiatives. Aetlas also supports green investors by enabling them to build fixed-income portfolios with a tangible environmental impact.

Carbon Asset Solutions

Carbon Asset Solutions (CAS) (https://carbonassetsolutions.com/) is out to help rid the planet of damaging atmospheric carbon dioxide. Its breakthrough measurement, recording, and verification technology platform creates a new, much more accurate way of measuring carbon sequestered in soil, verifying it efficiently and securely selling carbon credits to the rapidly growing net zero carbon markets. The company needed to capture and encrypt the precision carbon measurement data, protect against data tampering at both ends of the carbon credit process, and consider long-term global scalability. By enabling **Microsoft Azure confidential computing** in its IoT devices and data management, CAS is working to solve one of the earth's pivotal environmental problems.

Deforestation and agriculture create harmful greenhouse gases that accelerate climate change. CAS addresses this problem by focusing on a technology solution that encourages farmers to switch to sustainable agricultural practices that reduce greenhouse gas emissions and return carbon back to the soil from the atmosphere, where it improves soil fertility, so plants thrive.

Microsoft's cloud platform used by CAS provides a way to intensify the privacy and security of data in use with Azure confidential computing (ACC), a technology that enables sharing data while securing it. ACC incorporates highly secure hardware to create a trusted execution environment, protecting data during processing. Even a systems administrator cannot see the data in unencrypted form, which means that organizations like CAS which must share data can protect it from tampering.

CAS applies multiple layers of encryption to the raw data that is gathered from field scans. The encryption keys for this data are stored in Azure Key Vault while the hashes of measurement data and computation results are stored in Azure Confidential Ledger (ACL), a technology in ACC that provides a decentralized digital ledger and tamper-resistant storage for highly confidential data. CAS uses ACL to keep all their readings very secure and tamper-free. Because the confidential ledger runs on a hardware-encrypted trusted computing base, CAS customers can be confident that no-one at the company, and even Microsoft itself as cloud hosting provider, has the ability to change the data.

Figure 13.3 shows the gamma-ray carbon scanner developed by CAS in collaboration with the U.S. Department of Agriculture and Auburn University. The scanner is towed around fields with a tractor. It reads carbon at an atomic level better than many existing methods, it adds precise GPS coordinates and brings in other data to create a complete, accurate, and instantly available carbon profile of a field. As opposite to the commonly used method for sampling soil and measuring its carbon content, which takes months and lacks precision, CAS' scanner is fast and precise, and it does not interfere with farming operations.

Figure 13.3   Carbon Asset Solutions' field carbon scanner

The Mechanics of Carbon Tokenization

The Process of Tokenizing Carbon Credits

At the intersection of blockchain technology and environmental conservation lies the ground-breaking process of carbon tokenization. This novel system represents carbon credits in a digital format, making them tradable on blockchain platforms. But how does this transformation occur? Let's dive into the mechanics.

Before diving into tokenization, it is crucial to grasp what carbon credits are. A **carbon credit** represents the reduction of one metric ton of carbon dioxide or its equivalent in other greenhouse gases. They originate from projects or initiatives that reduce, avoid, or sequester emissions. These can range from renewable energy projects to afforestation initiatives.

The process for tokenizing carbon credits includes the following steps:

1. **Quantification and Verification**: The first step is measuring the amount of CO_2 reduced, avoided, or sequestered by a particular project. An independent body then assesses and verifies the reduction claims, ensuring they meet specific standards and criteria.
2. **Digital Representation**: Each verified carbon credit is then represented as a unique digital token on a blockchain platform. This process ensures that each token corresponds to an actual carbon reduction, avoiding double-counting or fraudulent claims. The token carries metadata about its origin, the project it represents, its date of issue, and other relevant details, ensuring transparency.
3. **Integration into a Marketplace**: Once tokenized, the carbon credits can be integrated into a digital marketplace where they can be bought, sold, or retired. Smart contracts ensure that transactions are executed only when specific criteria are met, automating the trade and ensuring trustworthiness.

4. **Trade and Redemption**: Interested parties can purchase these tokens as an offset for their carbon footprint or as an investment. When an entity wishes to use a carbon token to offset its emissions, the token is "retired" to ensure it is not reused. This action is recorded on the blockchain, certifying the offset.
5. **Monitoring and Reporting**: Blockchain's inherent transparency allows for continuous monitoring of the token's lifecycle, from issuance to retirement. Entities can seamlessly report their carbon offset activities, using the immutable records from the blockchain as evidence.

Carbon tokenization represents a confluence of technological innovation and environmental responsibility. By translating real-world carbon reduction into digital tokens, this system not only democratizes carbon trading but also amplifies transparency and trust. As industries and individuals worldwide become more conscious of their environmental footprint, understanding the mechanics of carbon tokenization becomes crucial for a sustainable future.

Standards and Protocols

The process of carbon tokenization relies on stringent standards and protocols to ensure authenticity, consistency, and transparency. These standards define the methodology for measuring carbon reductions, verifying them, and turning them into tradable assets on the blockchain.

The importance of standards and protocols is to **ensure authenticity**, that is to prevent fraudulent claims and ensure each token truly represents a metric ton of carbon dioxide reduction or its equivalent. Standards and protocols are also necessary for **facilitating trade** because standardized tokens can be traded across platforms and geographies without confusion. Lastly, they are beneficial for **instilling trust**, as adhering to globally recognized standards boosts confidence among stakeholders and encourages more participants to join the carbon trading ecosystem.

Currently, the key **standards** in carbon trading are as listed in Table 13.2.

The following list describes the four **protocols** (or processes) in carbon tokenization:

Table 13.2   Key de-facto standards for trading carbon credits

Reference	Description
Verified Carbon Standard (VCS)	Managed by Verra, this standard ensures the environmental integrity of carbon credits used in voluntary markets.
Gold Standard	Developed by WWF and other NGOs, it certifies carbon mitigation projects that also contribute to sustainable development.
Clean Development Mechanism (CDM)	An arrangement under the Kyoto Protocol allowing industrialized countries with emission-reduction commitments to invest in projects that reduce emissions in developing countries as an alternative to more expensive emission reductions in their own countries.
Climate Action Reserve (CAR)	A US-based carbon offset registry that sets protocols for GHG emission reduction projects.

1. **Measurement**: Define the methodologies to quantify emissions and reductions. They cover various sectors, from forestry to energy.
2. **Verification**: Determine the procedures through which third-party entities verify emission reduction claims.
3. **Tokenization**: Lay out the process for creating, issuing, trading, and retiring carbon tokens on blockchain platforms.
4. **Interoperability**: Ensure that different blockchain platforms and carbon markets can interact seamlessly, allowing for broader and more efficient trading.

While the maze of standards and protocols can seem intricate, they form the backbone of the carbon tokenization process, ensuring credibility and consistency in the market. As the world moves toward a more sustainable future, it is imperative for stakeholders to understand, adapt to, and shape these frameworks to maximize their impact on combating climate change.

Verification and Validation

Ensuring the integrity of carbon credits and tokenized carbon assets is paramount. This calls for robust verification and validation processes, which play crucial roles in ensuring the credibility, authenticity, and effectiveness of carbon offset projects. These processes are central to building trust in carbon markets, especially when utilizing blockchain and tokenization technologies.

Verification vs. Validation: Understanding the Difference

Validation is the process by which a project's design is assessed and approved. It ensures that the project, if executed as planned, will produce the expected carbon reductions in the future.

Verification refers to the periodic review of ongoing or completed projects. It confirms that the actual carbon reductions have occurred and align with what was predicted during validation.

There are four steps typically taken in a verification process:

1. **Documentation Review**: Scrutinizing project data, methodologies, and results to ensure accurate reporting of emissions and reductions.
2. **Site Inspections**: On-site assessments of projects to confirm that the documentation aligns with actual activities and results.
3. **Stakeholder Consultations**: Engaging with local communities and other stakeholders to understand the project's impact and ensure no discrepancies exist.
4. **Issuance of a Verification Report**: A detailed report confirming the project's emission reductions is published. If discrepancies exist, they are highlighted and need to be addressed.

Similarly, the validation process includes the following steps:

1. **Assessment of Project Design**: Evaluating the proposed methodologies, technologies, and practices to ensure they meet recognized standards.
2. **Stakeholder Engagement**: Ensuring local communities and other interested parties are consulted, and their concerns and suggestions are addressed.
3. **Issuance of a Validation Certificate**: Once the project design is deemed satisfactory and meets the necessary standards, a validation certificate is issued.

The role of third-party entities is to keep independence and objectivity. Maintaining trust, verification and validation are usually conducted by independent third-party entities. They bring objectivity and eliminate potential conflicts of interest. External parties should also bring specialized knowledge. These entities possess expertise in carbon markets, environmental sciences, and relevant sectors like energy, forestry, and transportation.

Challenges in verification and validation are represented mostly by geographical constraints. Some projects, especially those in remote locations, may be challenging to inspect physically. Comprehensive verification and validation can be time-consuming and costly, potentially deterring smaller projects.

Varied standards and evolving metrics are also a deterrent. Different carbon markets and standards may have diverse requirements, causing potential inconsistencies. As scientific understanding advances, the metrics used to measure carbon reductions may change, requiring continuous adaptation.

Verification and validation act as the twin pillars that uphold the credibility of the carbon tokenization process. Without rigorous checks and balances, the trustworthiness of carbon credits, tokenized or not, would be in question. As the importance of carbon markets grows in the global fight against climate change, ensuring the robustness of these processes becomes even more critical.

Chapter 14

The Metaverse

As we stand on the precipice of a new digital era, the concept of the **Metaverse** is emerging as a transformative force reshaping our understanding of reality, society, and connectivity. Imagine an expansive, shared digital universe, encompassing countless interconnected 3D virtual worlds, augmented realities, and digital spaces. In this realm, the boundaries between the physical and digital blur, offering users immersive experiences, where they can work, socialize, create, and play in ways previously confined to the realms of science fiction.

Originating from Neal Stephenson's 1992 novel "Snow Crash", the term metaverse has since evolved, transcending its fictional roots to represent a convergence of physical and virtual reality. Powered by rapid advancements in technology, such as virtual reality (VR), augmented reality (AR), blockchain, artificial intelligence (AI), and high-speed connectivity, the Metaverse is positioned to be the next significant phase of the Web3 internet.

Within the Metaverse, users can adopt digital personas, called **avatars**, interact with both AI-driven entities and real-world participants, and traverse between diverse virtual environments. Beyond entertainment, the Metaverse promises to revolutionize fields like education, business, healthcare, and art, offering new mediums for expression, collaboration, and innovation.

However, with these endless possibilities also come challenges. Issues related to privacy, digital rights, governance, and the digital divide loom large. As we delve deeper into this chapter, we will explore the technical intricacies, potentials, and concerns surrounding the ever-evolving Metaverse, preparing readers to navigate and shape this bold new frontier.

What Is the Metaverse?

At its core, the Metaverse represents a collective virtual shared space created by the convergence of virtually augmented physical reality and physically persistent virtual worlds. It is often regarded as a successor to the internet, a three-dimensional space where users can interact in real-time with digital environments, assets, and other users through avatars, transcending the limits of physical geography.

The nature of the Metaverse can be summarized by the union of its core and technical attributes, as displayed in Figure 14.1.

DOI: 10.4324/9781003491934-14

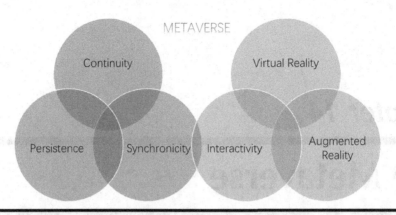

Figure 14.1   Core and technical properties of a Metaverse

Core attributes refer to properties of the Metaverse that are common irrespective of its technical implementation:

- **Continuity**: Unlike disparate websites or applications on the internet, the Metaverse offers a continuous digital universe. It is envisioned that a user could, for instance, walk from a digital concert into a virtual business conference, and then explore a digital recreation of a historic city, all without logging off or switching between platforms.
- **Synchronicity**: Events in the Metaverse happen in real-time. This synchronicity makes the digital experience closely resemble the spontaneity and unpredictability of the real world.
- **Persistence**: Even when individual users log off, the Metaverse continues. It is a world where actions have consequences, and history can be built. If a user builds a digital monument, it remains for others to see, just as in the real world.

On a technical level, the key components on a Metaverse world include:

- **Virtual Reality (VR)**: The use of VR headsets allows users to immerse themselves fully in the digital landscapes of the Metaverse, providing an experience that feels real in many senses.
- **Augmented Reality (AR)**: Rather than immersing users in a wholly digital space, AR overlays digital elements onto the real world. In the Metaverse, this could mean seeing digital information or creatures as if they're part of the physical world.
- **Interactivity**: The Metaverse is not just a space to observe but to interact with. Users can change, create, or manipulate environments and objects, allowing a dynamic experience.

Origins and Cultural Influence

The concept of the Metaverse has roots in science fiction, most notably from Neal Stephenson's novel "Snow Crash" and later from Ernest Cline's "Ready Player One". These literary works, among others, envisioned vast, immersive digital universes where users interact, work, and live parts of their lives.

While the Metaverse concept is not new, the technological advancements of the 21st century are bringing it closer to reality. As we understand more about its potential, its implications span far beyond just gaming or social interaction. The Metaverse holds the potential to revolutionize business, education, social dynamics, and even the very nature of what we understand as "presence".

The Metaverse and Blockchain

We can find many synergies between the Metaverse and blockchain technology. As the Metaverse continues its trajectory towards becoming the next significant phase of the digital realm, one technology stands out as an essential enabler: blockchain. This decentralized ledger system, originally popularized by the advent of cryptocurrencies like Bitcoin, has found profound synergies with the Metaverse in areas like digital ownership, authentication, and decentralized governance. A closer look at the connection between Metaverse and blockchain will highlight the following characteristics of both technologies:

- **Digital Ownership**: Often represented as a Non-fungible Token (NFT), true ownership of digital assets like virtual land, clothing, art, or even pets in the Metaverse can be owned outright, much like physical assets in the real world. This contrasts with the traditional model where digital assets were licensed, not owned, by users. One of the most significant blockchain innovations relative to the Metaverse is NFTs. NFTs can represent unique digital items, ensuring their scarcity and verifiability. This has led to the monetization of digital art, collectibles, and even parcels of virtual real estate.
- **Decentralized governance** and autonomous organizations that lead to decentralized decision-making: As vast digital spaces, Metaverses can benefit from decentralized decision-making processes. Blockchain enables the creation of Decentralized Autonomous Organizations (DAOs) where users can vote on rules, modifications, or events in a digital space.
- **Transparent Rule Enforcement**: Smart contracts implement self-executing rules with the agreement directly written into lines of code. These contracts run automatically and ensure adherence to rules and agreements without intermediaries.
- **Authentication and Identity Protection**: Blockchain can provide a secure way to verify user identities in the Metaverse, granting access to specific areas or ensuring users are who they claim to be. This adds also to identity privacy: With cryptographic security measures, users can maintain anonymity or selectively share attributes of their identity without exposing their entire digital footprint.
- **Economic Systems and Cryptocurrencies**: It goes by itself that blockchain can enable virtual economies based on cryptocurrency in the Metaverse. Many indeed envision the Metaverse to have a thriving economy that will eventually even replace the real world, and cryptocurrencies can serve as the financial backbone for these digital transactions. Not only a new economic market but a more inclusive one through cross-world trading. This is the promise of blockchain and the Metaverse, to enable a seamless trade of assets across different platforms, making the Metaverse more interconnected and economically dynamic.
- **Interoperability and Standardization**: Lastly, cross-universe identities and asset portability will enable a global Metaverse that is not limited to a single platform. Here again, blockchain can help standardize assets and identities across various Metaverse environments. A user's avatar or assets from one virtual world could potentially be used in another one. A user's inventory of digital assets can be securely and transparently moved between different platforms or games.

In essence, blockchain empowers users in the Metaverse, granting genuine ownership, providing secure identity verification, and fostering decentralized and transparent governance. As both technologies evolve, their intertwined relationship is likely to deepen, shaping the socio-economic structures and user experiences in the digital universes of tomorrow.

With this introduction to the Metaverse, let's now go into more detail about the foundational technologies, and principles of architecture and design that represent an ideal Metaverse platform.

Foundational Technologies

We mentioned virtual reality (VR) and augmented reality (AR) at the foundation of a Metaverse world. The shift from "reality" is a key aspect of a digital Metaverse, where people, or actually their avatars, meet and greet. Additional technologies, such as artificial intelligence (AI) and blockchain can enrich the experience, but the fundamental concept of a Metaverse lays in its abstraction from the real world.

Virtual Reality

Virtual reality (VR) serves as one of the pivotal pillars underpinning the Metaverse's vast potential. At its essence, VR immerses users in a fully digital or simulated environment, where interactions feel as close to real-life experiences as technology allows. VR has a key role in shaping the Metaverse in providing multiple experiences:

- **Immersive Experience Creation**: Engulfing senses, VR offers a 360-degree spatial environment, allowing users to "look around" and immerse themselves fully. Through the integration of haptic feedback and 3D audio, VR can stimulate multiple senses, making the digital realm feel tangible. VR is also about enhancing the presence: One of VR's most profound offerings is the sensation of "being there". This feeling of presence makes interactions within the Metaverse more authentic and engaging.
- **Enhanced User Interactions**: Spatial awareness enables users to experience a depth perception akin to the real world. This spatial understanding makes interactions like picking up objects, participating in events, or even socializing more intuitive. In the Metaverse, a user's representation, typically an avatar, becomes crucial. VR allows for full-body tracking, enabling avatars to mirror users' movements, gestures, and expressions. This ability is also a big factor of inclusion in the digital world, where people with different abilities can represent themselves differently. The Avatar movie anybody?
- **Bridges between Real and Virtual**: Yes, not everything is just digital. Real-world integration using simulations of real-world locations, events, or training scenarios can be rendered in the Metaverse, offering immersive education, tourism, or training experiences without the constraints of physical presence. VR can also enable real-time collaboration in a shared digital space. Professionals can work together in digital studios, students can learn in virtual classrooms, and friends can meet up in digital hangouts.
- **Gaming and Entertainment Evolution**: This obviously leads to enhanced gaming worlds: The gaming industry has been at the forefront of VR development. In the Metaverse, VR gaming takes on a new dimension, allowing players to be "inside" the game, changing the very fabric of gameplay narratives and mechanics. It is truly an immersive storytelling: VR

in the Metaverse can revolutionize the way stories are told, letting users step into movies or series, experience events from different perspectives, and even influence story outcomes.

■ **Economic Implications and Virtual Commerce**: VR facilitates unique commerce opportunities in the Metaverse. Users can "try on" clothes, "visit" real estate properties, or "attend" product launches, paving the way for new business models and revenue streams. Also, professional training already benefits industries such as healthcare or aerospace, that can harness VR to create hyper-realistic training simulations in the Metaverse, ensuring professionals can practice without real-world risks.

In conclusion, Virtual Reality serves as the foundational interface for the Metaverse, bridging human cognition with digital constructs. As VR technology continues to evolve, so too will the depth, realism, and breadth of experiences within the Metaverse, cementing VR's role as a cornerstone of this new digital frontier.

Augmented Reality: Bridging Real and Virtual

While VR immerses users entirely within a digital realm, AR overlays digital information onto the real world, serving as a bridge between the tangible and the virtual. AR's unique ability to merge these two domains has significant implications for the evolution and usability of the Metaverse. Let's analyze how AR is reshaping the interface between reality and digital space:

■ **Seamless Digital Overlays**: AR enhances the perception of real-world experiences by superimposing digital elements such as visuals, sounds, or haptic feedback. This enhancement can be as simple as displaying metadata about an object or as complex as integrating animated holograms into a physical space. Through AR devices, users can interact with these digital elements, adjusting settings, querying for information, or playing augmented reality games.

■ **Real-World Contextualization**: Spatial computing is an AR feature that enables devices to understand and map the environment, enabling digital assets to be placed accurately in real-world spaces. This can transform industries from interior design (visualizing furniture in your room before buying) to navigation (directional arrows on the road in front of you). This leads to the generation of adaptive content: Based on location, personal preferences, or real-time events, AR can present customized digital content, creating a tailored experience for every user.

■ **Enhancing Daily Tasks**: Similarly to what is already described for VR for professional assistance, education, and training, AR can turn a traditional classroom into an interactive learning environment. Imagine a history lesson where historical events play out on the student's desk or a science lesson where molecular structures can be explored in 3D. AR can play a pivotal role in fields like medicine, where surgeons can have overlay guides during procedures, or mechanics can view schematics while working on machinery.

■ **Social and Collaborative Interactions**: Shared digital experiences extend with AR, by which multiple users can view and interact with the same digital object or information in a physical space, fostering collaborative efforts or social interactions. The impact on digital art and public spaces is significant: AR allows artists to create digital sculptures, murals, or interactive pieces in public spaces that can be viewed through AR devices, reimagining public art and community experiences.

■ **Infrastructure and Real-World Alignment**: As cities become more connected, AR can provide real-time data overlays about traffic, pollution levels, public transport schedules, and more. This is at the foundation of the concept of Smart Cities.

In essence, while VR might transport users to entirely digital universes, AR seeks to enhance and augment our existing world with layers of digital information. By doing so, Augmented Reality plays a critical role in the broader Metaverse ecosystem, merging the boundaries of what is real and what is virtual, and providing tools and experiences that seamlessly integrate into our daily lives.

Artificial Intelligence: Driving Interaction

AI has evolved to become a cornerstone of modern technological innovation, and its application in the Metaverse is no exception. In the context of the Metaverse, AI is not just another tech layer; it is the driving force that brings depth, adaptability, and sophistication to user interactions, making virtual experiences feel authentic and dynamic. What follows is an exploration of AI's pivotal role in shaping the Metaverse's interactive landscape.

In sum, AI is set to be the silent orchestrator of the Metaverse, weaving together complex systems and ensuring that user interactions are not just passive engagements but are instead dynamic, responsive, and continually evolving. By integrating AI, the Metaverse transitions from a static digital space to a living, breathing, and ever-adapting universe that mirrors the complexity of human interaction.

High-Speed Connectivity: 5G and Beyond

As we dive deep into the digital realms of the Metaverse, a fundamental pillar underpins its functionality and fluidity: **connectivity**. Our transition from mere digital users to active participants in expansive virtual worlds necessitates bandwidth, speed, and stability on an unprecedented scale. The rise of 5G and the promise of technologies beyond are pivotal in this journey. Table 14.2 lists how advanced connectivity is transforming the Metaverse's potential.

In conclusion, just as the Internet's backbone was fundamental to the digital revolution of the late 20th and early 21st centuries, high-speed connectivity like 5G and beyond will be foundational to the Metaverse. As we stand on the cusp of this new era, the interplay between connectivity and virtual realms will redefine our understanding of community, interaction, and even reality itself.

Architecture and Design

This section intricately weaves the technicalities of Metaverse architecture with the more philosophical aspects of digital design. Architecture and design together represent spatial computing and digital landscapes in the virtual world, to create more immersive and seamless user experiences.

Table 14.1 AI-powered experiences in the Metaverse

Feature	Experiences
Personalization and Adaptability	**Tailored experiences:** AI can analyze users' behaviors, preferences, and histories to customize their Metaverse experiences, from the appearance of their avatars to the events and spaces they might be interested in. **Dynamic environments:** The Metaverse can use AI to automatically adapt and evolve. For instance, a virtual forest might change its seasons based on collective user actions or real-world data.
Enhanced Avatar Interactions	**Emotion recognition and replication:** Through facial recognition and sentiment analysis, AI can allow avatars to mirror users' real-world emotions, making interactions more genuine. **AI-powered NPCs (Non-Player Characters):** NPCs within the Metaverse can be imbued with AI, enabling them to have realistic interactions, hold conversations, and respond dynamically to user actions.
Assistive Features and Guides	**AI assistants:** Just as Siri, Alexa, or Google Assistant help users in the real world, AI-driven virtual assistants can guide users within the Metaverse, assisting with navigation, information retrieval, or event participation. **Automated moderation:** To ensure safe and respectful interactions, AI can be used for real-time content monitoring and moderation, flagging inappropriate behaviors or content.
Learning and Skill Acquisition	**Adaptive learning environments:** Education in the Metaverse can be enhanced by AI, providing learners with adaptive scenarios and challenges based on their progress and needs. **Skill training simulations:** For professionals, AI-driven simulations can recreate real-world challenges, adjusting complexity in real-time based on the user's performance.
Economic and Market Dynamics	**Predictive market analyses:** Within the Metaverse's virtual economies, AI can help predict market trends, assisting users in making informed decisions about digital assets or virtual real estate. **Automated transactions:** AI can facilitate and optimize trade, sales, and purchases in the Metaverse, ensuring users get the best deals or match with the right buyers.
Real-world Data Integration	**Dynamic event generation:** The Metaverse can use AI to pull real-world data (like weather, news, or social trends) to generate corresponding events or changes within the virtual environment. **Real-time feedback loop:** Users' actions in the Metaverse can influence AI-driven systems in the real world. For instance, collective decisions in a virtual city planning game might provide insights to real-world urban planners.

Table 14.2   High connectivity-powered experiences in the Metaverse

Feature	Experiences
Low Latency – Real-Time Interactions	**Instantaneous feedback:** High-speed networks like 5G drastically reduce latency, making interactions in the Metaverse near-instantaneous. This is particularly crucial for tasks requiring precise timing, such as virtual concerts, gaming competitions, or collaborative projects. **Synchronous multi-user activities:** Multiple users can partake in events, discussions, or challenges simultaneously without lags or disruptions, fostering genuine global communities.
Enhanced Data Throughput	**High-definition worlds:** With increased bandwidth, the Metaverse can support high-resolution graphics, making virtual realms more detailed, realistic, and immersive. **Complex simulations:** Advanced connectivity allows for intricate simulations encompassing myriad data points, from physics engines mimicking real-world properties to vast ecosystems with millions of entities.
Reliability – A Seamless Metaverse	**Consistent uptime:** 5G and its successors promise a robust connection. This reliability ensures that users' virtual experiences remain uninterrupted, preserving the continuity of the Metaverse. **Dynamic load balancing:** With smart networks, traffic can be intelligently routed to avoid congestion or overloads, ensuring smooth experiences even in densely populated virtual areas.
Edge Computing – Localized Processing	**Reduced latency:** By processing data closer to the source (i.e., the user's device), edge computing further reduces latency, facilitating real-time Metaverse interactions. **Efficient data handling:** Not every bit of data needs to travel back to a central server. Localized processing can handle routine tasks, reserving bandwidth for more crucial data transfers.
IoT Integration – Merging Physical and Virtual	**Real-world data infusion:** High-speed networks can seamlessly integrate data from billions of IoT devices into the Metaverse. This can manifest as real-world weather affecting a virtual environment or a user's wearable health device influencing their avatar's capabilities. **Augmented reality enhancements:** Advanced connectivity will bolster AR's potential in the Metaverse, ensuring real-time overlays without lags, based on constant streams of real-world data.
Beyond 5G	**6G and futuristic protocols:** Even as 5G becomes mainstream, research into 6G has commenced. With potential features like sub-zero latency, terabyte-per-second speeds, and advanced AI integration, the future holds even more promise for the Metaverse. **Global satellite networks:** Initiatives like SpaceX Starlink aim to provide high-speed internet globally via satellite constellations, potentially expanding Metaverse access to remote and underserved areas.

Spatial Computing and Digital Landscapes

Navigating the vast expanses of the Metaverse requires more than just high-speed connectivity and interactive avatars. The very essence of this digital universe hinges on its architecture, how it is designed, how spaces are interconnected, and how users interact with and perceive their surroundings. Central to this architectural marvel are **Spatial Computing** and the crafting of intricate **Digital Landscapes**. As we dive into the technicalities that shape the Metaverse, we will look at understanding Spatial Computing as the intersection of digital and physical space. This involves computing methods that can understand and process physical spaces, objects, and humans and allow digital systems to interact with and influence the real and virtual worlds seamlessly. Advanced sensors and cameras, often incorporated in AR and VR devices, capture and process real-world spatial data. This data is then translated to create corresponding digital representations or augmentations. Beyond traditional input methods (like keyboard and mouse), spatial computing leverages gestures, voice, eye-tracking, and other natural interfaces, enabling intuitive interactions within digital spaces.

Digital Landscapes are the building blocks of crafting virtual realms. Instead of manually creating every element, algorithms can generate vast, intricate, and diverse terrains, cities, or ecosystems, making the Metaverse expansively dynamic. To enhance realism even further, digital landscapes often simulate real-world physics. This includes elements like gravity, light propagation, fluid dynamics, and material interactions, providing an authentic feel to virtual spaces. This is an entirely adaptive ecosystem: Digital landscapes do evolve. Depending on user interactions, AI inputs, or real-world data integration, forests might grow, cities might expand, and weather patterns might shift, to give an example.

It is in this context that Digital Landscapes also represent ownership of **virtual real estate**: As the Metaverse grows, certain virtual spaces, due to their design, location, or significance, gain value. Users can buy, develop, or sell these digital lands, similar to real-world property. At this point, we can see the value of blockchain-backed titles: Digital property ownership can be secured and verified using blockchain technology, ensuring that land titles are tamper-proof and easily transferable.

Design aesthetics and the user experience also change in the Metaverse. The first type of feedback we receive is immersive sensory, that is, beyond visual and auditory design, haptic feedback enhances tactile interactions, making digital experiences feel more tangible. Digital architecture considers socio-cultural implications, creating spaces like virtual outdoor "piazzas", theaters, concert venues, or community centers that foster a more inclusive interaction and cultural propagation. These digital landscapes are often adapted to user preferences or needs, reconfiguring spaces or aesthetics based on collective or individual inputs.

What's next? Future directions are challenged by the need for scaling nearly at the infinite: As the Metaverse expands, ensuring smooth navigation, interaction, and adaptability across its boundless realms becomes a technical challenge. Sustainability and the digital carbon footprint of this process are also at stake: As digital landscapes grow in complexity, their energy consumption and environmental impact need consideration, driving research into green computing solutions for the Metaverse.

In wrapping up, the architecture and design of the Metaverse represent a beautiful blend of art, science, and technology. Spatial computing provides the technical bedrock upon which dreamlike digital landscapes are erected. As users step into these realms, the lines between the virtual and real blur, making us architects, inhabitants, and storytellers of a new universe we're only beginning to comprehend.

Creating Immersive Experiences: 3D Design and Haptics

In the digital playground of the Metaverse, immersion is paramount. It is not enough to merely observe or navigate these realms; users need to "feel" them, to be genuinely engrossed. This experiential depth is accomplished through advanced 3D design and haptic technologies, harmoniously melding to simulate reality or even surpass it. Table 14.3 lists features and related experiences that can be enabled in 3D worlds.

In essence, the Metaverse's allure stems from its promise of experiences that transcend ordinary digital interactions. Through meticulous 3D design and the tangible touch of haptics, it beckons users into realms where boundaries between the tangible and the digital dissolve, crafting moments that are felt as much as they are seen.

Interoperability: Seamless Movement between Worlds

In the grand tapestry of the Metaverse, countless worlds, platforms, and realms coexist. But for the Metaverse to realize its full potential as a cohesive, expansive digital universe, these disparate spaces must interact seamlessly. Interoperability, or the ability for different systems and applications to work together harmoniously, emerges as a key technical and philosophical cornerstone. As we observe the intricacies of ensuring smooth transitions and interactions across the vast Metaverse, let's now focus on understanding interoperability and its technical foundation in the context of the Metaverse.

At its core, **interoperability** in the Metaverse refers to the ability of users, assets, or experiences to transition and function smoothly across different virtual environments, platforms, or applications. From a user perspective, interoperability means carrying their digital identity, achievements, or assets across various realms without friction or loss of value.

At the technical foundation of Metaverse's interoperability there are **standardized protocols**: Just as HTTP and HTML serve as universal standards for the web, the Metaverse requires shared protocols to ensure different virtual spaces "speak the same language". Embracing open-source principles can accelerate the development of interoperable tools and platforms, fostering collaboration and transparency. Application Programming Interfaces (APIs) and Software Development Kits (SDKs) facilitate smooth interactions between different Metaverse platforms, allowing developers to build complementary tools or extensions.

Creating a metaverse with interoperability based on open source libraries is a complex task that involves several components, including 3D rendering, networking, user authentication, and asset management. For this example, let's focus on a simplified scenario where two different virtual worlds can interoperate through a shared user authentication system and asset exchange. We will use open-source tools and libraries such as Three.js for 3D rendering, Node.js with Express for the server, WebSocket for real-time communication, MongoDB for the database, and OpenID Connect for user authentication. All the source code is on the GitHub repository for the book. At a high level, Figure 14.2 describes the components of the Metaverse interoperability solution.

Interoperability impacts also **digital assets**, as we mentioned earlier for blockchain technology. Blockchain, and particularly NFTs, enables assets to have verified authenticity and ownership. These digital assets can move between various Metaverse platforms, retaining their uniqueness and value. Universal digital wallets can store a wide array of assets from different platforms, serving as a hub for users' digital possessions and identities.

Achieving seamless interoperability is not immune from challenges. The big debate of platform centralization vs. decentralization is a constant reminder of the technology underpinning

Table 14.3 3D-powered experiences in the Metaverse

Feature	Experiences
3D Design	**Realism vs. stylization:** While some Metaverse spaces prioritize photorealistic representations, others lean into stylized, fantastical, or abstract designs. This spectrum allows for diverse experiences, from near-replicas of reality to the entirely imaginative. **Dynamic environments:** 3D design in the Metaverse is not static. Trees sway, shadows shift, water ripples, and characters exhibit lifelike movements, thanks to dynamic simulations and advanced rendering techniques. **Depth and dimension:** Depth cues like parallax, occlusion, and perspective are meticulously incorporated, ensuring that users perceive depth and distance as they would in the real world.
Haptics: The Science of Touch in Digital Realms	**Haptic technology** recreates the sense of touch by applying forces, vibrations, or motions to users, allowing them to "feel" digital objects or interactions. **Tactile feedback devices:** Gloves, suits, and controllers equipped with haptic feedback systems provide sensations ranging from the gentle brush of virtual grass to the jolt of a virtual car crash. **Kinesthetic feedback:** Beyond tactile sensations, haptic devices can reproduce larger movements, offering resistance or guidance. For instance, pulling a virtual bowstring might feel tense due to kinesthetic feedback.
Synergy between 3D Design and Haptics	**Consistency in interaction:** When a user reaches out to touch a 3D-rendered raindrop, the haptic response should match the visual—a light, fleeting sensation. This coherence between visual and tactile feedback deepens immersion. **Enhanced simulations:** Advanced training or gaming scenarios in the Metaverse can harness this synergy. A medical training simulation, for example, might combine detailed 3D anatomical models with haptic feedback to mimic the feel of a procedure. **Emotional amplification:** The fusion of visual and tactile cues can intensify emotional responses. Feeling the heat of a virtual sun or the vibration of a virtual concert amplifies the sense of "presence" within the Metaverse.
Challenges and Evolution	**Complexity in reproduction:** While some sensations are straightforward to replicate (like vibration), others like temperature, pressure, or pain are intricate and remain areas of ongoing research. **Universal design standards:** As diverse Metaverse platforms emerge, a challenge lies in creating universal haptic and 3D design standards to ensure consistency and compatibility across experiences. **Reducing intrusiveness:** Current haptic systems can sometimes be bulky or invasive. Research aims to make them more user-friendly, compact, and integrated seamlessly with everyday wearables.
Beyond Visual-Tactile Symbiosis	**Olfactory and gustatory integration:** The next frontier lies in integrating smell and taste into the Metaverse, striving for holistic sensory experiences. **Brain-Computer Interfaces (BCIs):** Cutting-edge research into BCIs might someday allow direct neural interactions with the Metaverse, bypassing traditional sensory mediums altogether.

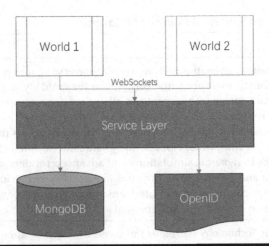

Figure 14.2 Metaverse interoperability components

the Metaverse. While centralized platforms may offer polished experiences, they often restrict open interoperability. Balancing user experience with open access poses also security concerns: Interconnecting different platforms introduces potential vulnerabilities. Ensuring robust security while promoting interoperability is crucial.

Initiatives for promoting interoperability may include **cross-platform transactions**. For example, some online games now allow players from different platforms (PC, console, mobile) to interact in shared environments, laying groundwork principles for broader Metaverse interoperability. Projects focused on inter-blockchain communication aim to enable different blockchains to exchange information, a foundational step towards interoperable digital assets and collaborative Metaverse consortia. As a result, various industry stakeholders are forming groups to discuss and define interoperability standards, ensuring diverse voices shape the Metaverse's foundational principles.

In conclusion, interoperability represents both a technical challenge and a vision for the Metaverse's future. As we design this digital frontier, the choices we make around interoperability will define not only the user experience but also the very ethos of the Metaverse – a fragmented collection of worlds or a harmonious digital symphony.

Digital Identity in the Metaverse

This section offers a comprehensive view of digital identity within the Metaverse through the lens of **avatars**. We will shed light on the intricacies of identity security and privacy within the Metaverse, delve deeper into the use of **digital twins** in the virtual world, and explore the broader societal implications of privacy in a digital-first world.

The Role of Avatars

In the vast expanse of the Metaverse, where physical appearances are rendered moot, how does one represent oneself? How does one ensure their uniqueness, express their personality, or convey their emotions? The answer lies in the concept of digital identity, embodied most prominently through avatars. These digital manifestations act as users' representatives, their faces and forms in the virtual realms. Let's delve into the nuances of digital identity and the pivotal role avatars play.

Understanding Digital Identity in the Metaverse

Digital identity encompasses the representation of a user's attributes, characteristics, and behaviors within the digital environment of the Metaverse. Components of identity go beyond mere visuals, as a digital identity may encapsulate a user's preferences, historical interactions, achievements, owned assets, and affiliations in the virtual space.

Avatars: The Faces of Digital Identity

Avatars allow users to tailor their appearance, from facial features and attire to body language and voice. This customization offers an avenue for self-expression, much like fashion or hairstyle in the real world. Modern avatars are equipped to convey emotions, respond to stimuli, and interact dynamically, thanks to sophisticated animation and AI-driven behavior modeling. Beyond aesthetics, avatars serve functional roles, such as interacting with objects, navigating environments, or performing tasks.

Diversity and Inclusivity in Avatar Design

Representation matters! Given the global audience of the Metaverse, it is imperative that avatar customization options reflect diverse races, cultures, body types, and abilities. Gender fluidity and non-binary representation are sown in the fabric of avatars: The Metaverse offers a space where traditional gender norms can be transcended, allowing for a spectrum of identities to be represented and celebrated.

Challenges in Crafting Digital Identity

With all this virtualization of ourselves, and taking a distance from our own look like, maintaining authenticity is a challenge. While the Metaverse permits boundless self-expression, it also raises questions about the authenticity of the people/avatars that interact. How does one discern genuine interactions from artificial or deceptive representations?

Privacy and security may be at stake too. With detailed avatars potentially revealing personal preferences and experiences, safeguarding users' data and ensuring their privacy becomes paramount. What are the ethical implications of balancing authenticity, privacy, security with freedom of expression? The very freedom to choose any identity can lead to issues like appropriation or misrepresentation. Setting guidelines without stifling creativity poses eventually challenges.

Evolving Identity: The Future of Avatars

Future avatars might incorporate real-world biometric data, like heartbeat or eye movement, to enhance realism and responsiveness. As technology advances, the 2D or 3D avatars of today might evolve into full-fledged holograms, merging the digital and physical realms even further. Leveraging blockchain could ensure each avatar's uniqueness, making replication or theft near-impossible and solidifying digital identity.

Figure 14.5 shows an example of avatars in the Metaverse. There are several tools you can use to create avatars in a Metaverse. **Ready Player Me** (https://readyplayer.me/) is a website that offers free, 3D full-body avatars that can be used across multiple virtual worlds. You can customize your avatar's skin, face, eyes, hair, clothes, and accessories. **Synthesia** (https://www.synthesia.io/) is a service that allows you to create a digitized version of yourself that looks less like a cartoon and more like a real person. **Ethereal Engine** (https://www.etherealengine.com/) is another free and interoperable end-to-end framework for metaverse development that offers a modular set of open-source tools, such as 3D world creation, complete world editing, voice- and video-based communication, and user management.

In summation, as gateways to the Metaverse, avatars bear the weighty task of conveying our complexities, desires, and identities in digital form. They are more than mere pixels; they are a reflection of who we are, who we aspire to be, or sometimes, who we choose to be in alternate realities. As the Metaverse expands, so will our understanding and appreciation of digital identity, pushing boundaries and redefining self-representation in the digital age.

Digital Twins: Replicating Real-World Assets

Amid the plethora of technologies shaping the Metaverse, the concept of digital twins stands out as a revolutionary paradigm. Digital twins offer a bridge between our tangible reality and the virtual realm, replicating real-world entities in intricate detail within the digital domain. From industrial machinery to entire cities, the applications of Digital twins are as vast as they are transformative. This section delves into the intricate world of digital twins and their role in mirroring real-world assets.

Defining Digital Twins

At its core, a digital twin is a dynamic, virtual representation of a physical object or system, built using real-time data from sensors attached to the corresponding real-world entity. Think of them as "synchronized realities": Digital twins constantly evolve and change based on data inputs, ensuring they remain accurate representations of their physical counterparts.

The key components of digital twins include:

- **Data Collection**: Sensors, IoT devices, and other data-gathering tools constantly monitor the physical entity, feeding this information into the digital twin.
- **Simulation and Modeling**: Advanced algorithms and simulation tools allow a digital twin to emulate real-world behavior, predicting how the entity might react under various circumstances.
- **Feedback Loops**: Changes in a digital twin can offer insights into the actual physical asset's status or potential issues, creating a bi-directional flow of information.

The following Python code snippet demonstrates how data might be collected from sensors and IoT devices and fed into a digital twin. This example uses the MQTT protocol, which is commonly used in IoT applications for real-time data transmission.

```
import paho.mqtt.client as mqtt

# The callback for when the client receives a CONNACK response from
    the server.
def on_connect(client, userdata, flags, rc):
    print("Connected with result code "+str(rc))
    # Subscribing in on_connect() means that if we lose the
        connection and
    # reconnect then subscriptions will be renewed.
    client.subscribe("sensor/data")

# The callback for when a PUBLISH message is received from the server.
def on_message(client, userdata, msg):
    print(msg.topic+" "+str(msg.payload))
    # Here is where you would add the code to feed the sensor data
        into your digital twin.
  # This will depend on the specifics of your digital twin platform.
client = mqtt.Client()
client.on_connect = on_connect
client.on_message = on_message

client.connect("mqtt.example.com", 1883, 60) # Connect to the MQTT
    broker.

# Blocking call that processes network traffic, dispatches callbacks
and handles reconnecting.
client.loop_forever()
```

In this example, the on_message function is where you would add the code to feed the sensor data into your digital twin. This will depend on the specifics of your digital twin or metaverse platform. The MQTT client is set up to connect to an MQTT broker and subscribe to the sensor/data topic, where it is assumed that your IoT devices are publishing their sensor readings.

Applications in the Metaverse

Urban planning and **smart cities** are hot topics in the Metaverse. Entire city layouts can be replicated as digital twins in the Metaverse, aiding in urban planning, disaster response simulation, or infrastructure development. This can be extended also to real estate, with properties mirrored in the Metaverse, enabling virtual tours, property evaluations, or design modifications. Virtual smart cities can even be modeled on real cities, bringing cultural heritage into the virtual world: Historical sites or artifacts can be immortalized as digital twins, ensuring preservation and offering virtual tours or educational experiences.

Predictive maintenance is another typical application of digital twins. For industrial assets, digital twins can forecast wear and tear, suggesting maintenance before a real-world breakdown occurs. By interacting with a digital twin, stakeholders can test various scenarios or strategies without impacting the actual asset, leading to data-driven decisions.

In the following example, we are using a random forest regressor to predict the time to failure of an industrial asset based on sensor readings for temperature, pressure, and the number of hours since the last maintenance. The model is trained on historical sensor data, with the time_to_failure column indicating the number of hours until the asset failed after each set of sensor readings.

```python
import pandas as pd
from sklearn.ensemble import RandomForestRegressor
from sklearn.model_selection import train_test_split

# Load sensor data
data = pd.read_csv('sensor_data.csv')

# Assume we have columns for temperature, pressure, and
hours_since_last_maintenance
features = data[['temperature', 'pressure',
'hours_since_last_maintenance']]

# And a column for time_to_failure that we want to predict
labels = data['time_to_failure']

# Split the data into training and test sets
train_features, test_features, train_labels, test_labels = train_
test_split(features, labels, test_size = 0.25, random_state = 42)

# Create a random forest regressor
rf = RandomForestRegressor(n_estimators = 1000, random_state = 42)

# Train the model
rf.fit(train_features, train_labels)

# Now we can predict time_to_failure based on new sensor readings
new_sensor_data = pd.DataFrame([[75, 300, 50]],
columns=['temperature', 'pressure', 'hours_since_last_maintenance'])
predicted_time_to_failure = rf.predict(new_sensor_data)

print('Predicted time to failure: ', predicted_time_to_failure[0])
```

This is a very simplified example, and a real-world predictive maintenance solution would likely involve more complex models, additional features, and various other considerations such as data preprocessing, feature engineering, model validation, and more. But overall, it gives a generic idea of a potential approach to take, using Python libraries like pandas and scikit-learn.

The Road Ahead: Digital Twins and the Expanding Metaverse

Combining AI algorithms with digital twins can further enhance predictive capabilities and introduce automated decision-making. Augmented and virtual reality tools can elevate the interaction experience with digital twins, allowing for immersive explorations or modifications. Furthermore, economic models and ownership can be developed with the emergence of blockchain, along with opportunities for trading or monetization of digital twins in the Metaverse.

To conclude, digital twin technology represents a harmonious blend of the tangible and virtual, encapsulating the essence of real-world assets within the boundless expanse of the Metaverse. As technological advancements continue, the fidelity, application, and importance of digital twins will undoubtedly grow, further blurring the lines between our physical reality and the digital universes we construct.

Economics of the Metaverse

We are now going to explore the economic dynamics within the Metaverse, centered around virtual goods and services. This section also offers a comprehensive look at the interplay between the Metaverse and the world of digital currencies, with an eye on potential business models and monetization strategies that can leverage the power of the Metaverse.

Tokenization and Cryptocurrencies

As the Metaverse gains momentum, so too does its deep integration with the burgeoning world of **tokenization** and **cryptocurrencies**. These digital tokens and currencies not only facilitate transactions within virtual realms but also fundamentally alter the nature of ownership, value exchange, and the decentralization of economic power. Understanding this intertwined relationship between the Metaverse and the world of digital currencies is crucial for grasping the future trajectory of virtual economies.

Tokenization involves the conversion of rights to an asset, whether physical or digital, into a digital token on a blockchain. While many types exist, the most prevalent in the context of the Metaverse include **utility tokens**, that offer access to specific services or functionalities within a virtual environment, or **security tokens**, that represent ownership in an asset or entity, often subject to regulatory frameworks. **NFTs** are a special type of token that describe unique digital assets verified using blockchain, making them distinct and ensuring their scarcity.

Tokenization, especially through NFTs, grants users verifiable ownership of virtual goods, real estate, or experiences. Artists, creators, and service providers in the Metaverse can directly monetize their offerings, bypassing traditional intermediaries.

As the Metaverse expands, ensuring seamless transfers and interactions between different virtual realms and their associated tokens will be pivotal. As more people engage with the Metaverse, we can anticipate a broader acceptance and understanding of cryptocurrencies, leading to deeper integration into everyday life.

The concept of "**Green Crypto**" is also raising to a broader attention. Environmental concerns, especially tied to energy-intensive proof-of-work mechanisms, will drive the adoption of more sustainable cryptocurrency models.

The symbiotic relationship between the Metaverse and the world of tokenization and cryptocurrencies represents a paradigm shift in how we conceive value, ownership, and decentralized economic systems. As virtual and real-world economies become increasingly intertwined, staying attuned to the evolving dynamics of digital currencies within the Metaverse will be paramount for stakeholders ranging from casual users to institutional investors.

Business Models and Monetization Strategies

The growth of the Metaverse has catalyzed new ways of thinking about business and value creation. Much like the early days of the internet, the Metaverse offers a fertile ground for innovation and entrepreneurial ventures. However, given its unique characteristics, such as immersiveness, persistent presence, and intertwined virtual-physical realities, business models need to evolve. There are myriads of business models and monetization strategies that are taking shape within the Metaverse. Figure 14.3 lists a few of the most significant.

Virtual Goods and Services

- Sales of digital assets in the Metaverse, which includes avatars, clothing, accessories, virtual real estate, and other assets. Many of these might be tokenized as NFTs, adding provable rarity and uniqueness.

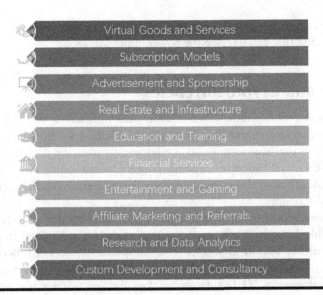

Figure 14.3 **Metaverse's most common business models and monetization strategies**

- Provision of virtual services ranging from guided tours in virtual worlds, hosting virtual events or conferences, to offering classes or training sessions.

Subscription Models

- Access passes: Some areas or experiences in the Metaverse might be gated, requiring users to pay a subscription fee to gain access.
- Premium memberships, offering enhanced features, exclusive content, or preferential treatment in virtual settings for subscribers.

Advertisement and Sponsorship

- Virtual billboards and ad spaces made available to brands for purchase of advertising spaces within popular zones of the Metaverse.
- Event sponsorships of virtual events, concerts, or competitions, enabling businesses to weave their brand into the virtual experience.
- Branded virtual goods by creating and selling virtual merchandise that promotes real-world brands.

Real Estate and Infrastructure

- Land sales and leasing: Virtual real estate has emerged as a lucrative market, with individuals and businesses buying, developing, and leasing virtual lands.
- Infrastructure development: Building and maintaining essential structures or tools within the Metaverse, akin to building roads or utilities in the real world.

Education and Training

- Virtual campuses, that is education institutions can set up campuses in the Metaverse, offering courses and degrees.

- Corporate training for companies that might use the Metaverse to conduct training sessions, workshops, or team-building activities.

Financial Services

- Virtual banks and financial institutions that offer banking and investment services tailored to the Metaverse's unique economies.
- Exchange platforms facilitating the exchange of one virtual currency for another or for real-world currencies.

Entertainment and Gaming

- Ticket sales: Charging users for attending concerts, shows, movies, or gaming events in the Metaverse.
- In-game purchases: Offering in-game items, powers, or advantages for a fee.

Affiliate Marketing and Referrals

- Promoting goods and services by recommending virtual (or even real-world) products and services to users.
- Earning a commission on sales generated through such referrals.

Research and Data Analytics

- Consumer behavior analysis: Given the richness of user interaction data in the Metaverse, companies can gather insights on consumer behavior, preferences, and trends.
- Selling aggregated data, providing anonymized data to third parties, ensuring user privacy is maintained.

Custom Development and Consultancy

- Tailored virtual experiences by designing custom Metaverse spaces or experiences for clients.
- Metaverse strategy consulting by advising businesses on how to establish and grow their presence within the Metaverse.

In conclusion, the Metaverse is proving to be a hotbed for innovative business models and monetization strategies. With its confluence of realities, technologies, and cultures, it offers an expansive playground for businesses to experiment, iterate, and redefine the concept of value. However, with opportunities also come challenges. Ethical considerations, user privacy, regulatory landscapes, and sustainability are areas that businesses will need to navigate carefully as they stake their claim in the Metaverse's evolving economy.

Social and Cultural Impacts

The profound ways in which the Metaverse is influencing societal structures are here to last. In this section, we would like to expand on the ethical implications of virtual spaces and explore the potential long-term societal impacts of a more (or less) inclusive Metaverse.

Ethical Implications and the Digital Divide

The advent of the Metaverse carries with it not only promises of immersion and global connectedness but also a host of ethical concerns. Chief among these is the digital divide, the gap between those who have ready access to computers and the internet, and those who do not. As the Metaverse becomes an integral part of our socioeconomic fabric, it is imperative to address these disparities and their broader ethical implications.

We need to start from understanding the **digital divide**, that is the unequal access to and use of new information and communication technologies. This encompasses hardware (like computers and VR headsets), software (apps and platforms), and connectivity (internet access). Factors contributing to the divide include socioeconomic status, education, geographic location, age, and disability, among others.

The implications of the digital divide in the Metaverse augment economic disparities that people may already experience in real life. As the Metaverse becomes a hub for commerce, education, and employment, those without access are at risk of missing out on emerging economic opportunities. There is also a risk of **social isolation**. The Metaverse promises new ways to socialize and connect. A lack of access could exacerbate feelings of social isolation or exclusion. Increased isolation will deepen cultural representation and educational gaps. A homogenized Metaverse dominated by privileged groups could misrepresent or underrepresent diverse cultures and experiences. And with institutions exploring virtual campuses and classes, students without access face potential disadvantages in learning opportunities and outcomes.

There are also broader ethical concerns about **data and identity protection** in the Metaverse:

- **Data Privacy and Security**: The Metaverse will gather vast amounts of user data. Ethical concerns arise around data collection, storage, usage, and potential misuse.
- **Misinformation and Manipulation**: Virtual realms might be used to spread misinformation or propaganda, making media literacy paramount.
- **Identity and Authenticity**: The freedom to choose and alter one's identity in the Metaverse brings forth questions about authenticity, trust, and potential misrepresentation.

Cases of impact on **mental health** have also been reported. Over-reliance or over-immersion in the Metaverse might lead to addiction, disconnection from physical reality, or other mental health concerns.

Addressing the Divide and Ethical Challenges

To address the divide and ethical challenges in the Metaverse, we should design platforms and experiences within the Metaverse with inclusivity in mind, catering to diverse user needs and capabilities. Table 14.4 lists a series of usability patterns that can be considered, and the technologies to implement them.

By considering these examples, platforms within the Metaverse can become more inclusive and accessible, ensuring that a wider range of users can participate and benefit from the digital experiences offered.

Let's make a couple of code examples, namely for an implementation of voice control and multi-language support.

Table 14.4   Usability patterns for a more inclusive Metaverse

Usability Pattern	Supporting Technologies
Accessibility Features	• Voice control and navigation: Implementing voice control for users with mobility impairments or those who find traditional controls challenging. • Screen readers and text-to-speech: Ensuring compatibility with screen readers for visually impaired users and providing text-to-speech options. • Haptic feedback: Utilizing haptic feedback to enhance the experience for users with visual impairments, allowing them to sense interactions through touch.
Diverse Avatars and Representation	• Customizable avatars: Allowing users to create avatars that reflect their identities, including diverse body types, skin tones, and cultural attire. • Inclusive gender options: Providing a wide range of gender options and allowing users to define their gender identity freely. • Cultural representation: Including elements from various cultures to ensure that users from different backgrounds feel represented.
Multilingual Support	• Language options: Offering multilingual support so that users can navigate and interact in their preferred language. • Real-time translation: Implementing real-time translation services to facilitate communication between users who speak different languages.
Economic Accessibility	• Affordable access: Creating affordable or tiered subscription models to ensure that users from different economic backgrounds can access the Metaverse. • Freemium models: Providing basic functionalities for free while offering premium features for a fee to lower the entry barrier.
Educational and Skill Development Programs	• Digital literacy programs: Offering programs to improve digital literacy, helping users understand and navigate the Metaverse effectively. • Skill training: Providing training modules for users to develop new skills or improve existing ones within the Metaverse environment.
Safe and Inclusive Spaces	• Anti-harassment measures: Implementing robust anti-harassment and reporting systems to protect users from abuse and ensure a safe environment. • Moderated spaces: Creating moderated spaces where users can interact without fear of discrimination or harassment.
Adaptable Environments	• Adjustable interfaces: Allowing users to customize the interface to suit their preferences and needs, such as adjusting text size, color contrast, and control schemes. • Assistive technologies: Integrating assistive technologies like eye-tracking for users with severe mobility impairments.

Voice Control and Navigation

Implementing voice control and navigation in the Metaverse involves integrating speech recognition libraries with your platform. Below is an example of how to use JavaScript along with the Web Speech API to create a simple voice control navigation system. This example will demonstrate recognizing voice commands to navigate between different sections of a web page. The full source code is available, as usual, on the GitHub repository for the book.

The following HTML structure includes the Home and About sections, with buttons to navigate between them. The JavaScript code will listen for voice commands to perform these navigations.

```
<nav>
    <button onclick="navigateTo('home')">Home</button>
    <button onclick="navigateTo('about')">About</button>
 </nav>

<section id="home">
    <h2>Home Section</h2>
</section>
<section id="about">
    <h2>About Section</h2>
</section>

<script src="voice-control.js"></script>
```

The following JavaScript (voice-control.js) script uses the Web Speech API for speech recognition. The webkitSpeechRecognition type is the primary interface for speech recognition, which implements the start() function to start a speech recognition service. The recognition object handles two events of the speech recognition process: onresult, which handles the result of the speech recognition; and onend, which restarts the recognition service automatically after it ends.

```
const recognition = new webkitSpeechRecognition();
recognition.lang = 'en-US';
recognition.start();

recognition.onresult = function(event) {
    const transcript = event.results[0][0].transcript;
    handleVoiceCommand(transcript);
};

recognition.onend = function() {
    recognition.start(); // Restart recognition automatically
};

function handleVoiceCommand(command) {
    if (command.includes('home')) {
        navigateTo('home');
    } else if (command.includes('about')) {
        navigateTo('about');
    } else {
     console.log('Command not recognized:', command);
    }
}
```

```
function navigateTo(section) {
    const sections = document.querySelectorAll('section');
    sections.forEach(sec => sec.style.display = 'none');
    document.getElementById(section).style.display = 'block';
}
```

This example is a basic demonstration and can be expanded with more complex navigation and error handling as needed.

Multilingual Support

Implementing multilingual support in a Python web application can be done using Flask and Flask-Babel, which is a library that helps with internationalization (i18n) and localization (l10n). Below is an example of a simple Flask application that supports English and Spanish languages.

```
from flask import Flask, render_template, request
from flask_babel import Babel, _

app = Flask(__name__)
app.config['BABEL_DEFAULT_LOCALE'] = 'en'
app.config['BABEL_SUPPORTED_LOCALES'] = ['en', 'es']
babel = Babel(app)

@babel.localeselector
def get_locale():
    return request.accept_languages.best_match(app.config['BABEL_
        SUPPORTED_LOCALES'])

@app.route('/')
def index():
    return render_template('index.html')
```

Actual language translations are stored in a messages.po file, for example, for English language:

```
msgid "Welcome"
msgstr "Welcome"

msgid "This is a multilingual support example."
msgstr "This is a multilingual support example."
```

And for Spanish language, a similar file with equivalent message "id" and "str" translations.

```
msgid "Welcome"
msgstr "Bienvenido"

msgid "This is a multilingual support example."
msgstr "Este es un ejemplo de soporte multilingüe."
```

The .po files will need to be compiled into .mo files using the following bash command:

```
pybabel compile -d translations
```

The .po files for the different languages are saved in a translations folder that contains language-specific subdirectories with the pertinent messages.po files.

This setup provides a basic multilingual support framework for a Flask application. You can expand the translations and customize the behavior further as needed.

Representation and Inclusion in Virtual Spaces

The Metaverse and other virtual realms promise a future where individuals can represent themselves without the physical-world constraints of geography, socio-economic status, or biology. However, the choices we make, and the systems we put in place, will determine whether these digital dimensions are inclusive utopias or simply reproduce the biases of the real world. As we step into this new frontier, understanding and emphasizing representation and inclusion becomes crucial.

Importance of Representation

Seeing oneself represented in virtual worlds validates one's identity and experiences. It sends a message that every individual, regardless of background, has a rightful place in the Metaverse. Diverse representation fosters a richer cultural mosaic, allowing users from different backgrounds to learn from and about each other. Varied perspectives lead to diverse thought processes, enhancing creativity and innovation in virtual designs and interactions.

Challenges to Representation in Virtual Spaces

Avatars and virtual personas may inadvertently perpetuate or exaggerate racial, gender, or cultural stereotypes. If the creators of a platform have a homogenous background, their unconscious biases may influence the design and rules of the virtual world, potentially excluding or marginalizing certain groups. Access to high-quality, customizable avatars or prestigious virtual real estate might be tied to real-world economic power, potentially replicating economic disparities in virtual spaces. Also, in a realm where anyone can adopt any appearance or cultural symbol, there is a risk of cultural elements being used superficially or disrespectfully.

Promoting Inclusion in the Metaverse

Ensuring that those who create virtual platforms come from diverse backgrounds will lead to more inclusive designs and features. Allowing users complete autonomy over their avatars promotes self-expression and helps avoid pigeonholing individuals into predefined categories. Holding workshops or informational sessions on cultural sensitivity, appropriation, and digital etiquette can foster understanding and respect among users. Empowering users from diverse backgrounds to participate in decision-making processes can ensure that policies and norms reflect a broad spectrum of needs and perspectives.

Celebrating Diversity and Fostering Allyship

Encourage and support the organization of cultural events, parades, and festivals that celebrate diversity. Create designated spaces where minority groups can come together to share their experiences, while also welcoming allies to learn and support. Platforms should be proactive in seeking feedback and be ready to evolve based on the diverse needs and concerns of their user base.

Representation and inclusion in virtual spaces are more than just checkboxes to tick; they are foundational to creating a Metaverse that is genuinely universal. As we stand at the dawn of this digital age, we have a unique opportunity to design systems that recognize, value, and celebrate the kaleidoscope of human identity. The choices we make now will shape the cultural and social fabric of virtual worlds for generations to come.

Privacy and Protection

The emergence of the Metaverse, a vast digital cosmos where assets, identities, and experiences intertwine, brings forth a need for structured governance and regulation. Within this realm, the issues of digital rights and ownership stand out as paramount. Addressing these concerns ensures the protection of users, fosters trust, and paves the way for the Metaverse to reach its full potential.

Digital Rights and Ownership

Digital rights refer to the privileges and entitlements users have over their virtual assets, identities, and activities within the Metaverse. This encompasses rights related to ownership, privacy, free expression, and more. As virtual assets gain real-world value and digital interactions influence real-world outcomes, safeguarding digital rights becomes as crucial as protecting rights in the physical world.

Digital ownership involves having exclusive rights over a digital asset, be it land, art, attire, or even aspects of one's avatar. These assets can have economic, social, and sentimental value. Leveraging blockchain technology allows for assets in the Metaverse to be tokenized, ensuring authenticity, scarcity, and verifiable ownership. With true ownership, users should have the ability to sell, trade, or transfer their digital assets as they see fit, potentially in decentralized marketplaces.

Table 14.5 shows a few strategies that can be considered for better digital rights and ownership protection. By combining these strategies, platforms and users within the Metaverse can create a secure and fair environment for managing and protecting digital rights and assets.

As the Metaverse becomes an increasingly significant aspect of our lives, establishing robust governance and regulatory structures is not just preferable but essential. The challenges are manifold, but with collaboration, transparency, and foresight, we can create a digital realm that respects rights, honors ownership, and nurtures innovation.

Privacy and Data Protection

In an era where digital transformation dominates, the Metaverse stands out as the epitome of this shift. As users navigate, interact, and transact within this expansive virtual universe, vast amounts of data are generated, collected, and analyzed. With such a wealth of information at stake, privacy and data protection emerge as primary concerns, demanding thorough examination and diligent action.

The nature of data in the Metaverse is multifold:

■ **Personal Identifiers**: Details linked to a user's real-world identity, such as names, addresses, and even biometrics.

Table 14.5 Technologies for digital rights and ownership protection in the Metaverse

Strategy	Implementation
Blockchain Technology	• Decentralized ledger: Use blockchain to create a tamper-proof ledger for tracking ownership and transactions of digital assets. • Smart contracts: Implement smart contracts to automate the execution of agreements and ensure that digital assets are transferred or used according to predefined rules.
Non-Fungible Tokens (NFTs)	• Unique identification: Use NFTs to assign unique identifiers to digital assets, ensuring their authenticity and ownership can be verified. • Immutable records: NFTs provide an immutable record of ownership and transaction history, which is essential for proving provenance.
Digital Rights Management (DRM)	• Encryption: Encrypt digital assets to protect them from unauthorized access and distribution. • Access control: Implement robust access control mechanisms to manage who can view, use, or transfer digital assets. • Usage tracking: Use DRM to monitor and track the usage of digital assets to ensure compliance with licensing agreements.
Secure Authentication Methods	• Multi-Factor Authentication (MFA): Use MFA to secure user accounts and prevent unauthorized access to digital assets. • Biometric verification: Implement biometric verification (e.g., fingerprint, facial recognition) to enhance security.
Watermarking and Fingerprinting	• Digital watermarks: Embed digital watermarks into assets to track their distribution and usage without altering their appearance. • Fingerprinting: Use digital fingerprinting techniques to create unique identifiers for digital assets, helping to trace and verify them.

■ **Behavioral Data**: Information about a user's actions, preferences, and interactions within the virtual environment.

■ **Transactional Data**: Records of economic activities, including purchases, trades, or any form of value exchange.

■ **Social Interactions**: Conversations, affiliations, and networks that a user establishes and maintains.

■ **Spatial Data**: Details about where a user goes, the spaces they frequent, and their navigation patterns.

Without proper data privacy protection in place, there is potential for continuous surveillance, leading to detailed user profiles that can predict or influence behaviors. Data breaches may represent a threat too. Unauthorized access to data can lead to personal information being stolen, misused, or sold.

With comprehensive data, platforms or third parties might manipulate user experiences, pushing particular agendas or products. Lastly, the blending of virtual and real identities could endanger the anonymity that many seek in digital spaces.

Existing laws like the General Data Protection Regulation (**GDPR**) in Europe or the California Consumer Privacy Act (**CCPA**) in the United States provide frameworks that could be extended or adapted for the Metaverse. There is a jurisdictional challenge, though. The decentralized and global nature of the Metaverse creates complexities in determining which regulations apply and where. Traditional laws might need to evolve to address the unique challenges and intricacies of the Metaverse.

What best practices can we put in place for effective data protection? Some of the most common strategies include:

- **User Consent**: Platforms should ensure that users provide informed consent before collecting or processing their data.
- **Data Minimization**: Only collect data that is necessary for the platform to function or provide a service.
- **Transparent Policies**: Clearly communicate how data is used, stored, shared, and protected.
- **End-to-End Encryption**: Implement encryption protocols to protect data during transit and at rest.
- **Regular Audits**: Periodically review and assess data protection measures to ensure their effectiveness and address vulnerabilities.

Remember, the Metaverse is all about user empowerment. Users should have the ability to view, modify, and delete their data, as well as have access to anonymity tools. That means the Metaverse should offer tools that allow users to navigate the virtual worlds anonymously, without linking to their real-world identity.

We can conclude by stating that the Metaverse, with its boundless potential, also brings forth novel challenges in the realm of privacy and data protection. While the virtual world offers unparalleled opportunities for interaction and immersion, it is crucial to ensure that these experiences do not come at the cost of individual privacy. Balancing innovation with protection will be key in fostering a Metaverse that is both exhilarating and secure.

Future Prospects

The concept of the Metaverse is continually evolving, driven by technological advancements and innovative approaches. As we look to the future, several emerging technologies hold the potential to significantly reshape the Metaverse's landscape, enhancing its capabilities and making it more immersive and accessible than ever before.

Quantum Computing

Unprecedented processing power brought by quantum computers can process vast amounts of data simultaneously, potentially enabling real-time simulations of unprecedented complexity. Quantum encryption could also bolster the Metaverse's security, making data breaches almost impossible.

Neural Interfaces and Brain–Computer Integration

Direct brain interfacing with technologies like Elon Musk's Neuralink might allow users to connect directly with the Metaverse, bypassing traditional input devices. This can even lead to emotion recognition: Advanced neural interfaces could detect users' emotional states, allowing the Metaverse to respond and adapt in real-time. Future wearables might integrate directly with the user's body, offering tactile feedback and sensation in the Metaverse.

Advancements in Holography

Advances in holographic projection could enable the creation of rooms where virtual and physical realities merge seamlessly. In the next years, we can expect portable holographic devices, that is, personal devices that could project 3D holograms, enhancing AR experiences without the need for wearable tech. Even further, advanced robotics can enable virtual presence with physical avatars. Advanced robots could act as users' physical proxies in distant locations, allowing for real-world interactions driven by one's virtual presence.

Improved AI and Machine Learning

Advanced AI could allow the Metaverse to adjust to individual user preferences and needs dynamically (Adaptive Environments). Realistic NPCs (Non-Player Characters) powered by AI could behave indistinguishably from human users, enhancing immersion.

Decentralized Systems and Web 3.0

The nature of the Metaverse is going to be more and more decentralized. Leveraging blockchain and decentralized technologies, parts of the Metaverse could operate without a central authority, promoting autonomy and reducing monopolistic control. Web3 technologies could facilitate peer-to-peer exchanges and interactions in the Metaverse without intermediaries.

In conclusion, the future of the Metaverse is dazzling, with technological frontiers waiting to be explored. These advancements will not only redefine the user experience but also challenge our very perceptions of reality, opening doors to possibilities once confined to the realm of science fiction.

Chapter 15

The Road Ahead for Web3 and Beyond

As we stand on the cusp of this transformative era, the road ahead for Web3 and beyond is paved with boundless potential. This journey promises to redefine our digital landscape, fostering an internet where power is decentralized, privacy is paramount, and innovation knows no bounds. It is a future where our digital identities are truly our own, where communities thrive on trustless networks, and where technology empowers rather than controls. As we venture forward, let's embrace the spirit of collaboration and creativity that will drive this revolution. Together, we can build a web that not only reflects our highest ideals but also unlocks new horizons of human potential, forging a brighter, more inclusive digital world for all.

"The best way to predict the future is to invent it" – Alan Kay

As Alan Kay, a renowned computer scientist and visionary who has made significant contributions to the fields of computer science and software development, reportedly said, the best way to predict the future is to invent it. Kay has been a strong advocate for using computers in education. He has worked on numerous projects aimed at enhancing learning experiences through technology. In 2003, he received the Turing Award, which is often regarded as the Nobel Prize of computing, for his contributions to personal computing and the development of object-oriented programming languages, particularly Smalltalk.

Throughout his career, Kay has been known for his forward-thinking vision and emphasis on the potential of technology to transform society. His famous quote encapsulates his belief in proactive innovation and the power of creativity to shape the future. Today, Alan Kay's ideas and innovations continue to influence the tech industry and inspire new generations of computer scientists, developers, and visionaries.

Roadmap for Web3

A plausible roadmap for Web3 encompasses several stages and milestones that span technological, regulatory, and adoption aspects. Figure 15.1 is an overview of what the roadmap could look like.

DOI: 10.4324/9781003491934-15

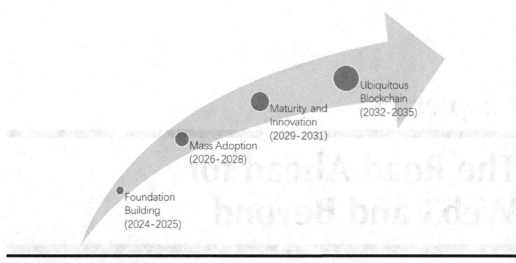

Figure 15.1   Roadmap for Web3

Currently, we are in Web3's **phase 1**, the building of the foundation technologies: Scalability solutions, interoperability systems, and security and privacy frameworks. The adoption of Layer 2 scaling solutions like optimistic rollups or ZK rollups to handle increased transaction volumes is pivotal to addressing the scalability requirements. Additionally, the implementation of sharding in blockchain protocols like Ethereum 2.0 has enhanced transaction throughput.

No blockchain network will survive in total isolation. Interoperability and cross-chain solutions are essential to success: The development and adoption of cross-chain bridges like London Bridge (https://londonbridge.io/) will enable seamless asset transfers and communication between different blockchains. Communication needs to be supported by protocol standardization, with the creation of interoperability standards to ensure compatibility across various blockchain platforms.

Not the least, security and data privacy is a growing concern. Many blockchain networks run advanced cryptographic techniques to enhance security, including hardware-based data protection strategies like confidential computing, boasted by Obscuro (https://obscu.ro/).

Phase 2, the phase of mass adoption, will follow immediately after, expected between the years 2026 to 2028. This is the phase of improvement of the Web3 user experience supported by simplified interfaces. The development of more intuitive and user-friendly interfaces for decentralized applications (dApps) and better wallet integration will bring Web3 to the masses. Wallets will also see improved functionalities, including multi-asset support and easy recovery mechanisms.

A larger adoption means more governance and the adoption of regulatory frameworks that bring clear regulations in the Web3 space. Essential is the establishment of clear regulatory frameworks in major jurisdictions to provide legal clarity and encourage institutional participation. This phase will also see the development of compliance tools to help projects adhere to increasing regulatory requirements.

At this point, the road is ready for institutional adoption of Web3 enterprise solutions. The adoption of blockchain solutions by enterprises for supply chain management, financial products, and asset tokenization will see the growth of an integrated ecosystem that unifies decentralized finance (DeFi) with traditional financial systems to provide hybrid solutions.

Following mass adoption is **phase 3**, the phase of technology and market maturity, in the years 2029 to 2031. With the foundation technologies settled, it is time to bring innovation in Web3 and create the opportunity for startups to introduce new concepts, such as:

- **Internet of Things (IoT)**: Integration of IoT devices with blockchain for enhanced automation and data security.
- **Smart Cities**: Development of smart city solutions utilizing blockchain for efficient urban management.
- **Artificial Intelligence (AI)**: Combining AI with blockchain to create intelligent, autonomous systems for various applications, including predictive analytics and automated decision-making.
- **Generative AI**: Decentralized content creation that is free from copyright infringement and royalties, or it can use security tokens for managing such royalty payments.
- **Data Marketplaces**: Establishment of decentralized data marketplaces where users can securely monetize their data. Generative AI can be used to create synthetic data that preserves privacy while retaining statistical properties of real data. This synthetic data can be shared on blockchain networks without compromising individual privacy.

This is the phase where we will see the next evolution of the Internet toward a truly global decentralized network, where data and applications are not controlled by central entities. This is the foundation for interplanetary networks, a system of interconnected land and satellite networks, for decentralized peer-to-peer communication and data transfer.

The vision goes on with **phase 4**, the ubiquitous blockchain after year 2032. At this point, we have reached universal adoption and global participation. The widespread adoption of blockchain technology across various sectors and regions, and the universal implementation of decentralized digital identities for secure and verifiable user authentication, is the norm.

Continuous innovation will not stop. Quantum computing will be a reality by then, making quantum cryptography a thing, that is the implementation of quantum-resistant cryptographic techniques to safeguard blockchain networks against future quantum computing threats.

Sustainability and green blockchain will be imperative. New and more efficient and environmentally friendly consensus mechanisms will be invented. Emphasis is all on sustainability, with blockchain networks focusing on minimizing their environmental impact.

This roadmap outlines a progressive path for the evolution and adoption of Web3, aiming to create a decentralized, secure, and user-friendly digital ecosystem. Each phase builds upon the previous ones, addressing key challenges and paving the way for future advancements. Will it become a reality? As Alan Kay said, the best way to predict the future is to invent it. What are we waiting for?

Key Web3 players

The success and evolution of Web3 hinge on the contributions and innovations of various key players across different segments of the ecosystem. Figure 15.2 lists some of the most influential players likely to make a significant impact.

Blockchain Platforms and Protocols

- **Ethereum**: Vitalik Buterin and the Ethereum Foundation continue to lead in smart contract capabilities and DeFi applications. Ethereum 2.0 has focused on scalability and energy efficiency with the transition to Proof of Stake (PoS).

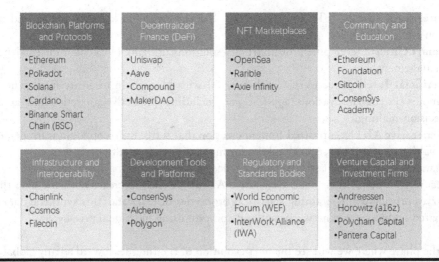

Figure 15.2   Key players in Web3

- **Polkadot**: Gavin Wood and Web3 Foundation are pioneers in interoperability and multi-chain technology, enabling different blockchains to communicate and share data.
- **Solana**: Anatoly Yakovenko and Solana Labs are known for high throughput and low transaction costs, gaining traction in the DeFi and NFT spaces.
- **Cardano**: Charles Hoskinson and IOHK focus on academic rigor, scalability, and sustainability, with a strong emphasis on formal verification and peer-reviewed research.
- **Binance Smart Chain (BSC)**: Changpeng Zhao first, before his troubles with justice, and Richard Teng as his successor as CEO at Binance, offer a parallel blockchain to Binance Chain, providing smart contract functionality and fostering a growing DeFi ecosystem.

Decentralized Finance (DeFi)

- **Uniswap**: Hayden Adams is leading decentralized exchange (DEX) using automated market-making (AMM) to enable peer-to-peer trading.
- **Aave**: Stani Kulechov is also leading a decentralized lending platform that offers flash loans and liquidity pools.
- **Compound**: Robert Leshner is at the reins of a decentralized lending protocol that allows users to earn interest on their crypto assets and borrow against them.
- **MakerDAO**: Rune Christensen is the creator of DAI, a decentralized stablecoin, and a cornerstone of the DeFi ecosystem.

NFT Marketplaces

- **OpenSea**: Devin Finzer and Alex Atallah have built the largest NFT marketplace, offering a platform for buying, selling, and creating NFTs.
- **Rarible**: Alex Salnikov and Alexei Falin drive a community-owned NFT marketplace, emphasizing user governance and decentralized decision-making.
- **Axie Infinity**: Sky Mavis is a blockchain-based game that has popularized play-to-earn mechanics and NFT-based gaming assets.

Community and Education

- **Ethereum Foundation**: Vitalik Buterin and team provide grants and resources to support the development and education around Ethereum and Web3 technologies.
- **Gitcoin**: Kevin Owocki has founded a platform for funding open-source projects, promoting collaboration, and supporting developers in the Web3 space.
- **ConsenSys Academy**: The ConsenSys team has developed a rich collection of tutorials and code samples from beginners to advanced Web3 developers.

Infrastructure and Interoperability

- **Chainlink**: Sergey Nazarov provides decentralized oracles, enabling smart contracts to securely interact with real-world data.
- **Cosmos**: Jae Kwon and Tendermint focus on interoperability and scalability, facilitating communication between different blockchains.
- **Filecoin**: Juan Benet and Protocol Labs offer a decentralized storage network that aims to store humanity's most important information.

Development Tools and Platforms

- **ConsenSys**: Joseph Lubin provides a suite of tools for Ethereum development, including MetaMask, Infura, and Truffle (now sunset from ConsenSys).
- **Alchemy**: Nikil Viswanathan and Joe Lau offer a development platform that powers many leading DeFi and NFT projects with robust APIs and infrastructure.
- **Polygon**: Jaynti Kanani, Sandeep Nailwal, and Anurag Arjun aim to provide scalable and interoperable blockchain solutions with its Layer 2 scaling solutions for Ethereum.

Regulatory and Standards Bodies

- **World Economic Forum (WEF)**: The work of the Global Blockchain Council influences global policies and promotes the adoption of blockchain technology through various initiatives and frameworks.
- **InterWork Alliance (IWA)**: Ron Resnick focuses on creating standard frameworks for tokenization, interoperability, and enterprise use cases.

Venture Capital and Investment Firms

- **Andreessen Horowitz (a16z)**: Chris Dixon is a major investor in blockchain and Web3 projects, providing capital and strategic support.
- **Polychain Capital**: Olaf Carlson-Wee focuses exclusively on investing in blockchain-based assets and technologies.
- **Pantera Capital**: Dan Morehead is one of the first institutional asset managers to invest exclusively in blockchain technology.

These key players, among others, are instrumental in shaping the future of Web3. Their contributions span from foundational blockchain protocols and infrastructure to innovative DeFi applications, NFT marketplaces, and regulatory frameworks. As the Web3 ecosystem evolves, these entities will continue to drive innovation, adoption, and integration of decentralized technologies into mainstream applications.

Toward a More Secure Blockchain

The Pentagon found concerning vulnerabilities about blockchain. Should we also be concerned? The "Are Blockchains Decentralized, Unintended Centralities in Distributed Ledgers" report (available at https://www.techrepublic.com/article/pentagon-finds-concerning-vulnerabilities-on -blockchain/) was commissioned by the Pentagon and published in June 2022. The report concluded that blockchain is not that decentralized after all, and it is vulnerable to attacks, also because it is running outdated software. The report found that a subset of participants can exert excessive and centralized control over the entire blockchain system.

The Pentagon's research arm, Defense Advanced Research Projects Agency (DARPA), engaged Trail of Bits, a security research organization, to investigate Bitcoin and Ethereum, the two leading cryptocurrencies in the global market. According to Trail of Bits, it only takes four entities to disrupt Bitcoin and only two to disrupt Ethereum. Additionally, 60% of all Bitcoin traffic moves through just three ISPs.

In another article, Microsoft investigates a new type of phishing attack called "Ice Phishing" on the blockchain. The article is available on the Microsoft website at https://www.microsoft.com /en-us/security/blog/2022/02/16/ice-phishing-on-the-blockchain/.

The term "Ice Phishing" refers to a type of scam targeting users of cryptocurrency or blockchain. The goal of Ice Phishing is to trick a user into signing a malicious smart contract that would let the attacker steal cryptocurrency tokens from wallets and send them to their own address instead of the rightful owner's address.

Microsoft's Threat Intelligence team has analyzed a phishing attack connected to the blockchain, which reaffirms the durability of these threats and the need for security fundamentals to be built into related future systems and frameworks. The article discusses the Badger DAO attack, a phishing attack that occurred in November–December 2021, during which the attacker was able to steal approximately 121 million US dollars from users.

Both reports are just examples of sources that have raised concerns about the security of blockchain technology, especially for sectors like security, fintech, big tech, and the crypto industries. We know that while blockchain technology has its vulnerabilities, it also has its strengths and continues to be an area of active research and development. Best practices for data security can be applied, starting by building security into Web3 while it is in its early stages of evolution and adoption.

The application of common cybersecurity principles and controls, derived from industry guidance and regulations, is critical to an effective cybersecurity program for a blockchain system. As a final summary, these principles and controls include:

1. Access controls on any information systems, including controls to authenticate and authorize individuals to access and participate in the network's activities.
2. Threat modeling is conducted by software developers to analyze threats and put in place the necessary mitigation actions.
3. Encryption of documents, records and any type of digital asset, when data is at rest, in transit, or in use by smart contracts as well as external applications.

4. Systems and procedures to detect attempted and actual attacks on or intrusions into blockchain networks, including machine learning-powered anomaly detection systems.
5. Application of secure software development life cycle practices that adhere to industry's recommendation for cybersecurity protection.
6. Regular audit programs to evaluate cybersecurity risk management practices, internal control systems, and compliance with laws, regulations, and corporate policies.
7. Response programs that specify actions to be taken when suspicious activity is detected, including unauthorized access to the network, data leakage, and execution of code.

The application of all, or most, of the aforementioned cybersecurity standards and guidance provides a strong foundation for protecting blockchains from cyber-attacks.

Web5?

Web5 is an advanced conceptual evolution of the web, combining elements of Web3 and decentralized digital identity to further decentralize the internet, enhance user control over data, and integrate advanced technologies like AI and IoT. It envisions a more autonomous and intelligent web where the physical and digital worlds are deeply intertwined. We can think of Web5 as Web2 + Web3 (that's why there is no Web4), that is, the union of the core technologies of the interactive Web2 as we know it today, and the decentralized nature and focus on data ownership of Web3.

Figure 15.3 shows the key elements of what Web5 could encompass, followed by a breakdown of each element.

Web5 is about **full decentralization** and the creation of an enhanced decentralized infrastructure. Building on the foundations of Web3, Web5 would have an even more robust decentralized infrastructure, minimizing reliance on centralized servers and intermediaries. Central to this vision is having **decentralized identity** management and authentication. Decentralized identity solutions ensure users have complete control over their digital identities and can authenticate across platforms seamlessly.

Enhanced user control and data ownership result in self-sovereign identity and credentials. Users will have complete ownership and control over their data, deciding who can access it and how it can be used. New business models may emerge for data marketplaces where users can monetize their data while maintaining privacy and control.

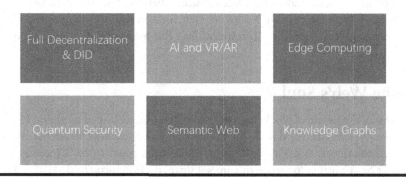

Figure 15.3   Key elements of Web5

The new Web to come cannot exist without a deep **integration with AI** services. This will go beyond text and image generation, well into autonomous systems that leverage artificial intelligence for creating self-operating systems that can make decisions and execute tasks autonomously. Users will also benefit from AI-powered personalization features, and they will be able to utilize AI to provide highly personalized user experiences, dynamically adapting to their preferences and behaviors.

Along with AI power, it comes a seamless human-computer interaction in the space of Augmented Reality (**AR**) and Virtual Reality (**VR**): Integrating AR and VR in the Web5 will create immersive and interactive experiences that blend the physical and digital realms. Natural Language Processing (**NLP**) capabilities will be heavily used to facilitate more natural and intuitive interactions between humans and machines.

Web5 will boost advanced **system interoperability** with better and more robust cross-platform compatibility thanks to enhanced protocols for seamless interaction between different blockchains, networks, and platforms, and thanks to universal standards that will ensure smooth data transfer and compatibility across various technologies and systems.

At the forefront of innovation in Web5 there is **edge computing**. Leveraging edge computing to process data closer to its source will reduce latency and improve efficiency. Deeper integration of Internet of Things (IoT) devices will allow for real-time data collection and processing from the physical world.

Web5 will look at quantum computing for enhanced **security and privacy**. Quantum-resistant cryptography is going to deliver cryptographic techniques resistant to quantum computing attacks, ensuring long-term data security. Zero-Knowledge proofs will evolve even further into using advanced cryptographic methods to enhance privacy without compromising transparency and security.

An old vision of the World Wide Web, unfortunately rarely fully attended, is the creation of a **Semantic Web**. Can Web5 attend this promise now? Improved data interoperability and understanding, employing AI technologies to enable machines to understand and interpret data more effectively, will certainly lead to more intelligent and context-aware applications. Another great concept not fully realized in the current Web is **Knowledge Graphs**, which can be addressed in Web5. Utilizing knowledge graphs, it is possible to interlink information and provide deeper insights and more accurate search results.

For those of you curious about more sources of information on Web5, the "What is Web5?" article available at https://developer.tbd.website/blog/what-is-web5/ is interesting and controversial at the same time. The interesting part is the identification of the pillars of Web5: Decentralized Identifiers, Verifiable Credentials, and Decentralized Web Nodes. The controversial portion is storing DIDs on ION (a Layer 2 DID network that runs on top of Bitcoin). The idea of storing elements of personal identity on Bitcoin is innovative. But it opens to a lot of other questions.

Finding the Web's Soul

As we understood, the future of blockchain and Web3 is strongly linked to digital identity and the struggle to own its elements. In May 2022, E. Glen Weyl, a Microsoft researcher, Puja Ohlhaver, an independent researcher, and Vitalik Buterin, published a paper titled "Decentralized Society: Finding Web3's Soul": https://papers.ssrn.com/sol3/papers.cfm?abstract_id=4105763.

Finding's Web3's Soul is close to becoming one of the top 50 most downloaded papers on the SSRN scholarly research platform. The paper discusses the concept of non-transferable soulbound tokens (**SBT**) representing the commitments, credentials, and affiliations of "souls". SBTs appear to be something like blockchain-based curricula vitae, while "souls" are basically people, or strictly speaking, individuals' crypto wallets. The authors illustrate how these SBTs can encode the trust networks of the real economy to establish provenance and reputation. The authors also envision a world where most participants have souls that store SBTs corresponding to a series of affiliations, memberships, and credentials. Key points of soulbound tokens include:

- **Non-transferable**: SBTs are non-transferable tokens (would they rather call them NTT then?). This means that once issued to a wallet, they cannot be transferred to another wallet, exactly like identity documents such as passport or driving license cannot be transferred to another person.
- **Representation of Identity**: SBTs represent a person's identity using blockchain technology. This could include address(es), medical records, work history, and any type of information that makes up a person or entity.
- **Issued by Souls**: The wallets that hold or issue these records are called "souls". Souls can represent individuals, companies, or institutions.

The concept of SBT is still relatively new and is an active area of research and development in the blockchain community. The mentioned paper has received praise for describing a decentralized society that is not mainly focused on hyper financializaton but rather encoding social relationships of trust by emphasizing the potential of blockchain technology in creating a more decentralized and trust-based society. It is an interesting read for anyone interested in the future of Web3 and blockchain technology.

~~Conclusion.~~ Carry on!

As we turn the final page of this journey through the application architecture patterns for Web3, we stand on the brink of a digital renaissance. The patterns and principles outlined in this book are not just blueprints for building decentralized applications; they are the foundation stones for a new era of innovation, trust, and empowerment. The world of Web3 holds the promise of an internet where users control their data, communities self-govern, and creativity knows no bounds. This is a call to architects, developers, and visionaries alike: to embrace these patterns, to push the boundaries of what is possible, and to build a future where technology serves humanity with transparency and integrity. Let this be the beginning of your adventure into the boundless potential of Web3, where your contributions can shape the digital landscape for generations to come. The future is decentralized, and it awaits your imagination and ingenuity!

Decentralized yours,
Stefano

Index

Printed in the United States
by Baker & Taylor Publisher Services